L.M. Montgomery's Complete Journals

The Ontario Years, 1911–1917

Edited by Jen Rubio
Preface by Jonathan F. Vance

Rock's Mills Press

PUBLISHED BY
Rock's Mills Press

L.M. Montgomery's Complete Journals, The Ontario Years 1911–1917

For information, visit us online at www.rocksmillspress.com or email us at customer.servicerocksmillspress.com.

Contents

Preface

1911 was an important year in Canada. The coronation of King George V was the occasion for an outpouring of imperial fervour, as was the arrival in Canada of the Duke of Connaught to begin a term as Governor-General; he would go on to become one of the most popular in the nation's history. Provincial elections in Nova Scotia and Ontario returned the governing parties to power. In the federal election in September, however, Robert Borden's Conservatives played the loyalty card to campaign against free trade with the United States, inflicting a crushing defeat on Sir Wilfrid Laurier's Liberals. The Dominion Parks Branch was established, giving Canada the world's first national parks service. The Dominion Census sketched a portrait of a nation that had grown by almost two million people since the previous census in 1901. Some of Canada's favourite authors had new offerings—Stephen Leacock's *Nonsense Novels* and Robert W. Service's *The Trail of the Ninety-Eight*—while a new face burst onto the literary scene with the publication of Pauline Johnson's *Legends of Vancouver*. And L.M. Montgomery, with *The Story Girl* soon to hit bookshops, left her beloved Prince Edward Island to move to Ontario.

For a woman as passionately attached to place as Maud, it was a terrible wrench. The village of Leaskdale was too small for her liking (Zephyr, the other community in Ewan's charge, was even worse), and the people appalled her: "There isn't one interesting or really intelligent person" in either place, she concluded (September 24, 1911). The manse in Leaskdale was comfortable enough, or could be made so under her watchful eye, but how would she cope with being uprooted from Cavendish and Park Corner? "Oh, how I miss Lover's Lane and my old woodland haunts!" she lamented. "Can I ever really *live* without them?" (October 21, 1911). But over time Maud began to adjust, and especially after her son Chester was born, she began to see Leaskdale—rather than Prince Edward Island—as her home. On later visits to the Maritimes, she would surprise herself by wishing she were back in Ontario.

This journal begins with more than three years of relative calm—or as much calm as Maud's troubled mind could conjure up. She was rarely happy, or even contented, and often expressed disappointment when a place that she remembered or imagined failed to live up to its perfection in her mind. Chester filled her with an exquisite joy, but in her depression she found almost everything else—the people in Scott Township, the duties of a minister's wife, many of her relatives and old friends, her domestic help—to be a source of annoyance. Having filled her novels with sunlight and optimism, it seemed that there was little left to brighten her own days.

It is impossible to read that early part of the journal without a sense of foreboding. Maud knew nothing of what lay ahead, of the trials and tragedies that would soon enough make her complaints about servants and neighbours seem trivial. And ironically, the summer months of 1914—the legendary Golden Summer before war—saw her in unusually high spirits. She rhapsodized about "the open glade" with its "big elms and its carpet of white and pale purple violets." She relaxed on "the flower-starred grass" and gazed up "into the green arches above" (May 24, 1914). For a moment, it might have been an idyll of her youth.

And then came the war, "like a thundercloud." Maud admitted that until that fateful weekend in August 1914, news of the deteriorating situation in Europe had made almost no impression on her. She recalled reading of the assassination of the Austrian archduke Franz Ferdinand in June, but paid little attention to it. She was no more interested in the rising tensions in the Balkans. "Who in this hemisphere cared?" she wrote. "There is always war somewhere among the Balkan States. It seems to be their normal condition" (August 5, 1914). Before August 1914, there is hardly a mention in any of her journals of news from the outside world; after, her life hung on every scrap of information from the far-flung battle fronts. Maud was in a constant state of tension as she waited for the newspapers to arrive from Uxbridge to bring her to the heights of elation or the depths of despair.

From that August weekend, the war became the central force in Maud's life. Her mental health was inextricably linked to the situation at the front, and her psychological state came to depend on the news from overseas. Looking back a century, it is difficult to appreciate the panic that Maud, like countless other Canadians, must have felt. Historians have drawn a complex picture of the First World War over the years—a war motivated by imperial and economic competition, a dynastic struggle between European oligarchies that shared family connections, a failure of the international system for which all of the great powers must accept blame, a European civil war needed to release pressure so an uneasy equilibrium could reassert itself. But for onlookers like Maud, it was so much simpler than that. It was the eternal struggle between good and evil, a fight to the finish, a 'death grapple' as she often called it – one civilization would survive, the other would be destroyed. Like most Canadians, Maud believed that, if Britain were defeated, Canada would become a German colony, the Union Jack would disappear, King George V would be replaced by Kaiser Wilhelm II, and British culture would yield to German *Kultur*. It was almost too terrible to contemplate, but Maud could not resist. It is hardly surprising that her journal entries so often take on apocalyptic overtones.

Calamity and illness, Maud wrote in January 1914, have "a way of 'staining backward' through the pages of life's volume—and forward too" (January 10, 1914). World War I would stain the pages of her life's volume in both directions. To recall her youth meant looking back through the war; to imagine her future meant peering ahead past it. Like so many Canadians, L.M. Montgomery would get through the war, but she would never quite get over it.

Jonathan Vance

The Ontario Years, 1911–1917

++Sunday, July 2, 1911
Park Corner, PEI[1]

... I suddenly realized how tired I was. A very wave of utter weariness submerged me. The preceding sleepless night, the excitement of the day, the worry and confusion of the Custom House, all took effect at once. And I was homesick—suddenly, wretchedly, unmitigatedly homesick!

Arch of St. John's
Chapel, Chester

Up to this time I had not been once homesick since leaving Park Corner. The novelty and the excitement of the voyage across had prevented that. Amid a constant series of new impressions there was no time or change for the old to make themselves felt. But now, in my physical collapse, homesickness came. I wanted Cavendish—Lover's Lane—Park Corner—the girls—and I was thousands of miles away from them, with a waste of ocean between us! I could have dissolved into a fit of crying—but one thing saved me. In the hall outside my room I found a pussy cat—a big black pussy-cat—and most friendly pussy cat, who allowed me to take her up in my arms and cuddle her. I thought of poor gray Daffy, far, far behind in Canada and I was comforted. I went down to tea and the "crying" feeling passed away. But I was so tired that night I couldn't sleep for a long time. I lay there, a stranger in a strange land, and thought of a thousand things.

The next day was Sunday. As there was nothing very interesting about Liverpool, which is merely a commercial city, we went to Chester and spent most of the day there. Chester is a quaint old down, dating back to Roman days and still surrounded by its old wall. We enjoyed our ramble around it hugely. The appended photo is the first one I took on the ould sod. As my first ruin St John's chapel stands out in

---

1 This entry begins during LMM's honeymoon in Britain. It is part of a much longer entry dated January 28, 1912, written from her new home in Leaskdale, Ontario. The last journal entry before had been written almost a year earlier, March 4, 1911, when she had been living with her grandmother in Cavendish, Prince Edward Island. LMM's entry of January 28, 1912, recounts the events of the previous year. The entry begins by recalling how the day following her journal entry of March 4, 1911, her grandmother became seriously ill and died several days later. Following her grandmother's death, LMM relocated to the home of extended family in Park Corner, Price Edward Island. She records being so busy preparing for her marriage to Ewan Macdonald that she could not keep up her journal, but did compose "some stray entries" in a notebook. From this point to her entry of March 22, 1912, the longer entry of January 28, 1912 is retrospective; here LMM recounts her marriage and honeymoon, partly from memory and partly from the aforementioned "stray entries." The symbols "+ +" are used to indicate a retrospective.

memory, although it was not to be compared to those we saw later on.

On Monday, July 17, we went to Glasgow and made it our head-quarters for eleven days, while we "did" various points of interest. We stayed at St Enoch's hotel. I like the British hotels very well, but I detest the tipping system which infects them. It is not that I grudge the money. It is the wretched uncertainty of it. You never know whether you have given enough, too much, or too little. The whole thing is a constant worry and vexation—one of the worst of the annoyances which detracted from the pleasure of travelling in Britain.

As soon as we arrived in Glasgow I began using my notebook again. The first entry as follows:

++Tuesday, July 18, 1911
St. Enoch's Hotel, Glasgow, Scotland

This morning we went out shopping. Glasgow is a big, prosperous-looking city but there is very little about it that is interesting in any way. The names on the shops gave me a nice "at home" feeling, though—McKenzie's, McLeods, Simpsons, Macneills, and so on, just like an Island street. I like shopping here—the clerks are so deferential and attentive.

In the afternoon we went to the Cathedral—St. Mungo's. This is one of the few interesting places in Glasgow. Moreover, the crypt was the scene of one of Francis Osbaldistone's adventures in Rob Roy. We saw the pillar by which he is supposed to have stood when warned of his danger by the mysterious voice.

From there we went to the Fine Arts Museum. I cannot say, however, that I enjoy visiting picture galleries, much as I love pictures. I get horribly tired, walking on stone floors and gazing at miles of canvasses. If one had unlimited time and could give an afternoon of leisurely survey and study to each room it would be very different of course. But even then the eye becomes glutted with so many pictures and ceases to take pleasure in any.

++Glasgow, Scotland
Wednesday, July 19, 1911

This has been a very interesting day. We spent it on the grounds of the Scottish Historical Exhibition which is being held here now.[2] The forenoon we passed in the Palace of History, where hundreds of relics, brought from all over Scotland, many of them from private collections,

---

2   Glasgow had hosted International Exhibitions in 1888 and 1901. In 1911 organizers responded to the growing Scottish national consciousness of the early twentieth century, staging an exhibition of Scottish National History, Art, and Industry in Kelvingrove Park.

Clock Tower and fountain at Exhibition

Mr. Geo. B. MacMillan

are shown.[3] The two I found most interesting were the cradle of Mary, Queen of Scots,[4] and a letter written by Sir William Wallace.[5] I delight in seeing curious old things like that.

The most interesting part of the afternoon was that we met Mr. MacMillan—my Scottish correspondent[6]—by tryst at the fountain in the fairy court. We were on the lookout for each other but, although I thought I would know Mr. MacMillan from his photograph, I did not recognize him until he accosted Ewan—having met the latter when he was in Scotland before. He is a slight, fair, nice-looking chap and one of the best conversationalists I have ever met. He dined with us this evening at St. Enoch's and we are to visit him in Alloa later on.

++*St. Enoch's Hotel, Glasgow*[7]
July 20, 1911, Saturday

Thursday afternoon we left on an excursion to Oban,[8] Staffa[9] and Iona.[10] We went by rail to Oban and the scenery was certainly beautiful, especially along Loch Awe, with its ruined castle. Beautiful—yes. And yet neither there nor elsewhere in England or Scotland did I see a

---

3   The six Palace of History galleries contained a huge collection of Scottish historical relics and artefacts, including weapons, clothing, and documents.

4   Mary, Queen of Scots (1542–87; also known as Mary Stuart), was Queen of Scotland from December 1542 to July 1567. After living through considerable political intrigue, Mary Stuart was found guilty of plotting to assassinate Elizabeth, and executed in 1587.

5   Sir William Wallace (c.1270–1305) was a member of the lesser Scottish nobility who played a key role in the First War of Scottish Independence (1296–1328). Wallace's troops defeated an English army at the Battle of Stirling Bridge in September 1297. In August 1305 Wallace was captured, handed over to England's King Edward I, and executed. Wallace would become the subject of both literature and poetry—particularly the fifteenth-century epic poem *The Wallace*.

6   George Boyd Macmillan had corresponded with LMM beginning in 1903. LMM's letters to Macmillan are brought together in F.W.P. Bolger and Elizabeth Rollins Epperly, eds., *My Dear Mr M.: Letters to G.B. Macmillan* (Toronto: McGraw-Hill Ryerson, 1980).

7   The Saint Enoch's Station Hotel was a landmark in central Glasgow until 1974.

8   Located on the west coast of Scotland, Oban has long been a popular tourist destination. Archaeological evidence suggests that the site has been occupied since at least Mesolithic times.

9   Staffa is an island of the Inner Hebrides. The name derives from the Old Norse for stave or pillar island. A key feature of the Island's geology is its columnar basalt.

10   Iona is a small island in the Inner Hebrides off the larger island of Mull, long a tourist destination; Iona was a centre of Gaelic monasticism for four centuries.

scene more beautiful than can be seen any fine summer evening in Cavendish standing on the "old church hill" and looking afar over the ponds to New London Harbor. But then we have no ruined castles— nor the centuries of romance they stand for!

Oban is a picturesque little town—a fringe of houses, built along the shore of a land-locked harbor, with steep wooded mountains rising directly behind them. Next morning we took the boat to Iona. It was a typical Scottish day—bright and sunny one hour, showery and misty the next. For a few hours I enjoyed our sail very much. The wild, rugged scenery of Cape and bay and island and bleak mountain—the whole, of course, peppered with ruined, ivy-hung castles—was an ever-changing panorama of interest, peopled with the shades of the past.

We had a most entertaining "Cook's Party"[11] of French tourists on board. They "jabbered" incessantly. There was one nice old fellow, in particular, with a pleasant, bronzed face and twinkling black eyes, who seemed to be the expounder-in-chief of the party. They seemed to get into repeated arguments on some subject, and when the discussion reached a certain pitch of intensity, he would spring to his feet, confront the party, wave his arms and umbrella wildly in air, and lay down the law in a most authoritative tone and fashion.

Oban

At first I enjoyed the day. But as the forenoon wore away I began to lose interest in everything. Ruined castle, towering mountain, white torrent, beautiful bay— even the French tourists, were as a tale that is told.

Climbing over the Staffa rocks to Fingal's Cave

In the morning I had been anxious because they said it might be too rough to stop at Staffa, and I wanted so badly to see Fingal's Cave.[12] But now I did not care a hoot for Fingal's Cave—or any other earthly thing.

---

11   "Cook's Tours" was a popular name for organized group travel to tourist locations; the Thomas Cook Travel Agency, founded in 1841, is still extant.

12   A famous basalt sea cave on Staffa. The original name arose from James Macpherson's *Fingal, an Ancient Epic Poem in Six Books, together with Several Other Poems composed by Ossian, the Son of Fingal, translated from the Gaelic Language* (1761). However, Macpherson's claims of historical origins have long been disputed by experts. Fingal's Cave was the inspiration for much Romantic art, including Felix Mendelssohn's *The Hebrides*, Op. 26 (known also as *Fingal's Cave*

I was horribly seasick!!

The boat stopped at Staffa, however, and two rowboat-loads went ashore. I let them go. What cared I? The waves would not have daunted me—the pouring rain would not have appalled me. But seasickness!!!

But the boat was now still and I began to feel better. By the time the row-boats came back for the second load I was feeling quite all right and once more it seemed a thing of first importance to see Fingal's Cave. I joyfully scrambled down into the boat and was rowed ashore to the Clam Shell Cave.[13] From there we had to scramble and clamber for what seemed an interminably long distance—but really I suppose it was no more than a quarter of a mile—over the wet, slippery basalt columns that fringe the shore, hanging in the worst places to a rope strung along the surface of the cliff. Owing to my much scrambling over the rocks of Cavendish shore in early life I got on very well, but some of the tourists slipped and sprawled to an alarming degree. Nobody fell off, however, and eventually we found ourselves in Fingal's Cave.

Entrance to Fingal's Cave [Staffa]

'Tis a most wonderful and majestic place—like an immense Gothic cathedral. It is hard to believe that it could have been fashioned merely by a freak of nature. I think everyone there felt awed—even those irrepressible French tourists were silent for a space. As I stood there

[St Columba's Trail and St. Oran's Chapel] Iona

and heard the deep solemn echo of the waves in it the memory of some Bible verse came to me—"he inhabiteth the halls of eternity"[14]—and it seemed to me that I stood verily in a temple of the Almighty that had not been builded by hands.

We went on to Iona and landed there for a brief, hurried, guide-ridden exploration. Iona is interesting as the scene of St. Columba's ministry.[15] His ancient cathedral is still there. To me, of greater inter-

---

Overture) and artist J.M.W. Turner's 1832 painting "Staffa, Fingal's Cave." The cave was also visited by William Wordsworth, John Keats, Alfred, Lord Tennyson, and Walter Scott.

13   The columns on the Clam or Scallop-Shell Cave appear bent like the ribs of a ship.

14   Isaiah 57:15.

15   Irish abbot and missionary St Columba (521–597 CE) was a key figure in establishing

Tomb of Kings

est was the burial place of the earliest Scottish kings—about sixty of them it is said, finishing with that Duncan who was murdered by MacBeth.[16] They were buried very simply, those warriors of ancient days. There they lie in their island cemetery beneath the gray sky. Neither "storied urn or animated bust"[17] mark their resting place. Each grave is covered simply with a slab of worn carved stone. But they sleep none the less soundly for that, lulled by the eternal murmur of the waves around them.

I would have liked to spend several days in Iona, prowling by myself around its haunted ruins and getting to know its quaint inhabitants. There is really small pleasure in a hurried scramble around such places, in the midst of a chattering, exclaiming mob of tourists. For me, at least, solitude is a necessary thing for real enjoyment. I must be by myself, or with but one or two congenial spirits, before I can dream and muse, and bring back to life the men and women who once dwelt there and made the place famous.

We sailed back to Oban by a different and less interesting route. The scenery was monotonously rugged and bleak. I was very tired when I reached Oban but I thought the day was worth it.

We returned to Glasgow yesterday by water and were glutted with scenery. The Crinan canal[18] was beautiful and interesting. I was wretchedly tired when we got "home". But weariness fell away from me when I found letters from Frede and Stella awaiting me here. How good those home letters tasted in a foreign land! I answered them to-day and thought bridged the gulf of ocean between us and took me home. I saw the Cavendish hills and the green gloom of the beech woods around Aunt Annie's. Ah, beautiful as the old world is, the homeland is the best!

Christianity in present-day Scotland. The abbey he founded on Iona was a dominant religious and political institution in the region for centuries.

16   The abbey graveyard contains the graves of many early Scottish Kings, as well as kings from Ireland, Norway and France including Donnchad mac Crínáin, king of Scotland ("Duncan I") and Mac Bethad mac Findlaích, king of Scotland ("Macbeth").

17   From Thomas Gray's meditation on death and remembrance, "Elegy Written in a Country Churchyard" (1751).

18   Linking Crinan and Ardrishaig in the west of Scotland, the 14-km/9-mile long Crinan canal was opened in 1801 to create a navigable route between the industrial region around the River Clyde and the Inner Hebrides.

++*Sunday, July 30, 1911*
Royal Hotel, Prince's Street, Edinburgh

If we "count time by heart throbs"—by our experience for delight and suffering—it is much more than a week since my last entry. This week has been a mixture of pleasure and misery.

Last Monday we went out to Ayr with a "Cook" guide. As a rule we dislike the Cook parties and go alone whenever we can. But this expedition was pleasant as there were only two besides ourselves and they were Canadians—a Mr. and Mrs. Thorpe from Guelph, Ontario. We had a nice—a very nice—guide. Two things, however, subtracted from my

[Auld and New Brigs o' Doon]

pleasure in the day—it rained quite heavily much of the time and I had a grumbling toothache all the time. But in spite of both drawbacks I enjoyed myself—"where'er we trod 'twas haunted holy ground."[19] We saw the room—the low, humble little room—where "a blast o' Januar' wind blew hausel in on Robin"[20]—and we explored the ruins of "Alloway's Auld Haunted Kirk" where Tam O'Shanter saw the dance of witches.[21] Then we went to the Burns' Monument[22]—just because it was on the list of "sights" and the guide would have been aghast if we hadn't gone. I have no interest whatever in monuments. They bore me horribly. But there were two interesting things in the monument—a lock of Highland Mary's fair hair and the Bible upon which she and Burns swore troth in their parting tryst.[23] Poor Highland Mary, I don't suppose she was anything more than a sweet little country lass, no sweeter or prettier than thousands of other girls who have lived and died, if not

---

19   From Canto II of Byron's *Childe Harold's Pilgrimage* (1812–1818), a long poem about the travels of a world-weary young man.

20   From Scottish poet Robert Burns' song, "Rantin' Rovin' Robin" (1787), a witty description of a momentous storm on January 25; according to Robert Burns the storm damaged his family's house when he was only a few days old.

21   From Robert Burns' *Tam o'Shanter*, a long poem about a farmer named Tam who, returning home one night following an evening of heavy drinking, happens upon a local church where a party of witches and warlocks is taking place, with the devil playing the bagpipes. The church—Alloway Kirk—is thought to be based on a ruin in Alloway, South Ayrshire, Scotland.

22   The Burns Monument, opened in 1879 in Kay Park, Kilmarnock, commemorates poet Robert Burns (1759–96).

23   Robert Burns had an affair with a young woman named Mary Campbell (known as Highland Mary), to whom Burns dedicated several poems. Mary, who died suddenly in 1986, possibly engaged to Burns. They are said to have exchanged Bibles.

unwept, at least unhonored and unsung. But a great genius flung over her the halo of his love, wrote a few verses about her—and lo, she is one of the immortals—one of the fair ladies of old romance who will be forever remembered because of the men who loved them. She is of the company of Laura and Beatrice, of Stella and Lucasta, of Julia and the unknown lady of Arvers' sonnet.[24]

We walked over the "auld brig" that spans "Bonnie Doon."[25] It is a beautiful spot. I don't wonder Burns loved it.

My teeth were worse in the evening and I spent a miserable night. We had intended to go the Trossachs[26] Tuesday but it was out of the question. I spent the day in bed instead. Wednesday, however, I was better and we went. This was one of the expeditions I have looked forward to all my life—ever since I read "The Lady of the Lake" in schooldays. Sitting behind that old brown desk in school I dreamed out the panorama of mountain and lake and pass, where Ellen lived and Fitz-James wandered and Roderick Dhu brooded like a stormcloud over a Highland hill.[27] And I promised myself that some day I would go to see it.

We sailed up Loch Lomond to Inversnaid. That the scenery is beautiful goes without saying. At Inversnaid we took coaches for a five mile drive across to Loch Katrine—a delightful experience. Of all the ways of locomotion I have ever tried I like coaching best. It beats motoring "hollow."

Loch Lomond [Loch Lomond from Luss (Mist Effect)]

---

24   All references to literary expressions of unrequited love. Italian poet Petrarch (Francesco Petrarca, 1304–74) wrote some 366 poems about a woman named Laura, who apparently he had seen once in a church. Dante Alighieri's (1265–1321) *Vita Nuova* (1295) is a long prose and verse composition said to be about Beatrice di Folco Portinari (1266–90), a Florentine woman who had married another man, and died young. Philip Sidney's (1554–86) *Astrophel and Stella* (1591) is a long sonnet sequence describing enduring but unfulfilled passion. Richard Lovelace's (1617–57) "To Lucasta, Going to the Warres" (1649) is a shorter poem about love, chastity and honour. Robert Herrick (1591–1674) was an English poet and cleric who devoted several short love poems to a character named Julia. Félix Arvers (1806–50) was a French poet and dramatist, most famous for his poem "Un secret" (c.1831) about a secret, one-sided love.

25   The "auld brig" refers to a medieval bridge across the river Doon in Ayrshire, Scotland. It is said to be the inspiration for Tam o'Shanter's escape from the witch chasing him and his horse. Nannie the Witch reaches out at the last moment, grabbing only the tail of Tam's horse Meg.

26   A scenic region of woodland glens made popular by Sir Walter Scott's (1771–1832) long poem, *The Lady of the Lake* (1810).

27   One of the plots of *The Lady of the Lake* is the contest of three men for Ellen Douglas.

Coaching [Loch Katrine]

We soon reached Stronachlacher—which, in spite of its name is a most beautiful spot, and took the boat down Loch Katrine. At the lower end we passed "Ellen's Isle," Benvenue and the "Silver Strand" and came to the Trossach's pier.[28]

I have never been able to decide whether Loch Katrine disappointed me or not. I think it did—a little. It was as beautiful as I had dreamed it—but it was not *my* Loch Katrine—not quite the Loch Katrine of my estates in Spain. And I resented the difference, as one would resent a change made in his childhood's home on going back to it after a long absence.

The lower portion of the lake is certainly much smaller than the impression I received of it from the poem. And the famous "Silver Strand" is a poor affair now. Since the instalments of the Glasgow water works, the lake has risen several feet and covered the "beach of pebbles white as snow." All that is left of it is a dull gray strip along the bank with a few pebbles scattered over it. They certainly are as white as snow. I brought a handful home with me as souvenirs. But I think I shall keep the Loch Katrine of my dream in my geography of the "Lady of the Lake." I like it better than the real one.

Stronachlacher Hotel

Lower end of Katrine

"Silver Strand" [path by the Loch, Loch Katrine]

28   Sites on Loch Katrine commemorated in *The Lady of the Lake*.

[Path by the Loch Katrine]

[Katrine Path, Trossachs]

We coached through the Trossachs to the Trossachs Hotel. The Trossachs is most beautiful and grand—and perhaps before the carriage road was made it was wild enough, especially to some benighted wanderer who had all too good reason to fear Highland plunderers. But it is far from being the wild, precipitous, riven dell of my fancy. No, it was not the Trossachs where I have so often wandered with Fitz-James!

The hotel is in a lovely spot on the shore of Loch Achray.

Loch Achray

Hotel

"Where shall we find in foreign land,
So lone a lake, so fair a strand?"

Yet Loch Achray, too, was on a much smaller scale than I had expected. We walked along it that evening as far as "the brig of Turk," gathering bell-heather and bluebells as we went. Scottish bluebells are certainly the sweetest things. They seem the very incarnation of Scotia's old romance.

Next morning we walked through the Trossachs to Katrine in a pouring rain and hired one of the old boatmen to row us out and around

[Ellen's Isle, Loch Katrin]e

Ben Venue

"Ellen's Isle." I don't think I liked it because it too was not the islet of my dream. It was beautiful but it "wasn't my idea of a diamond"— and so I was conscious of a certain disappointment.

But Ben Venue[29] did not disappoint me. It dominates the landscape. Everywhere we went there was old Ben Venue, rugged and massive, with a cloud wreath resting on his "summit hoar." I was very sorry that the night we spent there was wet. I should have loved to have seen a sunset effect on Ben Venue.

We coached to Aberfoyle that afternoon—another enjoyable trip—and reached Glasgow at night, pretty well tired out. Friday we came to Edinburgh and are at a very nice hotel in Princes Street.[30] Princes Street is another disappointment to me. It *is* a fine street—and the more I see of it the more I realize how fine it really is. But it isn't the Princes St. of my dreams—the fairy avenue of gardens and statuary and palaces. Probably no such street exists in the world—but I can't quite forgive it for that.

Saturday was a nightmare of a day. We went with a Cook's Excursion around Edinburgh. It poured rain the whole time and I was the victim of a peculiarly annoying and misery-producing ailment—to wit, cystitis,[31] of which I had an attack several years ago in Halifax. It completely robbed the day of all pleasure for me. I went through Edinburgh

29 Ben Venue is a well-known mountain in the Trossachs, with two peaks (one at 727 m/2,385 ft above sea level and the other at 729 m/2,392 ft). The name translates to the "miniature mountain" in Scottish Gaelic.

30 Princes Street is a main thoroughfare in Edinburgh, named after the sons of King George III. It was originally laid out in 1770 as the outer edge of Edinburgh's new town, facing Edinburgh Castle. Princes Street Gardens had been created out of the draining of Nor Loch, a flooded hollow that had once been part of the original defense of Edinburgh Old Town.

31 Inflammation of the urinary tract and/or bladder, usually caused by a bacterial infection.

castle[32] and Holyrood Palace[33] like one in a bad dream. Even the famous cabinet where Rizzio was murdered[34] left me indifferent. I only wished to get back to the hotel and go to bed—hide myself away from every eye. Besides my physical discomfort my trouble produced a singular nervous effect. I shrank from being seen by anyone—to be looked at by anyone was absolute torture—to be compelled to speak to anyone, or have a remark addressed to me was agony.

I feel quite well to-day. I do hope I shall not have as long an attack of this as I had in Halifax. If I do my trip will be completely spoiled.

++*Sunday, Aug. 6, 1911*
Royal Hotel, Princes St.
Edinburgh, Scotland

Sightseeing is really horribly hard work. I'm fagged out—though I suppose it was more the physical and nervous misery of parts of the week than the knocking about that has wearied me.

Last Monday we went by train to Melrose and coached over six miles of most beautiful road to Abbotsford.[35] Although we went on our own account we could not avoid falling in with a Cook excursion and this somewhat spoiled the day for us. But the scenery is

Abbotsford [Walter Scott's House]

exquisite along the road, and we saw the Eildon hills, cleft in three by the spells of wizardry.[36] Abbotsford is most interesting and crowded with relics. I should have loved to dream over them in solitude. But that

---

32   Human occupation of Castle Rock, the site of Edinburgh Castle, has been dated to the second century AD. A royal castle has been sited here since at least the twelfth century, and several sieges have taken place; the original twelfth-century castle was mostly destroyed in the sixteenth century. Its more recent role is mostly administrative and ceremonial.

33   The Palace of Holyroodhouse was built as a royal residence in Scotland between 1671 and 1678.

34   Italian courtier David Rizzio (1536–66) was private secretary to Mary, Queen of Scots. Mary's husband, Henry Stuart, Lord Darnley, suspected Rizzio of being her lover (and the father of her unborn child); Darnley conspired with several others—probably including Queen Elizabeth I—to murder Rizzio, who was stabbed 53 times next to the seven-months' pregnant Mary.

35   Large country manor built by Scottish novelist Sir Walter Scott on the banks of the River Tweed.

36   Hills near Scott's home, south of Melrose, Scotland, comprising three peaks; the highest is 422 m/1,386 feet.

might not be. The rooms were filled by a chattering crowd, harangued by a glib guide. I wondered if Scott would have liked this—to see his home overrun by a horde of curious sight seers. I am sure I would not.

We then drove over another magnificent road to Dryburgh Abbey[37] where Scott is buried. As we were able to get away from the "cookies" and prowl by ourselves here we enjoyed this. It is a beautiful old ruin and must have been a wonderful place before Cromwell and the Reformation completed its destruction.

Then we returned to Melrose and explored the ruins of the Abbey. We could not follow Scott's advice—which I will never believe he failed to take himself, as is asserted by some—and view it by moonlight. But in that golden-gray mellow evening light it was beautiful enough—beautiful and sad, with the little bluebells growing in its ruined courts and over its old graves.

Ruin of Dryburgh Abbey

Scott's Burial Place

Michael Scott is reputed to be buried there,[38] and then the heart of Robert Bruce was buried—and doubtless rests as quietly as if it had, according to his wish, been laid in the soil of the Holy Land.[39]

There is some wonderful hand-carving still left in Melrose— and the little hand high up on one

[Melrose Abbey from SE]

---

37   Dryburgh Abbey was first occupied by a sect of Roman Catholic canons in 1152. It was a site of conflict throughout the centuries. The abbey closed in 1600 and the land was purchased by the twelfth Earl of Buchan in 1786.

38   Michael Scot (1175–1232?) was a medieval mathematician and scholar, famous throughout Europe. A footnote in Sir Walter Scott's *The Lay of the Last Minstrel* credits Scot (misspelled as "Scott") with conquering a demon that had split Eildon Hill into three cones.

39   Robert the Bruce (1274–1329) was King of Scots from 1306 until his death in 1329. He led Scotland in battle against England during the Wars of Scottish Independence. A friend and lieutenant, Sir James Douglas, had agreed to take the late King's embalmed heart on crusade to the Holy Land, but he was killed in battle en route. Bruce's body and the casket containing the embalmed heart were returned to Scotland.

of the arches is as suggestive as it was beautiful. What fair lady's hand is chiselled there in lasting stone? For one cannot but think it was wrought by a lover.

Up to this time I had enjoyed the day. But when we went to the station I was again visited by a sudden attack of my malady and the trip back to Edinburgh was another nightmare. When we reached our hotel I yielded to Ewan's entreaties and had a doctor—who looked wise, ad-

vised a day's rest, wrote out a prescription and pocketed his fee. I hope it did him some good. His prescription really did not do me any. But I felt better again the next day and after spending most of it in bed we went

The Den

The Den

out in the evening, visited—and climbed— the Scott Monument[40] and then motored out to the Forth Bridge.[41] Everyone feels bound to see this because it represents one of the en-

gineering feats of the world. But I most enjoyed the drive out.

On Wednesday we started on an expedition to Inverness, but stopped off during the afternoon to visit Kirriemuir, the "Thrums" of J.M. Barrie's delightful stories.[42] In particular, I wanted to see "The Den," where *Sentimental Tommie* and his cronies held their delightful revels.[43]

The Den

---

40   The Scott Monument on Princes Street, started in 1840 and opened in 1844, is the largest monument to a writer in the world, rising 61 m/200 ft.

41   The Forth Bridge, completed in 1890 after 8 years of construction, is a cantilever railway bridge over the Firth of Forth, 14 km/7 m west of Edinburgh. The bridge spans a total length of 2,529 m/8,297 ft; until 1917 it was the longest cantilever bridge in the world.

42   Scottish author J.M. Barrie (1860–1937) set several novels in a fictional town of Thrums, based on Kirriemuir in Angus.

43   J.M. Barrie is best known for his 1904 play, *Peter Pan; or, the Boy Who Wouldn't Grow Up*

We explored it thoroughly. It is a most beautiful spot. One thing about it made me feel at home— its paths—"the pink paths" Barrie called them—are the very red of our own Island roads. I could have fancied myself prowling in the woods around Lover's Lane. The "Den" was one of the things that did not disappoint me and one of the few places in Britain to which I look back with a longing to see it again. It is not yet famous enough to be spoiled.

Hut on Culloden Moor where Cumberland spent the night before the battle

We spent the night in Aberdeen and reached Inverness the next afternoon. Of all the places we visited in Scotland I liked Inverness best. In itself it is only a small gray town, but the surrounding scenery is magnificent.

Cumberland Stone, Culloden Moor

We drove out to Culloden that evening and it is one of the drives that, for sheer pleasure, stand out in my memory. The road was exceedingly lovely and we were fortunate enough to have a nice old driver who knew all the history and

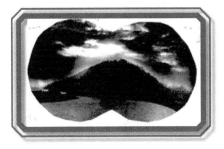

Tomnahurich

legend of everything and was very willing to tell it in delightful "broad Scotch." Culloden is almost covered with beautiful pine trees now, but in the days when the Bonnie Prince made his last throw for the crown of his fathers it was a bare heathery moor.[44]

The next day we visited "Tommahurich," the famous cemetery of Inverness.[45] It deserves its fame for I am sure it must be the most

---

(written as a novel in 1911). *Sentimental Tommy* (1896) is a tragic novel with similar themes, in which a young man clings to boyish fantasy.

44   The Battle of Culloden in 1746 was the last battle in the Jacobite Uprising (and also the last battle to be fought on British soil). Forces loyal to Charles Edward Stuart (sometimes known as Bonnie Prince Charlie) were beaten by British Troops led by the Duke of Cumberland. The battle took place on Culloden Moor near Inverness, lasting only about an hour. Some 2,000 Jacobites were killed, many of whom were Scottish Highlanders. British losses were comparatively light.

45   Tomnahurich cemetery, on the outskirts of Inverness, is associated with many legends. The

Scene on the crest of Tomnahurich

beautiful graveyard in the world. It is a large hill outside the city rising in a conical point and thickly covered with trees. The name is a Gaelic word meaning "the hill of the fairies" and surely it must once have been a spot meet for a fairy kingdom and the revels of Titania.[46] Seen at eventide against a sunset sky it seems a veritable outpost of the Land of Old Romance. I said to Ewan as we roamed about it "When I die bring me over here and bury me"—and if it were not that it is so far from home, I think I should have meant it.

But no! When I die there is but one place I wish to be buried—in that old graveyard down by the Atlantic waves where so many of my dear ones lie.

We spent that evening in "The Islands" and imagined ourselves in Fairyland. The Ness is the river which flows through Inverness and along one of its banks is a chain of small wooded islands connected with the bank and with each other by bridges. They are the pleasure ground of Inverness and at night are lighted up by Chinese lanterns. I shall never forget our walk through them and then back to town along the bank of the river in the beautiful northern twilight.

Yesterday morning we went down to Fort William by the famous Caledonian Canal.[47] The scenery was very fine but I could not enjoy it. In the morning I had another attack of cystitis and was utterly wretched until we reached Fort William, when it departed for the time as suddenly as it had come and I enjoyed the rest of the journey by train to Edinburgh. The sunset effects on the mountains along our way were too grand and beautiful for description. The ever-changing effects of cloud and mist and sunlight on their lofty brows were wonderful. If I were to live near mountains for any length of time I should learn to love them *almost* as much as I love the sea.

All this forenoon I was miserable but have felt well again this afternoon, though very tired.

---

name actually means "hill of the yews"—not, as LMM claims, "hill of the fairies."

46   Queen of the Fairies in Shakespeare's *Midsummer Night's Dream*.

47   A 97-km/60-mile canal connecting the Scottish east coast at Inverness with the west coast near Fort William.

++*Sunday, Aug. 13, 1911*
Berwick on Tweed

We have certainly "lived" this week, if getting over the ground and "seeing things" constitute life. It was all so interesting that I *had* to enjoy it, though much of the time I was tortured by my trouble.

Berwick on Tweed

Last Monday morning I was too miserable to leave the hotel but in the afternoon I felt better so we coached out to see Roslin Castle and Roslin Chapel.[48] The road was *not* beautiful but very tame and uninteresting. Roslin Castle was not uninteresting, however—quite the reverse, although in ruins. The Chapel is in a perfect state of preservation and is a wonderful specimen of Gothic work. The carving is certainly marvellous. This is the

[Roslin Chapel]

chapel made famous in Scott's ballad of "Fair Rosabelle"—

"Seemed all on fire that chapel pond
Where Roslin's chiefs uncoffined lie."[49]

After dinner that night we went out for a walk. I was not feeling very well and I was filled with a sudden unreasoning hatred for all the crowded streets where every face was unknown. Ewan had to go into the station to find out about trains and while he was away I walked up and down Princes St., alone. I was homesick—miserably so. I

Arthur's Seat

---

48   There has been a castle on the site near Roslin, Midlothian, Scotland since the early fourteenth century, but the castle LMM visited was rebuilt in 1544. Nearby is a fifteenth-century chapel.

49   In Scott's poem (1805), Rosabelle is drowned crossing the Firth in spite of warnings.

wanted my own land, my own solitudes, my own sea, my own familiar friends. And I was thousands of miles away from them all!

The next day, however, I felt pretty well all day and life seemed less gray. In the afternoon we drove out to Arthur's Seat, the famous hill which watches over Edinburgh and, from one point of view, looks much like a couchant lion.[50] We left the carriage at its base and climbed to the top of it. A stiff pull it was and we were totally out of breath when we reached the top. But the view repaid us for it was magnificent.

Wednesday afternoon we left Edinburgh and went to Alloa, Mr. MacMillan's town. We had been invited to spend a few days with the family of his *fiancée*, Miss Jean Allan. When we started I was so miserable I did not see how I was going to endure it at all. But fortunately by the time we reached Alloa I was so much better that I could hide my indisposition from others, though not feeling well enough to enjoy myself really.

Ewan, Miss Allan, M. McMillan

Miss Allan is a very pretty girl, owing most of her beauty however to her bright golden hair and to her complexion which is simply exquisite. I have read of "dazzling" complexions but I never have seen one before. "Dazzling," however, is exactly the word to apply to Miss Allan's. Her skin is snow-white, with a most delicious wild-rose pink in her cheeks. *I* have always

On the path to Gartmoor Dam   The Lake at Gartmoor Dam

been reputed to have a good complexion, as complexions go, but Miss Allan positively makes me look brown and sallow. It is a wholesome corrective of vanity to look into a mirror when she is before it, too, but I don't do it when I can help it, for all that!

After dinner Mr. MacMillan came and we all walked out to Gartmorn Dam, by way of a lovely wood-road, companioned by a beautiful

---

50   Lying to the east of Edinburgh Castle, Arthur's Seat is the 250-m/820-ft peak of a group of hills; it has been considered to be a possible location for King Arthur's Camelot.

brook.[51] I was not well enough to enjoy it, lovely as it all was. But in the evening I felt quite well and really enjoyed the long walk we took out to Tullibody.[52] (Isn't that just such a name as a Scotchman could invent?) It must have been nearly five miles out there but the night was moonlight and Mr. MacMillan is a delightful companion for such an expedition. He knows all the legends and traditions of the surrounding country and is a most congenial conversationalist.

I doubt if poor Ewan, walking behind us with Miss Allan, enjoyed the walk as much as I did. Miss A's stock in trade is her twenty-year-old freshness and her charming complexion. She has little else—no intellect, and certainly no conversational powers.

Thursday morning was fine and as I felt well Ewan and I started on an expedition by ourselves. We first went out to "Rumbling Bridge" and "The Devil's Mill."[53] The Devil, by the way, seems to have a vast deal of property in Scotland. Everywhere we find places called by his name.

The scenery at the Bridge is wonderful. Then we came back to Dollar to see the Dollar Glen.[54] I had never heard of the place until Mr. MacMillan told me of it. Yet it is one of the finest, wildest, grandest spots we saw in all Scotland. If Scott had touched it with his genius it would be as widely known as the Trossachs. Indeed, one part of it is much like what I had imagined the Trossachs to be before I saw it. Dollar Glen is like a deep gash cleft down through the heart of the mountain, and there are many beautiful waterfalls in it, caused by two streams, bearing the peculiar names of "Care" and "Sorrow" which meet in the middle of the glen.

Dollar Glen

On Friday we visited Stirling—"the bulwark of the North"—a most interesting old place.[55]

---

51   Gartmorn Dam had been engineered by landowner John Erskine, Earl of Mar, to drain his coal mines near Sauchie.

52   Tullibody is located 2.9 km/1.9 mile north-west of Alloa.

53   The name refers to a rumbling noise heard beneath a bridge that crosses the gorge (in fact there are three bridges: an ancient bridge consisting of a stone slab crossing the gorge at the river level, one built 26 m/85 ft above the water in 1713, and a third bridge 10 m/33 ft above that, built in 1816). Devil's Mill is a deep basin of turbulent water located a 15-minute walk upstream from Rumbling Bridge.

54   A valley network in the Ochil hills along the Highland fault marked by deep gorges and waterfalls.

55   Given Stirling's historical position as the nearest crossing of the Forth river, the site has been occupied since at least the Stone Age. A bridge has existed here since the thirteen century; there

We first went to the Wallace Monument, built on a high steep hill called Abbey Craig, some two miles out of Stirling.[56] It is a steep climb up the Craig itself and then another steep climb to the top of the monument. But such a view as we had from the top! Beneath us like a map we saw half of Scotland spread and every acre of ground on which we gazed was saturated with historic interest. We could see seven noted battlefields and had a splendid view of the famous Links of Forth— one of the most curious freaks of Nature one could imagine.[57]

Then we motored out to Bannockburn[58] and on our

["And twined in lnks of silber bright
Her winding river lay."—Scott
River Forth, Wallace Monument]

Wallace Monument

Stirling Castle

return "did" Stirling Castle. Stirling Castle was the most interesting thing of its kind we have yet seen.[59] The old Stuart palace reeks with romance and tragedy.

Yesterday we came to Berwick. Mr. MacMillan had planned to spend his vacation here with us and we asked Miss Allan to come too, as

---

have been at least sixteen sieges of Stirling Castle.

56   Completed in 1896, the 67-m/220-ft monument commemorates Sir William Wallace. Wallace was a Scottish knight and military leader who helped defeat an English army at the Battle of Stirling Bridge in 1297 during the First War of Scottish Independence (1296–1398).

57   The Forth River is formed by two head-streams that form a confluence visible from the Wallace Monument.

58   Bannockburn is the site of a major battle during the First War of Scottish Independence. In 1314, Robert the Bruce led the Scottish army to re-take Stirling Castle, held by England since 1304.

59   Stirling Castle is located on a site surrounded on three sides by steep cliffs and has probably been occupied as a defensive position for as long as Britain has been peopled. Until the 1890s it guarded the most convenient crossing of the River Forth.

our guest, for his sake. Berwick is in the heart of the *Marmion* country.[60] We have lodgings at a certain Mrs. Pringle's in a suburb known as Spittal. They differ somewhat from the hotel in Princes St. but we can put up with them for a week. It is difficult to get good lodgings here unless spoken for far in advance, as it is a popular seaside resort. Berwick is a most quaint antiquated old town. As we "live" on the Spittal side when we want to go anywhere we have to be rowed over the river mouth by one of the half dozen quaint old ferrymen who have boats for hire.[61]

Berwick Pier

Spittal Cliffs

Last night we all went for a walk along the shore in the moonlight. It was beautiful but so like the Cavendish shore that it made me bitterly homesick.

++*Carlisle, August 20, 1911*
Sunday

We are spending Sunday in Carlisle perforce, since we could not get any further last night, owing to the big railway strike which has been paralysing England this past week. We, in our seaside seclusion at Berwick, did not suffer from it or heed it. We let the outer world go by and lived in realms of romance.

---

60   Berwick-upon-Tweed is the northernmost town in England. For over 400 years Berwick was central to border wars between England and Scotland, and changed possession several times (it finally landed in English hands in 1482). The Battle of Flodden Field—a key event in Walter Scott's long poem *Marmion*—took place nearby in 1513. A Scottish army led by James IV invaded England as part of an alliance with France, but was defeated by an English army commanded by the Earl of Surrey. James IV of Scotland was killed in the battle.

61   The River Tweed empties into the North Sea off the east coast of Britain, not far south of the England-Scotland border. In 1911 when LMM was there, there was one bridge—the Berwick Bridge, built in the seventeenth-century. Spittal is on the south-east side of the river, a long way from the bridge.

[Lindisfarne Priory, Holy Island]

Last Monday we went by boat to Holy Island, or Lindisfarne, where we explored the ruins of the old Abbey there, which was the scene of *Constance De Beverley's* trial and death in *Marmion*.[62] Holy Island itself is a quaint interesting little spot. The old Abbey is in a very ruinous condition.

View on Holy Island

Only one of its arches remains entire. But over it all hangs the glamor of "unhappy far-off things."

Marmion Gateway

We had an enjoyable sail down to Holy Island but the return home was sadly different. It was quite rough and how that little excursion steamer rolled! Both our gentlemen became so sick that they had to retire temporarily from the scene while Miss Allan and I only fought surrender off by an effort of will and would have suffered less I think, had we just allowed ourselves to go!

Luckily seasickness is never fatal and we were all right next day and ready for another excursion to Norham Castle.[63] This is splendidly

62   Lindisfarne has a recorded history since the sixth century. Of little interest to Roman settlers, this island—accessible only in low tide—has been known as "Holy Island" because it became an important establishment of Celtic Christianity in 634 BCE.

63   Founded between 1099 and 1121, Norham Castle was the site of much Scottish-English

situated on the Tweed but is now in a very ruinous condition. "Marmion's gateway" is a pretty bit.

Growing all over the grounds was a little blue flower which I never saw anywhere else save in the old front orchard at home in Cavendish. Grandmother Woolner had brought it out from England with her. It gave me an odd feeling of pain and pleasure mingled to find it growing there around that old ruined mediaeval castle which seemed to belong so utterly to another time and another order of things.

The Tweed

We walked from Norham to Ladykirk, a very interesting old church, and then back by the Tweed.[64] When we grew tired we sat down on its twilight banks and rested—and dreamed dreams. What the others thought of I do not know. *I* was arranging furniture in Leaskdale Manse.

Next day we went to Flodden Field. We had to walk three miles from the station and as the day was fine and the scenery beautiful this agreed with all of us except Miss Allan, who didn't seem to like walking and sulked the whole way. That same young lady, in spite of her angelic appearance, has a temper which promises ill for Mr. MacMillan's future felicity. She contrived to spoil our Flodden expedition to a certain extent, for she gave a certain thunderstormy feeling to our mental atmosphere. Ewan had previously remarked to me that he thought Miss A. felt rather "out of it" while Mr. M. and I were absorbed in long literary discussions. So on this day I was at pains to walk and talk with Miss Allan or Ewan. But this did not seem to agree with her either, so that my painstaking self-effacement was quite thrown away.

Flodden Field disappointed me unreasonably—it was all so peaceful and harvest-hued and agricultural. I felt as aggrieved as if I had had any right to expect to see a real mediaeval battle being fought under my eyes.

That evening we had a delightful moonlight walk along the shore. It

conflict over the centuries.

64   Inland from Berwick, the boundary between Scotland and England is the River Tweed. Opposite Norham Castle is the village of Ladykirk, formerly known as Upsettlington Green, where important negotations between the two kingdoms during the Scottish Wars of Indepddendence were held.

was the best part of the day.

Thursday morning Ewan and I took Mr. M. and Miss A. for a motor ride. In the afternoon we had a delightful little expedition. We went out to Coldstream Station and walked through a pretty by-path along a ravine to a romantic old deserted mill in Horncliffe Glen. It might have served as a model for a ghost story. But the dearest part of it was that in the midst of the ravine we came upon a clump of spruce trees literally loaded with gum—the first of the kind I had seen since leaving home. Spruce gum and the delights of picking it seem quite unknown in Scotland. Ewan and I had a lovely half hour then and there picking it and fancying ourselves in the homeland. To me, the gum tasted

House where we had tea

delicious but neither Mr. M. nor Miss A. liked the flavor, declaring it was "bitter". When I come to think of it—which I never did before—spruce gum *is* bitter. But it's a nice bitterness.

From the old mill we walked on to the Union Bridge, which crosses the Tweed where the latter forms the boundary between England and Scotland.[65] We had tea in a little house on the Scottish side—"tea" by the way, doesn't mean here what it means at home!—and then

we went for a boat row on the Tweed. This would have been the most enjoyable part of the day if Miss Allan, who had behaved very well up to then, had not chosen to make another exhibition of her temper. When Mr. MacMillan first proposed the row she seemed quite pleased, while Ewan and I expressed ourselves enthusiastically. But when we got into the boat Miss A. suddenly discovered that Mr. MacMillan was himself to be the oarsman, instead of the proprietor. She at once declared she was frightened to go on the water with him and demanded that he give up the expedition. Mr. MacMillan replied by pushing out. I think he wanted to give Mr. Macdonald and me the pleasure we had expressed ourselves as so eager for and I think he was a little nettled at Miss Allan's tone and manner. I had opened my mouth to say we would not go since Miss A. objected but I shut it again without saying anything. I had looked into her face and had seen that, if she had been frightened when she first spoke, she was no longer so. She was simply and solely furious. Really, I never saw anyone behave much worse. It

65   The Union Bridge connects Horncliffe, England, with Fishwick, Scotland. When it opened in 1820 it was the longest wrought-iron suspension bridge in the world.

all made me uncomfortable and yet I was hugely amused. She was so ridiculous in her futile rage. Mr. MacMillan, I verily believe, kept us out all the longer for the occasional sarcastic sentences she threw at him, as if she had bitten them off with a snap from some bitter cud, and she was quite beside herself in a white fury when we got back to land. We had to walk two miles to the station and Miss Allan tore off up the road the minute she sprang on shore. I felt that it would not do for me to linger behind with the men so I hurried off with her! 'Twas a pleasant walk! Miss Allan would not talk and finally I, exasperated at her unreasonable and ungrateful behaviour, gave up trying to talk to her and we strode over the last mile in complete silence. Poor MacMillan got a dressing-down later on. At least, the sole remark she vouchsafed to me was that she meant to give him one. He must be pretty deeply in love with her to tolerate her behaviour. And he *must* have felt rotten over it. But he behaved irreproachably.

Friday morning Miss A. had recovered her temper and we spent the day prowling about the shore and talking—and I think it was the most enjoyable day of all. Saturday we packed up and left. We were not sorry to depart from the Pringle establishment, since it was the reverse of convenient or agreeable. Nor did we deeply lament leaving Miss Allan; but we were genuinely sorry to see the last of Mr. MacMillan who is a very fine fellow and the best of company.

We had hoped to reach Keswick last night but could get no further than here, owing to the strike. Our journey here from Berwick was most uncomfortable, for ours was the only train that got through and it was crowded. Our compartment was only seated for eight but thirteen were in it and it was a very warm day. We had nothing to eat or drink from breakfast time till six last evening. I was so tired and worn out that I spent most of today in bed.

I find railway travel here even more fatiguing than at home in any case. I do not like the compartment system at all.

We heard tonight that the strike is over and we shall be able to go on tomorrow.

++*Sunday, August 27, 1911*
York, England

Last Monday we went to Keswick and stayed there until Thursday in the heart of the Lake District.[66] It was the most enjoyable and delight-

---

66   The Cumbrian market town of Keswick, whose recorded history dates back to the seventh century, was made famous by Romantic poet Samuel Taylors Coleridge and Robert Southey. One

[Keswick and Derwentwater]

ful part of our trip so far. It is impossible to describe or exaggerate the beauty of the Lake District.

"The haughtiest heart its wish might bound
Through life to dwell delighted here."[67]

[Grasmere and Helm Crag]

And then it is so interwoven with much of the best in English literature. The very spirit of Wordsworth seems to haunt those enchanted valleys, those wild passes and "fells," those fairy-like lakes. I would like to come over to England some time and spend a month in Lake-land exploring it a-foot, which is, after all, the only way you can explore any place or get really acquainted with it.

Monday afternoon we took a coach drive around Lake Derwentwater.[68] All was beautiful. The most interesting sight was the Castle Rock which figures as the magic castle in Scott's "Bridal of Triermain."[69] There is only one point where the resemblance to a castle—said to be very striking—can be seen and we were never fortunate enough to see it from that particular point.

Tuesday was, I am sure, the most delightful day we have yet spent. We took the coach drive to Buttermere Lake and back.[70] The road is beautiful, grand, awe-inspiring—and wild

[Buttermere and Honister Crag, Keswick]

---

of LMM's favourite poets, William Wordsworth, wrote some of the most famous poems in the English language about the Lake District.

67   From Byron's *Childe Harold's Pilgrimage* (1812–18).

68   One of the largest lakes in "Lake-land" or the Lake District, Derwentwater is almost 5 km/3 miles long and 1.6 km/1 mile wide.

69   Jutting out from a minor rise a ridge in the Lake District, Castle Rock is an almost vertical outcrop from the hillside with rock faces on three sides. Walter Scott set his long poem, *The Bridal of Triermain*, here; the knight, Sir Roland de Vaux of Triermain, must rescue the maiden Gyneth from an Enchanted Castle.

70   Buttermere is a small lake, 2 km/1.2 mile by 400 m/1,000 ft wide.

enough in places. We enjoyed the whole day. And I may as well admit that after all the best part of it was the two hours after lunch at Buttermere when we sat alone together on a little wooded eminence overhanging the lake and forgot all the rest of the world in a little bit of "honeymooning" in our green seclusion.

Wednesday morning we took a motor drive of 80 miles around Lake Windermere, calling at Wordsworth's grave and the quaint little cottage where he lived for twenty years after his marriage and where we talked with an old lady who in her girlhood had been a maid of Wordsworth's and his wife.[71]

Every foot of the road revealed new beauty. Some of the huge rocks on the mountain tops are of very peculiar shape. The most noted of them are named. One of them is "The Lady Playing on an Organ."[72] It is on the very top of a majestic mountain and certainly does, from one point of view, look exactly like a woman seated at a huge organ. Somehow, that captivated my fancy and I wove a hundred visions around it. Who was the player, sitting forever at her mighty instrument? And what wonderful melodies did she play on it when the winds of heaven blew about her and the mountain tempest thundered and the great stars stayed to listen?

That same evening we walked out to the "Druid's Circle"—a ring of large stones on a flat hilltop, supposed to have been in old time a temple of the sun.[73]

Nothing I have seen so far made such a vivid impression on me as this. The situation is magnificent. The hill is completely encircled by a ring of the most famous mountains in the Lake District—Helvellyn and Skiddaw among them[74]—and the sense of majesty produced was overwhelming. Certainly those old sun worshippers knew how to choose their sites of worship. To stand there at sunset in that temple of a dead creed, surrounded by that assemblage of mighty mountains, and picture the rites perchance dark and bloody, which must once have been celebrated there, in that peaceful spot where sheep were nibbling, was an experience never to be forgotten.

Thursday afternoon we went to Leeds and next morning motored

---

71 Windermere is the largest natural lake in England; it was made famous by Wordsworth's poem, "There Was a Boy" (1799).

72 Helm Crag is a well-known range with several distinctive rock outcrops. The north-western outcrop is the summit, and has been called "The old lady playing the organ" given the unique shape visible from a specific angle.

73 Now known as the stone circle at Castlerigg, this Neolithic site is currently thought to have been a meeting place, possibly part of wider ceremonies. There is ongoing debate about their astronomical alignment.

74 Helvellyn is the third-highest point both in England and Skiddaw is the fourth highest.

twenty miles through a very ugly country to Haworth to visit the home and burial place of Charlotte Brontë.[75] We could not see the interior of the old Parsonage where she lived her strange life and wrote her compelling books,

Druid's circle

[Ewan McDonald]

The biggest Stone in the Circle

Past and Present

but it was something to see it from the outside.

Friday evening we came on to York mainly to see the magnificent cathedral here.[76] It *is* magnificent—a dream of beauty made lasting in stone.

Yesterday we intended to go on to London but I was too miserable to travel. Since leaving Alloa I have been perfectly well but yesterday another attack of that wretched little trouble overtook me. I was most miserable in the morning but

---

75 Novelist and poet Charlotte Brontë (1816–55) is most famous for one of LMM's all-time favourite books, *Jane Eyre* (1847). The Brontë homestead in the village of Haworth remains a central tourist attraction in Bradford, West Yorkshire.

76 York has been a location for British Christianity for centuries. The first record of a church on the current site is 627. The current buildings were begun in the Gothic style in 1220, and restoration work is ongoing. It is the second largest Gothic cathedral in Northern Europe.

felt quite well in the afternoon and went out for a walk around York; in the course of which I became the proud and happy possessor of two pairs of china dogs!

I have been pursuing China dogs all over England and Scotland! When I as a little girl, visiting at Grandfather Montgomery's, I think the thing that

York Minster

most enthralled me was a pair of China dogs which always sat on the sitting room mantel piece. They were white, with green spots all over them; and father told me that whenever they heard the clock strike twelve at midnight they bounded down on to the hearth-rug and barked. It was therefore the desire of my heart

Gog and Magog

to stay up until twelve some night and witness this wonderful performance, and hard indeed did I think the hearts of my elders when they denied me. Eventually, I found out, I forget how, that the dogs did nothing of the sort. I was much disappointed at this but more grieved still, over the discovery that father—father!—had told me something that was not true. However, he restored my faith in him by saying that the dogs would come down if they *heard* the clock strike. But of course china dogs could *not* hear!

I have always hankered to possess a pair of similar dogs and as those had been purchased in London I hoped when I came over I would find something like them. Accordingly, I have haunted the antique shops in every place I have been, but, until yesterday, without success. Dogs to be sure there were in plenty, but not the dogs of my quest. There was an abundance of dogs with black spots and some few dogs with red spots, but nowhere the aristocratic dogs with green spots. I had about given up in despair. But yesterday in a little antique shop near the Minster I found two pairs of lovely dogs—and bought them on the spot, lest they be enchanted dogs which would vanish forever if I made them not mine immediately. To be sure, they had no green spots. The race of dogs with green spots seems to have become extinct. But one pair of them had lovely *gold* spots and were much larger than the Park Corner dogs. The others were white ones, cutely got up as half shaved poodles. They are over a hundred years old and in that Leaskdale manse, which is as yet only a dream to me, I hope they will preside over my hearth with "due dignity and aplomb."

++*Sunday, September 3, 1911*
Russell Hotel, London, England

This has been, for the most part, a really wretched week for me. Last Monday morning we left York for London. Just as the train started I was attacked by another fit of my malady and that ride to London was a nightmare to me. I never suffered such misery in my life. I had

[Russell Hotel, London]

looked forward to the journey through that historic country—but I do not now remember a single feature of it. It is all a blank of suffering to me. When we reached London we came to the Russell Hotel and have been here ever since. It is in Russell Square—the haunt of so many of the characters in *Vanity Fair*.[77] One expects to see *Amelia* peering out of a window, looking for George, or perhaps *Becky* watching for *Jos*.

But when I reached the Russell I was in no mood for literary reminiscences—though I would most devoutly have agreed with anyone who stated that all was vanity indeed. What mattered it to me that I was in London, where great kings and queens had walked and great writers lived. All *I* wanted was to get to bed, out of sight of anyone, and to bed I went. Tuesday morning I continued to feel badly; but I felt better in the afternoon and we went to the British Museum,[78] which is quite near the Russell. I had just began to feel the charm of its wonderful galleries when I became so miserable that we had to return to

---

77   Russell Square was part of the regions of London developed by the Earls and Dukes of Bedford in the seventeenth and eighteenth centuries. The square is the location of another one of LMM's favourite novels, William Makepeace Thackeray's *Vanity Fair* (1848), set c.1812. The Hotel Russell was built in 1898.

78   The British Museum, founded in 1753, is one of the largest collections of human history and culture in the world.

the hotel, where I went to bed and had a doctor in again—who looked even wiser than the Edinburgh one and did me just as much—or as little good.

Wednesday morning we spent in the Museum and I enjoyed it greatly. But at noon my ailment returned and I had to spend the rest of the day in retirement. Thursday, however, I felt fairly well all day and we finished exploring the Museum—at least, as far as superficial sight-seeing could go. I would like to spend a year there. I liked best to be in the Egyptian gallery and had the same feeling of being "back home" which I always have in reading the history of ancient Egypt.

Friday I was too miserable to go out at all but yesterday and to-day I have felt pretty well. Yesterday afternoon we walked to Charing Cross, Trafalgar Square—a very ugly place—Nelson's Monument, Whitehall, and the Embankment.[79] After all, the streets of London themselves are among the most interesting sights it has to offer. How alluring its shop-windows are.

This morning we went to the City Temple to hear R.J. Campbell of "New Theology" fame.[80] There is something very magnetic about the man which holds you while you are listening to him. But after we left the church I found that no lasting impression had been made on me. I cannot even now recall what the sermon was about or anything he said.

This evening we had a delightful walk through Hyde Park and Kensington gardens.[81] It is so much nicer when we can get around by ourselves than when we have to go in a taxi and be pestered by that necessary evil, a guide. The Park and the gardens are beautiful.

+ +*Sunday, Sept. 10, 1911*
Russell Hotel, London, England

This past week I have felt very well and have enjoyed myself, although we have crammed so much into it that I have a rather *overfed* feeling mentally.

Last Monday morning we went to the Tower. We did not know it was the "free" day, or we should not have gone. As a result we had to

---

79   Key tourist sites in central London.

80   Rev. Dr Reginald John Campbell (1867–1956) was a popular preacher at the City Temple, a famous "nonconformist" church in London. He was at the time that LMM was there a leading exponent of "The New Theology" movement. In this theoretical position, God can be readily seen and known through Creation but is not limited to or contained by Creation.

81   Created in 1536 by Henry VIII for hunting, Hyde Park is one of the largest parks in London. Kensington Gardens, originally part of Hyde Park, was separated in 1728 from the rest of the park by Queen Caroline and recreated as a formal landscape garden.

explore the Tower in company with a mob, which diminished the pleasure a great deal. The clatter and buzz interfered with my imagination and I could not picture to myself the centuries of history centered around that stern old fortress as I wished to do. Only when I stood by the spot where Lady Jane Grey and Anne Boleyn were beheaded did I succeed in conjuring up briefly the spirit of the past.[82]

Late in the afternoon we went to St. Paul's.[83] I think the thing I found most interesting there was the Whispering Gallery—because I had so often heard grandmother speak of visiting it when she was in London on her way out to Canada.[84]

Tuesday I spent for the most part shopping on Regent Street—a too fascinating occupation.[85] I had an interesting and delightful time;

"So Green and cool"
[Lover's Lane]

but once, as I stood amid the crowd that surged continually along the street I suddenly thought of Lover's Lane—so far away, so green and cool and sweet and remote. And I longed to be there. Sweeter the pleasure to be sipped in that wood solitude than any offered to me on the garish street of the world's metropolis.

Wednesday morning we visited Westminster Abbey.[86] In the afternoon we went by the river to Kew and revelled in the gardens there.[87] But when we got back at night I was so tired that it seemed to me I never wanted to see another "sight" again!

Thursday afternoon we went to the Crystal Palace.[88] I must admit

---

82   The Tower of London (properly Her Majesty's Royal Palace and Fortress) is a castle on the north bank of the River Thames. Founded toward the end of 1066 as part of the Norman Conquest of England, has been used as a prison for high-ranking inmates as well as a royal residence. Jane Grey (1537–54) was in line for the throne but imprisoned in the Tower for political reasons, and executed in 1554. Anne Boleyn (c.1501–36) was the second wife of King Henry VIII. She gave birth to the future Queen Elizabeth I, but failed to produce a son. She was investigated on Henry's orders for high treason and executed on May 19, 1536. The following day, Henry was betrothed to Jane Seymour.

83   St Paul's Cathedral is an Anglican cathedral built in the late seventeenth century, and was the tallest building in London from 1710 to 1962.

84   The Whispering Gallery in St Paul's Cathedral is a circular room in which sound waves travel around a concave surface.

85   A street famous for shopping in downtown London.

86   Construction of Westminster Abbey was begun in 1245 by Henry III, although the location has been a site of worship since at least 970 with the installation of a community of Benedictine monks.

87   Kew Gardens was first established in 1722 and became a national botanical garden in 1840.

88   The Crystal Palace was a cast-iron and plate-glass building first erected in Hyde Park for the

that to me this excursion was a disillusionment and a disappointment. Ever since Grandfather visited London this Crystal Palace, partly from his description and partly from some views of it he brought home, has seemed to me like some fairy palace of dreamland—a wondrous place of crystal avenues and sparkling fountains, gleaming statues and luxurious palms. But I found only a crowded bazaar and throngs of people.

The "Festival of Empire" is being held there now and the ordinary crowd was hugely increased that day by the fact of some special excursion being on.[89] We really—like *Yankee Doodle*—couldn't see anything for people—and there was plenty of interest to see, for the exhibitions of all the different colonies were very fine. But I felt defrauded because my enchanted chateau of dreams had vanished forever from me. I was the poorer for a lost illusion by reason of my trip to the Crystal Palace.

[The Ford, Kenilworth]

When all the buildings were lighted up at night the effect was quite fairylike and beautiful though.

On Friday afternoon we went down by train to Leamington and that evening we drove out to the ruins of Kenilworth Castle.[90] The five mile drive through the beautiful evening was delightful and Kenilworth Castle was the most interesting ruin we have seen. We spent a delightful hour prowling about it, even though we had to be pestered by a guide. Part of the time however I succeeded in forgetting him and roamed the byways of romance unhindered. I saw Kenilworth in its pride when aspiring Leicester entertained

[Entrance to Banqueting Hall, Kenilworth Castle]

Great Exhibition of 1851. At the time it was built, it was at the time the largest amount of glass ever seen in a building and became known as the "Crystal Palace." It was rebuilt near Sydenham Hill, where LMM would have seen it, in 1854. The building was destroyed by fire in 1936.

89   The Festival of the Empire was held at the Crystal Palace in 1911 to celebrate the coronation of King George V.

90   Leamington (properly Royal Leamington Spa) is a historic city in Warwickshire first mentioned in the Domesday Book of 1086. Nearby Kenilworth Castle was constructed from Norman through to Tudor times. It is the site of Sir Walter Scott's novel *Kenilworth* (1826), a favourite of LMM.

[Kenilworth Castle: The Banqueting Hall and Mervyn's Tower]

[Warwick Castle from the Mound]

haughty Elizabeth. I pictured poor Amy Robsart creeping humbly into the halls where she should have reigned as mistress. Back they thronged from the past, those gay figures of olden days, living, loving, hating, plotting, once again. Yesterday morning we went by 'bus to Warwick and visited the castle there—not a ruin but a very beautiful and interesting place—a good example of "the stately homes of England."[91] Then we took a taxi to Stratford to see Shakespeare's birthplace. The road lies through one of the loveliest parts of England— rural England at its best. On our way our driver pointed out the Lucy place—the residence of Sir Thomas Lucy, who earned a dubious fame for himself by fining Shakespeare for poaching.[92] I really think poor old Sir Thomas has been hardly dealt with. His was no prophet's eye to pierce futurity and see what this stripling was ultimately to become. To him, Shakespeare seemed merely and quite naturally, to be a young scapegrace who richly deserved the lecture and fine bestowed on him lest he come to worse things. Perhaps, too, he *would* have come to worse things had not his

---

91   The original Anglo-Saxon fortress on this site dates to 914. William the Conqueror began to redevelop the site in 1068. While parts of the castle have been rebuilt over the years it remains one of the best examples of medieval architecture.

92   English politician and magistrate Sir Thomas Lucy (1532–1600) was a Protestant; Shakespeare's relatives were Catholic. There is local legend that the two families clashed. Some legends maintain that as a youth in the mid 1580s Shakespeare published a lampoon of Lucy; another myth holds that Lucy prosecuted the young Shakepeare for poaching (possibly rabbits) from his estate.

deer-stalking escapade resulted in his being caught up thus sharply. It may be that the world owes a large and unacknowledged debt to poor pompous Sir Thomas. If he had let Shakespeare off the lad might have gone on sowing his wild oats until something really serious came of it and the poaching developed into some more reckless offence severely punishable by the drastic laws of the time. Shakespeare might have adorned a gallows instead of a stage and gone down to death "unwept, unhonored, and unsung" as a wild ne'er-do-well who had come to the end meet for him.

The church where Shakespeare is buried is most beautifully situated.[93] We visited it, his birthplace, and Anne Hathaway's cottage.[94] We returned to London last night and got here at eleven, woefully tired. Today, we went to Westminster Chapel to hear Campbell Morgan preach but heard Dr. Adams of Brooklyn, N.Y., instead.[95] I had wished to hear Morgan because of his celebrity; but I do not think I would have enjoyed his sermon nearly as much as the one I did hear. Dr. Adams preached on "Immortality"—the finest sermon I ever listened to.

After the service we walked back to our Hotel by way of St. James Park, Buckingham Palace and Pall Mall.[96] This evening we walked to the Embankment to see "Cleopatra's needle."[97] I looked at that mighty obelisk, carved over with its forgotten symbols and thought of all it had seen since it was erected in Egypt thousands of years ago. I think it was a shame to bring it to England. It should have been left in its own land where it belonged!

---

93   The full name of this church is the Collegiate Church of the Holy and Undivided Trinity, Stratford-upon-Avon, and dates from 1210; it is the location of Shakespeare's baptism on April 26, 1564 as well as his burial on April 26, 1616.

94   Shakespeare married Anne Hathaway (1555/56–1623) in 1582.

95   Westminster Chapel was established in 1840. George Campbell Morgan (1863–1945) was an evangelical preacher and Bible scholar.

96   St. James's Park in central London was established in 1532 by Henry VIII. When James I came to the throne in 1603, he had the park drained and landscaped; for a time he kept exotic animals, including camels, crocodiles, and an elephant, here. Buckingham Palace has been the main residence of the monarchy since 1837. The main house forming the architectural core was built in 1703. Pall Mall is a famous street in London that takes its name from a ball game—a kind of precursor to croquet—that was played during the seventeenth century. In LMM's day, Pall Mall was known for being the home of various gentlemen's clubs that include the Athenaeum, the Travellers Club, and the Reform Club.

97   Cleopatra's Needle is the popular name for an ancient Egyptian obelisk that stands on the Victoria Embankment in London (although there is in fact no connection with Cleopatra). Inscribed with Egyptian hieroglyphics, the red-granite obelisk is 21 m/69 ft high and weighs about 224 tons. It was originally erected in the Egyptian city of Heliopolis, and dates to around 1450 BCE.

++Monday, Sept. 18, 1911
Russell Hotel, London, England

This past week has been packed full—too full. I really can't enjoy things in such wholesale quantities. But when time is limited and "sights" unlimited what are harassed travellers to do? For one thing at least I have been most devoutly thankful—I have felt very well, having had no return of that most distressing ailment.

Last Monday we went to Hampton Court.[98] It is a beautiful place, but the beauty of the grounds is too artificial to be pleasing. I found the older portions of the palace the more interesting, especially the great hall which served as a ballroom for the court of Henry VIII and where Anne Boleyn and Jane Seymour and his other unfortunate wives must have disported themselves according to their several bents.[99] The modern portions of the palace serve now as a picture gallery and we saw many famous paintings. But pictures *en masse* like that please me not.

Tuesday we went to the "Zoo."[100] I sheerly enjoyed seeing all the animals. They were just as interesting as ancient relics and half-forgotten tombs. From there we went to St. Giles' church where Milton was buried.[101] But we couldn't

Salisbury Cathedral

As many days as in one year there be,
So many windows in this Church we see.
As many marble pillars here appear (8760)
As there as hours throughout the fleeting year:
As many gates as moons one year does view,
Strange tale to tell; yet not more strange than true.

---

98   Hampton Court Palace was first established in 1515 by Cardinal Thomas Wolsey, a favourite of King Henry VIII. When Wolsely fell out of favour in 1529, the palace was reclaimed by King Henry VIII. Located upstream of central London on the River Thames, it was inhabited by British monarchy until the eighteenth century.

99   Henry VIII (1491–1547), King of England from 1509 until his death, is rememberd by history for his six marriages as well as the Church of England's separation from the Roman Catholic Church. Anne Boleyn and Jane Seymour were two of his wives.

100   Opened in 1828, London Zoo is the world's oldest scientific zoo.

101   One of London's oldest churches. The full name, St Giles-without-Cripplegate, refers to its historical location outside of a gate in London's wall (the name may derive from the Anglo-Saxon

get in and nobody in the locality appeared to have ever heard of Milton. It was certainly a surprise to find his burial place so forgotten and neglected—the tomb of one of the greatest epic poets of the world. I should have expected that it would be as noted a shrine as Shakespeare's or Burns'.

Wednesday we went down to Salisbury. There is a fine cathedral there with the most beautiful old trees around it.[102] From there we motored out to Stonehenge to see the ruins of the great sun temple.[103] In its original state this Temple must have been a marvellous place. It is marvellous even now with all its unanswerable riddles. But in spite of the superior size of its monoliths it did not impress me nearly as strongly as the Keswick circle.

Thursday was, past doubt, the "fullest" day we have had this side of the "pond." We made every minute tell. In the morning we went to the Museum to see some things we hadn't seen before—among them the Magna Carta.[104] Then we went to the "Temple Church" to see Oliver Goldsmith's grave.[105] We saw the grave and the church is a delightful old place set in a leafy square which, despite the fact that Fleet Street is roaring just outside of it, is as peaceful and silent as a Cavendish road. But when I recall that square it is not of the quaint old church and "poor Noll's"[106] grave that I think. No, it is of a most charming and gentlemanly pussy cat, of exquisite manners, who came out of one of the houses and came across the square to meet us as if recognizing a lifelong friend. He was large and handsome and dignified, and anyone could see with half an eye that he belonged to the cat caste of Vere de Vere.[107] He purred most mellifluously as I patted him and rubbed him-

---

term *crepel*, a covered way or underground passage). The current building was first established in 1394. Author and poet John Milton (1608–74), one of LMM's favourit poets, is one of many English notables buried here.

102   Salisbury Cathedral has the tallest church spire in England to this day, at 123 m/404 ft. The building of the Cathedral began in 1220 and was mostly completed by 1258.

103   A prehistoric monument consisting of a ring of standing stones and burial mounts. Radio-carbon dating suggested that the first stones were raised between 2400 and 2200 BCE (another theory holds that the site may date from 3000 BCE).

104   The Magna Carta was a charter first issued by King John of England in 1215 as a set of limitations on royal power (including the protection of church rights and protection against illegal imprisonment). In 1297 it became part of England's statute law.

105   A twelfth-century church, located between Fleet Street and the River Thames, was originally built for the Knights Templar as their English headquarters. It is the burial site of author, poet and playwright Oliver Goldsmith (1728–74).

106   Eighteenth-century actor and playwright David Garrick composed these lines as a mock epigraph for Goldsmith, who was said to have unrefined speech: "Here lies Nolly Goldsmith, for shortness called Noll,/Who wrote like an angel, but talked like poor Poll."

107   From one of LMM's favourite poems, *Lady Clara Vere de Vere* (1842) by Tennyson.

self against my dress as if we were old acquaintances—as perchance we were in some other incarnation. Nine out of ten cats would have ambled on with us to the grave and perhaps been too hard to get rid of. Not so this Marquis of Carabas.[108] He sat gravely down and waited until we had gone on, seen the grave, and returned to where he sat. Then he stood up, accepted several more pats, waved his tail amiably, and walked gravely back to the door from which he had emerged, having done the honours of his domain in the most irreproachable fashion. Truly, he did give the world assurance of a cat.

Then we went to lunch in a noted Strand restaurant with Mr. Hynes, the business manager of the Pitman firm who publish my books in England.[109] He was a very nice man and we enjoyed our lunch with him muchly. That over we rushed to a station and went down to Windsor to see the castle and palace there. When we came out we saw the crowd looking excitedly upward. Following their glances we beheld a flying machine soaring across the sunset sky like some huge bird. This was the first time we had seen one and I was quite excited over it.[110]

When we got back to London we went to see "Macbeth." Beerbohm Tree played the name part.[111] He was excellent and the staging was good. *Lady MacBeth*, however, was poor and they "played to the gallery" in the supernatural parts, which were just vulgarly "spooky" and entirely lacking in the real weirdness and mystery and subtlety which should characterize the scenes. Still, on the whole, it was exceedingly enjoyable.

Friday we went to Oxford and saw as many of its interesting old colleges as we had time for. This involved a great deal of walking and I was dreadfully tired when we got back to London. I am beginning to feel that I have had enough of sight seeing and knocking about, for one time. I am tired of living in a trunk—and I am tired of hotel cookery. And I want a *home* again. I am tired of living under stranger roofs. We sail for home next Thursday on the *Adriatic* and I feel heart glad at the thought. I want to get back to Canada, to build my nest and gather my scattered household gods all about me for a new consecration.

---

108   A fictional nobleman in the fairy tale *Puss in Boots*.

109   A British publishing house best known for educational and business materials founded in 1886.

110   According to the RAF Museum, Samuel Franklin Cody, an American entrepreneur, made the first officially recognized airplane flight on October 16, 1908. By 1910, Winston Churchill was encouraging interest in aerial reconnaissance for warfare.

111   Sir Herbert Beerbohm Tree (1852–1917) was an English theatre impresario and actor, especially noted at the time of LMM's visit to London for extravagant and popular productions of Shakespearean plays. His production of *Macbeth* (first mounted in 1911) later served as the basis for a film (since lost) by D.W. Griffith (1916).

However, "to resume and to continue":—

Saturday morning we visited the Houses of Parliament[112] and in the afternoon we started on what was, to me, the most interesting of all our expeditions. We went down to Dunwich, the little seashore village on the coast of

[A Bird's Eye View of Dunwich]

Suffolk where grandmother was born and lived until she was twelve.[113]

I had always been determined to hunt this place up if ever I came over to England. My fancy had always clung around the idea of it. Grandmother, with the reserve that always characterized her, very seldom spoke of her old home; but she did so occasionally and her remarks always lingered in my mind. I learned more of it from Grandfather, though, who often repeated what he had heard of it from Great Grandfather Woolner. From one hint or another I had built up a well-defined picture of it—which, I need not say, proved to be quite unlike the reality.

We reached Darsham station in the afternoon and got a cab to take us over to Dunwich, a distance of six miles. I looked at everything as we drove along with keen interest and eagerness. Very likely grandma and Aunt Margaret,[114] when they

Lover's Lane

---

112   The British Houses of Parliament—the House of Commons and the House of Lords—are located in the Palace of Westminster. The site itself is of great historical significance through the centuries: it may have first been used as a royal residence by Canute the Great between 1016 and 1035.

113   Dunwich is a village on the Suffolk coast of England.

114   "Aunt Margaret" (actually LMM's great-aunt) was Margaret Woolner Mackenzie. She was the sister of Lucy Ann Woolner Macneill, LMM's grandmother, and mother of Tillie Mackenzie Houston.

were little girls, had looked on those very scenes and may have driven over that very road. Half way to Dunwich we crossed a belt of waste land or "commons" which was very bleak and uninviting. But beyond that it was pastoral England again and presently we found ourselves in Dunwich—the quaintest, sleepiest, most out of the world little village imaginable, right down on the crumbling Suffolk coast. We went to the "Ship Inn" and got quarters with difficulty for they were full and we had to take an attic room of few conveniences. Then, after tea, we started out to try to find some trace of the whereabouts of the old Woolner farm. At first I was in despair. It seemed as if the race that knew Joseph

Old Woolner House

had utterly passed away. Nobody had ever heard of the name of Woolner or had any idea where his home had been—or any other idea, apparently, for the natives of Dunwich seemed the most hopelessly stupid folks I have ever tried to extract information from.

But at last, after persistent inquiry I located an old man of 86, named Samuel Scarlett, who gave me all the information I required. He said he remembered perfectly being at the Woolner auction when he was a

Granary of old Woolner Place

boy of twelve. The farm where they had lived was about ten minutes walk from the village and he said the buildings were all in good preservation and exactly as the Woolners had left them. Much excited over this, I rewarded old Mr. Scarlett with a half sovereign and we started off, soon reaching the long lane

with its hawthorn hedges, leading up to the old place. The house is a building of red brick surrounded by beautiful trees, with an old garden in front, hedged in by hawthorn. It is not occupied at present. By good fortune the man of the next farm, who had the key, was at the barn when we got there, and he unlocked the house and let us go all over it.

I cannot describe my feelings—nor account for them. I had expected to feel an interest in the place, naturally; but I had the strangest sensation of *coming home*. My emotion almost overpowered me. It seemed to me that grandmother and Aunt Margaret *must* be somewhere around, little laughing girls of twelve and fourteen—such as I had never been able to picture them before. Their bright eyes seemed to me to peep around the corners—I seemed to hear the patter of their flying footsteps, the rustle of their whispers and laughter. I was homesick—and yet I felt as if I had come home. It seemed to me that the Woolner auction must have been a thing of yesterday—as if the family had just moved out of the house, leaving it still warm from their presence. If the house had been occupied I might not have felt like this. But as it was, it seemed as if the Woolners had just gone.

[Woolner house]

We left it in the twilight and walked back to the inn. Then we went to the shore and sat there for a long time, watching the peculiar and beautiful phenomena of phosphorescent waves—such as I had never seen before. My heart was full. It seemed to me that back there, behind that village, was a home—a home empty and deserted, with no light gleaming from its windows, just as another home, thousands of miles to the sunsetting was also blank and empty and fireless. I thought of grandmother and how interested she would have been in hearing from her old home. It was a bitter thought

Old Church Tower, Dunwich

that I could never tell her. I cried myself to sleep that night—tears of longing and homesickness that seemed partly my own and partly some long-dead emotion of the vanished years.

The next morning we went again to the old place and I took several photos of it for Aunt Margaret. Then we went into the field behind the house and sat down for a couple of hours talking and eating bramble-berries from the hedge. I loved to be there and when we had to go I felt as I had felt when I left the old home of Cavendish.

We walked back to the village by way of the shore, seeing on our way the ruined tower, right on the very brink of the crumbling cliff, of the old church built hundreds of years before.[115]

After dinner we hired a pony and trap—and oh, how slow that pony was! Slow!!!—and started out to hunt up a place called Knodishall, seven miles away, where lived a certain Mrs. Robert Collins of whom Mr. Scarlett had told me.[116] Great grandfather Woolner was married twice. His first wife, Margaret Tuthill, died, leaving a daughter Caroline. This Caroline was grown up and married to one James Rous, when the Woolners "went foreign," as the saying is in Dunwich. The aforesaid Mrs. Collins was one of Caroline Woolner's children and therefore a cousin of sorts. We found her home eventually. Mr. Scarlett had told us that she had married beneath her and that her father never forgave her. So I was not surprised to find her living in a rather humble way, though quite comfortable. She was very glad and interested when she found out who I was and she showed me her mother's picture and gave me a good deal of information about her family.

On our way back to Dunwich we stopped at Westleton churchyard, where we found several Woolner graves, including that of Margaret Tuthill and a certain "Lucy Ann Woolner" who died in 1812—a hundred years ago almost—aged sixteen. I think she must have been a sister of Grandfather Woolner's and that Grandmother must have been called after her. *He* sleeps far from the wife of his youth. He is buried in the graveyard of the old English church at South Rustico and she sleeps alone in that quaint old English burying ground.

This morning we came back to London. We had planned to pack up this afternoon and go over to Ireland in the morning, to see the Lakes of Killarney[117] and join our boat at Queenstown. But on arriving here we found that a big railway strike was on in Ireland and that it would be too "risky" to go. I daresay when I am home and thoroughly rested I shall feel sorry that I did not get a glimpse of Ireland also. But at pres-

---

115   A few years later, this ruin fell into the sea.

116   Another small village in Suffolk.

117   A famous setting near Killarney in Country Kerry that consist Lough Leane, Muckross Lake, and Upper Lake.

ent my feeling is one of unmitigated satisfaction. I am horribly tired. I am sated with sight seeing. I had dreaded the task of packing up this afternoon and starting off again in the morning. Now I shall have a good rest before we start for home.

++*Sunday, Sept. 24, 1911*
Deck of the Adriatic
Mid-Atlantic

Homeward bound! Leagues of tossing ocean behind us, leagues of tossing ocean before us! And beyond it our ain countree and the "old familiar faces." Though, for me, there will be no familiar faces in the new home to which I am going. The thought is a little bitter.

Tuesday and Wednesday we put in packing up and visiting one or two places we had not been able to see before. Thursday afternoon we did our duty in the way of tips and after lunch took the boat train for Liverpool, which we reached at seven, and went on board the *Adriatic*.

We had had a beautiful summer but we were both heart-glad to be going home. As I stood on deck and watched the splendid scene made by the lights of Liverpool and the docks as we steamed down the Mersey in the darkness I said good-bye to the wonderful old land and turned my thoughts joyfully westward.

The *Adriatic* was not so nice a boat as the *Megantic*, we did not have such a nice stateroom, and the voyage as a whole was not nearly so pleasant as the voyage over. On Friday morning we called at Queenstown and had an interesting hour or so, when the Irish women came on board with bundles of lace to sell. They were certainly beautiful—the laces I mean—though the prices were quite wild. But they would take the half of what they asked if you offered it with an air of finality.

One day was very rough and I was seasick all day—not so very bad but just bad enough to lie still in my berth. The next day I was able to be on deck again, but I didn't go down for meals.

The rest of the voyage was quite uneventful. It continued cold and damp and rough but I was not again seasick. We got into New York on Friday morning in such a driving downpour of rain that we could not see anything. Although our boxes went through in bond

Uxbridge Station

we had to wait a long while in the Custom House, and the horrible hurly-burly made my head ache. Then we waited in N.Y. station for our train. We travelled all night, getting to Toronto in the morning. Marjorie MacMurchy met us and we had lunch with her and her sister.[118]

At five we took the train for Uxbridge, our home station, and reached it at dark.[119] Two or three of Mr. Macdonald's friends met us and it was nice to be welcomed. But I was dreadfully tired; it was a damp, murky autumn night, and when we started on our muddy seven mile drive I felt discouraged, heartsick and homesick.

Ewan's boarding house, Leaskdale.

The next time I went over that road it was glorious with October sunshine and crimson maples, with snug, prosperous farmsteads along it, and I thought it a very pretty road indeed. But that night in the starless darkness it was merely one long *blot* of wet shadow and seemed hopelessly dismal.

Leaskdale Church Outside and In

When we arrived at Ewan's boarding house—where we were to live until we could get the manse furnished—we found that our telegram had

never reached them and we were not expected. "They" are two old maids, Mary and Lizzie Oxtoby, who would have delighted Dickens. No pen but his could do them justice. And oh, they are queer—at least, it

---

118   Marjory MacMurchy (1870–1938), whose first name LMM spells as "Marjorie," was one of Canada's most prominent early female journalists, was first published in *Saturday Night* and other magazines of the day in the 1890s. One of the founders of the Canadian Women's Press Club, she served as literary editor of the Toronto News from 1903 to 1917. LMM met MacMurchy when the latter visited Prince Edward Island in 1910.

119   A town in south-central Ontario about 75 km/47 miles northeast of Toronto, Uxbridge was about 11 km/7 miles from LMM's new home in Leaskdale. Uxbridge was first settled in the early nineteenth century, and the town was incorporated in 1885.

was only their queerness I saw that first night. And I have never liked Lizzie who is a narrow-minded gossip, but there is a sort of innocent sweetness—without a grain of flavor—about Mary, which makes me like her now as I would like a child. But that night I thought "Is *this* the kind of people I must live among?" And when we went up to the tiny little bedroom, more inconvenient than any place I have ever been in since I boarded at Fraser's in "Sixteen," I was homesick and tearful and blue. I felt that I would *never* like Ontario and that existence here would be impossible.

Next morning was very wet, but there was a fair turn-out at church. Curiosity, I suppose, was strong to see the "new minister's wife". I passed through an ordeal of handshaking and good wishes. How I

Leaskdale Manse

View to left of lawn

View to right of lawn

would be talked over at the dinner tables of the congregation that day!

Ewan's congregation has two sections—Leaskdale and Zephyr.[120] The Leaskdale church is new and is a nice little one of white brick.[121] The Leaskdale people are all

---

120   Zephyr is a small community about 10 km/6 miles north of Leaskdale. First settled in the mid-1800s, it grew considerably after the coming of the railway in the 1880s, but today is a village of only about 500 people.

121   St. Paul's, the Presbyterian church in Leaskdale, traces its origins to the first congregational meeting in 1862. A first church building was erected in 1864, to be replaced by a brick building in 1906 (the church moved to new premises exactly a century later, in 2006). St. Paul's initially shared its minister with a congregation in Uxbridge, but with the creation of a congregation in

quite nice, being for the most part well-to-do farmers. It is not quite so in Zephyr. The church is old and unattractive, with windows whose panes are—or were—of "frosted" glass; half of the "frosting" has worn off each pane, producing the effect of a dull day in winter time, no

Front Walk

matter what the season of the year. Some of the people are nice; but there are many who are not attractive in any way and, taken as a whole, I do not like the Zephyr section. Ewan finds it unsatisfactory—lacking in "church spirit" and incapable of taking leadership.

The manse is quite prettily situated.[122] It is not an ideal house by any means, but it will do, and it is certainly much more comfortable and convenient than my old home. It is built of white brick in the ugly "L" design so common among country houses. My greatest disappointment in connection with it that it has no bathroom or toilet. I *had* hoped that I might have a home with these at least. But what is to be will be! It is Allah! We must submit.

Leaskdale proper is a small—a *very* small—village, called after the Leasks who originally settled here. I have always hated the idea of living in a small village. But Leaskdale is *so* small—only about ten or twelve houses—that it is almost as good as the pure country. It is quite a pretty little place. There are no young people in it—absolutely none. The residents are all oldish—or else mere children. There isn't one interesting or really intelligent person in it.

The first Sunday evening we slipped down in the dusk to see the manse—for I was eager to see my new home. As I have said, it is quite prettily situated—though a tumble-down old building on either side of it—the crumbling remains of old shops—detract terribly from the appearance of the place. We are much too close to the road for my liking—I love solitude and remoteness. We have a rather pretty little

---

Zephyr (the church building opened in 1881) Leaskdale and Zephyr were united in a "joint charge."

122   The church manse was about 25 years old when the Macdonalds moved in. Four prior ministers and their families had occupied it.

lawn. I wish it were eight times as large but we must make the best of it. It has some pretty trees in it and I plan to have some flower-beds in the spring. There is enough ground at the back for a fair sized kitchen garden.

When we came in that first night and surveyed the place by lantern light it didn't look very home-like! Boxes of goods and chattels were scattered about and torn paper was hanging in strips from ceilings and walls. But I had a mental vision of what it would be when we got it all in order and I ran over the house like a pleased child. It was *our* home and I was its mistress. No woman ever forgets that delightful sensation—especially if, like me, she has never lived in any house before where she had any rights or privileges beyond those of a dependent child. I was sorry to leave it and go back to the Oxtoby domicile. *En deshabille* as it was it was more like home to me than the latter place. The Misses Oxtoby had been very kind to me, but I did not like living there. The table was poor and our room terribly inconvenient. I longed to get into my own home. But before that devoutly wished consummation could come to pass there was some work to be done!

I spent Monday in the manse unpacking some of my boxes and occasionally suffering agonies of homesickness over some of their contents. But it was nice to see my own little household gods once more.

++*Tuesday, Oct. 3, 1911*
Leaskdale, Ont.

To-night the congregation gave us a reception in the church. We had a rather nice time, though I was dreadfully tired when it was over, meeting and talking to so many strangers. One of the names, however, was not unknown to me. Two of the men I met were Hugh and James *Mustard*.[123] By the oddest of coincidences I have come to live in *John Mustard's* old home.[124] These men are his brothers. They are nice, intelligent men, much superior to John. The Rev. John himself is now in charge of a small mission church in Toronto. He has married and has one son. He is coming out to see his relatives before long and we are to meet him. I really never expected that life would thus double back on itself and bring me into touch with John Mustard again.

The next day we drove to Uxbridge—where, by the way, my step-

---

123   Hugh and James Mustard were grandchildren of Hugh Mustard, who in 1831 was among the Township of Uxbridge's first settlers.

124   John Mustard had been LMM's high school teacher and (unwelcome) suitor in 1890–91 when she lived in Prince Albert, at that time the capital of the District of Saskatchewan, which made up part of the Northwest Territories as then constituted. Mustard became minister at the Dufferin Street Presbyterian Church in Toronto in 1911.

mother attended High School—and went up to Toronto where we stayed until Friday, getting paper and furniture for our house. The two months that followed were months of hard work—work that was made harder by well-meant invitations to tea from the families of the congregation. To work hard all day, trying to get the manse in order and then in the evening, aching with fatigue, to dress and go out to tea spending the evening "making small talk" or looking at photographs of people I hadn't the slightest interest in, was something of a weariness to the flesh. Sometimes I would be so wretchedly tired that in spite of the most determined efforts, I could hardly keep my eyes open.

The manse had to be papered all over from top to bottom and while the man we got to do it was on the job we could not make much headway in getting settled, especially as we had the most aggravating delays in getting our stuff out from Toronto. However, I got my boxes unpacked and the contents ready to be put in place when place was made for them.

++*Friday, October 13, 1911*
Leaskdale, Ont.

I had quite a surprise to-day. My half-sister Kate suddenly appeared at my boarding house![125] It seems that she and Ila are in Toronto on their way to spend a year in Europe. Kate had come out to Beaverton to visit cousins of hers there and her cousin had motored her over to see me. They had only a short time to stay.

When I last saw Kate she was a child of three and beyond doubt the most beautiful child I have ever seen, with golden curls and wonderful eyes of violet blue. She is now twenty-three and has no trace of her childish loveliness. She is merely average in appearance—very short, dark haired and insignificant, but with a rather pleasant smile. Her eyes are pretty still but are her only good feature. She looks more like her mother than any of father's people but is better looking than her mother, who was a very plain woman.

From her letters and the reports of my P.A. correspondents I had formed a pretty clear idea of her personality and my idea approximated pretty closely to the reality.[126] She seems a rather frivolous little creature whose sole aim in life seems to be to "have a good time." This is

---

125   Hugh John Montgomery, LMM's father, remarried after the death of LMM's mother. Kate was born of this second marriage to Mary Ann McRae.

126   "P.A." is LMM's abbreviation for Prince Albert, where she visited her father and his second family in 1890–91.

natural and excusable enough in a girl of fifteen or sixteen but from twenty-three one expects some real development of character, if there is ever going to be any. I found nothing congenial in Kate. We had nothing in common and her call could not have been any more a pleasure to her than it was to me.

++*Wednesday, October 18, 1911*
Leaskdale, Ont.

Tonight we had our first meal in the manse under somewhat ludicrous circumstances—certainly not quite as I had fondly imagined would attend our first meal in our new home. The cookery of the Misses Oxtoby is not the highest expression of culinary skill. So, though I have a capital appetite, I cannot eat very heartily thereof, and am generally in a state of chronic hunger, especially at bedtime. To-day the table was particularly poor and I was uncommonly hungry, having been employed most of the day in scrubbing manse floors and getting my kitchen into order. In the evening we went to prayer-meeting and when we came out I was really ravenous. I knew that if I asked the Miss O's for anything to eat some "sweet stuff" would be forthcoming and that I could not eat.

The Side Road

But I remembered that in the manse pantry was a box of eggs which Mrs. Hugh Mustard gave me the night we were there to tea. So Ewan went down to the store and got a box of crackers. We went down to the manse, lighted the oil stove, boiled a couple of eggs, broke them into cups, as we had not egg cups and with the aid of salt and the dry crackers ate what was quite as delicious and satisfying a meal as I have ever enjoyed! Truly, there is no sauce like hunger!

It was an exciting time. Every day something arrived—wedding presents, things we had bought, belongings of mine left at various places until sent for. We had no place ready for them and had to move about in terrible confusion. The kitchen was the only solace I had, for it was in order and things in their place. We worked from early morning until late at night. The work was delightful and interesting because we were home-making but it was none the less physically fatiguing.

++Saturday, Oct. 21, 1911
Leaskdale, Ont.

There is the prettiest "side road," running down from the manse, through trees and woods. Every time I pass it on my way back and forth between here and the Oxtoby domicile it holds out to me an almost irresistible lure. It beckons me—"Come, I have trees and solitude and the woodland beauty you love." But I have to resist it, because I have no time to spare for it just now. Yet it tugs at my heart strings. Oh, how I miss Lover's Lane and my old woodland haunts! Can I ever really *live* without them?

++Sunday, Oct. 22, 1911
Leaskdale, Ont.

When we go out to tea I *wish* people wouldn't ask us to play "Cro-quinole"[127] or insist on showing me all the photographs they have! They don't seem to have any other way of entertaining. I loathe "croquinole" with a deadly hatred. As for the photos—well if they would just give me the photos and let me look over them in peace, it wouldn't be so bad because human faces have always a certain interest. But somebody must sit beside you and explain them all—"That is my Uncle Rich-ard"—"that is my grandfather"—"that is my cousin in Chicago"—"that is a hired boy who worked for us." And you feel as if you were called upon to make some comment upon Uncle Richard and the hired boy and the Chicago cousin and you wonder miserably what in the world you can say, not knowing or caring anything about them and rarely finding any inspiration in their commonplace phiz's.[128]

++Tuesday, Oct. 24, 1911
Leaskdale, Ont.

Yes, we have really "moved in"—set up our own Lares and Penates.[129] The great event happened yesterday. I really couldn't endure the Oxto-by *menage* any longer, not to speak of the inconvenience of our double

---

127   "Croquinole" (usually spelled "crokinole") is a board game first invented in southwestern Ontario in the 1870s. Players flick disks across a circular playing board in a game rather like a miniature version of curling or shuffleboard. The game has in recent years made something of a comeback.

128   An abbreviation of "physiognomy," the face or countenance.

129   "Lares" were guardian deities in ancient Rome; their origin is uncertain but they were likely guardians of the hearth. They are often linked with "Penates," deities associated with the household.

existence. We had planned to move in last Friday, the papering being done and the floors all scrubbed. But, although some of our furniture had come no bedstead had made its appearance. We hoped one would come yesterday. None did. But I declared desperately that I wasn't going to wait any longer. So after tea last night down we came. I have twenty right good fat feather cushions. I put them on the floor of a bedroom, made them up with sheets and quilts and pillows, and there we slept! It was somewhat hilly and hollowy, but I have slept on many a worse couch!

We did not seek it early however. We stayed up and worked till one o'clock, Ewan painting the border of the library floor and I getting various "jobs" done. We were so tired when we went to bed that we could have slept soundly on a bare floor. But we were "at home" and in spite of the wild confusion of every apartment save kitchen and pantry, it really is home-like.

The next fortnight we worked slavishly. Most nights we worked till one, two and even three o'clock. But by November 2nd we had things pretty well in order at last, and I was ready to "receive." Much still remained to be done for our furniture came out from Toronto in driblets and delayed us terribly. But eventually we got all done. Room after room was rescued from chaos, and at last my longed-for home was an accomplished fact—no longer a dream but a reality.

I am pleased with my home. I think it is furnished as comfortably as its limitations permit and in good taste, with things we will

Inside the Manse

not tire of. At first, all our new possessions seemed to me to be a little strange to each other. But now they have got acquainted. Up to New Year's I was so busy all the time that I really had no time to *enjoy* my home—to *realize* it. But now I have more leisure and am beginning to realize the delight and comfort of many things that have been long absent from my life—or were never in it.

This doesn't mean that I do not even yet have agonizing hours of homesickness—hours where nothing seems to me able to make up for the loss of my old beloved haunts and the wild sweetness of solitary dreaming therein. Such hours come very often when I am alone. But

[Corner of Parlor]

they are not continuous. I am contented—I may say happy. There is an absolute happiness and comparative happiness. Mine is the latter. After the unhappiness and worry of the past thirteen years this existence of mine seems to me a very happy one. I am—for the most part—content.

Three rooms open off our entrance hall—parlor, library and dining room. The parlor is a large, square, bright room but not one which lends itself to decoration. It consists of nothing but a floor, a ceiling and four walls broken only by two doors and four high, narrow windows. Nevertheless, I think I have

made a rather pleasant room of it. The wall-paper is creamy yellow, my curtains are of lace, with straight green brocade over-curtains, and I have a moss-green rug on the floor. The furniture is of Heppelwhite design,[130] in mahogany done in brocade. I have some pretty pictures in it, and my big China dogs

Parlor view showing dogs and jug

sit in state, one on either side of the little bookcase—for alas, I have no fireplace in my home. I want one too much ever to have it, I suppose. Great-Grandmother Woolner's old jug, filled with pot-pourri, stands on the table. This old jug has quite a family history. Great-Grandmother Woolner had a sister named Harriet Kemp. This Harriet had a sailor lover who, on one of his voyages—to Amsterdam I think—had this jug made expressly for his lady-love. Her name and the date—1826—were engraved on it, along with several verses of poetry. On his voyage home he was drowned but the jug was sent to Harriet. Instead of

---

130   George Hepplewhite (1727?–1786) was a prominent English cabinetmaker known for a distinctive style of light, elegant furniture. Reproductions of his designs were popular well into the twentieth century.

prizing it, as one would rather expect her to do, she could not endure the sight of it, so gave it to her sister, Great-Grandmother Woolner, who brought it out to Canada filled with black currant jam from her English garden—perhaps the same

Library view—my secretary in corner

garden we saw when we were there last summer. For many years thereafter she used it in her dairy to hold her cream—for 'tis a jug of no mean proportions! Once it met with an accident and was badly fractured. Great-Grandmother Woolner mended it with white lead and, though the mending is not very artistically done, being all too evident, it was at least done thoroughly and holds good to this day. At her death it passed to grandmother who, as far back as I can remember, kept it on the top shelf of the old china cabinet in our sitting room. It had by then attained to the dignity of heirloom and was never used for anything, but was generally brought out and displayed

Library view showing entrance door

[Interior of manse]

to visitors, while grandfather told the story. When we broke up the old home last winter I packed the jug most carefully and it came safely up to Ontario. I prize it beyond all similar possessions.

Our library is a large room similar to the parlor, but with only two windows. It is papered with golden brown paper, has a brown rug and is furnished with Early English oak. I have at last bookcases for all my books and a desk where I can keep all the notebooks and "utensils" of my trade together. At home I had to keep them in different

Dining Room showing sideboard

Interior of manse

Dining Room showing china cabinet

My Dressing Table

Corner of our room

The Landing

places. But I did as good work there as I will ever do at my spandy new desk with all its shelves and pigeon holes. Nevertheless, they *are* convenient. On the library walls I have several enlarged photos of Lover's Lane and several other Cavendish views. I don't know whether they delight or pain me most. Over my own desk I have the framed pictures of *Anne, Kilmeny* and the *Story Girl*.[131]

The dining room is my most unsatisfactory room, having almost every vice a room can have. It is too small; it is the only way of getting from the kitchen to the other part of the house and so cannot be kept clean easily. It opens into the kitchen and so gets too warm and too smelly. The furnace pipe goes up through it and is *not* decorative. It has five doors and only one window which gives a view of several ugly back yards including our own.

Fortunately these things do not affect the flavor of our food!

Upstairs there are five rooms. Ours is a large, pleasant one, with two windows looking south but no closet. I have a pretty set of pearl-gray furniture in it, a crimson rug, and intimate home pictures on the walls. I do not think it possible that I can ever love it as I loved my little room at home. It can never mean to me what that room did. But I like it very much—*especially* after that awful room at Oxtoby's.

Spare Room

The "landing" is quite a nice size and I have furnished it as a sewing room. The other four rooms are small. One which I call the "rosebud room" is done in tones of pink, with a set of white furniture and the

---

131   LMM's early novels, published respectively in 1908, 1910, and 1911.

other is in blue with Circassian walnut.[132] This one is to be my spare room. One of the others we use to keep trunks and "junk" in and the remaining one is to be furnished later on for a maid.

On November second and third I went through the farce known as "receiving." I had many callers, who came, drank a cup of tea and ate a piece of cake, left oblongs of pasteboard and went away, believing themselves acquainted with me. Later on I returned the calls and left oblongs in my turn—at least, in Uxbridge. Zella Cook, one of the Leaskdale girls, helped me "receive."[133] She was Hobson's choice. I do not care for her greatly; I have not found nor did I expect to find any really "kindred spirit" here. Of course, a minister's wife is, or in the interests of discretion should be, barred from making an intimate of any one person among her husband's people. But even if that were not the case there is no one here whom I could admit into my inner circle. To all I try to be courteous, tactful and considerate, and most of them I like superficially. But the gates of my soul are barred against them. They do not have the key.

Early in November I began to suspect that what I had intensely longed for was to be mine and now I know it. I am to be a mother. I cannot realize it. It seems to me so incredible—so wonderful—so utterly impossible as happening to *me*!

But I am glad—so glad. It has always seemed to me that a childless marriage is a tragedy—especially in such a marriage as mine. I realize that maternity is a serious thing and all the more serious to a woman of my age. But not for that would I wish to avoid it. I want to have a child—something to link me with the future of my race. I want to give a human soul a chance to live this wonderful life of ours. I want something of my very own—bone of my bone, flesh of my flesh, to love and cherish. This desire, and the joy in its now probable fulfilment, overpowers all the fears and anxieties that sometimes creep in to disturb me. And above all is the *wonder* of it. I cannot get used to it. The thought that within me I carry *life*—a *soul*—a human being who will live and love and suffer and enjoy and struggle—is so amazing that I am lost before the marvel of it.

But, though thus mentally and emotionally uplifted by it, *physically* I don't seem to be taking to it quite so kindly. While so far my discom-

---

132   Light brown irregularly black-veined wood of the English walnut used for veneer and cabinetwork.

133   Cook had served as organist at the Leaskdale church since 1902. Her family, originally from England, settled on a farm located to the west of Leaskdale in the late 1860s.

fort has not been so great as many women have to undergo, still it has
been pronounced enough. I generally feel very miserable in the mornings and very little exertion tires me out completely.

As soon as my house was "set in order" we had to begin a series of
"pastoral visitations" which are not yet concluded. I detest this "visiting" since nine out of ten of the visits are wearisome beyond description, both mentally and physically. I have never thought it a very
enviable lot to marry a minister but when I did it I made up my mind
to perform as best I could such duties as are commonly expected of a
minister's wife. Of these, "visiting" is one. Then there are three Missionary Societies here—the Foreign Missions, the Home Missions, and
the Mission Band. I am expected to attend all these, of course, and I
do it—but!!!

I believe in Missions, especially in Medical Missions—and in giving
as one can afford to them. And it may be necessary to the success of
Missions—at least from the financial aspect—that these societies exist. But they are most deadly dull affairs. At least, I find them so, and
I feel sure I shall never find them anything else. Some women have a
natural leaning to them—a sort of *flair* for them, so to speak—and I
believe they really enjoy it. I have not, and never will find such meetings anything but unpleasant duties. We meet—the President, Mrs.
Geo. Leask—a hopelessly dull and uninteresting woman—opens with
a hymn and follows it with a stereotyped prayer. After a little business
someone reads a dull chapter out of some book on missions, we sing
another hymn, take up a collection and go home. The only part I enjoy
is the collection. I like to give the money—and it comes near the last!

During the first three months after coming here I was pestered by
letters from women all over the country asking me to "give an address"
before some Missionary Meeting or convention of some kind. Really,
such women must be geese. They could not, of course, be expected
to know that I never give "addresses" on any topic, least of all on missions. But they might have had sufficient common sense to realize
that, when I was just home from my wedding trip, with all the work
of "getting settled" on my hands, I would certainly have no time or
strength to career around the country giving "addresses."

To one and all I sent a polite refusal. I said that the claims of my own
special work would take all my spare time and that *I* could not under-
take any active mission work beyond the bounds of my husband's congregation. To this resolve they will find I shall firmly adhere. I am not
going to waste my time and strength on work for which I have no ap-

titude, to the neglect of my own work which has been as truly "given" to me to do as any missionary's or minister's.

Besides these aforesaid Societies I teach a class in Sunday School and do a good deal of work for our Young People's Guild, which meets fortnightly. This I rather like however. It is more in my line. We have a very good guild and the young fry take a great interest in it.

Thursday, November 23rd we spent visiting in Zephyr. I

Daffy

arrived home, very tired, late at night, to find a telegram from George Campbell—"Valuable box shipped today." I felt quite excited at once, despite my fatigue, for I knew that the "valuable box" contained—Daffy.

Of course I must have Daffy sent to me! I couldn't keep house without him. So they shipped him from Kensington by Express, in a box properly provided with air holes and food! Knowing what a nervous animal Daff is, I was really afraid the journey would terrify him to death and at any rate I expected he would make his entire journey vocal with shrieks. Thursday night I knew he must be travelling between Moncton and Montreal, probably half dead with terror, wondering in misery why he had thus been torn from his home again, consigned to the ignominy of such narrow imprisonment, and carried he knew not where. Such a picture of the wretchedness of his little cat mind did my imagination draw that I almost repented having sent for him at all. I felt sure he could never get here alive! He would be smothered or starved or frightened to death. I hoped he would get into Toronto Friday night in time to come out on the last train, so Ewan and I drove into Uxbridge to meet the "Flyer." But no Daff came, so we had to drive home again. Next morning, however, we phoned down to the station and learned that a box "containing a pet" had come for us on the morning train. Ewan could not go down for him then but a neighbour promised to bring him out. He arrived about five o'clock. When Ewan went out to get the box Mrs. Cleland said, "Your kitty is very quiet. There has never been a sound from him since we got him." I heard this and said to myself, "Daff is dead. Otherwise he would never be so quiet as that."

It had, however, probably been the silence of despair for when Ewan brought the box in I saw Daff's bright eyes peering wistfully through a slit in the top. In a few minutes he was free and I had my own gray pussy again. He knew me and seemed quite contented. He was not hungry but terribly thirsty. We kept him in the house and cellar till Monday night when we put him in the coach house loft. There was no Daff in the morning and I spent a most unhappy day and night. But next day Daff walked coolly in and has been perfectly at home ever since. It makes me feel "at home" to have him, too, for he is a living link with the old life, and Cavendish does not seem so far away when I see Daffy curled up on his cushion in perfect feline contentment.

On Tuesday December 5 I went up to Toronto for a short visit with Marjorie MacMurchy, mainly to attend a reception given by the Canadian Women's Press Club to "Marian Keith" and me.[134] On Tuesday evening Marjorie, Jane Wells Fraser, and I went to see John Drew in "A Single Man."[135] This was enjoyable although the play is a silly backboneless affair. On Wednesday "Marian Keith" and I lunched

Marjorie MacMurchy

134 The Canadian Women's Press Club was organized in 1904 by Margaret Graham, with LMM assuming duties as the Toronto branch's vice-president in 1912. Mary Esther Miller MacGregor (1876–1961), who wrote under the pen name "Marian Keith," was like LMM a prolific novelist who was also a Presbyterian minister's wife. She and her husband served in many charges across Ontario, including 22 years at St. Andrew's Presbyterian Church in London.

135 A stage comedy play by playwright Hubert Henry Davies; the play opened in Broadway in 1911 and travelled across North America. John Drew (1853–1927) was from a well-known family of actors.

Frede

Hugh Mustard's House

Cuthbert McIntyre

with Marjorie at their club rooms. The former is Mrs. Duncan MacGregor in private life and has written several novels. I have read only one, "Duncan Polite,"[136] and cared little for it, so I felt very uncomfortable when she praised *my* books enthusiastically. I liked the lady herself very much though. She is a bright little soul, full of fun and humor. The reception came off at the King Edward[137] that afternoon and was pronounced by all a great success. In reality it was the wearisome, unsatisfying farce all such receptions are and, in their very nature, must be. Thursday I did enjoy myself at luncheon Mr. and Mrs. Beer gave for me at the National Club.[138] But I was heartily glad to get back home that night. There is no

---

136   Keith's first novel, published in 1905. It was followed by 16 others.

137   The King Edward Hotel in downtown Toronto was opened in 1903 with 400 rooms.

138   G. Frank Beer (1864–1949), businessman, philanthropist, and first president of the Toronto Housing Company, was, like LMM, originally from Prince Edward Island, and was mar-

Mr Fraser

Mr McKay

place where I enjoy myself more than at home and the older I grow the less inclination I have to go away—at least, on other folk's invitations. Some outings I like. But they are such as I plan myself and are not of the conventional kind at all. Stella and Frede came to spend Xmas with me, Stella coming up from home and Frede from Macdonald College. It was good to see them.

Christmas day we spent at Hugh Mustard's and John Mustard and his wife and son were there. John has not changed much, except to get very gray—almost white. In personality he has not changed at all. He is just the same slow John Mustard, with the same old irritating habit of assuring you that he is "going to tell" you something "awfully funny" and then telling you some flat commonplace thing in which you cannot discern anything even to smile at. His wife, however, is a jolly soul and can talk enough for two. She has a rather pretty face with sparkling black eyes but is so very fat that her appearance isn't especially attractive.

On New Year's night I had a dinner party of "down-easters." Cuthbert MacIntyre came out from Toronto where he is in the bank of Nova Scotia. Rev. Mr. McKay of Wick and his wife came also.[139] She was of

---

ried to Annie Weeks of Charlottetown. The National Club, a private social club for Toronto's business elite, was established in 1874 and exists to this day. Since 1992 women have been admitted as full members.

139   W.A. Mackay served as a minister in Blackwater Junction, about 11 km/7 miles from Leaskdale.

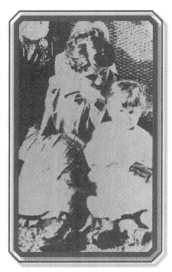

Mrs McKay

Ch'town and a chum of Margaret Ross![140] Rev. Mr. Fraser of Uxbridge is a Nova Scotian and a friend of Ewan's.[141] He is a widower and a clever, intellectual man. Win Ross was also here—Margaret's sister. She was visiting with the McKays. I think they all had a nice time and we had a splendid dinner—which I could not enjoy at all. I was just getting over an attack of grippe and felt very miserable and appetiteless. Frede and Cuthbert went away the next day but Stella decided to stay here for the winter. I had to have somebody so I offered her a good salary to help me out.

After New Year's I began my long neglected literary work again. I had been craving to get back to it but it was out of the question previously. I am now re-writing and revising several of my magazine stories. Mr. Page is going to bring out a volume of them in the spring under the somewhat delusive title "Chronicles of Avonlea."[142] Short story volumes never amount to much, so this must just be regarded as a "filler." Nevertheless, I never like to put out work that is not the best I can do, so I have put just as much painstaking into these stories as into my more important books.

---

140   Margaret Ross, who was married to the Rev. John Stirling, was one of LMM's friends from Cavendish, P.E.I.

141   James R. Fraser, minister at Chalmers Presbyterian Church in Uxbridge, may have played a role in bringing the Macdonalds to Leaskdale as the local presbytery's interim moderator in 1910.

142   Collection of twelve stories centring on the village of Avonlea. Though Anne Shirley plays only a minor role in the book, *Chronicles of Avonlea* (Boston: Page, 1912) was marketed as part of the vastly popular Anne series. LMM dedicated the book in memory of her friend Mrs. William A. (Tillie) Houston, "who has gone beyond."

March 22nd, 1912
Leaskdale Manse, Ont.

The winter is wearing away—for which thanks be. It has been an unusually cold and stormy one. The roads have been dreadful and this

has made our visiting
very difficult. It seems
to me that we have
been doing nothing all
winter but "visit." How
I loathe these "visits."
It seems to me that I
waste time horribly
thus which would be
far better spent on
other things. I get
home from these calls

Winter view from front door

tired out physically and mentally. The bad roads prevent any pleasure
even in the drive.

To-day I finished re-writing the short stories for my new book. It has
been hard to find time for it and it is a great relief that it is at last done.

Thursday, Mar. 28, 1912
The Manse, Leaskdale

This has been such a wretched sort of day that I must growl it off in
my journal. Being Thursday we went to Zephyr in the afternoon. As
Thursday is Guild and Prayer-meeting night there we generally go over
that day to do our visiting. I think I hate Zephyr more every time I go
to it. It has become inseparably associated in my mind with long wearisome drives over dreadful roads, mixed with calls on the most uninteresting and in many cases ignorant people. I should not have gone
today for the roads were beginning to break up. But it was fine and mild
and I had promised to go. We made several calls and as the roads were
very "pitchy" I began to feel very miserable physically, with a return
of cystitis.[143] We had tea with a Mrs. Urquhart—who, by the way, is a
woman I dislike and distrust.[144] After that came Guild; I was not fit to

---

143   With the coming of spring and the frost leaving the ground, gravel and dirt roads in the
Ontario countryside were rendered virtually impassable by ruts, potholes, and mud. Even today
rural roads often carry load restrictions that are in effect in March and April.

144   The reference is to Sarah Heise Urquhart, wife of township assessor and carpenter John
Urquhart. John's father had emigrated to Canada from Scotland in the 1830s and was among the
original members of the local Presbyterian church.

go—but anything was better than further endurance of Mrs. Urquhart. So I went and endured such misery all through the evening that when the meeting was out I was on the verge of collapse. Had I been near home I might have avoided it. But I had seven miles to drive over a dreadful road and my courage quailed at the prospect. I simply did not see *how* I could endure the drive home—nor did I endure it! I held up until I got away from the people. But as soon as we were alone on that horrible road, where our horse plunged to the bottom at almost every step I gave way and burst into a wild fit of crying—the culmination of my physical discomfort and nervous stress. I *couldn't* stop crying, try as I would. Every bit of courage and strength went out of me and left me limp as a rag. Poor Ewan was dismayed, not being used to "nerves" in women. But he was very patient, understanding what a fearful strain the day had been on a woman in my condition. But I shall never forget that horrible drive home. I suppose it is quite unfair to charge it to the account of Zephyr, but certainly the two will always be associated in my mind.

Still, I have never this winter suffered from any of those distressing nervous attacks which used to harass me in winter. My health is better than it has been for many a year and I am fatter than at any time since I taught in Bedeque. Tonight was simply the climax to a very trying day. One of the little ailments of pregnancy from which I suffer a good deal just now is one that is very trying to the nerves and when an attack of it comes on when I am away from home it almost wears me out, since I cannot yield and explain the trouble but must sit up and talk brightly, pretending that nothing is the matter.

Oh, how besottedly thankful I was to get home tonight! The peace and rest of my own room seemed like a haven of Paradise to a storm-tossed soul. And I am also thankful that "visiting" has come to an end for a time. The spring break-up is on and I shall have a vacation.

Thursday, April 4, 1912
The Manse, Leaskdale, Ont.

Have had such a lovely week of home life and work. I feel like a new creature. To shut the door of my soul on the curiosity and ignorance displayed by so many and retreat into a citadel of dear thoughts and beautiful imaginings—this it affords me peculiar satisfaction to do.

I am very busy just now sewing—making *tiny little dresses* and garments of materials very nice and soft. It is a very sweet and dear occupation—though it doesn't make it seem any more real to me that *my* baby is really coming. *That* continues to seem like a dream. I imagine dimpled little hands coming out of the lace-edged sleeves, dimpled little toes kicking beneath the flounces, laughing eyes gleaming over the frills. Eyes—what color will they be? Brown like its father's, or blue like mine? And will it be a little son or daughter? Of course I want a boy first. But I shall be satisfied with either if all goes well. I feel very nervous when I think of the ordeal before me. It cannot be easy at the best. But I try not to think of it. The pain will not be lessened by living it through a hundred times in anticipation.

The little basket which is to serve as a cradle came to-day and I fixed it all up with pillows and tiny sheets and blankets. How strange it all is—this life coming out of the silence—out of the unknown. My child at least will "come desired and welcomed into life."

Tuesday, April 30, 1912
The Manse, Leaskdale, Ont.

April—and spring! Spring comes a good three weeks earlier here than down home. The last fortnight it has been so delightful to get out and feel the good dry ground underneath my feet instead of wading through snow. April has been a good month. I did not have to go anywhere and I sewed and read and wrote, none daring to make me afraid. I have begun work on a second "Story Girl" volume, though I don't expect to get on very rapidly with it.[145] However, if I can get the skeleton of it blocked out before my confinement I shall be content.

This last fortnight in April I have been miserable enough physically—at least in the afternoons and evenings. I don't suppose I shall be much better until it is all over. I do not mind it so much when no one is here and when I do not have to go anywhere. But when company comes or I have to go to meetings etc. I really suffer a martyrdom of misery, partly physical, partly nervous. This last week, too, we have been housecleaning and I find it doubly hard for a number of reasons. I always liked housecleaning before, but this spring I certainly did not like it.

May 31st, 1912
The Manse, Leaskdale, Ont.

May has been a most interesting month. We began our garden and it is flourishing. It is so delightful to have a garden again. It is so many years since I had one. In the backyard we have our vegetable array and

---

145   Published as *The Golden Road* (Boston: Page, 1913), the new novel featured the same characters as *The Story Girl.*

on the lawn our flowers and shrubs. We have had a lot of work getting the place into tolerable shape—for it had been pretty well neglected for several years—but it was pleasant work. Our little "lot" looks so pretty now, when the trees are out and the grass is green. Every morning I make a pilgrimage over our domain to see what has come up during the night.

Oh, how I missed the mayflowers this year! They do not grow here— and spring does not seem wholly spring without them. To be sure, we have some lovely flowers in their place—delicate white and pink "spring beauties," looking very like mayflowers at a little distance, beautiful white and pink trilliums, like hot house blossoms, and long-stemmed blue violets. The children hereabouts kept us supplied with bouquets and one delightful evening we had a still more delightful stroll—Ewan, Stella and I—along the side road and up through Mr. Leask's woods to gather trilliums ourselves. 'Twas in wild cherry time and the world was abloom. Memories of Lover's Lane in springtime tugged at my heart.

But all the loveliness of trillium and violet could not quite atone for the lack of mayflowers.

The first two weeks of May I continued subject to attacks of "misery." Since then, however, I have been very well. But I am beginning to feel the inconvenience of increasing size. It is difficult for me to move about. I am not nearly so ungainly as many women are. The "old women" say I "carry it well." Nevertheless, I am decidedly not the slight creature I was a year ago. I seem big all over now—not misshapen but just a big woman. I find it is becoming hard to get up and down, or change from one posture to another. All this however is very little. If it were not for the anguish of the final ordeal, these discomforts would be a small price to pay for the delight of a child. Perhaps, if all goes well and my baby comes to me safely, I shall think even the pain of birth not too large a price. But now, when the end is coming so near, I cannot avoid feeling dread and anxiety. I have never had to endure any intense physical pain. So I fear I shall not bear it well or be very brave and patient. And then—it may even mean my life. The thought is a strange one. To-day I found myself thinking, "Will I be here this day two months?"—"or shall I be lying in Cavendish churchyard?" And I sowed not a seed this spring without wondering if I should live to see it blossom and bear. I want to live—I have many things I want to do and accomplish and enjoy—and oh, I want to live for my child's sake, if it lives. It is my greatest dread that I may die and yet leave a living child to suffer and lose what I have suffered and lost by being motherless! If I am not to live I pray that my child may not live either.

I do not allow these thoughts to master me or make me morbid. But all contingencies must be faced calmly and provided for. I think I have made all such provision as fully as possible. My business affairs are all in order, my personal wishes written out clearly. If I have to go those who stay behind will know what to do.

But I hope all will go well, both with my child and me. If I were to live but lose my baby I think the disappointment would almost kill me.

Ewan went home for a flying visit of ten days in May. How I wished I could have gone with him! It is my only regret that I cannot go home this summer. And yet it is not so poignant as

A weird picture of Stella and myself at Niagara

I would have expected. It is the *old* Cavendish that I long for in my homesick hours. And the changes there are so great that, in one way, I have a strange shrinking from going back. Home, as it was, I can never see again.

After Ewan came back Stella and I took a jaunt to Niagara, as Stella wished to see it before going home. The falls are, of course, magnificent though much spoiled by the power houses and buildings along the brink of the gorge.[146] If one could see the falls in the midst of their green primeval wilderness! But with all drawbacks their grandeur is indisputable and I could gaze upon them endlessly. Yet would I rather look out from Cavendish shore upon a gulf storm!

Sunday, June 30, 1912
Leaskdale, Ont.

June has been, on the whole, a very pleasant month of fine weather and interesting occupations. A busy month, too—gardening, sewing etc. I have been remarkably well—much better than in May and am quite active and "spry" yet. But my time is drawing very, very near and—what will be the outcome?

---

146   By 1912 there were a number of hydroelectric plants operating on both the Canadian and the American side of the falls. While these stations helped to power industrial development in Ontario and Quebec, many felt they undermined the natural beauty of the falls.

My new book "Chronicles of Avonlea" came the other day. It is got up like the others. The reviews have been very kindly so far. There is less of "real life" in it than in any of the others—in fact, all the tales and personages are "compact of imagination" only and have no prototypes in actual existence. To me, from much re-writing they are very stale but to those to whom they come newly they may give pleasure.

A corner of our lawn

But just now one thought dominates my mind. In a little over a fortnight comes "my hour." How shall I meet it? What will it bring me? Will I pass safely through the valley of the shadow and bring therefrom a new life? Or shall I remain among the shadows?

I shall not write in this journal again until all is over. Perhaps I may never write again. If not, Old Journal—greeting and farewell!

Sunday, Sept. 22, 1912
Leaskdale Manse, Ont.

This is the first time I have had a chance to "write" up my journal. The past three months have been packed so full of busy doings and wonderful experiences that journal writing has been out of the question. Now, however, on this quiet afternoon of the waning year, I find myself at liberty to take it up again. Ewan is away to afternoon service in Zephyr—Frede is asleep in her room upstairs—and down the hall in my room, in a white-lined basket with soft little blankets tucked around him, wide-awake, cooing to himself, and playing with his little hands is the dearest, sweetest, darlingest, loveliest little son—yes, he is!—whose coming ever made a mother glad and thankful.

I am indeed a most happy and thankful woman. Motherhood is *heaven*. It pays for all.

I laid down my pen that afternoon in June, not knowing if I should ever again take it up to write in this journal. I was expecting my confinement shortly. I was thirty-seven years old and I was a slight woman, never very robust. All my life I had heard and read of the anguish of childbirth, its risk, its dangers. There were times when I could not believe that I would get safely through. In the dead, dim hours of night fears and gloomy dreads came to me. I put them resolutely away, but always they lurked in the background of my mind. Would I escape with my life? Would I, as some of my friends have done, suffer so dreadfully that the remembrance would always be a horror? Would my child live? Would it be "all right"? What if it were *not* right—if it were some monstrosity—or if it were blind or deaf, or crippled mentally or physically? These and a score of other fears haunted me. And not the least dreadful among them was the quiet, persistent, secret dread that I would not *love* my child when it came.

As I said once before, when writing of Kenneth Ritchie I do not, as a rule, love children merely *as* children. Some I *like* very much because I love their parents or because they are really attractive in themselves. One or two, like Kenneth, I have loved because they are lovable and beautiful. But would I love my own? My reason told me I would—that a child, according to the old saying "brings its love with it"—but I could not quite convince myself. And if I did not love it—how terrible! This nightmare dread haunted me like a spectre that refuses to be laid by any exorcism.

The first ten days in July were really dreadful. A "heat wave" struck Ontario, and earth and air were like a burning fiery furnace, day and night.

On July second Frede and my nurse, Miss Fergusson, arrived.[147] Frede graduated in Household Science in June and came here for her vacation. Miss Fergusson was a Toronto nurse—originally belonging to the West Indies—who had been recommended to me by Dr. McMurchy.[148] The first sight of her was quite a shock to me. She looked so young—and was young, being only 28. My idea of a confinement nurse was that of an old or middle aged woman, such as I had always seen in such cases. I *knew* perfectly well that trained nurses are as often young as not, and that it is experience that counts, not years. But unconsciously I had been expecting to see a motherly middle aged sort of person, and girlish, black-eyed, curly haired Miss Fergusson was a surprise to me that I couldn't get over.

It was *good* to see old Frede and have her by me in those critical, anxious days.

The schedule date for baby's arrival was July fifteenth but Miss Fergusson cheerfully assured me it couldn't be so near—I was "too spry." She thought I'd certainly be a week and possibly a fortnight later.

---

147   Isabella W. Fergusson had been trained as a nurse at the Toronto General Hospital.

148   Helen MacMurchy (1862–1953) graduated from the University of Toronto's faculty of medicine in 1901 with first-class honours. The first woman to carry out post-graduate work under William Osler at Johns Hopkins and to intern at Toronto General Hospital, she was a pioneer in reducing infant mortality rates, wrote best-selling books on baby care and other areas of medicine, and shortly before her death was named one of the world's ten foremost female doctors. She was the sister of journalist Marjory MacMurchy.

I *was* spry. Wednesday afternoon I attended a meeting of the W.F.M.A. in the church and that evening I went to the Guild and read a paper on *Paradise Lost*.[149] Thursday and Friday passed. The heat was excessive and we all sweltered and groaned. Saturday came, hotter than any preceding day. I worked about at odd jobs all day until three in the afternoon, when I felt the heat so terribly that I went upstairs to lie down a little while. I did not come down again for nearly three weeks. Soon after I went upstairs I began to feel faint, transient little pains in my back. When I mentioned this to Miss Fergusson, she looked at me.

"I think labor has begun," she said.

The next day, Sunday, July 7, at 12.40 my little son was born.[150]

I have heard much of the agony of the birth chamber. That such agony is the rule rather than the exception generations of suffering women have testified since the dawn of time. But I know no more of it than I did before my child's birth. From first to last I had *no* severe

pain. I have suffered more many a night with toothache. If I knew I was to have another baby tomorrow it would not worry me in the least, as far as the ordeal itself goes. I felt nothing but cramp-like aches in the back and had it not been for the dreadful stifling heat and several hard and exhaustive attacks of vomiting I would not have minded it much at all. Dr. Bascom[151] said he could not understand it. He said it was perfectly marvellous, in a woman of my age, at a first birth, and with a child having such a large firm head.

Ever since I knew I was to have a child I persistently took, every day, a set of exercises recommended in a medical book for pregnant women. These exercises were said to affect all the muscles used in parturition, making them flexible and elastic.

Frede, Miss Fergusson and Daffy

Perhaps it was because of this I suffered so little. Personally, I have

---

149 John Milton's epic poem, *Paradise Lost* (1667; 1674) is a literary classic that LMM had studied at Prince of Wales College. The W.F.M.A. is the Women's Foreign Missionary Association.

150 Born in 1912, Chester Cameron Macdonald lived until 1964.

151 Horace Bascom (1863–1956), an 1884 graduate of the Toronto School of Medicine, practiced medicine in Uxbridge from 1888 to 1912, when he moved to Whitby, Ont., where he served as county court clerk and a member of the board of education. He also served as a medical officer in the First World War.

Frede at time of her graduation

First pictures of Chester, three weeks old.

another opinion but I do not tell it to all and sundry.

A few years ago I read Hudson's "Law of Psychic Phenomena."[152] Ever since I have had a strong belief in the power which the subconscious mind can exert over physical functions. Every night, as I was dropping off to sleep, and frequently through the day I repeated over and over the command to my subconscious mind "Make my child strong and healthy in mind and body and make his birth safe and painless for me."

Well, his birth *was* safe and almost painless for me and whatever he may develop into he is certainly strong and healthy now. I believe it was the "psychic suggestion" which produced my "easy time." But it *may* have been the exercises—or *both*—or *neither*. It is one of the things that can't be *proved,* believe what we will. I have said that I had been afraid that I would not *love* my child. And for a few hours after his birth I did *not* love him—or rather, I was not conscious of loving him! I heard his first cry with emotions of wonder and delight; but when the nurse brought him to me, bathed and dressed, and laid him on my arm, it was *not* the great moment I had dreamed of its being. I looked at him with interest and curiosity, as I would have looked at the child of a friend, but I felt nothing more than interest and curiosity, and I lay back on

152   Thomas Jay Hudson's *The Law of Psychic Phenomena: A Working Hypothesis for the Systematic Study of Hypnotism, Spiritualism, Mental Therapeutics, Etc.* (Chicago: A.C. McClurg, 1893) was reprinted dozens of times before the First World War. Hudson posited that supposed spiritual contacts were actually the product of the subconscious mind.

my pillow with a sickening sensation of disappointment and shame and dismay! I did not love my child! I did not feel like a mother. And how was I ever to care for and train that child with the requisite patience and tenderness when I did not

Leaskdale Manse where Chester was born

love him? I was appalled at the prospect. The first few hours after my baby's birth held for me some of the keenest mental suffering I have ever experienced. That night I could not sleep. I lay alone in my room—Miss F. having taken baby to the spare-room with her—and cried bitterly.

I understand now why it was so. The strain through which I had passed had robbed me temporarily of almost all power of sensation, physical and emotional. Although I had just given birth to a child I felt quite well and strong with no feeling of weakness or soreness. It seemed to me that I could get right up if it were allowed. But by next morning sensation had returned. I felt weak and bruised and every movement was an effort. And with the return of physical feeling came the power of emotion. When the nurse again laid my baby beside me my "great

Chester and Miss Fergusson

moment" came—the exquisite moment of the realization of motherhood. It seemed to me that my whole being was engulfed in a wave of love for that little blinking mite of humanity that lay cuddled to my breast. Love—such love! I never dreamed there could be such love. It seems blent and twined with the inmost fibres of my being—as if it could not be wrenched away without wrenching soul and body apart also. And, ever since, that love has grown and deepened. Oh, how I love him! At times I am terrified that I love him *too* much—that it is a defiance of God to love any created thing so much. *How* can a mother bear to lose her child! It must be possible, since mothers *do* bear it and live. But I cannot believe that I could go on living if anything happened to my darling. The mere thought of it sends a thrill of agony to my very soul. The love of motherhood, exquisite as it is, is full of anguish, too. I see and realize deeps of pain I never realized before. Motherhood is a revelation from God.

In reading tales of the martyrs I have shuddered with horror—and been lost in wonder. How, for instance, could any human being face the prospect of death at the stake for his religion? I knew I could never do it. I would recant anything in the face of such a hideous threat. *Nothing*, I thought, could fortify me to endure it. And now—I know that for the sake of my child I could and would undergo the most dreadful suffering which one human being could inflict on another. To save my child's life I would go to the stake a hundred times over.

Always when I read of a child being neglected or ill-used I would thrill with indignation and horror. But now I can scarcely endure to read such a thing because of the anguish it causes me—for in every child I see my own child—and I picture him undergoing that. I have cried aloud with the pain that came with such a picture.

Oh, my darling little son, you make up for everything I have suffered and missed in life. Everything led to you—and therefore I feel that all has been for the best.

I recovered strength with normal rapidity and never had any trouble of any sort. But it was unpleasant enough lying there in the extreme heat and having to have everything done for me by the nurse. I hate to be waited on in little personal offices. How glad I was when I was able to brush my own hair and wash my own face! Miss F. was a capital nurse, capable and efficient, but with the drawback common to most trained nurses—a Procrustean determination[153] to fit every patient to the same set of rules, leaving all individuality out of the question. I suppose it is unavoidable, since not one nurse in a thousand could be trusted to discern clearly just how far any rule might be relaxed for a certain patient. But I suffered some as a result. For example, I craved for a bit of beef ham. But Miss F. decreed that I must not have any salt meat and no decree of Mede or Persian was ever more relentless than she. I lost my appetite completely. I could eat nothing and this continued until she became worried. Finally she became so alarmed that she let me have some ham as the lesser evil. Result—it not only did me no

---

153 Procrustes is a character from Greek mythology who mutilates people so that they can fit the size of an iron bed. LMM uses the term to suggest a misguided determination to force individuals into an arbitrary standard.

harm but my appetite for other things returned and thenceforth I had no trouble in that respect. Frede and I are alike in this. There are certain times when our digestive tracks seem to *demand* a bit of beef ham as a sort of tonic or stimulant and when we get it we are all right again.

Baby was—and is—so good. I had dreaded having a "cross" baby but from his birth the precious little soul has been as little trouble as any baby could possibly be. Miss Fergusson started him in good habits and I have kept them up. He sleeps, or lies and coos to himself. The only time he ever cried was when the nurse was bathing him. *Then* his shrieks of protest would ring through the house. I saw him bathed for the first time the second day I sat up. Never shall I forget it. I laughed and cried. The naked little body, trembling and cringing as the nurse put him in the water was both comical and pathetic. But after a time he learned it was not a fatal affair and he became reconciled to it; then he began to like it. Now he loves it and it is so delightful to sponge his dear, firm, plump little body and work with it, and see him splash in the water, crowing with delight. He has learned to smile and he has such a pretty smile. His whole wee face lights up and his eyes gleam with mirth. Such a moment as it is when one catches "the earliest ray of intellectual fire." At first his eyes were the blank indifferent eyes of all babies. But one day he looked at me—*looked*, with an expression of intelligent wonder in his eyes. It passed quickly but I had caught it while it was there and I realized with a thrill that the little mind in that little body had begun to develop—and what would the full development be?

I gaze at my child often with an aching wonder as to what germs of thought and feeling and will and intellect are unfolding in that little soul. I can see what he is externally. I can see that he is plump and shapely and sturdy, with long-lashed dark blue eyes, chubby cheeks, lacking his father's dimples but with dear wee waxen fingers and toes. But I cannot peep into that baby brain and discover what is hidden there. He is my child—"bone of my bone and flesh of my flesh"[154]—but his little individuality is distinct from mine. He is the captain of his own little soul and must live his own life as we all do from the very cradle.[155]

It is heavenly to stand by his basket and watch him when he is asleep. I am sure there is nothing on earth so unutterably sweet as a sleeping baby. And then to waken up in the night and hear his soft regular little

---

154   From Genesis 2:23, these are the words spoken by Adam upon the creation of Eve: "The man said, 'This is now bone of my bones, And flesh of my flesh; She shall be called Woman, Because she was taken out of Man.'"

155   This phrase echoes William Ernest Henley's famous poem "Invictus" (1875).

breathing—and to think with a thrill of pain, how awful it would be to waken and *not* hear it. As long as the nurse was here she kept the baby at night, and when she carried him out at bedtime I could hardly bear it. The room seemed so very lonely and empty.

Miss F. would not let me go down stairs until July 26th. How strange and nice it was to be down again. I felt as if I had been away a very long time. The garden looked so beautiful. The flowers were in their prime. We have literally revelled in flowers all summer, especially sweet peas.

In a month after baby's birth I was as well and strong as ever and Miss Fergusson left. I felt considerable trepidation at her departure, especially when I thought of giving baby his bath. But I got on all right. I daresay I was awkward enough at first but I am quite expert now and it is lovely to do everything for him myself. I really feel jealous of everyone who does anything for him!

We had him baptized on September 8th—Chester Cameron Macdonald. Chester was my choice—not "after" anyone but because I have always liked the name and Cameron after the family name of Ewan's mother. I really would have liked to call him "Sidney Cavendish," Sidney being my favourite masculine name, but I couldn't get Ewan to see it that way.

Rev. George Millar was up from the Island, visiting friends in Ontario, and as he is an old friend of both of us, we got him to come over and baptize our small son. I should have liked to have had Mr. Stirling christen him but that could not be, and Mr. Millar was next best. Baby behaved well and looked sweet. He wore a little dress I had made for the occasion. It was a very simple little gown but every stitch was set in it with a prayer and a blessing.

Well, I have my baby and none of my forebodings have been fulfilled. I can smile at them now—

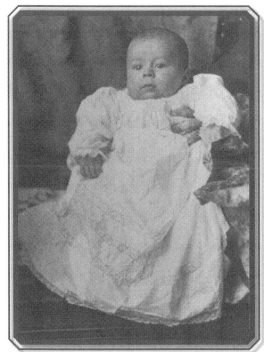

Chester in his christening robe

but they were nonetheless harrowing while they lasted. I remember one dreadful dream I had in April; and I could not help feeling strangely over it for it is an undeniable fact that some of my dreams have been strangely fulfilled.

I dreamed that I wakened in the night, sat up, and looked over the footboard of the bed. On the floor between the box couch and the wardrobe lay a big empty black coffin, with a man standing at the foot and another at the head. As I fell back on the bed, overcome with the horror of the sight, the men lifted the coffin and laid it on my bed across my feet. The pressure of it wakened me, but for a few minutes I could hardly distinguish between the dream and reality. That dream haunted me. From that out I saw that hideous empty coffin waiting for me at the end of my months.

In the days that followed baby's birth I was surrounded by kindly living friends. But in the night the dead companioned me. I dreamed of almost everyone I ever knew who had passed on—my father, Mrs. Houston, Pensie Macneill, Grandfather and Grandmother, Herman Leard, Uncle John Montgomery and many more. I saw them as in life and heard them speak and laugh as in the olden years. When I wakened it was always with a curious sense of really having been with them again—especially when I dreamed of father.

How father would worship my baby if he were living! It would be his first grandchild and I know just how his eyes would shine over it! And poor Tillie, too—she would have been almost as much interested in it.

How strange I felt the first time I left the house and went to a neighbor's after baby's birth! It was the first time we had been separated—the first of the little tragedies of motherhood. When I came home I rushed to see him as if I had been away for a year.

And how fussy and anxious I was the first time I took him out driving. I nearly smothered the poor darling with clothes, lest he be cold. How besottedly pleased and proud I was when people told me I had a lovely baby! And how fiercely I hated the woman who remarked to me that he did not have much hair! I feel sure I can never forgive that woman either in this life or that which is to come!

Yes, I am just as big a goose over my baby as any mother ever was. But I shall try to hide my folly in the pages of this journal. I shall *not*—if it be humanly possible—bore my friends with my raptures.

On August 21st Stella went home. Poor Stella, I am afraid her departure caused very little real regret in the heart of anybody in Leaskdale manse.

Last fall I invited Stella to visit me at Xmas, when Frede would be here—and sent her the money for her ticket also. For a visit Stell is a good thing. She is full of fun when she likes, the jolliest of the jolly. But when she wrote back and asked me if she couldn't stay with me for the winter—well, I was honestly dismayed!

There was no way out of it. To refuse was out of the question. It would have turned Stell against me forever and I would not have a family row for anything, especially with one of Aunt Annie's girls. But I felt very dubious as to the outcome.

When a young girl Stella was "livable" enough, though always with a quick temper. But during the past fifteen years she has been developing along wrong lines. I had heard a good deal about the sort of person Stella was to live with and had seen enough in my Park Corner visits to verify it; and last spring during the four months I spent there I realized to the full just what a disposition the poor girl had.

Stella

We did not clash at all, because I did not interfere with her in any way. I was only going to be there for a short time and I had my own work to do. So I held my tongue and possessed my soul, though many a time my blood boiled over Stella's behavior to the rest of the people in the house, especially her brother's wife.

In the first place she is the most tyrannical creature who could be imagined. She must have her own way in *everything* or there is no living with her. Even to express an opinion on an indifferent subject which differs from hers is taken as an insult. Then she has an *infernal* temper—a temper which she never tries to govern and which explodes on the slightest provocation. She continually makes the rudest and most insulting remarks to everybody, and yet if anyone, driven to desperation, retorts with even the mildest rebuke or protest Stell is outraged—and sulks and bawls for hours as if she considered herself the most injured of mortals. All this is bad enough, yet I do not think it is as bad as her ceaseless endless complaining. Stell is the picture of health. She is as fat as a seal and as strong as a horse. Yet from the time she gets up in the morning until she goes to bed at night she complains ceaselessly of aches and pains. She has almost every ill known to human existence. She pores over patent medicine ads. and "doctor books" and discovers in herself every symptom recounted there. And she is furious if everyone does not take her agonies as seriously as she takes them herself. Her ceaseless complaints are farcical enough to outsiders but when you have to listen to it day after day it is really dreadful.

Therefore, I felt, as I have said, dismayed. But as I saw no way out of it without creating family bitterness I tried to look on the best side of it. I determined to offer Stella a salary to be my "assistant house-keeper," so that—as I fondly hoped—she could not presume too much, as she would undoubtedly do, if she just "helped around" as anyone living with me might; and I got Frede to give her a preachment on the difference between living in her own home and in a house where another woman was mistress. Stella is good company when she chooses to be, a capable though not a dainty housekeeper, and a good, though extravagant cook. I was not well and was dubious about my prospects of getting a good maid. Perhaps when Stella was away from George—who certainly was as hateful to her as she to him—she would not be so irritable and unreasonable. In short, I made a virtue of necessity and hoped against hope.

Stell is an odd compound. She would work her fingers to the bone for you, complaining bitterly of it all the time and furiously resentful if she is not allowed to do it. She insults and derides you to your face, but behind your back she is the most loyal of friends and would defend you against the world. But everyone who ever has to live with her will be miserable—there is no doubt of that.

Well, Stella came. For about a month or six weeks all went fairly well. And then the leopard showed that its spots were quite unchanged. From that out she got worse and worse until it is hardly believable what she was like.

She was "boss" here. I was nothing more than a cipher in my own house, existing on sufferance. I hardly dared venture into my own kitchen to concoct a cake. Stella was angry if I did. Everything had to be done her way and all the work planned in accordance with her convenience. If she were crossed in the slightest degree she was furious. To Ewan she was as impudent and insulting as to her own brother and father. And oh, her complaints—her ceaseless complaints! They were dreadful. I was not very well and sometimes it seemed to me that I *could not* bear them. She never stopped talking of "the untold agonies" she was enduring. But let anyone 'phone down asking her to go for a drive or some such outing and we heard no more of "the untold agonies" just then.

And nothing suited her! Everything about the house and place was inconvenient or useless. Nothing in Leaskdale pleased her, from the weather up. I shall certainly never forget last winter.

I endured it all in silence for two reasons. As aforesaid, I did not want a fight with her; and I was determined for my coming child's sake not to give way to anger and have any upsetting fuss that might affect it unfavorably. These considerations also restrained Ewan, whose patience was sorely tried. He never said anything to her, but he hated her and it could not be wondered at. The way she bullied him and insulted him, even at his own table, was absurd.

And her *noisiness*—oh, her noisiness! She could do nothing without racket and fuss. She seemed to live, move and have her being in the centre of a whirlwind. Everything banged and slammed and rattled and clattered when Stell was working.

Unpleasant as it was to be home with Stella it was almost as bad to be out in company with her. To be sure, she was on such occasions genial, witty, jolly. People congratulated me on having her—she was "such good company etc. etc." They did not notice the grim smile with which I responded to such remarks. But Stell could not remember her place any better abroad than at home. She was constantly humiliating me. For example;—one evening we were out calling. The lady of the house said to me, "When are you going to begin housecleaning, Mrs. Macdonald?" Before I could reply Stella, as was her custom, spoke up "*I* am going to begin next week."

This was news to me. Housecleaning had not been mentioned between us. I was nettled and could not refrain from saying drily, "*I* am not going to begin until the need for furnace fires is past." And then poor Stella sulked for the rest of the evening.

Again, one evening when we had company to tea and I was pouring out the tea Stella rudely exclaimed to me, "Put more cream in the tea, Maud." I am *not* niggardly in regard to my rations of cream—do I not remember Oliver Wendell Holmes' dictum, "Big heart never loved little creampot"[156]—but even if I had been it was not Stella's place to insult the mistress of the house like that. She really resented the fact that *she* could not sit at the head of the table and pour the tea herself. I could hardly keep the tears of mortification out of my eyes. To be

---

156   From Oliver Wendell Holmes's 1861 novel *Elsie Venner: A Romance of Destiny*.

insulted like that in the presence of members of my husband's congregation was really too much!

And if I asked anyone here to tea without first getting her approval I was made to repent it. Oddly enough, I think this was what I found hardest of all—perhaps because it was what I had had to endure all my life with grandmother.

I was in terror lest Stell would just stay on until she was told to go. Rant as she might, at Leaskdale she was very well satisfied with the place and in no hurry to return home where George would give her as good as she sent and where she would have to work three times as hard as she did here without any fat dollars coming in every week. When she began throwing out hints about staying on I said nothing; but I wrote to Frede and begged her to get Stella to go home without a fuss if it could be managed. Frede accordingly convinced Stella that she ought to go home because Aunt Annie was not well—as is really the case—and much to my relief Stella finally announced that she meant to go home after baby came.

She was very good to me when I was ill. She had everything her own way then, without any irksome shadow of authority over her. I do not deny that it was a comfort to know that someone I could depend on was running the house. But I consider that last winter was too high a price to pay for that comfort.

Stella liked baby, too, and was wondrously gentle and tender with him. When she went away I forgot temporarily how she had acted and thought only of our mutual jokes and laughter and the bonds of olden days and interests. And I cried sincerely, thereby leading poor Stella to suppose, I fear, that I was quite incon-

A flashlight photo of our supper table—very weird of me, poor of Ewan and Baby, excellent of Frede.

solable over her departure. But my tears were soon dried; and since then peace and harmony have reigned in Leaskdale manse. Frede and I work together in beautiful concord and at last I have the home I had dreamed of having. Stella writes us the most doleful epistles of her aches and woes and crosses at home; but her shadow lies not on our threshold.

Thursday, Sept. 26, 1912
The Manse, Leaskdale

This morning, Frede and I, with fear and trembling, feeling as guilty as if we were committing murder in the first degree, chloroformed a cat![157]

Ever since coming here last fall I have been persecuted by starving cats. It has been a joke and a by-word with us. Last fall two hungry cats, a handsome gray "Tom" and a lean little Maltese, contracted the habit of coming here, because I, in the weakness of my heart, threw out some scraps to appease their ravening hunger. They came all winter and literally camped on the back veranda. We could not go out of the door without falling over a starving cat, with eyes of wolfish hunger and bones sticking through its skin. How poor Stell raged at them! We did not like to do away with them, because we knew they belonged to some near-by neighbors who might be annoyed if we disposed of them—though certainly they did not seem to prize them much! And they were such thieves—the cats, not the neighbors! We couldn't leave a door open but one of them darted in and decamped with something, or sneaked down cellar and stole the cream.

However, we bore with them all winter. But in the spring another cat adopted us—the most forsaken looking feline I ever saw—ragged-eared, and her two sides almost slapping together. She was worse than the others. The gray tom had lost an eye through the winter and "One-eyed Oxtoby," as we called him and the forlorn old spotted cat used to sit on our door mat and swear at each other by the hour. As for poor Daff, he fought valiantly, but he was harried from home and mother. He would not stoop to fight with "The Dweller on the Threshold"—as we called the spotted cat—but she clawed him viciously whenever he passed near her. I have borne with her all summer but the other day my patience gave way. She got down cellar and drank up a whole pint of cream—all there was and poor me expecting "company to tea." I hied me to Uxbridge and got two ounces of chloroform. Even then it was in the house a fortnight before I could get up my courage to use it. But today we've been and gone and done it. We decoyed her in this morning, gave her a good meal and then—guiltily, for the poor old thing looked so confiding and trustful—we clapped a box down over her, slipped the uncorked bottle of chloroform under it, and put

---

[157]   A similar incident was incorporated by LMM into Chapter 16 of her novel *Anne of the Island* (Boston: Page, 1915), but in the novel the cat actually survives.

"The Dweller On The Threshold" and "One-Eyed Oxtoby"

a weight on top. We heard two faint "mews"—then silence. We dared not lift the box till evening however, and then did it with set teeth. But the poor old Dweller On The Threshold had gone where good cats go—very painlessly and peacefully to judge from appearances. She was curled up as if asleep. We buried her in the back yard. May her rest be sweet! But alas, One-Eyed Oxtoby and the Maltese are still at large; and the latter has had two brisk kittens that are running about the yard. I foresee more expenditure for chloroform and more harrowing executions—for I cannot have these pests around here another winter, no matter who they belong to.

Friday, Sept. 27, 1912
The Manse, Leaskdale, Ont.

This evening was fine and crisp and I drove in to Uxbridge to meet Ewan who has been away all the week attending a conference in Toronto. We have a dear little mare "Queen," who is not afraid of motors or anything of that kind and I can drive her without fear. We had a pleasant drive home through the moonlight and a delightful home-coming, with Frede and Sonny Punch, a bright fire and a good supper awaiting us. I am beginning to have a very nice "home" feeling in connection with Leaskdale manse. I like to get into it and shut the door behind me in the world's face.

Queen

Punch [Chester]

Wednesday, October 2, 1912
Leaskdale, Ont.

On Monday Punchkins had his first little journey into the "big World." Frede and I went up to Toronto to do some shopping and of course had to take him along. He was very good but it is a fatiguing thing to travel with so young a baby and I was pretty well tired out when I got to Uxbridge station last night. But the worst was to come. Ewan could not meet us because of a meeting with the Bible Society which was held that night, so Fred Leask, a stolid urchin of eleven or twelve met us. We stowed ourselves away in the buggy and started on a cold dark drive home. Punchie remained good for five miles. Then the poor mite's patience gave out. He must have been desperately tired. He began to cry and for the remaining two miles he shrieked blue murder. I thought every inch of those two miles a league. Never was I more thankful than when we got home. I was so tired I could hardly stand and my arms ached as if they would drop off at the shoulder. But we got in, got a fire on, and got poor baby undressed and fed. When I put the dear mite down in his basket he looked up at me and laughed as if he appreciated his nest. Then Frede and I had to fly round and get the house in order, for the Bible society man was coming to stay all night and Ewan had been keeping bachelor's hall for two days!!

McKenzie-Naughton was his name. He was here all night and half to-day and is about as conceited, self-assured a young snip as I have ever encountered. He was quite clever and good-looking and Lord, but he knew it! And oh, how seriously he took himself and his hyphenated name and his pet theory that the English people are the descendants of the lost ten tribes! He was really furious, I think, because I would not discuss it seriously. As for Frede, she shocked him so badly with some of her heretical remarks that I fear he will never get over it.

But I'm glad to get home. Wow! (As Punch would say, it being the sole extent of his vocabulary at present.) No more of Toronto for me until Punch is able to stand on his feet and play the game!

Monday, Oct. 7, 1912
Leaskdale, Ont.

To-day there was a tragedy in Leaskdale Manse. We "shortened" our baby! Joking apart, I could have wept. It made such a change in him. My little baby disappeared and in his place was just a big fat chubby-legged "bouncing boy." I felt as if he were dead as I folded up his dear little long dresses and put them away in a trunk—little dresses I made last winter when I hoped for him. His short ones I bought and they have nothing of the sacredness that pertains to the others.

Frede and I have such fun in the mornings when I bathe and dress him in the kitchen while she is washing the breakfast dishes. We talk the most delicious nonsense

Abbreviated Punch

to him, make all the funny impromptu rhymes we can about him, and act the fool generally, none daring to make us afraid. Here for example is this morning's classic on "The Pirate Wag"—which is one of Frede's nicknames for him.

"There was a pirate known as Wag
Whose Sunday name was Punch
He sailed upon the raging main
And ate his aunts for lunch.

He liked them fricasseed[158] and stewed
But sometimes for a change
He broiled them nice and tenderly
Upon his kitchen range.

But he preferred them piping hot
Served up in a tureen,
Fried in deep fat a golden brown
And decked with parsley green.

And when an aunt was saucier
Than usual Waggy said,
"I'll have you made into a hash
You gristly old Aunt Frede."

But when Aunt Stella was served up
Wag wouldn't touch a bite,
He said, "If I et her I'd have
Most awful dreams tonight."

When the supply of aunts ran out
Wag used to eat his fists,
And when he went to bed he put
His stockings on his wrists."

Frede calls Punch's basket "The Jolly Roger." Punch is "Captain" and she is "First Mate" and she rings endless changes on this theme. Her production today was,

"The jolly Roger put out to sea
In a terrible gale of wind,
They left the manse, they left the church
They left them far behind."

---

158   A way of preparing meat in which the meat is minced, braised and sautéed, and served in its own sauce (generally a white sauce).

Also her discovery that Daffy had been stealing cream resulted in the following impromptu, to which we both contributed.

"What's the matter with Daffy?
He's all wrong.
What's the matter with Daffy?
Big and strong.
Oh, he's the Cat Who Walks by Himself
And steals the cream from the pantry shelf—
What's the matter with Daffy?
He's all wrong."

It's all pure foolery but we get heaps of fun out of it all. Frede felt as badly as I did over the "shortening." But tonight when I put him in his long nighty, lo, there was my ownest little baby again. And I cuddled him in my arms and tucked him away in his basket and cosied the blankets and down puff about him. It is so lovely to make him warm and comfortable and happy. The very hardest thing I have to do is sometimes to steel my heart against him when he cries to be taken up at some hour when, per schedule, he is fed, warmed and should be asleep. I just have to hold on to myself to keep from rushing to him. And I sit there in misery and harrow my soul by thinking, "What—if—he were to—if anything should happen to him ever—I would be haunted to my death by the agonizing thought that I had let him cry his poor wee heart out without consoling him." And I see myself lying alone at night thinking of the little creature far away from me in his grave and his little basket empty—and the horror is often so great that I fly to him, rules and regulations to the contrary notwithstanding, and catch him up and cuddle him against my breast, with his darling head nestled on my shoulder. And then the sweet baby smiles and the blue eyes laughing through the tears!

Thursday, Oct. 10, 1912
Leaskdale, Ont.

To-day I received a letter containing the sad news of the death of Aunt Mary Lawson.[159] It was not unexpected for she has been ill for three or four weeks but it gave me a bitter sense of loss and sorrow. I do not grieve for Aunt Mary. She was almost 89. She was very lonely. All her dearest

---

159   Mary Macneill Lawson, the older sister of LMM's maternal grandfather, Alexander Macneill.

Aunt Mary Lawson

had gone and she had no home of her own. Life, to that high-spirited, sensitive woman had been a bitter thing for many years. For her sake I was thankful that she was at rest. But I am the poorer by another loss of a rich-souled, beloved friend. Aunt Mary was one of the "ancient landmarks" of my life. It seems strange to picture a world without her—hard to realize that I can never see her again. Somehow, when we last parted, although she was in good health and seemed as strong and bright as usual I had a feeling that I had looked my last on her strong, gentle, intelligent old face. She is gone and I shall not look upon her like again. Women of Aunt Mary's type are rare indeed. I wish she could have lived to have seen my baby. How she would have loved him! But for that matter how many friends have gone who would have loved him—father, Tillie, grandmother and my own young mother. In certain lights my baby's eyes and brows are strangely like my mother's in a little old picture I have of her, taken when she was a young girl. It gives me a strange ghostly feeling when I see it, as if something of mother were living again in my child. My mother! How near I feel to her now in my own motherhood. I know how she must have loved me. I know what her agony must have been in the long weeks of her illness when she was facing the bitter knowledge that she must leave me. My dear, beautiful young mother whose sun went down while it was yet day! I am glad my child has a resemblance to you and I hope it will be a permanent one.

Sunday, Dec. 1, 1912
Leaskdale, Ont.

Another seven weeks have slipped away. It is winter now—or the beginning of it. We have enough snow to shroud the dead summer and hide the desolation of field and garden. I do not look forward to the winter with the dread I used to feel the last few winters in Cavendish. Nevertheless I do not welcome it warmly. It is a dreary lonely time enough. Always with the first snowfall comes to me now a sense of desolation—of being cut off from the world—of being, as Frede says,

Winter on the Lawn [same photo as "Winter view from front door," March 22, 1912]

thousands of miles away from anybody or anything. When I look out on my little lawn, which was so pretty and green and flower-spangled in summer and see it white and cold and still I shiver with a sense of poignant loneliness.

I have had a very busy fall—too busy in some respects. I haven't had time to *be*, because I have so much to *do*. I have had a good many visitors. Not many of them were very interesting. But I don't mind seeing them come. Never shall I forget how I hated to see anyone coming to the house those last few years in Cavendish—the humiliation of not having fit accommodation for their horses, of them seeing the general tumbledown appearance of the place, and of the display of grandmother's peculiarities of age. Nor, at any time in my life could I welcome anyone very freely, for I never knew how grandfather and grandmother would regard their advent. All this is changed now. I can invite what guests I please and treat them properly. This is a great relief; but in my position as "minister's wife" I have to entertain, and waste my time and soul on, some awful bores!

But we have some interesting visitors once in a while. Mr. Fraser, the Presbyterian minister in Uxbridge, comes out occasionally and is a clever fellow. He is a widower and it has been rather plain of late that he has cast a tentative eye Fredeward. It has been great fun for us all— that wicked Frede included. Mr. Fraser stands no chance with her of course but she is quite willing to amuse herself and us with him.

I think these missionary society meetings will be the death of me. We

Mr Fraser

have three societies here—Woman's Foreign, Home Missions and Mission Band. And I have to attend all three every month. I grudge the time—for they are so deadly dull. And I have "to lead in prayer."

This is truly one of my greatest "crosses." I dreaded it more than anything else before I married and it is fully as dreadful as I feared. To me it seems a mockery. I am so nervous that I seem to be merely reciting—and reciting badly—the form of words I have "thought out" beforehand. There is no real "prayer" about it. Perhaps through time I may get so accustomed to it that the nervousness will cease but I will *never* be able to pray a *real* prayer before others. To me prayer has always seemed something very sacred—the intimate communion between the soul and its Great Source, hardly to be breathed into words, much less uttered before others. *I* cannot *pray* in any other fashion and therefore any public prayer on my part must forever be a sacrilege and a mockery. To me, a petition asking for various "blessings" of one sort or another is merely rather ridiculous. I do not believe that God is "a changeable Being whom our prayers can alter"—who will give or withhold according as we do or do not ask, and therefore I see no use at all in such prayers as are commonly "offered." To me, ten minutes alone in a great forest, or beside the sea, or under the stars would be filled with more of the essence of prayer than could be contained in a lifetime of "asking for blessings." Prayer to me is an aspiration and an up-reaching, not a string of more or less selfish and material requests.

Sonny Punch keeps well and good and sunshiny and happy. He is growing so fast. His dear little body is so firm and plump and shapely and comical. I love to handle it. And he has such darling funny smiles and chuckles, and the most enviable knack of always laughing at exactly the right place in your remarks! But happy and sheltered as he is he cannot escape the common foes of humanity. From the beginning he was acquainted with pain—yea, at his first breath he met that grisly enemy. And the other day the second greatest woe of our race came upon him—*Fear* entered into his little experience. I never saw him afraid before. But one morning I was nursing him in the dining room. Frede opened the kitchen door. Daff was just inside and on the threshold was a stray Tommy whom the soul of Daff hated. Both cats split the air with that fiendish shriek of conflict which only cats can give. Poor little Punchkins shrank away from my breast with a cry of terror—the pitiful, agonized cry I have heard him give when a spasm of pain shook his wee body. Into his little eyes came a questioning hunted look of dread. His darling face blanched and quivered. I caught him close to me and comforted him until he forgot about it. But ah, little son, some day there may come a Fear into your life such as not even your mother can charm away. The "twin Eumenides—Fear and Pain"[160]—they cannot be escaped by mortals.

As I hold little Punch's dear body in my arms I am lost in wonder—and awe—and terror—when I *realize* that *everybody* was once a baby just like this. All the

Punch "au naturel" [Chester]

great men, all the good men, all the wicked men of history. Napoleon was once a chubby baby, kicking on his nurse's lap—Caesar once smacked his lips over his mother's milk as does my mannie—Milton once squirmed with colic—Shakespeare cried in the night when he grew hungry. Yes, and—horrible thought—Nero[161] once looked up with just such dear, star-like innocent eyes and Judas cooed to himself with the same sweet noises and vocables. Nay, even that wondrous Person—so grand and wonderful and amazing that it seems almost sacrilege to call him man, even to those of us who can no longer believe him anything but the consummate flower of humanity at its best—even He was once a white, dimple-fisted, waxen-faced little creature like this, cuddled in his mother's arms and drawing his life from her breast. What a terrible thing it is to be a mother—almost as terrible as it is beautiful!

---

160   Greek deities of vengeance, also known as the Erinyes or the Furies.
161   Roman Emperor (37–68 CE), legendarily famous for extreme cruelty.

Oh, mothers of Caesar and Judas and Jesus, what did you dream of when you held your babies against your beating heart. Of nothing but sweetness and goodness and holiness perhaps. Yet one of the children was a Caesar—and one was a Judas—and one a Messiah!

Thursday, Dec. 12, 1912
Leaskdale, Ont.

Last night we had a "Kipling Night" in Guild and I read an old paper on "Kipling's Verse" which I wrote and read many years ago to the Literary Society in Cavendish. It made me homesick and my soul ached when I lay awake in the darkness afterwards and thought over the old days.

Letters from Cavendish tell me that the old Literary Society has finally died. It struggled poorly through last winter but this year no effort was made to revive it. The old set who organized it and the younger set who carried it on for so long have nearly all died or gone away. And it is a sad fact that there is not among the present young set in Cavendish enough of either ability or interest to carry it on. I am sorry. I hate to see that dear old spot degenerating in any way. Yet degenerating intellectually it certainly is. Most of the old "brainy" stock of Simpsons and Macneills have gone. Such of their descendants as still live there are indeed "degenerate sons of noble sires." The old Simpsons and Macneills, whatever their faults, were intellectual people with a keen interest in intellectual things. But the young folk in Cavendish now decidedly are not.

It must be twenty-five years since that Literary Society was first organized—soon after the hall was built. Walter Simpson and George Simpson, Arthur Simpson, "Will Effie" Simpson, George R. Macneill, John C. Clark and Rev. Mr. Archibald were its main supports then. It was a flourishing institution, beguiling the winter months with debates, lectures, and concerts. A good library was started in connection with it and grew to generous proportions. That society was a boon to us young people. It was the greatest social factor in our lives. For the first few years I was very rarely allowed to go and I was not allowed to join the society. After that I attended regularly and always enjoyed the meetings. The fortunes of "The Literary" ebbed and flowed, some winters being highly successful, others, for various reasons, being less so. But on the whole it flourished and was an excellent educational factor in our simple country life. As the older members grew too old or indifferent to run it younger ones came up to fill their place. But there is an end to all things under the sun and I fear the end of the old Literary has come at last. Nor do I think it will ever be resuscitated. The spirit is gone.

So tonight I read the Kipling paper to an Ontario guild. But I do not think it was as much appreciated as when I read it to "the Simpsons, Macneills and Clarks" on the old Cavendish benches.

Monday, Dec. 16, 1912
Leaskdale, Ont.

I feel sad—lonely—sick at heart tonight. Frede went away this morning.

Lily Reid

She goes to Alberta to take a position in the new "Ladies College" in Red Deer.[162] It seems so horribly far away. We have never been so far separated before. It makes me wretched to think of it. I shall miss her so horribly—our little chats, our mutual jokes, our delightful eye-to-eye vision of everything, our sympathy with and understanding of one another. Frede has a pet expression by which she denotes congenial souls—"the race that knows Joseph."[163] People, in her classification, either belong or do not belong to the race

---

162   Frede had earned a degree in Household Science from Macdonald College in 1912. The Alberta Ladies' College of Red Deer opened the following year, in 1913, then one of the country's finest residential buildings. Along with Macdonald College, it was built as part of a country-wide initiative to create educational opportunities for young rural women. However the College was overwhelmed by debt, and in 1916 sold the building to the provincial government for use as a psychiatric hospital for soldiers returning from the war.

163   Frede's expression reverses the description found in Exodus 1:8: "Now there arose up a new King over Egypt, which knew not Joseph."

that knows Joseph. And oh, how few and rare and precious are those who do! And how miserable it is when they are separated.

Now that Frede has gone I have absolutely no real friend near me—and that is a hard position for any woman. It seems just now as if I *couldn't* live without Frede. I'll get over this in a few days and life will be pleasant again, but something will always be gone from it. We have had such a happy, delightful summer since Frede came from Macdonald—so full of jokes and laughter and sweet simple little pleasures. And now Frede has gone—and it is winter.

I have got a very good maid—a Mrs. Reid[164] who has been here since the first of the month. She is a young widow, neat and efficient and as her home is near here everything fits in very nicely. I am very fortunate in having

Frede in her room at Leaskdale manse

secured her, but of course, she is no real companion for me in any way. No one can take Frede's place in that. Poor Frede! I hope life will be easier for her in the future than it has been in the past. She has had a hard struggle and many bitter experiences. Perhaps it will be make up to her yet as it has been to a great extent, made up to me.

But oh, I miss her—I miss her! The house seems so vacant and still without her—her room so lonely and deserted. A pang goes through my heart as I pass the door—and glance into the empty darkness.

"Friend after friend departs—
Who hath not lost a friend?
There is no union here of hearts
That finds not here an end."[165]

Alas, that it should be so! But who so accepteth human love must bind it to her soul with pain.

---

164   Lillis (Lily) May Reid had been married to Arthur Wesley Reid before the latter's death. She was George Harrison's daughter.

165   The verse is from the 1824 poem "Friends" by English poet and hymnist James Montgomery (1771–1854).

The Manse, Leaskdale, Ont.
Thursday, Dec. 19, 1912

I had a solitary walk tonight—a rare experience with me now. I miss my old-time walks in a beautiful solitude of dreams very much. It is so impossible to have them here—at least, just now. I can leave baby only very rarely. But tonight I went up to see old Mrs. Quigley for a few minutes. They live about half a mile from here. I drove up but I walked back alone through the dim, quiet white winter night. It was good. My soul fed itself once more on that old divine nutriment of fancy. It was easy in that dimness to imagine myself walking down the hill from Amanda's gate to "Pierce's Hollow," with the sea off to my left and the woods around Lover's Lane to my right.[166] Dear thoughts trooped into my mind. I had a very happy walk and was sorry when it ended.

Tuesday, Dec. 31st, 1912
The Manse, Leaskdale, Ont.

To-day I had a letter from Mr. MacMillan in which he told me that his engagement to Miss Allan was at an end. It seems that young lady went back to Berwick again last summer—having been so pleased with it during her first visit—for her vacation. There she met someone who pleased her fancy better, it seems, than Mr. MacMillan—or perhaps one who had more money! At any rate she coolly wrote the poor fellow that all was over between them. Mr. MacMillan seems to feel very badly over it. This is natural; but I must say that in view of the disposition Miss Allan betrayed more than once during that fortnight in Berwick I think it is really the best thing that ever happened him and that he will realize this when the first sting is over.

"Aunt Jane of Kentucky" says, "There are mighty few things that ain't little until you foller them up and see what comes of them."[167] It seemed a little little thing that we should have invited Miss Allan to be our guest at Berwick for that fortnight. Yet it probably has had and will continue to have tremendous effects on three lives. If we had not taken Miss Allan to Berwick she would have had no chance to be so charmed with it; it would never have occurred to her to go there this

---

166   Cavendish locations. "Amanda" is childhood friend and cousin Amanda Macneill; Pierce's hollow is a favourite location from Cavendish belonging to farmer Pierce Macneill.

167   The reference is to a character in a series of books by American humorist Marietta Holley (1836–1926) featuring Samantha and Josiah Allen, published between 1887 and 1913.

last summer. She would thus never have met the unknown and her engagement to Mr. MacMillan would be still unbroken. Though, if it comes to that and to go back further still, if Mr. MacMillan himself had not gone to Berwick a few years ago to spend his vacation and written me from it such a charming descriptive letter we, in turn, would never have thought of visiting Berwick. It's all like the old nursery rhyme of the stick that began to beat the dog and the dog that began to bite the pig.

This is the end of 1912. It has been the greatest year of my life—the year that brought me motherhood. I faced death in it—and came off conqueror, bearing as my guerdon a new and unspeakably precious life. So it to me must always be the *annus mirabilis*—the wonderful year.

Saturday, Feb. 1, 1913
Leaskdale, Ont.

I've been having a very miserable time ever since the 8th of January, having been sick off and on with that old harassing enemy of mine, cystitis. I really suffered wretchedly with it and am run-down besides. Nursing as big and lusty a baby as Punchie is of course rather a strain. I must soon begin to wean him although I hate to think of it. But I'm better again now and earnestly hope I have paid my winter's toll in this attack. It always seems to be exacted in one way or another.

Friday, Feb. 7, 1913

Punch was seven months old today—and signalized the date by getting up on his own wee feet in the basket holding on by a chair—and then alas, pitching out on the floor on his dear head. This means that he has outgrown his basket as an abode by day; the old "Jolly Roger" is done with, save as a pirate bark o'night,[168] and we must get a high chair for him, the dear wee adventurer. Every week brings him some addition of strength and knowledge.

But for me another of the little tragedies of motherhood took place today. I gave my little son his first meal of milk—the beginning of his weaning. I felt it bitterly. From his birth he has been wholly dependent on me. He has drawn all the sustenance his darling wee body demanded from me—he has been mine, wholly mine. But henceforth this is not to be so. He is beginning to owe his nourishment to an outside source and must continue to do so more and more. In one way it will be, I suppose, a relief. Certainly there are some aspects in which nursing is a nuisance, especially when one lives in an epoch of fashion which ordains dresses hooked in the back. But I hate to give it up. I am so thankful I have been able to nurse my baby and I cannot understand how any mother can refuse to do so if she is able. Yes, today it gave me a pang when I gave my wee man his cup of milk.

Saturday, Feb. 22, 1913
Leaskdale, Ont.

This has been that most delightful and rather rare thing—a quiet home day; and it was doubly delightful coming after a very strenuous week.

168　Jolly Roger was the eighteenth-century skull-and-crossbones flag used to identify a pirate ship.

The Hypatia Club[169] has been getting up "The Temple of Fame"[170] in aid of the Uxbridge Library and I had promised to take part in it in my own character as the author of "Anne." So I had to drive in last Monday night to a practice. It was a crisp, frosty moonlight night with excellent roads and I enjoyed the drive. But next morning I had to go over it again on a shopping expedition. Then Wednesday the Home Mission Society met in the afternoon and the Guild in the evening. Thursday I had two ladies here to tea and last night the concert came off in Uxbridge. It was capital but I had to take Chester and we did not get home, over bad roads, till two o'clock. Consequently, my "quiet home day" has been a boon and a blessing. I certainly want badly to get a good rest. But my life is very busy—almost too much so. There is always some duty waiting to be done— and all too often something unexpected

Punch and Mrs Reid

turning up to interfere with the doing of it. But motherhood pays for all. I don't complain—that is, I don't complain of all I have to do in connection with my home and dear ones. But I do grudge the time I have to give to outsiders for whom I don't care a straw.

Saturday, Apr. 26, 1913
Leaskdale, Ont.

We have had the most beautiful April. One thing I do like about Ontario and that is its early springs. They are fully three weeks earlier than down home and so mild and ungrudging. And yet—after all, there is an indefinable sweetness about an Island spring that is lacking here. What it is I cannot tell but I feel it and miss it. Perhaps it is in the very austerity of an Eastern spring that its charm consists.

---

169 Hypatia (c.350–415 CE) was a female philosopher and mathematician who became head of the Platonist school in Alexandria. The concept of a Hypatia Club, a self-improvement organization for women, dates to 1886. The Hypatia Book Club in Uxbridge continues to this day.

170 Alexander Pope's eighteenth-century adaptation of Geoffrey Chaucer's *House of Fame* (dated to c.1379). The long poem about the endurance of art provides a witty list of classical works. Each woman played the role of a famous historical figure, arguing that she was the most important in the "Temple of Fame."

We have been housecleaning furiously all April. We have finished all but the kitchen and I am not sorry. I used to love housecleaning down home. But it was a much easier affair there where all the furniture and appointments were so much simpler and plainer. The price one has to pay for having many nice things is the much harder work which it is to clean and care for them. Of course, I do not object to this for I love nice furnishings and always longed for them. I am quite willing to pay the price, but I may be permitted to state the fact that housecleaning here is hard work and that I am glad it is over. Hard as it was, however, it was easy compared to last spring's, with Stella's bad temper, complaining and "driving" ways. This spring the housecleaning was done as *I* wished it and in accordance with my convenience and plans. The difference is a huge one.

Thursday, May 1, 1913
Leaskdale, Ont.

To-day I got a box of Mayflowers from home! They were somewhat faded— but oh, they were Mayflowers; with all the old haunting woodsy sweetness. I buried my face in them and shut my eyes—and in fancy I was back again in those old barrens a thousand miles away, with the blue harbor gleaming westward and the spring winds tossing the fir trees. I don't know whether those mayflowers gave me more of pain or pleasure. But even the pain was very sweet.

[Chester in a high chair]

Lily and I papered the kitchen to-day and I got a young girl to come and look after Chester, so that I could work uninterruptedly. I had grown used so gradually to the increasing care he needs that I didn't realize until today what a care the little creature really is. He has to be constantly watched lest he get into mischief. But he is a precious care, the darling little star-eyed soul, and one I wouldn't be without for the world. And he is so good. Few babies are so little bother but the best of them need heaps of attention.

Tuesday, May 6, 1913
Leaskdale, Ont.

I weaned Chester finally today. How I hated to do it! It seems to me that the dearest bond between us has been broken. He is a little less my own now. And he is wearing creepers and looks so much the big sturdy man-child in them. I sometimes wonder if he can really be the wee white thing that nestled by me last summer. My moments of greatest happiness come when I stand by his little crib and look down upon him sleeping—the little, relaxed, perfect body, the bare, chubby limbs, the wee dimpled fists flung up by his head, the rosy cheeks, the shut, long-lashed eyes. I think he is going to be a handsome little lad. He has a fine complexion, starry, dark blue eyes, and dimpled cheeks. His hair is beginning to grow nicely and promises to be a golden-brown. My own dear little son! What a blessing you are to me! Will you always be so? (Oh, dear God! 1937!)[171]

Chester in creeperss

Sunday, May 18, 1913
The Manse, Leaskdale, Ont.

We have been gardening furiously since housecleaning was finished and I am besottedly happy in it. My tulips and daffodils are out most beautifully. Tulips are really rather a barbarous sort of blossom and seem as if they could not really belong to a spring, the season of delicacy and evasive charm. But they certainly make vivid patches of color on the lawn and "look well from the road." But it is the daffodils I love—especially the sweet "poet's narcissus" and the little starry jonquils. My garden is such a joy to me. I had to go without one for so many years and now I'm quite drunk with the joy of having one again.

---

171   LMM added this exclamation to the entry 25 years after first writing it. Chester's behaviour, troublesome as a child, had become an object of significant concern after he reached adulthood.

Wednesday, May 21, 1913

To-day I finished my new book "The Golden Road"—a second *Story Girl* volume.[172] I have not enjoyed writing it. I have been too hurried and stinted for time. I have had to write it at high pressure, all the time nervously expecting some interruption—which all too surely came nine times out of ten. Under such circumstances there is very little pleasure in writing. I often think wistfully of the quiet hours by my old window "down home," where I thought and wrote "without haste and without rest." But those days are gone and cannot return as long as wee Chester is a small make-trouble. I do not wish them back—but I *would* like some undisturbed hours for writing.

Nevertheless, the book is done and may be quite as good as those written more pleasantly. I am too *near* it yet to judge and having written it under stress and strain I have not that intimate sense of having *lived* it which made my other books seem so *real* to me.

Tuesday, June 10, 1913
Leaskdale, Ont.

A week ago Friday, Margaret and John Stirling and their little Doris arrived.[173] I had been greedily looking forward to their visit for some time as Margaret and I had planned that she should spend Assembly week with me. Oh, wasn't it *good* to see someone from home again and hear all the home news down to the least detail. How our tongues did go! I asked questions until my jaws ached. John S. stayed until Monday morning, when I drove him and Ewan to the station. Margaret and I had a good week of it. I had a lot of people in to tea and we visited some—and filled all the between times with talk!

[Montgomery, Chester, Mrs Stirling, and Doris]

---

172   Boston: Page, 1913.

173   Margaret Ross Stirling was a Cavendish friend, wife of the Reverend John Stirling.

Margaret went away today. I would have felt blue enough had I not expected to see her soon again. For I am going home in July! I can hardly believe it. It seems so long since I left—so much has happened since then.

I cannot help looking forward to being in Cavendish again. The thought of walking once more in Lover's Lane and by the shore thrills me with a delight not felt since I left them. And yet I fear it will seem very sad and bitter to be in Cavendish and not be *home*. Moreover, cold reason steps in and tells me that it will be a very fatiguing thing to visit about for weeks with an active, restless, ever-moving piece of mischief like young Chester.

Then I shall have to go to see dozens of people I don't really care much for. Of course in a way I shall enjoy seeing them but—oh! If I could only go to Cavendish and spend my time wholly in the woods and by the shore, visiting only a few choice spirits. That cannot be; even if certain folk did not have to be visited I could not have my dear old solitary rambles because I could neither take nor leave Chester.

Still, there will surely be some pleasure in my trip—and I have the pleasure of looking forward to it. And glory be, I will be free for five or six blissful weeks from the boredom of missionary societies and "pastoral visitations." That alone will be a great deal to be glad of.

Wednesday, June 11, 1913
The Manse, Leaskdale, Ont.

This evening I had to go to Will Cook's to a "Guild" Social. I am Vice President of the Social department of the Guild this year. I like running it well enough when the social evenings are held in the church but when they are held around at the homes of the members I don't like it. No doubt the young fry have a good time but I can't mingle with them on common ground. I have to sit around and talk to the older folk who go—and there is so little they can talk about. Tonight I exchanged commonplaces about the weather and the crops with two stout elderly ladies and despairingly wished myself home with Ewan and Chester, reading the volume of history I am studying.

I get almost no time for reading now. I miss it horribly; but then I have lots of other things worthwhile and my little man-child is far more interesting than any book. He stood alone the other day; but he is so expert at galloping about on all fours that he is not at all keen about walking. It is too funny to see him scuttling about in his "creepers." He runs like a little dog.

Sunday, June 29, 1913
Leaskdale, Ont.

I felt so tired to-night that I'm about "all in," to use a slang phrase. This past week has been one wild scramble to overtake a hundred "must be dones." Tomorrow we leave for home.

Punch trotting on all fours

Monday we had to go out to tea. Yes, there was no escaping it. It was a "Pastoral duty"—and hopeless boredom. Tuesday a heat-wave struck Ontario and we have been sweltering ever since, night and day. I had to go to Uxbridge, do a lot of shopping and then go out to tea again. Wednesday I had to go to a Home Mission Sewing Bee over on the 6th. Thursday I had company—more bores—to tea. But there was one very sweet thing about that evening to me. At dusk I was alone for a moment outside with Chester. I was standing on the walk and he was scuttling up and down the veranda on all fours. On the stand on the veranda was a large potted geranium brilliant with clusters of red blossoms. Chester came to a stop before it, put his wee face close to a scarlet cluster and smiled at it—the dearest little *companionable* smile, such as he might give a beloved playmate. I never saw anything sweeter or more spontaneous.

Friday I was busy packing and getting the house in order for leaving Saturday. I finished this and then went out to another tea-martyrdom. Oh, the precious time I have to waste utterly, going out to tea! It makes me wild to think of it. And if I even enjoyed it I wouldn't grudge it so bitterly. I would then have the pleasure at least. But as it is I find these

The veranda

visits insufferably dull. I force myself to chat and smile and make suitable comments when I am shown the family photographs. But I detest it all.

To-day brought little respite. I went to service in Leaskdale in the forenoon and then in the afternoon drove over to Zephyr service. I have to show myself there once in so long or the jealous Zephyrites would think they were not getting their share of my attention. This evening callers came in and stayed late. I am very tired and the heat is stifling. What will it be travelling? But it can't be any worse than going out to tea in the congregation!

Why do I go? Because the people expect it. If I did not go they would resent it and my husband's work would suffer in consequence. It is for his sake alone I go. Otherwise I would say—in effect—to those people, "Begone! I refuse to waste my precious time catering to your petty vanity—a vanity which makes you want to have the minister and his wife to tea so that you can say they visit you as often as they visit your neighbor. I have other and more important work to do. You have no right to expect me to sacrifice that work to your trivial round and common thought. I will not do it. I will live my own life—and the devil take you all!!!!"

But I can't and don't say it. What would happen to "Society as she is" if the truth were told always? It's an amusing speculation.

What a grand saying it is—"Ye shall know the truth and the truth shall make you free."[174] It is the greatest of the great Teacher's sayings. Were I a minister I would preach one sermon on that—only one for I would certainly not be permitted to preach any more! It would reek with heresy. The truth *does* make us free—but only when we have the honesty to accept it and the courage to tell it. I think I have the former but I have not the latter. I am a coward and dare not tell the truth as I see it and consequently I am not free—I am a slave to old customs and old conventions and old rules. But that is not the fault of the truth. It *would* make me free if I told it. But even freedom may be too costly a thing—for us weak ones at least.

Jesus told the truth—and he was free, as no man ever had or has been free. But his society cast him out—and his world crucified him for it. The world always has crucified those who tell it the truth. *That* is the price to pay for freedom on this planet.

Thanks be, I'll have a taste of freedom the next few weeks.

Thursday, July 3, 1913
Bellevue, P.E. Island.

As I write I breathe P.E. Island air—P.E. Island's blue skies are over me—P.E. Island's greenness is around me. It's almost "too good to be true."

Last Monday afternoon we left Leaskdale in a wave of blistering heat, spent the night in Toronto and left Tuesday morning for Montreal.

I am sure that that Tuesday was the most uncomfortable day, in regard to purely external discomfort, that I ever endured. It was incredibly hot and vilely dirty. Clouds of black cinders blew in at the windows and in a short time we were so dirty that I longed to hide me from the face of man. Anything like my face when we got to Montreal I never saw before surmounting my body. As for Chester's white dress and my white blouse—did I say *white*? Nay, like our faces they were inky black. To make matters worse it was Dominion Day and the trains were crowded. At every station new arrivals got on, all fresh and spick and span. And we hated them fiercely for half an hour and then forgave them because they were as dirty as ourselves.

At Montreal we struck a glorious cool wave and by the time we reached the Point next day it was positively cold and raining. It was dark before we reached "the Island"—but wasn't the tang of the salt air good! It is so different from Ontario's languid air.

---

174   "And ye shall know the truth, and the truth shall make you free" (John 8:32).

LOOKING SEAWARD   TEA HILL, P.E.I.

[Looking seaward, Tea Hill, PEI]

We went right down to Ch'town, getting there at eleven o'clock in a pouring rain. But next morning was glorious—clear, sunny, bracing. Ewan got a team and we drove out here to his old home, a distance of 24 miles. It was delightful to roll over the soft, easy red Island roads again. In Ontario the jar and rattle of the gravelled roads tires me out when I go driving.

We caught our first real glimpse of the sea from Tea Hill.[175] There is a very famous view, about which I have heard much all my life but had never seen before. It is certainly magnificent. I was not prepared for the flood of emotion which swept over me suddenly when I saw the sea. I was stirred to the very deeps of my being. Tears poured into my eyes—I trembled! For a moment it seemed passionately to me that I could *never* leave it again. I *belonged* here. No other land could ever claim me—in no other land can I ever feel satisfyingly at home. Somehow, I have always had a queer instinctive feeling that I shall yet come back to the Island to live.

Friday, July 4, 1913
Bellevue, P.E.I.

Today Ewan and I drove over to Point Prim to visit his brother. We had a delightful walk to the shore—though it is only the Strait shore and

---

175   Tea Hill is in central PEI. Tea Hill Park, at one time a provincial park, is now run by the town of Stratford.

not so beautiful as the north shore. We were away all day. Chester was left home with Ewan's sister Annie[176]—Mrs. John Gillis—and was exceedingly good. But he has been so ever since we left Leaskdale.

Saturday, July 5, 1913
Bellevue, P.E.I.

Ewan and I had a drive this evening—one of the most delightful drives I ever had in my life. We went along what is called "the county line road." For over three miles it winds through glorious maple woods where the trees met overhead and the green carpet of ferns comes out to the very edge of the red road. The evening was perfect besides. I shall remember that drive and the beauty of that road all my life. There are no such roads in Ontario. There are beautiful roads there, and beautiful landscapes. But they lack the indescribable charm which haunts the roads and landscapes of the Island. I have often tried to define the difference but I have not succeeded. It is too elusive—too subtle. Is it the touch of austerity in the Island landscape that gives it its distinctive beauty? And whence comes the austerity? Is it from the fir and the spruce? Or the glimpses of the sea? Or does it go deeper to the very soul of the land? For lands have personalities as human beings have.

Sunday, July 6, 1913
Bellevue, P.E.I.

To-day must be chronicled a very important and wonderful fact! Chester walked three steps alone! My wee man! And tomorrow is his birthday. For one whole beautiful year this little creature has been mine, growing and developing under my eyes. And how he has grown! The change has been so gradual that it is only by an effort of memory that I can recall him as he was a year ago—that tiny little mite, helpless and sweet and dimpled, that lay in the bed beside me that wonderful day.

Chester at one year old

176 Annie Macdonald Gillis and Christie Macdonald McLeod, Ewan's siblings, lived in Kinross, a community located in Queens County in central PEI.

And now he is getting on his own small legs and beginning to walk. Oh, my dear laddie, at first he needed me for everything; but he needs me less now and he will need me less and less as the years go, until he is wholly independent of me. It is a bitter thought; and yet it would be much more terrible if he did not become so.

Kinross, P.E.I.
Monday, July 7, 1913

We came to Kinross today to visit Ewan's sister Christie—Mrs. A.J. MacLeod. This evening at sunset John Gillis took us for another delightful drive. I enjoyed every minute of it. There are some very pretty roads hereabouts. And it was such a beautiful evening—dewy, cool, fragrant, with fairy tints in the western sky. And as we drove along everywhere we breathed the delicious scent of dying fir! I have not smelled it since I left the Island. Of all the fragrances the world over none is like to the odor of fir distilled on dew-damp twilight air. And there is no more exquisite sight than a field of ox-eye daisies in that same twilight. To be sure, those same ox-eye daisies are pestiferous weeds and their presence is an evidence of bad farming! But for airy, fairy, elusive, subtle grace and beauty there is naught to match a sunset field of them.

Park Corner, P.E. Island,
Wednesday, July 9, 1913

Again at Park Corner![177] We came up to Kensington yesterday evening and drove down here. It was a beautiful evening and our drive was delightful. Besides, for me it had the charm of old scenes revisited. And when we came over the Irishtown hills and saw the blue gulf again and heard its low distant murmur! I thought of another evening long ago—over twenty years ago—when I came home from my western exile[178] over that very road. I recalled the rapture and ecstasy that filled my heart when from that same hill the same glimpse of the purple evening sea flashed on my eyes. That same view always brings a resurrection of that old thrill and rapture.

---

177   John and Annie Campbell lived at Park Corner, on the island's north shore about 55 km/ 34.5 miles northeast of the provincial capital of Charlottetown. Annie was the daughter of LMM's grandparents, Alexander and Lucy Macneill, and the Campbell children were about the same age as LMM.

178   At age 15, LMM had spent most of a year in Prince Albert with her father and his second family. The visit was not overly successful. Back in Prince Edward Island, LMM hired a wagon team and drove to Park Corner to visit her aunt, uncle, and cousins.

Then we turned at the corner—and down before us ran the long, hilly red road—and a little further on we saw the pond—the "Lake of Shining Waters" and the trees that shut Uncle John's place in from the world. And then we were driving through the spruces by the gate and up the slope by the orchard. The big white house was before us, and I thought the last time I had seen it when we had driven away from it on that dream-like afternoon of our wedding day. It seemed as if it must be much longer than two years. And now I was coming back to it with my little blue-eyed man on my knee. I had often dreamed of this very thing—and now the dream had come true. Not all my dreams have come true,—not many of them indeed—but this one had.

As we rounded the maple curve Aunt Annie and Stell came running to meet us—and there was the old welcome and laughter and jests and chatter. And then in to one of Stell's famous suppers, to which we hungry travellers did full justice. Was there ever such a house as Uncle John Campbell's for "spreads"? Aunt Annie and her girls were all resplendent cooks and Uncle John C. had always the old Montgomery traditions of lavish hospitality.

The curve under the maples

This evening Stell took Ewan and myself for a drive around the harbor. Of course it was lovely. It *is* a delight to be back here in this old spot again. And yet amid all the pleasure there is a constantly recurring note of sadness—which must, I suppose, sound through most of the symphonies of life when we have left the golden road behind. For 'tis only on the golden road that music knows no minor key.

I can see poor Uncle John C. sadly failed. One cannot wonder that it is so—he is over eighty. But I cannot realize that Uncle John Campbell is eighty—or anywhere near it. My mind stubbornly refuses to conceive of him as being older than forty or fifty—the age at which I just knew him. It is as hard for me to realize that he is eighty as it is for me to

The spruces by the gate

realize that *my* next birthday but one will be my fortieth! Uncle John has failed in mind and body and I fear it cannot be long before he will be gone from the old home amid the orchards.

Another thing that hurts me here is this:—everywhere I turn I see something from the old home in Cavendish. And the sight of these things, divorced from the old surroundings of which they seemed a part, is painful to me. In the dining room is the old oval table which was in the sitting room at home, around which so many sat in the old days. In the hall is the bookcase which held our china at home and which was the habitation of "Katie Maurice" and "Lucy Gray."[179] It is now used more legitimately as a bookcase. Upstairs in the hall is the carpet we had in the parlor at home and the horse-hair rocker with the black and red cushion and the knitted red and white woollen tidy I thought so very wonderful in childhood. In the room I sleep in is the bedstead from the downstairs bedroom I used to occupy in childhood; and the feather bed on it is the very one I slept on always to the last.

---

179 "Katie Maurice" and "Lucy Gray" were imaginary childhood companions of LMM. They are mentioned in an earlier journal entry as well (January 27, 1911).

I used to think it a most comfortable bed. But truly last night I didn't find it so. I have become used to a spring mattress and alas, I found the old bed I used to think so soft and cosy very stuffy and smothery. So much depends on what we are used to!

Thursday, July 10, 1913
Park Corner, P.E.I.

This morning Ewan and Chester and I drove up to Malpeque to see Aunt Emily.[180] We had a pleasant drive both ways. But a queer little disappointment was my portion. I knew Lucy Ritchie was home with her two children and I was looking forward to seeing Kenneth.[181] Three years have passed since I saw him, a child of four. I *knew* he must have changed somewhat but I could not grasp it. Subconsciously, I suppose, I was really expecting to see the beautiful child I saw in Boston three years ago. I was utterly taken aback when Kenneth presented himself. I felt as if he were a total stranger. His hair was clipped to the bone. He wore a shapeless overall suit, the trousers reaching to his feet and making him look like a grown-up dwarf so to speak. The only thing I recognized about him were his beautiful brown eyes. Yes, I *was* disappointed. I daresay if I had stayed long enough to get acquainted with him all over again I would have found him lovable and charming enough in his new incarnation. But as it is I've lost the little dream boy I loved. The present Kenneth Ritchie seems as nothing to me.

Monday, July 14, 1913
Park Corner, P.E. Island

I had to-night one of those little psychological experiences which make an otherwise commonplace day stand out in memory as a beacon through the years. I had a walk over the pond tonight which I shall always remember.

To-day was showery but tonight the rain ceased to fall. It was a dull, damp brooding night. At nine o'clock, Chester being asleep, I slipped away for what is my rarest pleasure nowadays—as it used to be my commonest and almost my only one—a solitary ramble in the twilight.

As I went down the lane my very soul became penetrated with and

---

180   Emily Macneill Montgomery, daughter of LMM's maternal grandparents, married John Malcolm Montgomery, one of LMM's father's cousins.

181   Lucy Ritchie was the daughter of Uncle John Montgomery and Aunt Emily (Macneill) Montgomery. LMM had been quite taken with their son Kenneth on an earlier visit, discussed in her journal entry of November 9, 1910.

steeped in the mystic, sinister, uncanny charm of the night. It was close and shadowy and breathless and still—like the night of a forsaken world. Thickly in orchard and wood glimmered the goblin firefly lanterns. I walked through the dark belt of spruces and across the pond, lying silent and shadowy and deadly still beneath me. I lingered long by the railing—"doubting, dreaming dreams no mortal have dared to dream before,"[182] as I peered through that strange baffling twilight. And then fancy began to summon up from the vasty deeps of the old years many by-gone memories of mirth and frolic—and the imagined laughter of those memories seemed to echo alienly through the deserted haunts of those who had so laughed. Back they all came trooping—those I had walked over that bridge with years ago—in their merry youth they came, their forms were around me, their voices whispered half-mockingly, half tenderly through the gloom, their viewless hands plucked at me, drawing me into their charmed circle once more. They were all there—Clara, Stella, Frede, in their youth, Lem and Ed and Howe and Ev and Irv and Jack[183]—all the boys and girls who formed our "set" that gay winter at Park Corner. They seemed so oddly *near* to me—I felt that if I could only tear aside that thick curtain of twilight I could see them all with the body's eye. But I could not tear it aside—and presently my ghostly company left me sorrowfully—and I walked back to the house alone, save for an impish black kitten that frisked along before me, looking like the very incarnation of some witch's work. And those who saw me come in knew not that I had just come from that strange, weird borderland which parts the present from the past and where we can only wonder when dark meets light on a summer eve.

The Pond Bridge

---

182   From Edgar Allen Poe's long poem, "The Raven" (1845).

183   Clara, Stella, Frederica ("Frede"), and George Campbell were the children of LMM's Aunt Annie (Macneill) and Uncle John Campbell.

"Silent and shadowy and still"

Thursday, July 17, 1913
Park Corner, P.E. Island

After dinner this lovely day Stella and I got the hired man to row us down the pond to the shore. It was delightful. Oddly enough, in all the times I have been at Park Corner I have never once been on that pond in a boat. The views as one rows down it are charming. I took my bathing suit along with me but I really hadn't the least intention of going in. I was sure the water would be too cold. But when I got down there and saw the little white ripples crisping over the sands the old water lust awoke in me and would not be denied. I *must* go in—yea, though the water were as cold as ice. It *was* cold enough at first but soon that was over and I had a glorious dip.

Then the pleasure of the day was over. I had to come home and dress for a visit to Aunt Mary Cuthbert's.[184]

I have always liked Aunt Mary and have always liked to go there. But Aunt Mary, though the soul of kindness, has always been *fussy*. At first it was not so bad; but as the years went on it intensified. To-day she completely spoiled my visit for me. Not one moment could she leave me in peace. Did I feel a draft?—she asked me that half a dozen times and in spite of my desperate assurance that I hadn't even noticed

---

184   This "Aunt Mary" was the widow of Cuthbert Montgomery, brother to Hugh John Macdonald, LMM's father. Three Aunt Marys are mentioned by LMM in this volume of her journals: Mary Lawson, older sister of her maternal grandmother (see entry for October 10, 1913); the aforementioned Mary Montgomery; and Mary Montgomery McIntyre, LMM's father's sister (see entry for February 16, 2016).

Aunt Mary's

that the window was open she finally shut it down. Wouldn't I like a shawl?—did I find that chair comfortable—try this other chair, yes, I must—and so on and so on. At tea time it was still more awful. She urged and entreated me to eat—she *pestered* me to eat—she lamented that she had nothing nice for me—nothing that I cared to eat. And poor me eating furiously until I was ready to burst. I was so thankful when my visit came to an end. My nerves were almost frayed out and I was deadly tired when I got home. Why can't people have a little sense?

The Manse, Leaskdale, Ont.
Saturday, Sept. 27, 1913

I had to give up "journalizing" since the foregoing record, save for an occasional hurried entry in a notebook. I hadn't the time for it; and since coming home I have been so busy I had no opportunity to write it up.

I left Park Corner on Monday, July 21st—left it sadly and regretfully. I felt that it was all too likely that sad changes would have taken place before I could ever visit it again. And I had had a delightful sojourn there. Stella could always act the hostess' part very well and she did everything to make my visit pleasant. Chester was good all the time and Aunt Annie looked after him a good bit, thereby giving me a rest.

Stell

George took me down to Cavendish Monday forenoon. That beautiful drive is as beautiful as ever. And how exciting it was as we drew near Cavendish and began to meet folks I knew! It was delightful to see the old familiar faces again—and the dear old spots—the hills, the fields, the sea, the ponds! How my heart throbbed as we drove down the long hill from the Baptist church. There, off to the right, were

Ernest Webb's House from Back

Lover's Lane

Chester, the Webb children, and Polly

the woods where Lover's Lane lay hid—there to the left was the sapphire ring of the sea— before us the old "church hill," the graveyard where so many of my dear ones slept—and the trees around the old homestead. It gave me a pang when we turned into Mr. Webb's lane instead of going on.

But it was nice to see that old lane again, the poplar-shaded house, and Myrtle and the children.[185] Twenty years ago, had I been asked to

---

185   Myrtle Macneill had been born out of wedlock to a schoolteacher named Ada Macneill. Ada's

The row of wild cherry trees

name the least likely house in Cavendish for me ever to be a visitor in I should unhesitatingly have pitched on David Macneill's. It was quite unthinkable then that I should ever under any conceivable circumstances be a guest there. Yet it has come about.

Of course the first thing after dinner was Lover's Lane. How I wished I could have gone alone—or at least only with Chester. But Marian and Keith Webb must go, too.[186] They are nice little tots but oh, I didn't want them with me that particular time.

I went with fear and trembling. If the lane had changed! If it were not so beautiful as I remembered it. But my fears were groundless. It was as beautiful as ever and there were no changes, save such tiny ones as only the jealous eye of love could notice.

Yet there have been changes in that lane since the first time I saw it, that summer evening all of thirty years ago when the Nelson boys and I, bound on a fishing expedition walked through it and my beauty-loving heart hailed it as a path in Arcady. At that time the row of wild cherry trees on the left at the beginning of the lane were young and unbroken. Now they are old and several have rotted away and blown down. There are only a few left. Further on there is an avenue of spruce where the boughs meet in a dark roof overhead. That evening those spruces were merely a young close-set hedge over which we could easily see the field beyond.

aunt and uncle—Maud's Great-Uncle David Macneill and his sister Margaret—raised Myrtle, who was much beloved by them. In 1905 she married Ernest Webb, and the two inherited David and Margaret Macneill's farm. In some respects this kinship relation was part of the prototype for *Anne of Green Gables*—David Macneill was notoriously shy, like Matthew Cuthbert, and Margaret shared qualities with Marilla Cuthbert. LMM and Myrtle remained good friends all their lives, but Myrtle herself was not the model for Anne. Anne in fact was drawn more from LMM's own childhood personality, and Marilla also shared some characteristics with her own strict grandmother, who had raised her.

186   Myrtle and Ernest Webb's children. Marion, a favourite of LMM's, visited her in Ontario as an adult, and in 1934 married Murray Laird of Norval.

Midway the lane was a gate, crossing the road; and to the left of it a little gate for walkers, between them a huge spruce which served as a common post for them. These gates have long been done away with.

I was sorry, for I liked them, especially the little gate. Further on was another gate. When Mr. Webb came he shifted this gate to the second bridge. By so doing he spoiled a very pretty vista.

Soon after my first discovery of Lover's Lane David cut a huge gash out of the woods on the right, near its upper end. For a few years it was very unsightly. Then nature, after her dear fashion patiently began to make it beautiful again with ferns and maple shrubbery. Now it is almost forest again; in a few more years it will be wholly so.

Lover's Lane

We went right to the end of it, to that secluded field where I have often thought I'd like to have a house and live, "the world forgetting, by the world forgot."

The rest of the day Chester kept me pretty closely at home. By half past eight that night he was asleep. I was rather tired; outside it was damp and dark; common sense said I should go to bed myself. But a stronger emotion than common sense was drawing me. I *had* to yield to it. I had to go.

The other gate

Voices were calling to me that could not be resisted—voices of the past, fraught with all the past's enchantment. They summoned me imperiously and I obeyed the summons. I slipped out into the darkness of the summer evening and went to find the lost years.

In one way it was a bad evening for such a stroll. It was dark, damp, misty, brooding—a sorrowful evening such as might turn mirth into joy[187] and weigh down the gayest heart with nameless foreboding and regret. Yet, in another way, it was the very evening of such a pilgrimage to shrines forsaken and altars overthrown. There was nothing to detract from the sway of memory—nothing to clash with the dreams of

---

187   This is probably an inadvertent misquotation from Proverbs 14:13: "Even in laughter the heart is sorrowful, and the end of that mirth is heaviness."

A very pretty vista

The bridge over the brook

old days. Something about the night itself filled me with longing and pain—nearly broke my heart—but it was in keeping with my mood and my object. The result was an hour I can never forget—an hour whose pain was sweeter than joy, whose loneliness was dearer than delight.

In the dim, still, eerie twilight I slipped down the hill, over the bridge across the brook and up the dark path under the spruces. It was the old way home. I found the little gate in the fence and went through. Then I stopped in dismay, my soul rent with a pang of grief and indignation.

I was in Pierce Macneill's hill field.[188] As long as I can remember the north western corner of that field was occupied by a grove of spruce and maple. It was always one of my beloved haunts. The maples in the jutting corner were among my dearest tree friends. What then were my feelings to see that the grove was—gone. Only a desolation of stumps remained. That soulless Pierce Macneill had cut it down—may jackals sit on his grandmother's grave!

Really, it hurt me horribly. I felt lacerated and rent as I walked across the field to the main road. Arriving there I turned and walked up Laird's hill. How many times I had walked up that hill in the old evenings. At the top I turned to the gate in the hill field—and from there I looked down on home.

Yes, there it was. In the fading gray light I could see the old gray

---

188   Pierce Macneill was another of LMM's cousins on her mother's side. His wife was named Rachel, and their house served as the model for Rachel Lynde's home in *Anne of Green Gables.* The Macneills had adopted an orphan, Ellen, and LMM was annoyed when it was suggested that Ellen had served as the inspiration for Anne. On January 27, 1911, LMM declared in her journal that "There is no resemblance of any kind between Anne and Ellen Macneill who is one of the most hopelessly commonplace and uninteresting girls imaginable."

house hooded in shadows—I could see the little window of my old room—I could see the blot of dimness beyond that was the orchard.

I stood there long—and never have I felt keener pangs—never did my heart ache more bitterly with longing and sense of loss. And as I stood there I thought—not of home empty and forsaken—not of home as it was in the years before I left it—but of home as it was long years ago. It seemed to me that if I could only put out my hand and draw aside that gray veil of twilight that hung over it I should see it again as it was then—steeped in summer sunshine, surrounded by green, apple-bearing trees, filled with laughter and light steps and mirthful hearts with the homelight shining from its windows at night. Yes— yes, it was all there—only those cruel shadows hid it from me. They barred me out in the darkness—I could not pierce through them to my own—I could only hover longingly on the outside.

I wept bitterly. It seemed to me that my heart was broken with real- ization. I found no comfort in any thought. I thought of my husband down at Bellevue—thought of my little son asleep in the house behind the spruces. But they seemed unreal and far away. I had strayed back into a past which knew them not and where I could not find them but only the ghosts of old friends and companions. It was horrible—it was heartbreaking—but withal there was a certain luxury in it to which I abandoned myself until I knew that I must tear myself away from that gray kingdom of shadows.

As I walked down the hills I pleased and tortured myself with a bit of pretence. It was four years back. All was as it used to be. I had slipped away in the dusk, as was my custom, for a solitary ramble. Now I was going home again. I would go down the hill and up the "school hill." I would turn into the old lane. As I walked up it I would see the kitchen light shining through the trees. I would pass under the birches and then under the cherry trees and then around the curve. The old house would be before me; Daffy would come frisking across the yard and bound before me to the old red door. I would lift the latch and walk in, a little tired, and glad to be home again. Grandmother would be sitting in her old arm-chair by the table, reading, with her gray shawl about her shoulders.

It was very real to me. My vivid imagination can always deceive me— for a little while. When I reached the top of the school hill I thought I would go up the bank and look up the old lane once more, over the bars that were now across it. I had no thought of going further, but I would just look up the lane and spin out the thread of my fancy.

I went up to the bars and looked over. The shock of what I saw turned me quite faint. *There was no lane*—it was gone! All I saw were

The gate in the hill field

the rows of potatoes with which the field was planted.

Somehow, I had never once thought of such a thing. I had often thought of things that might and probably would happen to the old house. I had pictured it as torn down—I had pictured another house built there. But it had never occurred to me to think of the old lane being done away with. It seemed to me as much a part of the landscape as the hills or woods. Some men, indeed, would have hesitated before doing away with it—the old homestead lane their feet had trod in childhood, in farings forth and in returnings home. But such sentiment could, of course, have no power with a man of Uncle John's type—especially when weighed against the few bushels of potatoes the soil of the lane would grow!

I turned away. I pretended no longer that I was going home. To me, the disappearance of that old lane had a symbolism all its own. It was not only that the way to the past was closed—it was altogether gone. Only on the wings of imagination could I revisit it—could I cross the gulf of time and change that yawned between me and the spot I loved.

I walked on to the graveyard. I met no one. I seemed alone in a dark world upon which the sun would never more rise. I went into the graveyard. I stood by the graves of grandfather and grandmother, of mother and Tillie. And then I left them and wandered down the old church hill, choking with sobs. The tears poured down my cheeks in the darkness. I wished wretchedly that I had never come back to Cavendish—the pain of it was unbearable. I would not enjoy a minute

"Home as it was long years ago"

of my stay. I only wanted to get away—far away from those haunting memories. On the hill there had been a strange, mysterious pleasure mingled with the pain—but now it was all pain.

Not until I found myself back beside my little son and felt his dear warm chubby arms go round my neck clingingly did my heart stop aching. And even then I cried myself to sleep.

But next day all was magically changed. It was bright and sunny; with the darkness had fled the eerie unwholesome charm the night had woven over my soul and my senses. I drove myself up to Bay View post-office and I did not hurry, either going or coming for it was delightful to be on that pretty road once more and see the blue sea sparkling beyond in every break of tree and hill. In the afternoon was another dear walk up Lover's Lane and through the woods to "the devil's punch-bowl" and beyond it out through the wood-path to the fields again. Then a merry call from Margaret—and finally a blissful evening of berry-picking in the grove of maple and apple trees they call "the old orchard" closed a flawless day.

I had been craving wild strawberries. Never since I left the Island had I so much as seen one. And all the time I was there I revelled in them. It was a banner year for wild berries there. The very roadsides were red with them. Almost better than eating them was the picking them. Every evening that I was home Myrtle and I would take the children and hie us to the Old Orchard. The kiddies enjoyed it as much as we did. Chester tumbled and crept among the fragrant grasses, laughed and crowed, picked and ate his first wild strawberries, "tops and all." Below us we could see the pond and the sea—and away to the west glorious summer sunsets. After the first day it seemed quite natural to be at Myrtle's and I had no more visitations such as I had that first night. I was in Cavendish—that was enough.

Wednesday afternoon I went down and had tea with Tillie Macneill—who is now Tillie Macneill no longer.[189] She was married the next week to a widower, Mr. Bentley by name, and departed for Calgary with him. Cavendish was tremendously excited over her courtship. It really was all very funny. Poor Tillie is a good soul but she has always had a quite frantic desire to be married—it did not really matter much to whom, I think, so long as he was respectable. Tillie has had two or three affairs which came to nothing; and now in her 48th year she has achieved matrimony at last. I am glad she has because she would never be happy otherwise; but really it was all very comical and Tillie did make a goose of herself and her elderly lover.

---

189   Tillie was Amanda's Macneill's sister; see note 195.

The old lane

Tillie

I can't say I enjoyed the afternoon very much for it was a constant effort to keep Chester out of mischief. That house was never meant for children. Tillie has no idea what to do to amuse them; and I cannot picture her poorly-concealed anguish when Chester strewed crumbs from his cookie over the sacred parlor floor! But after tea came a lull when I took Chester outside and let him tumble harmlessly about on the grass, while I sat on the front doorstep. That was a favorite seat of mine in old days. How often had I sat there in summer evenings gazing on that self-same scene bathed in the golden after light. It was still the same—the pond between the gnarled old apple trees—Pierce Macneill's place—the red hill—the graveyard with its white stones—the trees beyond that shut in my old home. I had a happy half hour; but when I went back to Mr. Webb's I was horribly tired. That was the drawback to my vacation. I had to visit so much and it tired me so, looking after Chester-boy and keeping him out of mischief. But no afternoon was quite so hard as that one at Tillie's.

Ewan came that evening and left early the next morning for home. I must say I felt as lonely and forlorn over his departure as if I did not expect to see him again for years. I went with him as far as the top of Laird's Hill and waved him out of sight. Then I went to the gate in the hill field and looked down upon home again.

I could see it plainly then, in the fresh morning sunshine. But, although I gazed on it sadly, I felt none of the strange agony and desolation I had felt that first evening. Then I went across the fields to Lover's Lane and walked home by way of it.

In all the many walks of long years I had never been in Lover's Lane in the early morning. I had been in it in forenoons and afternoons, in evenings and twilights, even late o'nights. But never till that day had I seen it in the first morning sunshine. And it was very lovely; and I discovered a woodland secret I had never known before. The sunshine, striking down through the woods, revealed across the brook a charming woodland hill nook that had never been visible before. I explored it later on and found it lovely. And I had passed it a thousand times and never dreamed of it, though I thought I knew those old woods so well.

In my notebook I find written:

++Friday, July 25th, 1913[190]
Cavendish, P.E. Island

This afternoon I had the delight of a walk through Lover's Lane *alone*. It was so dear. All my old dreams came peeping out from covert of bough or fern or moss—every one of them that used to companion me there. That lane keeps them for me and I found them all to-day. There

The front door step

---

190   Two crosses signify a retrospective entry.

was a bit of a hurt when I came back down the slope of the wild cherry trees and turned up to Mr. Webb's instead of slipping across the fields home.

This evening I went to the manse to tea, as Margaret had some guests she wished me to meet. It was very nice to be there again—as nice as in that last year in Cavendish when I spent so many jolly hours there. Margaret and John are such nice friends. The "race that knows Joseph" is the salt of the earth!!

On the following Sunday I went to the Presbyterian church. It was very nice to be there and see so many old friends again. I saw little or no change in the folk who had been fully grown-up when I left. But the children and young fry generally had changed quite bewilderingly.

I recalled the last time I had been in that church—the second Sunday before grandmother's death. I had sat on the choir platform then and I had had no thought but that I should sit there for many Sundays to come. I went out of the church with not a backward glance—and now it was more than two years agone.

Sunday evening I went up to the Baptist church with Myrtle. They had a young student for the summer. The B. church is very weak in C. now. I hardly see how they keep it up at all. I hate to think of it going down because I hate the idea of *any* change in Cavendish.

The next day Myrtle and the children and I drove to the shore by way of the old "big lane" and had a dip. That was the only time I got to the old sandshore. This is one of my regrets. I should so have liked to walk down that lane some evening and wander at sunset along the sandshore. But I could not manage it because of baby and it was a real disappointment to me.

+ +*The Manse, Cavendish, P.E.I.*
Wed. July 30, 1913

To-day I shifted my trunk to the manse. I was sorry to leave Myrtle's where I had had a very enjoyable visit—and I hated to leave the neighborhood of Lover's Lane. But in some ways it is nicer to be here. And in some ways sad! Just out there, through the thin spruce bush is home! I never let myself look that way.

I had a dear farewell prowl all by myself over the back fields beyond Mr. Webb's to-day. It was lovely weather to roam afield in and I skimmed over those green solitudes "like a youthful hart or roe." And certainly I found "the hills where spices grow."[191] Methinks they are

---

191   From Song of Solomon 2. See also Caroline Richings Bernard's *Oldde Folkes Tune Book*

only to be found on "the hills our childish feet have climbed the earliest" and to which our childish eyes are turned in the first dawning of consciousness.[192]

This evening I went over to see George R's folks. They are just the same—just the same as I remember them for the last thirty years. I do love those places where Time

Chester and "Polly"

stands still. They give you such a comfortable sensation of getting the better of that change which is so rampant and insulting everywhere else.

++*The Manse, Cavendish*
Thursday, July 31, 1913

Margaret and I put in the afternoon today visiting Jas. Simpsons—of which visit nothing more need be said. But on our way home tonight I looked back from a certain hill—and I saw the sunset on New London Harbor. The beauty of it choked me. It was the finest sunset view I ever saw. One does not see more than a very few like it in a lifetime.

++*The Manse, Cavendish, P.E. Island*
Sunday, Aug. 3, 1913

This has been a rich day. This afternoon I got away for a little farewell walk by myself. I went along the school road and up "Laird's Hill" in the dreamy August sunshine. From the top of it I looked long at my old home. I knew that I might never see it again. It may not be there the next time I come back to Cavendish. But what matter? I can see it forever with my closed eyes as vividly as if I stood before it. In the Land of Dream—in the Valley of Lost Sunsets—that old spot is found,

(1873) in which a song by Kimball entitled "Invitation" uses both of these phrases ("Youthful hart or roe" and "hills where spices grow"). The phrase "where spices grow" is attributable to Isaac Waats in *Hymn and Spiritual Songs* (1773).

192   From John Greenleaf Whittier's poem "Home." LMM was very fond of Whittier's poetry.

with many another castle in Spain.[193] There years have no power over it, nor any change.

From it I went across the fields to Lover's Lane by a way I had not traversed since coming back. I had a beautiful walk through it as it basked in the afternoon sunshine—a walk threaded by sadness; for it was the last time I would be in it this summer; and who knows when, if ever, I shall walk through it again and what changes there may be in it—or in me.

This evening I went again to church and saw Jack Laird and his wife who are visiting in C. at present. I was glad to see Jack again. He hasn't changed much—except to grow stout and broad-shouldered—and there is a good deal of gray in his hair. Well, for that matter I have a good many gray hairs myself, scattered through my tresses, although as yet they show only

The Manse [Cavendish]

on close inspection. We of that old class are all getting on. It seems quite unbelievable that we should have gray hairs. Once gray hairs seemed so very very far away from us.

I remember acutely the anguish the discovery of my first gray hair brought me. It was ten years ago. One spring day I had washed my hair and in the twilight I went to the window of my room to examine the scalp to see if it was perfectly clean. I drew the comb through my hair, parting it midway. And there, cruelly distinct in the harsh light of the gray spring evening, was a white hair—snow-white. I gazed at it with incredulous eyes. It could *not* be. But it *was*. With

Basking in sunshine

shaking fingers I searched through my hair and found a second white

193 This phrase is used in Helen Maud Waithman's poem "Charybdis," published in an 1891 collection by that name. "The Valley of Lost Sunsets," in this collection, expresses similar sentiment as these passages.

one. Well, it seemed to me that I finally turned my back on youth that night. I cried myself to sleep and for days the thought of those gray hairs haunted me. Then I accepted them and became resigned. I found that life went on pretty much the same as ever in spite of those gray hairs. They have gradually increased since then but not so rapidly as I once feared; and they do not worry me much now—nothing ever does worry you much once you accept it. I admire gray hair—on other people; and when my own is all gray I daresay it will be very becoming. When I was a child my hair was very thick and long and of a very pretty shade of golden brown. When I began to grow up it began to darken and soon became a much less beautiful shade of dark brown. It was never curly, alas! I have always envied people who have naturally curly hair. When I had Typhoid fever[194] at the age of five or six the doctor wanted to cut my hair. Grandmother would not allow him to do so. She meant well but I have always wished she had not refused. If it had been cut it might have come in curly. But what matter? I don't suppose it would have made any great difference if it had—only it would have saved me much time and trouble curling and waving my hair.

++Wednesday, Aug. 6, 1913
Cavendish, P.E. Island

This morning I drove in and spent the day with Amanda.[195] She was very nice—more like her old self than I have seen her for years. I quite enjoyed the day. She talked much of old schooldays and frolics—something she would never do for years before I left home. I often used to try, in desperation for something to talk about, but she always avoided the subject. I think perhaps since I passed finally out of her life, she has realized the worth of the friendship she threw away and now would fain regain it. Alas, she cannot! Not because I would be unforgiving but sheerly because of the change in herself—the lack of all development, the dwarfed, stunted nature. Poor Amanda, she cannot be happy, with such a husband and such a home. Yet her young girlhood promised fair—and this thwarted, unlovely womanhood is the result. It is a pity she has not had a child. It might have made up to her for all. And yet, looking at her and at George Henry, we cannot but feel thankful for the child's sake that it was never born!

---

194   A bacterial disease that remained dangerous until the mid-twentieth century brought improvement in public sanitation and the development of a vaccine. LMM's *Rilla of Ingleside* (1921) begins not long after Anne's son Walter has survived a bout of typhoid.

195   Amanda Macneill, LMM's third cousin, was the same age as LMM and her closest friend around age nine.

Amanda's Home

On August 7th I left the manse and went to Alec Macneill's.[196] I had a good week there, though three days of it were rather spoiled by an attack of teething fever in Chester. But Alec and May and I had any amount of fun. It seemed like old times to be there. I used to spend so many jolly afternoons and evenings with them. May and I had some lovely drives and on Sunday afternoon Alec and I drove around the old shore road to the harbor. That night we all went to their shore for a walk, Alec carrying Chester. Both Alec and May idolized Chester. It is such a pity they have no children of their own. I visited friends on Monday, Tuesday and Wednesday but Chester was fretful and so they were rather hard days.

Thursday came—my last day. I hated the thought. I hated the thought of leaving Cavendish. It was so lovely to be there again, among all my own old friends. Somehow, I could not feel a bit glad to be going back to Leaskdale. I knew that by the time I got here the discomforts of travel would have made me heartily glad to be here, but as long as I was in Cavendish I didn't want to leave it. My heart clung to it and ached at the thought of leaving it again.

I packed up Thursday and made some farewell calls. Friday morning Mr. Stirling drove me to Hunter River, Alec taking my trunks. It was a lovely morning. Cavendish looked so beautiful as we drove through it—so green, for the season was late and the grain had not begun to ripen. I knew the harvest was on in Ontario and that it would seem like stepping from spring to autumn when I went back. We had a lovely drive to Hunter River. I went from there to O'Leary to see Mary Beaton.[197] I had not seen her for nine years. She has failed a good deal—is very thin and I do not think she is very happy. My namesake, Maud, who was a tot of two when I last saw her is now a big girl of eleven and quite nice-looking.

---

196   Alexander C. ("Alec") Macneill (1870–1951) was the son of May and Charles Macneill, whose other children were Russell and Pensie. A second cousin to LMM and also an early romantic interest, he was married to May Hooper and lived in Cavendish.

197   Mary Campbell, LMM's second cousin, was also her roommate in Charlottetown in 1893–94 while they attended Prince of Wales College. Tillie Macneill Houston and her husband, Will, are discussed by LMM in journal entries dated August 18, 1903, August 10, 1910, and February 10, 1911.

From O'Leary I went on Saturday to Elmsdale and stayed over Sunday with the William Macneills. I wanted to hear all about poor Aunt Mary's last days. How I missed her! How she would have loved to have seen my boy! But alas, how many others would have loved to see him, too, had they been there to welcome me. And Tillie most of all. Poor Tillie! It almost broke my heart to drive past her little home the first time I went to Rustico and recall all the happy hours I had spent there with her. I did not go there at all, though Will invited me the Sunday I saw him in church. It would have been too painful; and anyway I could not go. Will was very gushing that day and had been at Webb's the night before to see me but I had been away. I was furious with him, for I had been hearing things. It seems he acted insanely when he heard about my marriage and went about talking promiscuously in the most idiotic fashion—raving against Ewan, whose friend he had always professed to be. He has said unpardonable things and betrayed to everybody that he was mad with jealousy, thus opening their eyes to facts that otherwise would never have been suspected. He even went to Park Corner after I was married and made an absurd scene there. Aunt Annie thought he must be out of his mind. I was furious when I heard it all and resolved that I would never make any pretence of friendship for Will again. He has made it impossible. And yet I feel sorry. I liked Will in olden days and he was always so kind to grandmother. For Tillie's sake I would have forgotten his folly in the past and remained his friend. But that cannot be now. He seems to have sunk back to his old level since Tillie's death. Hilda McKenzie, a cousin of Tillie's whom she had with her a couple of years before her death, keeps house for him. He must have a lonely life. I would feel sorry for him if he had not behaved so outrageously.

On Monday, Aug. 18th, I went down to S'side and crossed in the boat. Stella came as far as Moncton with me to help me through the turmoil of changing cars there. From Moncton to Montreal I got on beautifully as I had a drawing-room compartment where Chester could range at will. Tuesday morning my troubles began again. The train was an hour late when we reached Montreal. Result—the train was gone which would have reached Toronto in time to catch the Uxbridge train and I could not get home that night. I had to come on in a slow train. Chester was a huge trouble owing to his roving tendencies. I was tired out when we reached Toronto at nine. There was no one to meet me, Ewan, as I learned later, having returned home thinking that I would not be along till next day. I stayed all night at the Walker House and Ewan came next morning. We reached home at 8 o'clock that night.

Up to the very moment of getting here I was not reconciled to coming back. The drive from Uxbridge home depressed me. The road was dusty and dry and white. The dim slopes on either hand were sere and harvested.[198] The air seemed dull and languid after the tang of the gulf breezes. There seemed a smouldering revolt in my heart at coming back. But when our gate shut behind us it vanished. I was suddenly glad to be back—to be home! Glad to see again my garden, grown out of all recognition in my absence, glad to see my flowers, gray Daffy, my books and pictures, my own comfortable room. My house looked pretty nice to me. I saw it with a stranger's eye after my long absence and when my impression of it was not blurred by familiarity. I liked it! Yes, it was good to be home again among my own household gods.

For a day or two it seemed odd to me to take up the reins of household government again after being a guest in other people's homes so long. And it was *not* pleasant to have to take up again the burden of boring congregational visits and missionary societies.

On the Friday night after my return I got a card from Frede Campbell saying that she would be at Uxbridge on the seven o'clock train that evening. I had been expecting her, as I knew she did not intend staying in the West another year. As Ewan was busy I drove down to meet her. In the excitement of our meeting we were only vaguely aware that a very heavy thunderstorm was coming up and that rain was already falling. For the first two miles of our homeward drive our excitement continued to burn so red-hotly and our tongues to fly so vehemently over the much matter we had to discuss that we did not realize our plight— and then suddenly we realized it with a vengeance! It was pouring rain; it was inky black, relieved by blinding flashes of lightning; we had no idea just where we were; we could not see our hands before our faces.

I have always had a dislike for afternight driving. And here I had to drive home from Uxbridge on a night like this!

Well, needs must when the devil drives![199] We had to keep on. We could not see any gate or place to turn in, or we would have gone to some house. The road was straight so we could not lose it. So perforce we kept on. Queen could only walk for the rain drove in her face and if she trotted she could not keep the road but diverged towards the gutter. I am sure neither Frede nor I will ever forget that nightmare drive home. Our greatest dread was that we might meet teams and have to

---

198   Dry and desiccated.

199   An old expression dating back to Middle English meaning to take action, however unwillingly, when there is no alternative. The clown in Shakespeare's in *All's Well That Ends Well*, explains why he must marry: "My poor body, madam, requires it: I am driven on by the flesh; and he must needs go that the devil drives."

pass. We welcomed the lightning flashes that at least served to show the road ahead clear. It seemed as if we would *never* get home. And yet we talked and jested through it all and by the time we did get home we had emptied our souls of all the accumulations of the past months. But heaven send I may never have another such drive!

I have been exceedingly busy ever since coming back—preserving, canning, sewing and visiting. That never-ending visiting! What precious moments it eats up!

On September first I began work on a third "Anne" book. I did not want to do it—I have fought against it. But Page gave me no peace and every week brought a letter from some reader pleading for "another Anne book."[200] So I have yielded for peace sake. It's like marrying a man to get rid of him!

I don't see how I can possibly do anything worth while with it. *Anne* is grown-up and can't be made as interesting as when a child. My forte is in writing humor. Only childhood and elderly people can be treated humorously in books. Young women in the bloom of youth and romance should be sacred from humor. It is the time of sentiment and I am not good at depicting sentiment—I can't do it well. Yet there *must* be sentiment in this book. I must at least engage Anne for I'll never be given any rest until I do. So it's rather a hopeless prospect and I feel as if I were going to waste all the time I shall put on the book. I might be doing something so much more worthwhile. Perhaps when I get fairly underway I shall warm up to the task but at present I feel very coldly towards it.

"The Golden Road" came out on September first—in appearance just like the preceding five. It is getting monotonous. I wish Page would make a change. It is my sixth book. Can I really have published six books! Some readers and critics think *"The Golden Road"* is the best since *Anne*. I rather like it myself now that I have got far enough away from the turmoil of writing it—the odor of its brewing. It is simply a continuation of the *Story Girl* and ends that series. There is not a great deal of "real life" in it. Some of the stories and anecdotes are "true."

The "Xavy" who had "never learned jogerfy" was Jerry Peters, who was hired with grandfather for several years—the nicest "hired boy" we ever had. Old *Highland Sandy* who said, "If she for go let her for went" was—and is—an old Scotchman down at Kinross. When I wrote the book I was blissfully certain that the old fellow was dead and buried these many years. This summer I discovered to my dismay that he is

---

200   *Anne of the Island*, published April 1915.

still living, and has a numerous progeny of children and grandchildren. May I never fall into their vengeful clutches! The man who wanted the brandy "oftener and more at a time" was a Mr. Miller, formerly teacher of Cavendish school for fourteen years. Those were the days when schoolmasters and ministers stayed long in one place. Afterwards he went to Ch'town and taught there for the rest of his life. He died only a short time ago. He was also the man who came to borrow the axe from grandfather—"more private still." Both those little yarns were often told by grandfather. *Dan King's* "worst adventure" was what happened

"The church beside."

to Dave Nelson when we were coasting at Charles Macneill's, and the story of "How Carlisle got its name" is said to be a true tale of Hunter River. "Oatmeal Frewen" was a certain awkward, long-legged Simpson who carried a bag of corn-flour into church. I think his name was Robert Simpson. Aunt Mary Lawson used to tell the tale with great gusto. Several of *Peg Bowen's* speeches in church were founded on the jokes of country gossip. I used the "Yankee Storm" and "Franklin Dexter" stories and quoted a couple of verses from the poem written by the Cavendish pedagogue at that time, James McLune. This poem, in

"The rock-bound land."

manuscript—the copy, I think, was written by my mother—was always kept in a scrapbook on the parlor table at home and I pored over it and loved it all through my childhood. It was not very "high-class" poetry, perhaps, and yet I believe there was in it that subtle touch which much finer verse often lacks—the "touch that makes the whole world kin."[201]

---

201 An echo of "One touch of nature makes the whole world kin ..." From Shakespeare's *Troilus and Cressida*, Act 3, scene 3.

Here is the whole poem, written from memory. To me, it is too precious to lose or forget, for it is a sweet, silver-clear note in the cherished symphony of childhood memories.

"Lines on the American fishermen who perished in the great storm, October 1851.

(Composed by James McLune, school teacher.)"

There are the fishers' hillside graves,
The church beside, the woods around,
Below, the hollow, moaning waves
Where the poor fishermen were drowned.

A sudden tempest the blue welkin tore,
The seamen tossed and torn apart,
Rolled with the seaweed to the shore
While landsmen gazed with aching heart.

No tolling bell in mourning strain,
No plaintive dirge nor service read,
Marked that procession on the main
Or graced the seamen's oozy bed.

The sandy shroud, the rocking graves,
The wild bird's cry was all their own,
They died like seamen on the waves,
They lay on foreign shores unknown.

That opening day was gay with hope,
Green waved the hillocks and the vales,
The songsters carolled down each slope
And land-birds fluttered round their sails.

The lover dreamed he saw his maid
Waving her welcome from the strand
Alas, by sunset lowly laid
And washed upon the rock-bound land.

In many a tower and wildwood bower,
The sun looks sad, the moon is drear,
Where love still weeps that fatal hour
While memory dawns the shipwrecked year.

A stranger's tears above them flow,
As wandering here he takes his round,
Where the rank grass and wildflowers grow
And silent evening shades the ground.

Poor fishers, how I weep your fate
Whose sails were prematurely furled,
Far from your home in old Pine State
You anchor off a stormy world.

Your loved wives' and children's feet
May never press your grassy graves,
Seen by your country fisher's fleet
While bounding gaily o'er the waves.

Stranger, whoe'er thou art draw near,
Here brother-strangers rest alone,
Come all, for all are brothers here,
The stranger's grave how soon our own.

Frail as the dust it seeks to guard
No stone is here their worth to tell,
Enough—the vile have their reward
And they have theirs who merit well.

No, it is not very good poetry. But, not "Milton's starry splendor"
or "sweetest Shakespeare" can call up for me the beautiful memories
which this poem can summon before

"that inward eye
which is the bliss of solitude."[202]

I see the old burying ground on the westward sloping hill in Cavendish where those grass-grown graves were, by which I often used to
pause dreamily, knowing that the unknown victims of the great storm
were buried there; I see the old church, the fields sloping to the shore,
the pond, the long stretch of sand-hills, and the sea beyond dotted with
fishing vessels and smacks. Or I see the old kitchen at home on a winter's evening when Grandfather and the men who had dropped in for

---

202   From Wordsworth's famous 1807 poem, "I Wandered Lonely as a Cloud."

the mail told tales of the "American Gale" or "the Yankee Storm" and sometimes Grandfather recited McLune's verses. I do not know what became of McLune. He is probably long since dead. But at least two of his verses have found their way into print long after they were written. Possibly they were printed in the Island papers when written.

I also used that beautiful fire I once saw at dusk in Geo. R's old orchard—only it is Ernest Webb's old orchard now—and Well Nelson's old story of "The Battle of The Partridge Eggs." I wonder if this last could be called plagiarism! Hardly, I think. Well little guessed when he wrote it that it would ever see print. I wonder if he will by any chance see it and recognize it. I wish he would. I have lost all trace of Well. I wonder if he has read any of my books and recognized them as the work of his old playmate. How very far away those days of old comradeship seem now! And yet how bright and vivid! At this very moment I can see Well's roguish hazel eyes and merry face and Dave's round, solemn, blue-eyed countenance. It makes me feel lonely. I'll think no more on them.

Lily was away for her vacation of seventeen days in October and I had few spare moments those days. And yet it was very nice to be alone. There was a sweetness in our home life then that cannot be present when a servant shares it—especially when said servant has to be treated as a member of the family, as is necessary here. Lily is an excellent maid and I am well satisfied with her. Still, any outsider is an alien. I wish I could do without a maid but it is impossible.

Not long ago I had a letter from May Macneill in which she informed me that Cavendish post-office had been closed.

I felt sorry—and a little indignant. It was a shame to close that historic old office. Of course the recent introduction of rural mail delivery all over the Island has done away with the need for many of the small offices. But they should not have closed an old one like Cavendish. It must have been one of the oldest country offices on the Island. Grandfather and grandmother kept it for forty years. Well, I am glad the change did not come there in my day. Up to about fourteen years ago we had mail only three days in the week—Tuesdays, Thursdays and Saturdays. It seemed quite wonderful when we got the daily mail; but soon it seemed as if we must always have had it. And now the old Cavendish office is closed. *Sic transit gloria mundi.*[203] It is another one of the little changes that make the big sum total of all change. Dear heart, how homesick it makes me to write anything about Cavendish!

---

203   A Latin phrase meaning "Thus passes the glory of the world."

Last Monday Frede left, going to Montreal to take a position in Macdonald College.[204] Again I missed her horribly but I am thankful she is comparatively near me.

Saturday, October 18, 1913
The Manse, Leaskdale, Ont.

Ever since my last entry I have been, so it seems to me, scrambling through the days striving to do a thousand things in the time that might comfortably suffice for a hundred—doing household duties, tending Chester, sewing, writing novels, and letters and "Guild" papers and lectures, visiting and being visited, attending missionary societies, running Mission Bands—and ending up most of the days by being woefully tired and rather disgruntled. But it is my "kismet"—therefore I must submit![205]

To-day in the Charlottetown *Guardian* there was an announcement of Uncle Leander's death.[206] It is not to be regretted by anyone for the past ten years have been to him death in life and he longed for release. I have never had any especial reason to be very fond of Uncle Leander but nevertheless I felt sad over his death. He was so largely a part of the old life that I feel as if something had been wrenched away in his going—a something not wholly pleasant perhaps but still a something so interwoven with the fibres of my life that tearing it from them meant pain, keen though transient.

Uncle Leander was the first-born of grandfather and grandmother. Great-grandfather Macneill gave him the name of Leander "after him who swam the Hellespont." He was never over-grateful to Great-grandfather for this—nor do I wonder at it! He was a clever and ambitious boy, noted for always getting his own way in everything and carrying out his plans, quite regardless, I have been given to understand, of anyone else's feelings in the matter. He went to Prince of Wales College and from there to Edinburgh University. When he graduated from it he took a position as teacher—of mathematics I think, although I am not sure—in Prince of Wales College, and soon after he was married to Janie Perkins of Charlottetown. I have no memory of "Aunt Janie" but I have been told that she was a very sweet woman. And now Uncle L.G.

---

204 See the entry and note for Monday, December 16, 1912. Located in Sainte-Anne-de-Bellevue, Quebec, Macdondald College was opened in 1907 by Sir William Macdonald as part of a larger initiative to provide education to students from rural backgrounds.

205 Derived from the Turkish word for fate, "kismet" suggests a power that is believe to control events of the future.

206 Leander George Macneill (1845–1913), an older son of LMM's maternal grandparents.

discovered that teaching was not his vocation. He hated it and he was so unreasonably severe with his pupils that many of them refused to go to school to him. He could not keep order without thrashing several of them every day which, as they were all nearly as old as himself, was rather too strenuous. So he resigned his position and went to Princeton to study theology. I do not think I do Uncle Leander any grievous wrong in saying that he had no over-loud "call" to enter

Uncle Leander [Grandma Macneill, Murray Macneill, Murray Macneill]

the ministry. He had a wife and child to support, so he must choose a profession that would promise subsistence from the start. There was certainly nothing "spiritual" about Uncle Leander. He was an intensely selfish man, keenly ambitious of place and supremacy, and neither in his life nor his ideals did he have much in common with the teachings of "the meek and lowly Jesus." But during my two years sojourn in the manse and consequent close association with many ministers I have been driven to conclude that this is not so uncommon as it should be.

Uncle Leander

He was strong and brilliant, with a charming society manner and so, from a worldly point of view, he succeeded. He had wealthy city churches and an unquestioned standing in the councils of "the cloth."

His first charge was in Maitland, N.S. Then he went to St. John's, Newfoundland. Here Aunt Janie died of consumption. Later, he married Annie Putman of Maitland. In my first recollection of him he was in Newfoundland, coming home every summer for his vacation. Uncle Leander was always very fond of his home and his "folks." He had the Macneill "clannishness." Unlike Uncle Chester, who never seemed to care for his home after he had left it, Uncle Leander never grew away from it. This was not only because it was a good and economical place to spend vacations in and send his boys for the summer. He really loved it.

Aunt Janie

I never was very fond of Uncle L.G. In society he could be very agreeable. In private life he was a domineering, selfish man and rode rough-shod over everyone's feelings. Aunt Annie was a very sweet woman and I always liked her. She was an excellent mother to her stepsons and fostered her husband's selfishness by adoring him and submitting to him in everything.

In course of time Uncle Leander was called to St. John, N.B. Here his only living daughter—three other daughters had died in babyhood—Edith died of consumption at the age of eighteen. This was a sad blow to him. In a few years it was followed by Aunt Annie's death. In three or four years time he married his third wife, Mary Kennedy. This was his fatal mistake. He lost his hold on his congregation by such a step. She was a very inferior, illiterate person, a jolly good soul enough, suited for some laboring man's wife but wholly unfitted for his position. His own family resented it bitterly also. Uncle Leander's decline dated from then. He saw his church going down and worried about it. Before long the first symptoms of *"paralysis agitans"*[207] became apparent and

---

207 There are many causes of the "shaking palsy," one being Parkinson's Disease, identified in 1817 by James Parkinson.

for the next fourteen or fifteen years he grew worse and worse until he was a hopeless wreck—a sad ending to a brilliant career.

In my childhood and young girlhood Uncle Leander took very little notice of me, except to hector and snub me, in season and out of season. Grandfather and grandmother, who idolized him, never attempted to check him in the slightest degree. He would never have dared to use me so if my parents had been there to protect me. He never meddled with Uncle John's children or Aunt Annie's. Having no one to defend me I was sometimes goaded to defend myself and so was considered "saucy and impertinent" by Uncle L.—whose own children often "answered back," precisely as I did, but were never so condemned for it!

For twenty years Uncle Leander and some or all of his family came to Cavendish to spend the summer. Yet he never once asked me to visit them. If he had asked me, now and then, to spend two or three weeks with them in the winter the advantages of such a visit would have been incalculable to me, especially from a social point of view. But no such invitation was ever given. I was only an insignificant "country cousin" whose mission in life was, or should be, to wait humbly upon Uncle L's family during the hot weather of July and August and feel myself honored! That sounds bitter. But I *did* feel bitter about it in those days.

But there was in Uncle Leander a rather decided disposition to worship the rising sun. It was not very long after the success of "Anne" until I was aware of a very pronounced change in his manner to me. He ceased to snub or patronize. He seemed to accept me as an equal—deigned to converse quite seriously with me and was really quite agreeable. But it was a little too late. Had he been one half as nice to me when I was a child or a young struggling girl I would have worshipped him. As it was, he could not quite blot out the old memories of him.

Yet those memories of Uncle Leander are not all bitter or unpleasant. He was not always disagreeable, even to me. On the contrary, there were occasional times when he was quite kind and companionable, and it was always a pleasure to me to listen to his conversation with others—he was so witty and polished and pointed. When I visited him on my return from Boston he was delighted. Nobody could have been kinder—nobody more the hospitable host. Uncle Leander had many fine qualities. Had it not been for his domineering habit he would have been a delightful and lovable person all the time, instead of only at intervals. And had he remembered that a child had feelings and rights as well as an adult he would have left a kindlier memory behind him in my heart.

But he is gone—not quite three years after the mother who so idolized him and whom, to do him justice, he loved most tenderly and faithfully. After her death he wrote a letter to Aunt Annie in which he said that, as head of the family, he felt that he ought to convey to me his thanks for the faithfulness with which I had stayed by grandmother to the last. It was a fair and just thing of him and I appreciated it—but what a pity the justice and fairness couldn't have been sprinkled along the way and not all reserved for a parting bouquet.

I am glad grandmother went before him. It would have been very bitter for her had he gone first. I understand now her love for him in the light of my own love for Chester.

Saturday, November 1, 1913
St. Paul's Manse, Leaskdale, Ont.

I have been rushing madly through the days since writing last. On Thursday, Oct. 23rd I went up to Toronto. Last spring the Women's Canadian Club of Toronto asked me to address them at their opening meeting this fall, taking as my subject, Prince Edward Island. I had never made a speech in public, had no wish to do so, was in a blue funk at the idea—and yet I consented. I do not know why I consented. It seemed as if I were compelled to do so by some psychic impulse, such as led to my going to Boston three years ago. In evangelistic jargon I was "led." At any rate I agreed to go. All through October I was getting my address ready and as aforesaid I went to town on the 23rd. I stayed with Marjorie MacMurchy while I was in and had a very delightful time. I do like Toronto. I almost think I would like to live there. I have always said and believed that I could never wish to live anywhere save in the country. But I now begin to suspect that what I meant by "country" was really "Cavendish." I would rather live in Cavendish than anywhere else in the world. But apart from it, I really believe I would like very much to live in a place like Toronto—where I could have some intellectual companionship, have access to good music, drama and art, and some little real social life. I have *no* social life here—none at all, not even as much as I had in Cavendish, for there at least I had a few "chums" whose society I really enjoyed. But here, though I am "visiting" and being visited half the time, there is no pleasure whatever for me. As "the minister's wife" I dare not talk gossip. It would be fatal. But there is nothing else the women here, even the nicest of them, can talk about—except market prices and crops—so conversation on these occasions is a dreary desert. Of course I can rattle on in "small talk" but in my inmost soul I am "cussing" the waste of time. Real enjoyment is never a waste of time; but these horrible "pastoral visits" are, I really believe, an invention of the devil himself.

But I had a good forty-eight hours in Toronto. I had no cares, no worries. I didn't have to watch over everything I said, lest it might be reported to my own or my husband's discredit. I could just "talk." And I had left Chester-boy home, so I wasn't obliged to watch him out of mischief every minute. I felt quite girlish again.

The first evening the MacMurchy girls had some friends in to dinner and after dinner we went to see an amusing little musical comedy at one of the theatres. It was silly and superficial enough but the music and costumes were pretty and it was certainly more interesting than

the dreary "inanities" of the Zephyr "guild," where I would have had to be if I had been home. Friday afternoon the MacMurchy girls gave an afternoon tea for me, which was very pleasant. Saturday afternoon I addressed 800 women in the Forresters' Hall. Mrs. Dickson, the president of the club, is a woman of notable distinction and charm. I have met few women who impressed me so favorably.

I was not at all nervous. My address lasted an hour and nobody seemed bored. Judging by the newspaper reports it was quite a success.

One paper said, "Her address lasted for over an hour

[Mrs. George Dickson, of Toronto]

during which she held the interest of her listeners without a moment of boredom intervening and her clear enunciation carried her every word to the far end of the hall, a feat seldom attained by women speakers unless they have had considerable training in delivery."

One paper described me as follows:—

"In appearance Mrs. Macdonald is slight, of medium height, with dark hair and eyes and a fair complexion. She wears her hair waved and drawn down over her ears. There is something quaint and taking in her whole personality. She is quiet, with a great deal of reserve force and strength. Few writers impress one to the same degree with the conviction that she lives in a mental world of her own.—She has a voice of admirable carrying quality."

The *Courier* said: —It was very delightful to find that this entertaining author is also an entertaining speaker.—L.M. Montgomery is a vari-talented woman who did not quite all go between the covers of "Anne of Green Gables."

I have no intention however of rushing into a career of platform speaking.

After my address the Club had an afternoon tea and I had to shake hands with and say something amiable to nearly all those women. So I was very tired when I got on the seven o'clock train for home. Rev. Dr. Gandier of Knox College came out with me. He preached the next day and was with us two days canvassing the congregation. Lily and I have been trying to get some housecleaning done this week and everything has been rushed.

Wednesday, Nov. 5, 1913
Leaskdale, Ont.

A beautiful wasted day. Wasted because I had to spend it attending a Home Missionary Convention in Uxbridge. It was deadly dull. All the good I got from it was learning how to pronounce "Heimweh" correctly—that is if the anaemic-looking lady who used it in her speech knew herself! I brought Mrs. Horne of Lindsay home with me. She is to speak before our Auxiliary tomorrow and we are going to have afternoon tea. Mrs. H. is hopelessly uninteresting and seems to have resolved to know nothing but Foreign Missions and them only. What a pity it is so hard to be both good and interesting.

I am not good—but I *am* interesting!

Monday, Nov. 10, 1913
Leaskdale, Ont.

A "dirty" day—snowing and raining by fits. This evening I had to spend calling on a cranky old maid who fancies herself sick and gets very angry and disagreeable if we do not visit her frequently. Both she and the Uncle and Aunt she lives with are very dull so it was only the bit of fancy work I had taken with me that saved the situation. Then I had to walk half a mile home, facing a driving sleet. But when I came to my own door I slammed it behind me in the world's face. I threw my clothes off my weary limbs, donned a comfy dressing gown and for an hour gave myself up to a real good "read." And the book I was reading transported me back to childhood. It was "The Wilds of Africa."[208] Years ago Amanda Macneill's brother Allan had a copy of it. I used to borrow and read the book every year. It had a perennial fascination for me. Recently I saw it in a catalogue and promptly got it for Chester's library. Much of its old-time fascination was lacking to my adult taste but enough remained to carry me back for a blissful hour into those vanished years "before the shadows fell." It is one of the best books of adventure for boys I have ever read.

Thursday, Nov. 27, 1913
The Manse, Leaskdale, Ont.

This being "black Thursday" again meant that I must visit in Zephyr. I loathe Thursday as much as I loathe Zephyr. This afternoon, too, I felt very miserable. I suppose I can expect nothing else for some weeks now. Chester's little sister—let us hope!—has, I think, started on her journey from "the kingdom of the future." I am very glad of this but that fact will not prevent physical discomfort. And it is a discomfort which one must hide, pretending to feel quite well. This afternoon was hateful to me. We were visiting an ignorant, bigoted family. I found it wretchedly hard to "make talk." And for tea we had cold roast pork and fried potatoes.

Normally, I am, I admit, very fond of pork and fried potatoes. This may be a very plebeian taste but it is undoubtedly mine and praise be that it is—for almost *everywhere* we go to tea—absolutely everywhere in Zephyr—we have cold pork and fried potatoes. What my fate would be if I did *not* like them I tremble to think. But lately I have turned against many things that I like and the mere thought of eating pork or

---

208   Probably *In the Wilds of Africa: A Tale for Boys* (1881) by W.H.G. Kingston.

fried potatoes nauseates me. Yet there was hardly anything else on the table tonight that I cared for. I made a miserable meal and my hostess watched me with an unfavorable eye. Doubtless she resented my not doing better justice to her viands.

After tea we drove to the village and I put in the evening talking to two deaf old ladies while E. went to prayer-meeting. We had a cold drive home, I felt sick all the way and very tired holding Chester. There, I've written a whole page of grumbles. Great is the relief!

Tuesday, Dec. 16, 1913
The Manse, Leaskdale, Ont.

Ever since my last entry I have been deathly sick with almost no intermission. "Deathly"—yes, that is the very word to express my feeling. I have been ten times worse than during the same period with Chester. The last three weeks have seemed like a nightmare to me. I have been sick with nausea almost unceasingly—I have the most horrible taste in my mouth—I loathe the thought of food—any food—*all* food—I have headache—I am miserably tired all the time and—hardest of all—I have not a spark of energy or interest in anything. Everything I have done in those three weeks I had to *drive* myself to do. I have done nothing except what had to be done. The rest of the time I have had to lie around like a log. Finally today I sent in desperation for Dr. Shier. If I do not get better soon I don't know what I'll do.

Saturday, Dec. 27, 1913
Leaskdale, Ont.

I have been no better—worse if anything. Really, it has been horrible. I am absolutely useless. Thanks be, Christmas is over. It was a hard one. I had to go to Uxbridge Monday morning to do some Christmas shopping. This tired me out; and then in the evening we had to go out to tea and have a family baptism. I was worn out when I got home and sick all the next day. In the evening I had to go out and take part in the Sunday School Concert. Wednesday I spent in bed.

Thursday was Christmas—the most doleful one I ever put in. Lily went home so I had to cook the dinner. When I'm well I love cooking. But just now the sight and odor of food is nauseous to me. Sick as any dog, I cooked that dinner and choked some of it down. Turkey—cranberry sauce—pudding—what booted it? One and all were vanity. Friday I had to cook all day again, preparing refreshments for the Guild executive which met here in the evening. To-day I've been doubly miserable.

I cannot describe how miserable I do feel—*all* the time, day and night. I had not expected this for I had not a great deal of trouble before. As it is, I look forward to the months of winter with dread. When I waken in the morning, I think, "Oh, how can I drag through the day?" At night I think "Oh, Thank God this day is ended."

Saturday, Jan. 3rd, 1914
Leaskdale, Ont.

This week I have had a visitation of Zephyr people—two days of them. In all the time I have been here hardly any of them have ever come— not that I lamented that, though I religiously invited them! But of course, now that I am sick, they will come. To talk to Zephyr folk when I am well is something by way of penance. When I am as sick as I have been all this week it is martyrdom. One family came and brought three children, two of them "enfants terribles."[209] The mother seems to have fashioned her views and conversation on the "Pansy" books.[210] She talks a sort of cant I never heard outside of those fairy tales. Evidently she expected me, as a minister's wife, to appreciate it and respond in like manner. But alas, I cannot talk Pansyese. I was indeed put to it to hide my amusement over her speeches. Had I not been so miserable physically I fear I could not have succeeded and the result would have been dire, for her husband is an elder and quite the most influential personage in Zephyr church, therefore has power to make it unpleasant for Ewan if he choose. So I tried to steer between Scylla and Charybdis and think I succeeded tolerably well.[211]

Saturday, Jan. 10, 1914
The Manse Leaskdale.

There is an old hymn with one line of which I have never, until lately, felt much in sympathy—"travelling through life's wilderness." In my normal health and condition I could never agree that life, lived sensibly and rationally, was a "wilderness," whatever occasional tracts of arid plain it might show. But really, of late, I have been tempted to think that it is. Certainly for the last two months I have been travelling through a wilderness that seems without beginning or end and devoid of even a cheering oasis. In these two months I have not felt well for one single moment and nearly all the time wretchedly miserable—a martyr to nausea, indigestion, and a general useless, dragged-out feeling. Like calamity, illness has a way of "staining backward" through the pages of life's volume—and forward, too. It seems to me as if I must have been sick all my life and must be sick all the rest of it. I cannot

---

209 "A child who embarrasses his elders by untimely remarks" (OED 2nd edn).
210 American author Isabella Macdonald Alden (1841–1930) wrote some 100 books under the pseudonym Pansy. Most of her work is didactic fiction illustrating religious principles.
211 An expression dreived from Greek mythology, meaning sailing between two terrible dangers.

imagine the sensation of feeling well or of taking an interest in anything. I drag through the days, compelling myself to do what has to be done, and then collapse on my bed, feeling as if I could never rise from it again. This past week a bad cold has been added to my other miseries. Wednesday I had to go to the W.F.M.S. at Mrs. Cook's and to the Guild in the evening, where I read a paper on *Esther*,[212] written in bitterness of soul. Thursday I went to Zephyr, had tea with a prosy family and went to Guild in the evening. As a consequence I felt utterly exhausted on Friday and doubly miserable.

Grave and ...

To-day was Mission Band day and the hour I spent at it seemed a year long.

Chester-boy, too, has been cutting teeth lately and has been quite restless at night, requiring several drinks and so disturbing my sleep. But he is a darling little lad. He is beginning to talk now and imitate everything he hears, and he has such funny, adorable little ways.

To be sure, it's an ill wind that blows no good. These past six weeks I have done more reading than in the preceding two years. I am good for nothing else, so when I finish what has to be done I lie on my bed and read—

... Gay [Chester]

when I *can* read. Sometimes I am too sick even to do that; and at the best I don't enjoy it as I would if well. Still, it passes the time and I have got through with quite a number of books. Among the rest I have read the twelve volumes of Grote's *History of Greece*.[213] I have

---

212   The main character of the Bible's Book of Esther.

213   British historian George Grote's (1794–1871) major work, A *History of Greece; from the Earliest Period to the Close of the Generation Contemporary with Alexander the Great* (1846–56).

never read a continuous history of Greece before. Grote's scholarship is quite marvellous and there are many "purple patches" in his work. But much of it is dry enough. Still, I am glad to have managed to read it. My knowledge of a very important part of ancient history has been much enlarged.

To employ a trite and bromidic remark, "dreams are curious things." I had one last night which illustrates this remark.

Long years ago, when I was about ten years old, grandmother took a monthly magazine called "Godey's Lady's Book."[214] She took it for several years. I do not know that I should think a great deal of that magazine now, but then I thought it very wonderful and its monthly advents were "epochs in my life." It was, of course, a fashion magazine. The first pages were full of fashion plates of the day and were as delightful to me as any other part. I hung over them with rapture and whiled away many an hour "picking" what ones I would have, had I but to choose. Those were the days of bangs, bustles, and high-crowned hats—all of which I considered wondrously beautiful. Past the fashion pages came the literary pabulum—short stories and serials. In those blissful days I read serials. I never read them now—I haven't the patience to wait from month to month. But I devoured everything then. One of those serials was "The Dreeing of the Weird" by *Helen Mathers*,[215] and a most exciting thing it was. I hadn't any idea what the title meant and nothing in the story explained it. But the story was easily understood—and I think it was of higher literary excellence than most of the stuff in the "Lady's Book." I enjoyed it immensely, re-read it many times—and then as years passed forgot it—forgot it absolutely. It was as if I had never read such a story. Not since I was fifteen have I thought of or recalled that story. But last night I dreamed I was reading it again and every incident, every name returned to my memory as clearly as if I had read the story yesterday. Nor did it flee with the visions of the night. Waking, I recalled it all from beginning to end.

Do we ever really forget *anything* in our lives? I do not think we do. The record is always there in our subconscious minds, to be suddenly remembered when something brings it to our recollection—perhaps never to be remembered, but always there.

One night, when I was about ten years old, I dreamed a curious and rather horrible little dream. I dreamed that there had been a terrific

---

214 This American fashion magazine had a widespread circulation of about 150,000 in 1860; it specialized in poetry, articles, and fashion.

215 Helen Mathers (1852–1907) was a popular English novelist and contributor to *Godey's Lady's Book*.

snowstorm and that I was walking to school through a low and narrow tunnel that had been cut through the enormous drifts from our house to the school.

This tunnel had many curves and turns in it. I turned around one sharp angle to find my path completely blocked up by a huge, hideous *face* which filled the tunnel before me. The horror of the face wakened me. I recalled the dream when I woke. Perhaps I remembered it for a few days. Then it passed completely out of my memory. For twenty years I never recalled it. Then one day I was reading *Undine*.[216] While the hero was riding through the Enchanted Forest his path was suddenly blocked by a hideous head and face. Like a lightning flash came back to me that old forgotten dream. As vividly as if it were of yesternight I saw the white walls of my snow tunnel and the huge face that barred my way. Last night the process was reversed and the dream recalled the tale.

Tuesday, Jan. 27, 1914
The Manse, Leaskdale, Ont.

Have been most miserable ever since last writing. I am beginning to feel discouraged. I have never felt well for a moment and most of the time wretched in the extreme. But it boots not to enlarge on the theme. If I did it would seem like a page from a patent medicine almanac.

To-day *I began to knit a quilt*. That sounds like an arrant folly in a woman who is as busy as I am. Yet there is a method in my madness. There have been so many days lately that I could do absolutely nothing, not even read, because my nerves got in such a state. Now, *knitting* has always had a good effect on me when I am nervous. I was always very fond of knitting and I find that it helps me greatly these bad days. So I began the quilt. It doesn't matter if I never finish it.

Quilt knitting, in this particular pattern especially always makes me think of Malpeque. I spent a winter there once with Aunt Emily. Every girl and woman in Malpeque had knitted, was knitting, or intended to knit a quilt—some of them several quilts. They possessed many patterns and considerable rivalry went on. Lace knitting was very popular also. I caught the fever and began a quilt. I think I was three years knitting it. It was very pretty but was worn out long ago. Ten years ago I knitted a second which I still have. Shall I ever finish a third? I feel so

---

216   Friedrich de la Motte Fouqué's novella *Undine* (1811) was a favourite of LMM's from an early age. In the story, a water spirit (Undine) marries a knight named Huldebrand in order to gain a soul.

blue and wretched just now that it does not seem to me as if I would ever be able to accomplish anything again.

Friday, Jan. 30, 1914
The Manse, Leaskdale, Ont.

Yesterday we went to Zephyr. A thaw was on and the roads were dreadful. We visited another rough, ignorant family living in a little log house at the back of beyond. At night we went to Guild. When we came out I thought of the drive home with dismay. The roads were so bad—and I was so tired and sick. How could I endure those endless seven miles of half bare hills and swamps? But lo, that drive home proved to be one of those peculiar psychological experiences I have by times. As we left the church something suggested to my mind a verse from "The Lady of the Lake." I began recalling the poem, which I have known by heart since childhood—and not only recalling it but *living* it. I roamed through its vivid scenery. I talked with its people. Other poems followed and them I also lived. The physical discomforts of the drive were quite unnoticed. I was snatched far away from them and in spirit lived "one crowded hour of glorious life" oblivious of all my surroundings, save only the stars shining over me. That drive home, instead of being the nightmare I dreaded, was a strange, scintillating, vivid dream of unearthly delight.

Nevertheless, the aforesaid physical discomforts were present, though for the time unfelt; and to-day I felt their effects. I have been exhausted and ill all day.

Wednesday, Feb. 11, 1914
The Manse, Leaskdale, Ont.

We are having an exceedingly cold snap and our sufferings from that cause are considerable. Yesterday we had the unusual experience of a slight earthquake shock. We did not know what it was at the time. Just after we rose from the dinner table all the dishes on and in, the sideboard began to shake and rattle in a very peculiar fashion, and continued to do so while one might have counted forty. We could not account for it, for nothing had touched it. To-day's paper announced that there had been a decided shock all over Ontario at that time.

It does seem to me that these past few days I have been slightly better. It seems too good to believe—I hope in fear and trembling. I am miserable enough still but my improvement is a blessing after the intolerable discomfort of the past three months. They seem like as many years.

Monday, Feb. 16, 1914

The improvement is certainly real. This past week I have felt a little like myself. Physical ills have been lighter and I have begun to feel an interest in things again. To-day I even enjoyed myself. I had the first little outing that I have found pleasant since October. Indeed, it was the first one I could have found any real pleasure in had I been ever so well.

I was to read a paper before the Hypatia Club this afternoon, so Mrs. Cooke of Uxbridge asked Ewan and me to have dinner with them. I enjoyed the drive down, for though frosty it was fine and the roads excellent. I enjoyed a dainty dinner which had more taste for me than anything I have eaten for months. And more than all I enjoyed a little free, *real* conversation with people of intelligence and culture. It was to me as the shadow of a great rock in a weary land.

Thursday, Feb. 19, 1914
The Manse, Leaskdale, Ont.

This isn't "Black Thursday," for I didn't go to Zephyr today. Instead, I went yesterday— to a rather awful sort of wedding. The day was beautiful and the roads good, so that the drive over was rather pleasant. But when we got there all enjoyment was over. The people were ignorant and hopelessly dull; the wedding baked meats were a poor affair; and I had Chester with me which meant that I was not to know a minute's peace of mind. For he is just at the worst age—able to get into all kinds of mischief and having no "sense" to keep him in bounds. The only thing to do is to watch him constantly, lest he do himself harm or annoy others. So I was tired out when we got away. But I had to

Chester and Lily

go to a Guild social last evening so I'm tired again today. But praise be, I haven't to go to Zephyr! Name of abomination!

Wednesday, Feb. 25, 1914
The Manse, Leaskdale, Ont.

I have had another bad cold for four days. It seems that I cannot throw off colds this winter. They cling to me closer than a brother. My other discomforts are, however, slowly lessening. I never feel *quite* well but the insufferable misery of the past three months seems to have passed and I do not know how to be sufficiently thankful.

To-day I finished re-reading Anthony Trollope's inimitable "Barset" series of novels.[217] I read them last six years ago down home. They *are* delicious. The glorious scene where "*Mr. Crawley*" turns upon "*Mrs. Proudie*" with his splendid, "Peace, woman!" is finer than anything in Dickens or Thackeray. As I am beginning to be able to work again I have scant time for reading now—a half hour or so after I am ready for bed. I ought to be asleep for I need all the sleep I can get. But man cannot live by bread alone. I *must* have a little sustenance for soul and mind and where can I get it here save in books. That half hour is well spent, sleep to the contrary notwithstanding. And as I am a fast reader I get through a good deal in it.

Friday, Feb. 27, 1914
The Manse, Leaskdale, Ont.

A case of "stolen goods" came to my knowledge today. In a current magazine I found some verses entitled "Come Back" purporting to be by one "Margaret Gibson," of Plainfield, New Jersey. The poem was written by me six years ago and published in the *Youth's Companion* in 1909, under the original title "The Old Home Calls." I must see to the matter, as I intend to include this poem in a published collection someday and can't permit its publication under another author's name to pass unchallenged. It was a bare-faced trick of "Margaret Gibson" and absurd as well. She must have known she ran a risk of being found out. "I can stand *wickedness* but I can't stand *foolishness*."[218]

Sunday, March 22, 1914
The Manse, Leaskdale, Ont.

I have been much better this month—but much of the time feel very weary and useless. I had a nice little time this week—I went in to Toronto Thursday morning and stayed till last night. I stayed with Mrs. Norman Beal[219] who lived in Uxbridge until recently and who is a nice jolly soul of the race that knows Joseph. I was glad of a short jaunt away from the cares and responsibilities of my daily routine—cares

---

217 English author Anthony Trollope's (1815–82) series of six novels are set in the fictitious English county of Barsetshire (located roughly in the West Country).

218 A favourite saying, used by (among others) Miss Cornelia in *Anne's House of Dreams* (1917).

219 Mary Beal came from an Uxbridge family and had been the Vice-President of the Hypatia Club in 1911–12.

and responsibilities which are pleasures when I feel well but have been a heavy burden this winter. Mary and Norman and I went to the theatre Thursday night and saw "Peg O' My Heart"[220]—one of the most charming little comedies I've ever seen. I enjoyed it so much. But some wretched newspaper reporter saw me there and put it in the society column of Friday's *Globe*—bad 'cess to him! All "the parish" will see it and what will the Zephyrites think!! Verily, that I am a brand, not yet plucked from the burning!

Mary gave an afternoon tea for me Friday. I suppose she wanted to show off a real live though small lion as her guest! Afternoon teas are such senseless things—satisfying neither to mind, soul, or stomach. I shopped a good deal, finding it very hard under existing conditions. But I had two glorious nights of unbroken sleep! Such are very rare with me now—and must continue to be rare for some time I suppose! "The gods don't allow us to be in their debt." That they do not!

Wednesday, April 15, 1914
The Manse, Leaskdale, Ont.

Verily these last few days have been to me as manna to a hungry soul. Frede came on Friday for Easter and stayed till yesterday. We emptied out our souls and rinsed them. I feel that I can go on again for awhile. I had bottled up various things so long that I was dangerously near exploding point.

We are into housecleaning and I am finding it desperately hard this year. I am very short of breath and if I am much on my feet my back aches woefully. I just drag through the days and am always very thankful when night comes. Yet people seem to expect me to do just as much visiting and attend just as many meetings as usual. At times my soul is sick within me. I remember in an old reading I used to give years ago there was one sentence "The life of a minister's wife is a sort of refined slavery." Bitter truth! Well, I always knew it and expected it; but when I am not well parish fetters are a little hard to bear.

This evening I read a rather entertaining article in the *Bookman*,[221] dealing with "Confessions in an Album." Such were in vogue years ago. You had to answer a series of questions on your preferences and dislikes. The article in question dealt with the answers of several noted people of bygone days. I amused myself mentally answering, or trying to answer, the queries myself.

---

220 Comic play by John Hartley Manners (1870–1928); the play was first produced in 1912, and sparked many popular touring companies.

221 An American literary journal founded by Frank H. Dodd in 1895. Its last issue appeared in 1933.

No. 1. What is your favorite flower?

Well, I love all flowers so much it is hard to choose. But of wild flowers I love best the shy sweet wild "June Bell"—the *Linnea Borealis,*—of Prince Edward Island spruce woods; and of garden flowers the white narcissus—the old "June lilies" of girlhood days. We did not have them but they grew in the grassy nooks of many old Cavendish gardens.

No. 2. "Your favorite tree?"

Most certainly the pine—though the fir runs it hard. There were few pines in Cavendish—an odd one or two back in the woods. Indeed, there are not many anywhere on the Island. It is the habitat of spruce and fir. I first got well acquainted with pines in Halifax Park.

We have a good many pines in Scott township but none very near the manse. Spruces are scarce. There is an abundance of scrubby cedar—a tree I despise. They seem like a wretched imitation of spruce when seen in the twilight. And they are generally so shabby and faded and draggled. There are many lovely elms, which are great favorites of mine, and some nice maples. White birch, which comes next to pine and fir in my affection, is rather scarce.

No. 3. "Your favorite object in Nature?"

Rather an obscure question. Many of the noted people aforesaid answered "the sea" and I am half inclined to also. But it seems incongruous to call that blue lone entity an "object in nature." After all, I think my answer to that must be "A Prince Edward Island wood of fir and maple, where the ground is carpeted thick with ferns." Specifically, my favorite object in Nature is *Lover's Lane*.

No. 4. "Your favorite hour of the day?"

—*day* presumably meaning the twenty-four hours. Sunset and the hour following for me. That time used to be my happiest at home—I hovered then between two worlds, forgetting all the cark and care of this one. Nowadays I have seldom a chance to enjoy the twilight; the sunset is generally swallowed up by Mr. Leask's woods. Once in a while though, I can enjoy the afterglow, sitting out on the lawn in the dusk.

No. 5. "Your favorite season of the year?"

Spring—spring—spring! The last two weeks of May in Ontario, the first two of June in P.E. Island. Who could love any season better than spring? And yet several in the aforesaid article answered "Autumn." Well, autumn is love-deserving, too. But it advances to decay while spring flies on to abundance of life.

No. 6. "Your favorite perfume?"
The fragrance of freesias.

No. 7. "Your favorite gem?"
The diamond, when all is said and done. But I love gems of all descriptions—all except turquoises. Them I loathe—the shallow, soulless, insipid things. The gloss of pearl, the frosty glitter of diamond, the glow of ruby, the tenderness of sapphire, the melting violet of amethyst, the moonlit glimmer of aquamarines—I love them all.

No. 8. "Your favorite poets?"
Byron and Scott.

No. 9. "Your favorite poetess?"
Jean Ingelow.[222]

No. 10. "Your favorite prose authors?"
Nay, nay, there are too many of them—Scott, Dickens, Thackeray, Collins, Trollope and fifty others. I love them equally well, one for one mood, one for another. When I was fifteen I should have answered unhesitatingly, "Lytton, first and last, and the rest nowhere."[223] Now he would not be on my list at all. *Sic transit gloria Mundi.*[224]

No. 11. "Where would you like to live?"
Cavendish, Prince Edward Island.

No. 12. "Your favorite amusement?"
Reading and walking in the woods are ties.

No. 13. "What trait of character do you most admire in a man?"
Justice.

No. 14. "In a woman?"
A sense of humor. I would also admire justice in a woman if I ever saw it.

No. 15. "What do you most detest in each?"
Deceit and love of meddling.

---

222   Jean Ingelow (1820–97) was an English poet, novelist, and children's writer.
223   Edward Bulwer-Lytton (1803–73); LMM's favourite novel as a youth had been *Zanoni* (1842).
224   A Latin phrase meaning "Thus passes the glory of the world."

No. 16. "If not yourself, who would you rather be?"

Humph! When all is said and done I don't know. I can't just now recall one person I would really like to be—though there are some *in whose place* I would like to be.

No. 17. "Your idea of happiness?"

A good novel and a plate of russet apples! Well, that is a flippant definition. But to give a faithful account would require pages. And yet—and yet—no! Holding my little son in my arms or feeling his chubby arms around my neck is happiness. Once I might have answered "To be in Herman Leard's arms." I would not so answer now. But to be in the arms of a man whom I loved with all my heart and to whom I could willingly look up as *my master* is, after all, every woman's real idea of happiness, if she would be honest enough to admit it. There are dear and sweet minor happinesses. But that is the only perfect one.

No. 18. "Your favorite dream?"

To write a book that will live. I can never do it—but dreams don't have to come true.

No. 19. "What do you most dread?"

Dying of cancer.

No. 20. "What is your motto?"

What is worth doing is worth doing *well*. It doesn't make for an easy life, though. The ability to *shirk* is really a desirable one, I believe—at least I think so when I am all tired out.

Saturday, April 18, 1914
The Manse, Leaskdale, Ont.

Having been, thanks to my ill health, ever since last September getting together material for "Anne III"[225] and blocking out the chapters I really began to write it today. *Beginning* a story is always a hard thing for me to do. I feel as if it were half done once it is really begun. And I *never* feel satisfied with my beginnings. In especial my beginning today seemed horribly flat. My pen dragged. I find it very hard nowadays, with all my manifold duties and interruptions to get into the mood for

---

225 *Anne of the Island*, still at this time with the working title "Anne of Redmond," based on LMM's year studying in Halifax.

writing. I seem to feel an undercurrent of hurry that spoils my work and my pleasure in it. I can't believe this third Anne book will be any good. I have no faith in it. It seems *going backward* to try to write it. I feel as if *Anne* and all pertaining to her had been long left behind.

I remember well the very evening I wrote the opening paragraph of *Green Gables*. It was a moist, showery, sweet-scented evening in June ten years ago. I was sitting *on the end of the table*, in the old kitchen, my feet on the sofa, beside the west window, because I wanted to get the last gleams of daylight on my portfolio. I did not for a moment dream that the book I had just begun was to bring me the fame and success I had long dreamed of. So I wrote, the opening paragraphs quite easily, not feeling obliged to "write up" to any particular reputation or style. Just as I had finished my description of *Mrs. Lynde* and her home *Ewan* walked in. He had just moved to Cavendish from Stanley, where he had previously been boarding and this was his first call since moving. He stayed and chatted most of the evening, so no more of *Green Gables* was written that night. And now today I began my seventh book, a thousand miles from that twilight window looking out into the rain-wet apple trees of the front orchard. The window by which I wrote today looked out on several unlovely, spring-naked back yards—for the only chance I have to write is to shut myself in my room where young

The west window

Chester cannot prowl. But then he is worth all the books in the world.

Sunday, May 24, 1914
Leaskdale, Ont.

We are in mid-spring now and everything is very lovely. Yesterday Lily and I took her two children, Archie and Edith, Jessie and Cameron Leask, and Chester back to Mrs. Leask's woods for a picnic. It was the first time I had been back to the woods this spring. It is lovely back there now—so green and cool and remote. The path under the trees along the old mill race is very pretty and the open glade where we had our lunch is beautiful with its big elms and its carpet of white and pale purple violets. My present physical clumsiness rather spoiled my enjoyment; but it was beautiful to sit there on the flower-starred grass and look up into the green arches above us, with Chester-boy, looking like a wee man in his red cap and blue sweater beside me. There is nothing of the baby about him now. I'm sorry, for he *was* an adorable little baby. Now he is just a big boyish boy. He has begun to talk at last. I don't think he has been very precocious about it all. But it is so inter-

[Chester]

[Chester]

esting to watch his little mind developing and broadening as he adds new words to his vocabulary. So far he deals only in single words and hasn't attempted to join them together. He makes one word in its time play many parts. "Door" means *anything* that opens—door, window, drawer, lid, box-cover. He pronounces such words as he has acquired very well and plainly.

I suppose in about two months more he will have a wee sister or brother—if all goes well. I *do* hope it will be a sister. I want a little daughter so much and I will be bitterly disappointed if the baby is not a girl—for at my age I cannot confidently count on having any more children, though I hope I will. And will all go well? Some-

[Picnic]

how, I look forward to this second birth with more anxiety than I did to Chester's coming—perhaps because I realize more clearly how many things *might* go wrong. Somehow, too, I can't believe that I shall have as easy a time as I had when Chester was born. And it will be so lonely. Neither of the girls will be here and I have to have both a new doctor and a new nurse. I wish it were all well over, for at the best, it is not a pleasant experience, especially in hot weather.

I have all my housecleaning and gardening done, for which praise be. I found both very hard this spring. Ewan leaves for P.E. Island tomorrow for a short vacation. It makes me lonely to think of his going without me. But I can't visit the dear old spot this summer, alas!

Sunday, June 28, 1914
St. Paul's Manse, Leaskdale, Ont.

This has been for once a real "day of rest." And I needed it sadly, for the past fortnight has been a decidedly strenuous one. Ewan returned from his holiday on June 9, and the next week the rush was on.

Last fall Ewan began to carry out his long-cherished project—getting the congregation to support a foreign missionary of its own. It was rather a big undertaking to engineer in a country congregation. I do not think there is another country congregation in Canada doing it. I did not think it a wise thing for him to attempt—and I don't think it a wise thing now. As soon as the initial enthusiasm wears off I fear it will mean a lot of extra work and worry for him if it is kept up or a certain humiliation if it fails. But at any rate he has accomplished it and the salary is pledged for five years.

"Our missionary" came on June 15 to spend a week in the parish. His name is Stewart Forbes and he is a young Knox graduate of boyish appearance and with just a tinge of the new-fledged collegian's comfortable assurance that he knows it all and a cheerful ignorance of human nature.[226] But he is nice and sincere, and improves on acquaintance. I found him an agreeable variant from the type of most foreign missionaries I have known. He is free from cant and narrow-mindedness and does *not* appear to think that foreign missions are the one thing needful and foreign missionaries the only people who are doing God's work in the world. On the other hand, he has no magnetism or enthusiasm and I don't think he is just the man for a "special missionary." He will not inspire zeal and interest in the congregation supporting him and that will be very necessary in this case.

He and Ewan plunged into an orgy of visiting. Then on Tuesday came the ordination and designation service. Monday Lily and I were very busy all day for we were to have three or four ministers to dinner Tuesday and had also to help prepare the supper which was served in the basement after the service. All Monday and Tuesday I was on my feet much more than I should have been. Result—utter weariness of soul and body on Wednesday and Thursday. But company came to tea on Thursday. Then on Friday we had to prepare for the S.S. picnic; that came off yesterday—the unholy thing! I believe S.S. picnics are necessary evils because the children enjoy them.[227] I used to enjoy them when I was a child. Now they are an abomination unto me. I started late after all the rest had gone. It was a cool pleasant day and I was all alone—something that happens so rarely nowadays that it is by way of a treat. I decided to walk as slowly as I could to prolong the enjoyment, going by the pretty mill-race path. It was the only pleasure the day offered me. Alas for my anticipations! Just as I turned into the side road I saw Mary and Lizzie Oxtoby. I walked still more slowly, praying that they might keep ahead. Not they! They stopped and waited—and I had to walk to the picnic grounds with them. I said it looked a little like rain—and Lizzie Oxtoby laughed. I said the path along the race was very pretty—and Lizzie Oxtoby laughed. I said there still seemed to be plenty of mosquitoes—and Lizzie Oxtoby laughed. If I were to say to Lizzie Oxtoby "My father has hanged himself, my husband has gone out of his mind, my children have been burned to death and I am suffering from an incurable cancer"—Lizzie Oxtoby would laugh. She can't help it—she was born so—but it is very awful!

Arriving at the picnic ground I picked out a soft stump and sat upon

---

226   The Rev. H. Stewart Forbes went on to work as a missionary in the central Chinese province of Honan (now known as Henan). The Leaskdale church, Zephyr church, and the Macdonalds themselves each contributed about one-third of his annual salary of $1,200.

227   Sunday School picnics were traditionally held in June, prior to the summer break. The first Presbyterian Sunday School had been organized in Brockville, Ontario, in 1811.

it. Moving about much or standing is a physical impossibility with me now. A lady sat beside me who will probably go into the kingdom before me, but who offers a horrible example of how not to converse. She passed a whole hour detailing to me the sayings of her three-year-old son—and all the sayings were commonplace to a sinful degree. Yet she seemed to expect me to laugh over them. I couldn't

The side road

and didn't—I had no desire to rival Lizzie Oxtoby. But I groaned in soul. If I could only have been there alone with winds and trees and clouds. Or if I could just have been at home reading a book or lying down to ease my aching back and tired muscles!

Then came the repast. I sat sideways on the ground and ate several sandwiches and a piece of lemon pie and one of gooseberry. I think I also ate several crickets who had got tangled up with the meringue of the pie. After that I concluded I might go home. I got Chester-boy and we

[Chester]

went. Thank heaven, there was no Lizzie Oxtoby this time. Chester-boy toddled by my side, clinging to me with his dear sun-burned hand and chattering about "orses" and "geesies" and all other objects he saw and if I had not been so horribly tired I would have enjoyed the walk.

To-day, therefore, my rest was as manna to a hungry soul.

August 5, 1914
The Manse, Leaskdale, Ont.

England has declared war on Germany!

Good God, I cannot believe it! It *must* be a horrible dream. It has come up like a thundercloud.

Sometime in June I picked up a *Globe* and read that a Serbian had shot the Archduke of Austria and his duchess.[228] The news was of little interest to me—as to most people on this continent. We dreamed not what was to come of it. But verily *that* was "the shot heard round the world"[229]—to be echoed and re-echoed by the death shriek of millions and the wails of heart-broken women.

Seemingly nothing much did come of it as far as we were concerned. A short time ago we read that Austria had demanded certain things of Serbia. Serbia refused to comply. Austria declared war on Serbia. Russia told Austria she would not allow Serbia to be attacked without coming to her assistance. So far, who in this hemisphere cared? There is always war somewhere among the Balkan States. It seems to be their normal condition.

But—Germany declared that if Russia mobilized she would back up Austria. When that news was flashed around the world the world suddenly held its breath and began to tremble. What did it mean? It meant that France, according to treaty obligations must stand by Russia—it *might* mean that England must fight, too.

For a few days we have hoped desperately that England's diplomats might succeed in averting the peril. Germany's wanton and utterly indefensible violation of Belgium destroyed that hope. England's honor was pledged to Belgium and to France. And yesterday she declared war.

The *Globe* came as we went to dinner. I sat down weak and unnerved. I could not eat. I could only sit there dumbly trying to realize it—to realize that our Empire was at war. And such a war! No paltry struggle in an out-of-the-way corner—no Boer conflict which we all thought so terrible at the time—but a death grapple. For Germany comes to conquer or to die.

Germany provoked this war because she wanted it and was ready for it. For the last twenty years she has been preparing for it. That fact

---

228   Gavrilo Princip (1894–1918), a student born in Bosnia and associated with the Yugoslav nationalist movement, assassinated Austro-Hungarian crown prince Franz Ferdinand and his wife Sophie in Sarajevo on June 24, 1914. Princip's ties to Serbian military authorities led Austria-Hungary to issue an ultimatum to Serbia that precipitated the outbreak of the First World War.

229   A phrase from Ralph Waldo Emerson's "Concord Hymn," marking the Battle of Concord near the beginning of the American Revolutionary War

has been open and notorious. Four years ago Earl Grey told me that war between England and Germany was surely coming in a few years. I said, "Don't you think that is one of the things that are expected so long they never come to pass? It is generally some other thing—the unexpected thing that happens." But he said gravely, "No. This is coming. We must get ready for it."

It has come. Britain or Germany must fall. But the death-grapple will be awful beyond anything ever known in the world before. Oh, if I could but waken up and find it all a dream! These last four days have seemed like a nightmare. Already Canada is ablaze. Volunteers are being called for Red Cross and patriotic funds are being started. The bottom has fallen out of the world's markets. Civilization stands aghast at the horror that is coming upon it.

The worst of it is that Germany is so fully prepared. England is totally unprepared as far as an army goes. Thank God, her navy is ready. That may save her—may save us all. If Germany wins Canada will become a German colony—there is no doubt of that. God save us!

As for me—I had expected that by this time I would have had my baby. But my hour has not yet come. I have been feeling very miserable and the days are long and trying. My nurse, Mrs. Aubin, has been here ever since July 17th. When she first came I did not like her. She was a voluble Irishwoman—by ancestry—knowing not the meaning of reserve, with an irritating habit of laughing nervously at the end of every sentence. I recoiled from the thought of having *her* wait upon me in the intimacies of childbirth. But that is past. I begin to like her very much. She is very kind and sympathetic and now that the edge of her is off I don't mind her chatter. She is the utter antithesis of Miss Fergusson in every way as far as personality goes.

I wish greatly that it was all over. I am full of forebodings. And now this war will make everything harder.

Sunday, Aug. 30, 1914
The Manse, Leaskdale, Ont.

Have the past three weeks been a dream of horror? No, they are a fearful reality. My heart seems broken. On August 13th a darling little son was born to me—dead.

Oh God, it almost killed me. At first I thought I could not live! All the agony and pain I have endured in my whole life heaped together could not equal what I felt when I realized that my baby was dead—my bonny sweet boy, so beautiful and perfect.

The cause of his death was a knot in the cord—an accident that could not be foreseen or prevented. It very rarely happens but when it does it is always fatal. Oh, I had never thought of this—strangely enough I had never once thought of it. I had thought of it in Chester's case but never in this. I had had dread forebodings—but they had been for myself—not for my child. Oh, will the pain ever grow less? My heart is wrung with the agony of it while I write. Oh, it was cruel—cruel—cruel!

Never shall I forget the misery of that afternoon, after I came out of the valley of the shadow to find that my darling was dead—that the reward for which I had suffered through long months and faced death had been denied me. I lay there—weak, broken in body and heart. And beside me lay that tiny waxen form clad in the little dress that had been Chester's christening robe. Oh, when I made it with happy dreams and hopes for my first born I little thought it would one day be a shroud. And he was such a lovely baby—so plump and sweet and dimpled. His dear eyes, that would never lighten with intelligence, were large and blue as violets, and so bright. His dear little feet that would never toddle to me—his dear little hands that would never reach out to cling to mine. Oh, it *was* cruel! I can never forget the horror of the night that followed. They had taken my baby away and laid him in a little white casket in the parlor. I was alone. I could not sleep. I could not cry. I thought my heart would burst.

My convalescence was a dreary time. If my baby had lived I would have been so happy, contented to take the days as they came and grow strong gradually. But to lie weakly there, enduring all the discomforts of my condition and nothing—nothing—to recompense me for it. It seemed as if the days crept by on leaden feet. Mrs. Aubin was a good nurse, skilful, tender, sympathetic. I was thankful I did not have Miss Fergusson who, with all her skill, was hard. But nothing could heal my deadly hurt. I fought my sorrow during the day but night betrayed me. I always broke down when twilight came and cried through the terrible hours until exhaustion brought sleep.

Oh, it is not fair—it is not fair! Children are born and live when they are not wanted—where they will be neglected—where they will have no chance. I would have loved my baby so, and cared for him so tenderly and tried to give him every chance for good. Yet I was not allowed to have him.

And while I was lying helpless bad war news began to come, too—news of the British defeat at Mons and the resulting long dreary retreat of the Allies which is still going on before the victorious rush of Germany's ready millions.[230] Everything seems dark and hopeless.

---

230   Belgian city taken by the Germans after defeating the British Army on August 23–24, 1914. Mons remained in German hands until liberated by Canadian forces at the very end of the war.

Chester

I was so thankful when I was able to sit up. Yet I dreaded with a sick dread going back to the routine of everyday life. I could not have faced it but for Chester. Oh, what a comfort that little creature has been to me!

I came downstairs today. And this evening Mrs. Aubin left unexpectedly. Dr. Shier wanted her for a typhoid case in Uxbridge. I miss her so much. The loneliness is terrible.

Birth

MACDONALD—At the Manse, Leaskdale, Ont., on Thursday, August 13, to Rev. and Mrs. E. Macdonald, a son, still-born.

[Newspaper announcement: still-birth, Hugh Macdonald]

Monday, Aug. 31, 1914
The Manse, Leaskdale

I tried to take up life again to-day and began work on my new book. It was very hard to go back to it but work and duty must be done. Perhaps they will help me to forget. To-day I put away the little muslin-lined basket and the little garments I had ready for my darling. His tiny limbs never rested in the nest I had prepared for them. They found a narrower, colder bed. "Little Hugh." That is what we call him to each other. If he had lived we would have called him Hugh after my father. He shall have his name at least. We can give him nothing else.

I wrote in this journal before his birth that I would be much disappointed if my baby were not a girl. It seems to me now that it was wicked to write or think such a thing. But I was *not* disappointed. In that brief moment when I knew my child was a boy and did not know that it was dead, I felt no disappointment—only gladness that I had another son. There must be something—some deep instinct in us women that makes us rejoice when we have brought a man child into the world, no matter what we have hoped for. Oh, what a proud, happy mother I would have been with my two boys! Too proud—too happy. The gods were jealous!

And Chester would have had a little brother. I suppose he never will have one now. If I were a younger woman I might not feel so terribly over it all. But I hardly dare hope for another child. And if God were pitiful and gave me again the chance of being a mother I tremble to think of the months of dread I would have to undergo for fear that the same hideous thing would happen again. Almost I would rather not run the risk. And yet—I *must* hope.

Thursday, Sept. 3, 1914
Leaskdale, Ont.

Today Ewan got a telegram announcing the serious illness of his father. He left for the Island at once. I am not at all strong yet and the excitement and worry of helping him to get away at an hour's notice has rather upset me. I feel very lonely and nervous tonight—as if he would never come back to me. This is foolishness. But physical weakness makes cowards of us all. Oh, if my darling baby had only lived! When I am alone now at night I am haunted by the thought of him, lying lonely in his little grave down the Seventh. My little, little son, how my heart yearns for you! You had no chance—not even a fighting chance for your little life. Oh, it was cruel—cruel!

Friday, Sept. 4, 1914

Another of those horrible "letters of condolence" came to-day. I have received so many. Two or three, written by friends who understand me and who think as I do in regard to the great mysteries, were helpful—or at least soothing. But the rest only opened the wound afresh and jarred every sensibility I possess. The writers meant kindly. But they hurt me as keenly as an enemy could have done—their blundering attempts to console, their trite, threadbare assurances only wounded me. Platitudes can never cover the nakedness of bereavement. One of the most common and most painful was, "the baby is better off." I do not believe it! Why should it be born at all—why should anyone be born?—if it is better off dead? I do *not* believe that it is better for a child to die at birth than to live its life out, and love and be loved, and enjoy and suffer, and do good work, and shape a character that would give it a personality in Eternity. And I do not believe that it was "God's will" either. Why blame every sorrow on God's will? I believe it is God's will that every human being born into the world should live and do its work; and if it does not it is not God's will but a crossing of His purpose by the mysterious Power of Evil that is manifest in the universe. I do *not* believe that we are called upon to be resigned to *that*. I believe we have a right to grieve when It accomplishes Its malignant purposes. And it is no comfort to me to be told that I shall meet my little son "some day." I cannot wholly believe that; and if I could it would still be little comfort. For it would not be my little blue-eyed baby but a personality that had developed and grown apart from me and so would be to me a stranger. Oh,

> "Not all the preaching since Adam
> Hath made death other than death."[231]

—nor ever will!

Saturday, Sept. 5, 1914
The Manse, Leaskdale, Ont.

The war news has continued steadily depressing. Every day brings the news of the steady advance of the Germans towards Paris. They are little more than thirty miles away now. They are steadily pressing back the British and French armies. It seems as if they were sweeping irresistibly to their goal. Oh, will they reach it? Will not some mighty arm even yet interpose? Will not God's finger touch them and say, "Here— but no further?" If Paris falls France will be crushed. She will have no heart to struggle further.

Tuesday, Sept. 8, 1914
The Manse, Leaskdale, Ont.

Oh, God's finger *has* touched them! The German Army, almost at the gates of Paris, has been foiled—driven back—forced to retreat!

This morning was a delightful one. Lily and I drove to Uxbridge. It was the first time I had been out for a drive since my illness and I enjoyed it as a child might. It was delightful to be a part of the sunshine and fresh air once more. And yet at one part of the drive my heart was wrung with agony. And through it all there was an underache of ceaseless worry—the thought "What will the war news be when we get to Uxbridge? Will it be that the Germans have hacked through to Paris?"

Down the Seventh, about half way from here to Uxbridge is a little

---

231   From "After the Burial," by American poet James Russell Lowell (1819–1891).

country graveyard, rather grassy and overgrown, with elms around its borders. It is called "Zion." Long ago there was a Methodist church near it but it is no longer there. Many of our Presbyterian families bury there, as there is no Presbyterian graveyard close at hand.

I have driven past this little graveyard many times, carelessly and indifferently. It never occurred to me that it was to become the saddest and most sacred spot on earth to me. But our wee darling lies there in a little green corner under the elms.

How my heart ached as we drove past it today! It seemed so cruel and bitter to go by without stopping. It seemed to me that Little Hugh was calling to me from his grave—"Mother, won't you come to me?" It was anguish not to respond. But I could not make my first pilgrimage to that little grave with anyone but Ewan. So I went on, my eyes burning with tears.

When we reached town I went to see Mrs. Aubin. She had just opened the morning's papers. And there was the headline—"General French Inflicts Great Defeat on the Enemy."[232] Oh, the relief was almost painful, coming after all these weeks of strain and growing dismay. I hardly dared believe it. But it is true. The Germans have been

["Zion" Cemetery]

232   Field Marshal John Denton Pinkstone French (1852–1925), Earl of Ypres from 1922, served as Commander-in-Chief of the British Expeditionary Force until December 1915.

hurled back from the Marne.[233] God be thanked! Oh, we all come back to God in these times of soul-sifting—humbly, starkly, unconditionally. Perhaps this is why this awful war has come. The world was forgetting God. It had to be reminded of Him.

Thursday, Sept. 10, 1914
Leaskdale, Ont.

The war news continues good. Every day since Monday I have opened the paper with fear and trembling; but each day brought the blessed news that the Germans were still retreating. There is but little fear of Paris ever being captured now.

But I have been so lonely to-night—so heart-broken. I wish Ewan were back. He seems so far away. I seem alone among aliens save for darling Chester. Last night I had the sweetest experience—one of those brief, fleeting joys that transform life and illuminate the meaning of motherhood.

It was a cold night with a touch of frost. When I went to bed I thought of taking Chester in with me but decided not to, as he seemed so warm and cosy in his own little crib. But in the night I wakened. Chester was whimpering softly and pitifully in the darkness. I rose and bent over him. The poor mite had thrown off his blankets and was curled up on his bed, a little round, cold, forlorn ball. I lifted him quickly into my own warm nest and snuggled down beside him. I thought he had dropped asleep but suddenly I felt the little head move near me in the darkness and the next moment his little lips were pressing the softest, sweetest little kiss on the back of my hand which I had up to my cheek. That little kiss thrilled my soul with its sweetness. I shall feel it on my hand forever.

Saturday, Sept. 13, 1914
The Manse, Leaskdale, Ont.

Ewan came back tonight. How glad I was!

The war news still continues encouraging. The Germans are still retreating. But oh, there have been such hideous stories in the papers

---

233   An eastern tributary of the Seine 514 km/319 miles in length, the Marne rises in the Langres Plateau and joins the Seine at Charenton, in the southeastern suburbs of Paris. It was at the Marne that British and French forces rallied in retreat, launched a counterattack, and threw the Germany army back, saving Paris from occupation.

lately of their cutting off the hands of little children in Belgium.[234] Can they be true? They have committed terrible outrages and crimes, that is too surely true, but I hope desperately that these stories of the mutilation of children are false. They harrow my soul. I walk the floor in my agony over them. I cry myself to sleep about them and wake again in the darkness to cringe with the horror of it. If it were Chester! Oh God, why do you permit such things?

Monday, Sept. 21, 1914
Leaskdale, Ont.

Last Friday Mrs. Alex Leask and I drove to Whitby to visit friends of hers and stayed until Sunday evening. It was a long and tiring drive for me, as I am not strong yet. But we met some nice people and I enjoyed it very much. Today Ewan and I went to Uxbridge and we went together to our darling boy's grave. I cannot write about it.

Saturday, Sept. 26, 1914

This has been a hard week. Three days of it Mrs. Alex Leask and I spent canvassing the Seventh on behalf of the Patriotic and Red Cross funds. As a rule I loathe asking people for money. But I did not mind it this time, for everybody seemed willing to give and did not convey the impression that they thought we were begging for ourselves. But physically it was very fatiguing to me and I feel rather played out today.

Another great battle is on along the Aisne, where the Germans have rallied and made a stand.[235] This means several days of agonizing suspense. Also this week came the news of the sinking of three British cruisers in the North Sea.[236]

---

234 German soldiers committed a series of war crimes in Belgium in the war's opening weeks and months. As many as 6,000 Belgian civilians were killed before the end of 1914. In the 1920s it was widely thought the atrocities were exaggerated by the British, but the current view among historians is that the so-called "Rape of Belgium" did in fact occur.

235 Following the battles along the Marne river in north-eastern France, the German advance into France was halted. Allied troops began a counter-advance along the Aisne river, with both sides hoping to reach the North Sea (this period of conflict was known as "the race to the sea"). Given the difficulty of the terrain, however, both sides became literally entrenched in their positions, a situation that continued for the next four years.

236 The German-designed U-9 submarine was a new and fearsome weapon. On September 22, 1914 three British armoured cruisers were sunk by a U-9 submarine in the southern North Sea. While the cruisers themselves were obsolescent, assigned to prevent German surface vessels from access to the eastern English channel, 1,459 British sailors died in the attack.

Tuesday, Oct. 13, 1914
Leaskdale, Ont.

Yesterday came news of the fall of Antwerp.[237] For a week it has been expected though we hoped against hope. The news seemed as bad as if it were entirely unexpected. I was all alone. Lily was away on her vacation and Ewan went to Toronto yesterday. When I went down for the mail I dared not open the paper until I got back home. Then I saw the head-line, "Antwerp has fallen."

I went all to pieces. I could eat no dinner. I walked the floor in nervous agony. When night came I could not sleep until nearly morning. The word "Antwerp" reiterated itself over and over in my brain until I thought it would drive me mad.

Friday, Oct. 30, 1914

Turkey has plunged into the war on the side of Germany.[238] Ultimately this can only mean that she has committed suicide. But it will prolong the war and harass the Allies—and so means more and longer strain and anxiety for us all. England is now reaping the fruit of her mistaken policy in always posing before Europe as Turkey's defender. She would not intervene to prevent the hideous Armenian massacres and now she must pay for that with the lives of her best.[239] Truly, the mills of the gods do grind small though slowly. National as well as individual sins are punished in the long run.

---

237   A major Belgian commercial centre and port, Antwerp was occupied by the Germans until 1918.

238   The Ottoman Empire (Turkey) refused diplomatic entreaties from the Entente (France, Britain, and Russia) and thus entered the war on the side of the Central Powers in the autumn of 1914.

239   The Ottoman Empire had carried out several massacres of its Armenian minorities in recent memory. During the reign of Abdul Hamid (Abdulhamit) II, a three-year bout of political violence now known as the Hamidian massacres took place across eastern Turkey, arising from Armenian protests at government brutality. The immediate spark of violence was the sacking of several hamlets in southern Armenia, the result of Armenian resistance to Kurdish encroachment. Armenian protests followed. (There were some European interventions to quell further disturbances, consisting of attempts to persuade the Ottoman government to adopt reforms for the Armenian-populated provinces.) Government reprisals ensued, involving a pattern of violence suggesting of a premeditated plan. A series of massacres spread south through nearly every major Armenian-inhabited town of the Ottoman empire. In August 1896, Armenian revolutionaries attempted to draw international attention to the situation, seizing the European-owned Ottoman Bank in Constantinople (now Istanbul). The government responded with reprisals during which 5,000 to 6,000 Armenians were killed in a short period, within sight of the European embassies. Estimates of the total death toll between 1894 and 1896 range from 100,000 to 300,000. Further violence was sparked in April 1909 in the province of Adana, with an estimated 30,000 Armenians reported killed, and (as with the Hamidian massacres) Armenian property destroyed or looted.

Wednesday, Nov. 4, 1914
The Manse, Leaskdale, Ont.

Bad news of German naval victory off Chile![240] It was only an encounter between a couple of small squadrons and can have no real effect on the war. But it is mortifying and a blow to British prestige. I feel depressed and *useless* tonight.

Tuesday, Nov. 10, 1914

'Tis a dark dreary night and snow is falling for the first. On such an evening I think always of the old home in Cavendish—that old deserted house I love so much. I have been haunting it in spirit all the evening. I could see it, gray and dark, through the falling whiteness. I wandered through its empty, cheerless rooms where the flakes spot-

The old home

ted against the bare windows. Its desolation and loneliness pierced my soul. I wish it were torn down. It would not hurt me then to think of it, for then it would exist only in the land of dreams and there is no

240   On November 1, 1914 German forces defeated a Royal Navy squadon off the coast of central Chile; two British armoured cruisers were destroyed. The defeat led to more British ships despatched to British bases in the region.

loneliness there. Old home, once warm and bright, now the November twilights are never starred by your out-glowing light.

Thursday, Nov. 12, 1914

Bad war news again! The Germans have crossed the Yser and captured Dixmude! I have been of no use since the *Globe* came. They are now only fifteen miles from Dunkirk. If they should win it and Calais! God forbid!

The Manse, Leaskdale, Ont.
Nov. 19, 1914

A week of anxiety! But better news has come. The Germans could not advance beyond Dixmude and now they have been driven back across the Yser.[241] The drive on Calais has failed! But oh, this constant strain is horrible!

Friday, Nov. 20, 1914

I finished "Anne of Redmond" to-day.[242] And I am very glad. Never did I write a book under greater stress. All last winter and spring I was physically wretched and all this fall I have been racked with worry over the war and tortured with grief over the loss of my baby. From a literary point of view I don't think much of it. Yet there is some fairly good material in it. But I cannot write of sentimental college girls. Anyhow, it is done, praise the nine gods!

Monday, Nov. 30, 1914
Leaskdale, Ont.

My fortieth birthday! Once I thought forty must be the end of everything. But it isn't! I don't *feel* any older today than yesterday—when I was only 39! Or the day before yesterday when I was—19! Thank God

---

241   "The Battle of the Yser" took place in October 1914 and marked the end of open warfare. The German army had been advancing into Belgium, but was finally halted before reaching the North Sea. Belgian troops held the line near the town of Diksmuide ("Dixmude") and after sluices were opened on the Yser River in back of the German lines, the German army pulled back. The armies settled into the flooded "Flanders mud" of the Belgian countryside for a winter of trench warfare. Casualties on both sides were heavy, and Germany controlled most of Belgian territory for the duration of the war.

242   Published in 1915 by L.C. Page as *Anne of the Island*, the novel drew upon LMM's own time studying English literature at Dalhousie University in Halifax in 1895–96 in portraying Anne Shirley's experiences at the fictional Redmond College in Kingsport, Nova Scotia (itself modelled on Halifax).

we don't *feel* old. Life is much richer, fuller, happier, *more comfortable for me* now than it was when I was twenty. I have won the success I resolved to win twenty years ago. It is worth the struggle—but I would not wish to be twenty again with the struggle still before me. No, I am quite content to be forty—though it does sound so impossible. And I suppose the next twenty years will fly even more swiftly. Then I shall, if living, be sixty. That sounds grandmotherly.

To-night brought me a bitter pang, though not on account of the vanished years. On our way home from Uxbridge Ewan and I stopped at Zion to see the tiny tablet we have had put down to mark the spot where "Little Hugh" sleeps. Oh, as I stood by that wee grave in the dim, dull November twilight, with the cheerless autumn landscape all around my heart ached agonizingly. Why, oh why must it be? My bonnie, blue-eyed darling. He would just have been beginning to be so bright and interesting.

Monday, Dec.7, 1914
Leaskdale, Ont.

A *Globe* headline to-day was "The Germans Capture Lodz."[243]

This war is at least extending my knowledge of geography. Six months ago I did not know there was such a place in the world as Lodz.[244] Had I heard it mentioned I would have known nothing about it and cared as little. To-day, the news that the Germans have captured it in their second drive for Warsaw made my heart sink into my boots. I know all about it now—its size, its standing, its military significance. And so of scores of other places whose names have been lettered on my memory in blood since that fateful 4th of August—Mlawa, Bzura, Jarolsav, Tomaskoff, Yser, Lys, Aisne, Marne, Prysmysl.[245] At the last mentioned the newspaper wits have been poking fun since the siege of it began. Nobody seems to know how it is pronounced. I daresay the Austrians would think that Saskatchewan and Musquodoboit were about as bad.[246]

---

243   After extended fighting between German and Russian forces in central Poland that resulted in high casualties on both sides, the German army surprised Russian positions on the Vistula with an attack in November 1915. 12,000 Russians were taken prisoner. Łódź fell on December 6; the Russian army was forced to retreat and form a stronger defense of Warsaw.

244   Łódź is a major industrial centre in the central region of Poland, which was a part of the Russian Empire until the First World War. Łódź was occupied by the Germans until 1918 when it became part of a newly independent Poland.

245   Names in Poland, France, and Belgium.

246   Saskatchewan is a province in Canada and Musquodoboit is in Nova Scotia.

The Manse, Leaskdale, Ont.
Thursday, Dec. 10, 1914

To-day at noon Ewan came in jubilantly. "Good news!," he said. I snatched the paper and read that a German squadron had been totally destroyed by a British one off the Falkland Isles.[247] Coming after the long strain of the recent series of Russian reverses I rather went off my head. I waved the paper wildly in air as I danced around the dining room table and hurrahed. Yet hundreds of men were killed in the fight and hundreds of women's hearts will break because of it. Is that a cause for dancing and hurrahing? Oh, war makes us all very crude and selfish and primitive!

Saturday, Dec. 12, 1914

To-day's war news was better than it has been for some time—the second German invasion of Poland seems to have been definitely checked. Ever since it began—a fortnight or so ago—I have been racked with dread. If Germany should smash Russia and then hurl her victorious army back against the French and British lines! That thought was the Dweller on my Threshold. All through the forenoons I could manage to work and hold my dread at bay. But when at twelve I saw Ewan going out for the mail my nerve invariably collapsed. I could not do anything—it was of no use to try. I could not even read. I could only pace the floor like a caged tiger, nerving myself to meet the worst. Then when he came back I would snatch the *Globe* and desperately tear over the headlines. It has been agonizing.

Saturday, Dec. 19, 1914
The Manse, Leaskdale

To-day I began re-reading Mrs. Hemans' poems.[248] I read them all through once before. In my childhood those sweet and tender lyrics of

---

247   Two days earlier, on December 8, a British naval squadron that included the two battle cruisers HMS *Invincible* and *Inflexible* had located and destroyed most of a German squadron of five ships, including two armoured cruisers. The battle took place in the South Atlantic, after the German squadron had attempted to raid a British supply base at Stanley, capital of the Falkland Islands.

248   English poet Felicia Dorothea Hemans (1793–1835) had been a favourite of LMM's for years. Considered a poet of good morality, her work was often included in children's schoolbook collections.

hers, many of which were in the old Royal Readers, were a source of great pleasure to me. I admit that I love them yet, partly for their own sake, partly because of the old associations connected with them. I think Mrs. Hemans has been hardly dealt with by our hurrying, feverish, get-rich-quick age. Surely sweetness and charm of sentiment have their place in literature as well as strength and grandeur. A violet is a dear thing though it is not a star and a ferny dell is delightful though it is not "a heaven-kissing hill." In one mood Mrs. Hemans gives me quite as much pleasure as Kipling does in another.

Friday, January 1, 1915
The Manse, Leaskdale, Ont.

When has a New Year dawned, freighted with such awful possibilities? Never did I ask with as great a dread of the answer, "What will the New Year bring"? Nineteen-fourteen has gone. Its sun which rose fairly has set in blood. It brought to me the greatest anguish of my life. Never shall I recall 1914 without a shiver of pain.

I am very lonely tonight. Frede left to-day on her return to Macdonald. She came on December 22nd. I had been counting the days till she should come—looking forward to her visit for months. And now it is over. But we *did* make the most of it. I have emptied and rinsed my soul and taken fresh courage.

In especial it was a great thing to have someone to talk over the war news with as it came each day. Hitherto I have had no one. Ewan refuses to talk about it. He claims that it unsettles him and he cannot do his work properly. No doubt this is so; but it is rather hard on me, for I have no one else with whom to discuss it. There is absolutely *no* one around here who seems to *realize* the war. I believe it is well they do not. If all felt as I do over it the work of the country would certainly suffer. But I feel as if I were stranded on a coast where nobody talked my language. While Frede was here I had the relief of thrashing everything out with her. We flayed the Kaiser[249] every day and told Kitchener[250] what he ought to do. Not but that we both have absolute confidence in K. of K.[251]—which is doubtless a great consolation to him! It seems to me that he has been predestined to the present crisis in the Councils of Eternity. My greatest faith in the ultimate success of the Allies consists in the fact that Kitchener is at the helm. I feel sure that Fate would never have wasted him on the losing side.

We had a quiet "homey" Xmas. Lily went home so we had no aliens. We had a good dinner and a satisfying afternoon of talk—*real* talk which is the best amusement in the world.

---

249   Wilhelm II (1859–1941) was the last German Emperor ("Kaiser"). He was a bellicose leader who supported Austria-Hungary and steered German foreign affairs toward the events leading to World War I. He was a poor war leader, and ultimately abdicated his position in November 1918, fleeing to exile.

250   Field Marshal Horatio Herbert Kitchener (1850–1916) was a senior British Army officer. At the outbreak of the war, Kitchener became Secretary of State for War. He was one of the few politicians to foresee a long war.

251   Kitchener had enoyed many military successes in east Africa, particularly Egypt and Sudan, which was then under British administration. *Daily Mail* journalist G.W. Steevens described Kitchener's adventures in *With Kitchener to Khartoum* (1898), which made him a household name throughout the British Empire. Kitchener became Governor-General of the Sudan in September 1898.

The day after Xmas I had a letter from Kate saying that my youngest half-brother, Carl,[252] was going with the Second Contingent. Kate announced the fact as airily and indifferently as if she were saying that he was going to a concert. Is she really as heartless and devoid of all feeling as her letters indicate? Her mother's daughter[253] might very well be, 'tis true—but how could her father's child be? As for Carl, I have never even seen him, poor little chap. But as I read Kate's careless lines my eyes suddenly filled with tears. My father's son was going to do what he could for our Empire.

Carl

"He goes to do what *I* had done
Had Douglas' daughter been his son."[254]

I wrote him at once a letter in which I spoke from my heart. If there is anything of father in him it will appeal to him. If he is solely of the mother and is going into this war from a mere hankering for change and adventure—which God forbid—it will mean nothing to him.

I remember, long ago, when I was a little girl, the Metis Rebellion broke out in "the North-West" as it was then called.[255] Prince Albert was in the fighting zone and all communication between it and the outside world was cut for months. During all that time I had no word from father and it was not known if he were living or dead. I was too young to fully realize the situation but oh, how glad I was when at last a letter came from father. A courier had crept into P.A. contriving to elude the rebels and when he crept out again father

---

252   Hugh Carlyle Montgomery, LMM's half brother, had been born to her father and his second wife in 1893. The first Contingent, a convoy of ships carrying nearly 33,000 Canadian troops, had departed on October 3, 1914. The second contingent of over 20,000 men departed for Britain in early 1915.

253   LMM had not gotten along with her father's second wife, Mary Ann McRae, when she had visited the family in Prince Albert in 1890–91.

254   From Walter Scott's long poem, "The Lady of the Lake," IV.

255   Toward the end of the nineteenth century, there was growing anger in the north-west among native peoples and the Métis for reasons that included inadequate long-distance governance, poor communication regarding the terms of land treaties terms, white settlement of traditional indigenous lands, and decimated buffalo herds. In 1885, the Métis people under Louis Riel, along with First Nations Cree and Assiniboine peoples, rose up against the government of Canada for failing to protect their rights, their land, and their survival as a distinct people.

sent a letter with him. Father was present at the battle of Batoche as a volunteer, though not actually in the fighting line.[256] I have not thought of all this for years until tonight. And now father's son is going to a war compared to which the Riel Rebellion was as a match-flare to Vesuvius.

I thank God that Chester is not old enough to go—and as I thank Him I shrink back in shame, the words dying on my lips. For is it not the same thing as thanking Him that some other woman's son must go in my son's place? "Without shedding of blood there is no remission of sins."[257] Without shedding of blood there is no *anything*! Everything, it seems to me, must be bought by sacrifice. The race has marked every footstep of its painful ascent by blood. And now torrents of it must flow! Stella recently wrote me that somebody she had met had said to her, "This war is the greatest tragedy since the crucifixion." Will some great blessing, great enough for the price, be the meed of it? Is the agony in which the world is shuddering the birth pang of some wondrous new era? Or is it all merely a futile

"struggle of ants
In the gleam of a million million of suns?"[258]

We would think lightly of a calamity which would destroy an ant-hill and half its inhabitants. Does the Power that runs the Universe think *us* of more importance? We *must* believe that it does or we could not live.

"Nothing can ever be quite the same again for any of us." I read the other day in a London paper. Oh, horribly true! The old order has passed away forever. Life can never again be for us what it was before that fatal day in August.

Last Wednesday Frede and I drove down to Uxbridge and spent a very enjoyable day at Harvey Gould's.[259] On New Year's eve I gave a little dinner for Frede—had Fraser and the McKays, Rev. John Mustard and Mr. and Mrs. Hugh. We had a nice, nice time. I do enjoy entertaining a little like this. It is such a contrast with my past life for

256   May 9 to 12, 1885, saw the deciding Battle of Batoche, in which government soldiers (both regulars, who had arrived via the newly built railroad, and volunteers, like LMM's own father) defeated the forces led by Louis Riel at the then-capital of the Province of Saskatchewan, Batoche.

257   The reference is to Hebrews 9:22, which in the King James Version reads: "And almost all things are by the law purged with blood; and without shedding of blood is no remission."

258   The reference (slightly misquoted) is to the second couplet of Tennyson's poem "Vastness" (1885): "Raving politics, never at rest—as this poor earth's pale history runs,—/ What is it all but a trouble of ants in the gleam of a million million of suns?"

259   Harvey Gould was born in 1857 and died in 1943. The Goulds were an old Uxbridge family; in fact, the town had originally been named after them ("Gouldville"). They ran a general store.

never, before I was married, could I ask my friends to my home and have things nice for them. To be sure I do *not* care much for the teas to which I must invite the newly-weds of the parish or the prosy old elders and their dames. Those are painful duties which I perform as gracefully as may be. I *can't* talk eggs and butter with the female of the species—and that is almost all the most of them can talk, apart from gossip with which I dare not meddle. However, "a reasonable amount of fleas is good for a dog."

But Frede had to go this morning. I watched her drive away drearily. Under what circumstances shall we meet again?

The Manse, Leaskdale
Wednesday, Jan. 6, 1915

The war news to-day was good in its way—the Russians have won a big victory over the Turks. If England were not an ally of Russia in this war the news of this victory would but faintly interest me. Yet the death and agony and horror of it would have been just the same. Oh, we are very selfish. There was one horrible account of a regiment of 900 Turks who were found frozen to death. The sufferings of the men everywhere in the trenches this winter must be dreadful.[260] I never go out on these cold dark nights without thinking of them miserably. I am ashamed that I am warmly clad and housed. When I snuggle down in my comfortable bed I feel ashamed of being comfortable. It seems as if I should be miserable, too, when so many others are.

The Manse, Leaskdale, Ont.
Sunday, Jan. 17, 1915

This has been a lonely afternoon. Ewan, of course, was away, wasting a good logical hard-hitting discourse on the stolid unappreciative Zephyrites who would no doubt infinitely prefer a Billy Sunday rant on hellfire and brimstone. Lily took Chester home with her. These pilgrimages to "the farm" are a delight to his small soul. Poor baby-man, I am sorry that he can't be brought up on a farm and have the birthright of green old orchards and clover meadows and big, dusky, sweet-smelling barns to romp and frolic in. Well, we shall have to make it up to him in other ways. I am very anxious that Chester should have a happy, *nor-*

---

260   Trench warfare was a prevalent feature of the Western Front from the fall of 1914 to the last German offensive in 1918. As the front stabilized, each side built increasingly elaborate excavated trenches that faced one another across "no man's land."

mal childhood, with all the simple world-old pleasures that are the right of children. I do not want him to be spoiled by over-indulgence but I do want him to have a childhood which will fit him, mentally and physically for life and which will be

[Chester]

a delightful memory to him. He is learning to talk rapidly now—and puts sentences together, with such a funny, triumphant note in his voice when he arrives at the end of one. So far all is concrete—no appearance of abstract thought yet, no attempt at reasoning or reflection. He has an affectionate little heart and very dear little ways. When he creeps into my lap, pats my cheek so softly with his chubby hands, and says in the softest and sweetest of voices, "Dear mo'er—poor mo'er, I mo'er's dear *son*"—why, the delight that sweeps over

my soul is the last revelation of the sweetness of motherhood. When a woman hears her own son call her "mother" she thanks God that she *is* a woman.

Oh, do I love my wee mannie too much? Sometimes, especially since that hideous 13th of August I fear that I do—that I will be punished for it. "Thou shalt have no other gods before me." It seems an almost instinctive fear. I am near kin to the heathen who call their children evil names that the listening spirits may hear and, supposing them unloved, work them no evil and afflict them not with disease. But I could not pretend, even to a God, that I did not love Chester. When I look at him lying asleep, dimpled and flushed, my love for him is almost agony, so intense is it. And yet children as sweet and dear as he have been cruelly murdered or have died from neglect in Belgium. Oh, motherhood is awful—motherhood is awful! I re-read Tennyson's *Rizpah* lately.[261] How could a *man* have written it? All the agony and

---

261   Dramatic monologue, published in 1880, about the Biblical figure of "Rizpah," who buries the bones of her sons, killed in political conflict.

"See my daffodil"

tragedy of motherhood is in it. I said once that Tennyson never hurt me. That was before I was a mother. To read *Rizpah* now tortures me. After I had read it the other night I walked the floor and wept wildly. It was as if *I* was that mother who collected the bones of her baby and buried them by the churchyard wall. Her soul, her sorrow entered into me and possessed me and wrung me.

I have wandered far from my subject. I began by saying I was lonely because I was alone this afternoon. It was dull and gray in the outer world, too, and the shadow of the war was over me. I felt dreary—as if life were all "gray rocks and grayer sea."[262]

I wrote to Stella. Writing to Stella was once a pleasure. Now it has become a painful duty. I have not for two years received a letter from Stella which I did not shrink from opening. There is no disguising the fact that Stella has become a very serious problem to those of us who are unfortunate enough to be closely connected with her.

Stella spent most of the winter of 1912–1913 in the hospital at Ch'town where she underwent several "operations," spent a great deal of money and drove doctors and nurses frantic. She came home no better and in every letter poured out her old complaints of "untold agonies." I grew sick to death of the phrase. There is really, so all her doctors have told me, very little the matter with her. But unbridled indulgence in bad temper seems to have unsettled her mind and she is really insane with "hallucination of disease." A year ago she took it into her head to go to California and spend the winter with Clara. She has been there ever since and poor Clara is almost wild. She has had a dreadful time. Stella has been absolutely outrageous. Ever since she

---

262   Title of a poem (1917) by Charles G.D. Roberts (1860–1943).

went to Los Angeles she has poured out to me in her epistles unceasing floods of complaints. She had hardly arrived there before she wrote me that she hated it, would not stay, and would likely come to Leaskdale before the winter ended.

Well, I could not and would not have her here. So I never once, in any letter to her, mentioned her coming. I was impervious to her broadest hints. But I go in mortal terror that, finding I will not "rise" to them, she will simply come without an invitation. If she does I really do not know what I will do. Stella has got to such a stage that *no one* can live with her. She is violently discontented everywhere. I really fear she will go quite insane before long. Clara is afraid she will commit suicide but Stella's threats along that line do not worry me much. It is one of her Satanic devices for getting her own way. But she obsesses us all like a nightmare. It is piteous and terrible.

The Manse, Leaskdale, Ont.
Friday, March 19, 1915

Have been very busy of late and very miserable physically. I do not complain of this latter fact, however. Nay, in one sense I rejoice in it. It means that I may hope to have another wee baby yet and I am so thankful and glad—and so frightened that I will lose it again. That dread companions me night and day.

But, though I bear the ceaseless nausea that seems my daily portion thankfully, that does not prevent it from making my existence rather difficult. I have so much to do—so many things to attend to—and I have to force myself to do them all without betraying my wretchedness. I am just as sick as I was last winter and I suppose will continue to be for many weeks yet. Before I suspected my condition I had embarked on the enterprise of training several of the Guild members in a little play for a Social night. I have to go through with it now as I have no excuse I can offer for backing out but I have to set my teeth every practice night.

The war drags on. The Allies are now trying to force the Dardenelles.[263] I cannot believe that they will succeed. It would be a great thing if they should. On the west and east the ceaseless trench warfare goes on— on—on. What will the spring bring? I dread it as I never dreaded a spring before.

---

263   The Dardanelles (known to the ancient world as the Hellespont) is a narrow strait that connects the Sea of Marmora (or Marmara) with the Aegean and Mediterranean. The Sea of Marmora is linked to the Black Sea; by forcing the Dardanelles, the British hoped to open up a more direct supply route to their ally Russia, and also to threaten the Ottoman capital of Istanbul (formerly Constantinople).

Sunday, April 11, 1915
Leaskdale, Ont.

In my new book "Anne of The Island"—as Page insists on calling it, much against my will—I used an expression—"She tasted the poignant sweetness of life when some great dread has been removed from it." That expresses my condition at present. I am tasting most thankfully the sweetness of life from which has been lifted a hideous dread.

On Saturday afternoon, March 20th, I was lying on my bed when I heard the telephone ring. I was physically most wretched, having had an attack of grippe the day before and suffering in addition the nausea of pregnancy. I got up and went down to the 'phone. The Uxbridge central was calling saying that a telegram had come for me. This it was:—Kensington, P.E. Island. Boat stuck. Go at once to Frede in General Hospital, Montreal. Aunt Annie.

In half an hour I was on the road to Uxbridge, with my agonized fancy imagining all possible illnesses for Frede. I had not heard from her for some weeks. She had just been recovering from a very severe attack of jaundice when she had written. I knew she must be seriously ill or Aunt Annie would never have sent such an urgent message. I caught the seven o'clock train to Toronto and arrived there in time to get the 11 o'clock to Montreal. I spent a wretched, sleepless night, physical misery and mental agony overcoming me in turn. I reached Montreal at 8 in the morning and drove through a snowstorm to the hospital where I found Frede's nurse. She told me that Frede had typhoid, had had two hemorrhages, and that there was very little chance of her recovery![264]

She would not allow me to see Frede until the doctor came. Besides, she said, Frede was delirious and would not know me. I doubted the latter statement but said nothing. I got a room, shut myself in, and tried to face the thought of a world without Frede!

I could not do it. With clenched hands I strode up and down the room wrestling with my agony. *Frede dying*! Frede, my more than sister, the woman who was nearest and dearest to me in the world! My mind refused to accept the decree. It pushed it away and mocked at it with such intensity that I became calm and met the doctor at two o'clock with outward composure.

Dr. Gordon was most sympathetic and confidence-inspiring. But he shook his head over Frede's case. He told me I might go in and see her but not to be surprised if she did not know me. She had been in the hospital a week and had at first refused to let her friends be told of her

---

264   Typhoid fever is a bacterial infection of the gastro-intestinal tract.

illness. But on Friday night, when the first hemorrhage occurred, Dr. Gordon had decided that he must send word to her parents.

I went across the hall and entered Frede's room. When I had watched her drive out of the manse gate at New Year's I had had a dreary presentiment that our next meeting would not be a happy one, and I had wondered when and where it would be. The question was answered.

Frede was lying on the cot. I can never forget the sight of her. Her face and eyes were as yellow as gold with jaundice, her cheeks were glazed and purple with the fever flush, and her mouth was surrounded with fever sores. For a moment my stricken consciousness re-echoed the dictum of doctor and nurse, "she cannot recover."

Frede opened her eyes, "Maud!" she said, in a tone which she might have used had she seen an angel from heaven. Afterwards she said that my face was the only one she had been able to see clearly since she had come to the hospital—all the others were clouds and blurs; and that no heavenly visitant could have been as welcome. She would not now die alone among strangers. She knew I would stay by her.

That night as I knelt to pray desperately for Frede's recovery there suddenly came to my mind, clear and distinct as if a voice had uttered them, the words, "Strength and honor are her clothing and she shall rejoice in days to come." From that moment I believed that Frede would live.

And she did. As Dr. Gordon said to me later on, "It is a strange thing, Mrs. Macdonald, but from the moment you came to this hospital Miss Campbell began to improve."

Well, perhaps that was only a coincidence. Or perhaps my coming did give Frede just the little impulse and stimulation she needed to start her on the road to recovery. At all events, she came up again from the valley of the Shadow.

But it was very slowly. Very slowly the fever ebbed. Again and again it came up and our hopes fell as it rose. I learned to watch in gnawing suspense when the nurse brought the basin of water to bathe Frede. If I heard the clink of ice rattling in it—I shall hate that sound forever—I knew that the fever had gone up again. If I heard it not—I knew that Frede was at least no worse. Finally the jaundice cleared away and the purple flush passed and Frede, worn and pallid, looked once more like herself. The day came when the doctor said, "If no set-back occurs she will recover".

For myself, I was also very miserable, if my anxiety about Frede had permitted me to think about myself. I had nausea night and day—I was always tired and drowsy—*and* I was in a chronic state of starvation.

The hospital rations, which may have been ample enough for invalids, seemed a mere bird's bite to me with the voracious appetite I always have in this condition. Frede, too, was beginning to be very hungry and of course could have nothing but liquid food. She and I whiled away many tedious hours planning out all the good old "down-east" dishes we would have as soon as she was strong enough to come to Leaskdale. The nurse must have thought us dreadful gourmands.

Frede's Macdonald friends kept her room a bower of flowers and came to inquire about her in shoals. At the end of a fortnight the doctor pronounced her out of ordinary danger and I decided that I must return to my forsaken family. Last Sunday night I left Montreal and got home the next evening a very weary but very thankful woman. Once more life is lovely to my eyes. My friend is spared to me.

To-night we all laughed over Chester's prayer. Last night for the first time I taught him a prayer ending up with the old petition, "make me a good boy." Tonight he insisted on saying it himself and ended up triumphantly, "Dear God, make me a good boy *in the hall closet.*"

The hall closet is where he is sometimes imprisoned when he is naughty until he promises to be good. I suppose he thinks God will adopt the same method of reforming him!

Monday, April 26, 1915
The Manse, Leaskdale, Ont.

I said I dreaded the spring for what the war news might be. My dread has been justified. Terrible news came on Saturday of the awful battle of Langemarck, the fearful slaughter among our—Canadian soldiers— who saved the situation at an awful cost—and the advance of the Germans by the aid of asphyxiating gases.[265] Today the despatches claim that their thrust has been checked but the situation is still terribly critical.

Thursday, May 6, 1915

Truly "the woman pays." Well, if all goes right at the east I shall not grudge the payment. But certainly I have found the last fortnight a

---

265   Langemarck is a village in Belgium roughly four miles north-east of Ypres. Around 2,000 Canadians died in this attack on April 22, 1915, the first time the Germans used poison gas. Officially known as the Battle of Gravenstafel Ridge, the event is commemorated by "the Brooding Soldier" statue.

hard one. I have suffered absolute agony with two ulcerating teeth. For a week I had no relief night or day. Then the abscess broke and left me five pounds lighter.

Then the war news has been bad. The Germans have been checked in the west but in the eastern theatre they are driving the Russians back and the prospects there are very disquieting.[266]

Frede is to come to Toronto tomorrow and I am going in to meet her. I am thankful she is to be here for awhile. I need her companionship in my present state of chronic discomfort and weariness.

Sunday, May 30, 1915
The Manse, Leaskdale, Ont.

In one way May has been a pleasant month. It has not been the usual delightful May of Ontario—more like an Island May, coldish and grudging. But Frede has been here and we have had a month of delightful companionship.

I went to Toronto to meet Frede on the evening of May 7th—a date that must ever seem of hideous import to many heart-broken people. For it was the day the *Lusitania* was sunk by a German submarine and the whole world shrieked with horror and rage over the hellish deed—a deed that will brand the name of Germany with indelible infamy through generations yet unborn.[267]

When I got to Uxbridge station I saw the announcement in the evening papers. But at that time it was supposed that nearly all on board had been saved. It was not until the next morning that the terrible truth was known. I shall never forget the scene as I walked up Yonge Street the next morning. As usual it was crowded and every man and woman on it held a morning paper and blundered along reading it, indifferent to everything but the news it contained. For myself, when I read of those scores of murdered babies and pictured their dear little dead bodies floating about in that pitiless ice-cold water I felt a hideous nausea of life. I wanted to get out of a world where such a thing could happen and shake its accursed dust from my soul. Can there be a God?

---

266 Allied forces struggled in late 1914/early 1915 in the eastern theatre of World War I, particularly in the Straits of Dardanelles in western Turkey and the Carpathian Mountains in Romania, where Russian forces battled Austro-Hungarians. Russia did cross the Carpathians in February and March 1915, but the Germans sent relief to Austro-Hungarian forces, which halted the Allied advance.

267 The RMS *Lusitania* was a large British ocean liner, probably carrying munitions. Torpedoed by a German U-boat on May 7, 1915, the *Lusitania* sunk quickly; 1,198 passengers and crew were lost, with 761 survivors. The event turned many countries against Germany and contributed to the United States' entry into war.

For weeks the papers have been full of the details. Some of the things I have read have left an indelible brand on my heart. May Wilhelm of Germany go down to the deepest hell haunted by the cries of the babes he has murdered and the women whose hearts he has broken!

The war news of this month has been disquieting. On the Western front the German drive has failed but in the east they are driving the Russians back.[268] I don't like the situation there.

To-morrow we leave for the Island and Frede returns to Macdonald. Somehow I do not look forward to my trip with much pleasure. I feel a conviction—probably born of my physical discomfort—that I shall not enjoy myself. And I feel loathe to leave my home. It is so beautiful just now—the fresh luxuriance of the young leaves, the garden coming up so nicely, the splendor of blossom and grass. I want to stay here and enjoy it. But if I do not go down home this summer I don't know when I may get again and I must go early because later on it would be out of the question. I think it is because of my hunger for the sea that I am going. I *must* look on it again.

Monday, June 7, 1915
Kinross, P.E. Island.

We left Leaskdale the evening of May 31st and went to Toronto, spending the evening at the Walker House. We met and had a chat with Uncle Leander's son Eric.[269] I had not seen him for seventeen years. He was a little boy when I saw him last and now he is verging on baldness. He is very nice—always was the nicest of Uncle Leander's boys. He looks like his father and has his father's agreeable society manner. Looking at him I recalled with a pang of homesickness that long-ago day I saw him first, when Uncle L. and his family arrived to spend their vacation in that old farmhouse by the eastern sea. Eric was an adorable chubby youngster of about two then, with a round face, golden hair, and big brown eyes. Of that old group grandfather and grandmother and Uncle Leander and Aunt Annie have gone. And we who were children then are men and women now, with our own heartaches and

---

268   Germans had pushed forward into north-west Belgium with several surprise attacks in April and May 1915. They gained ground but were pushed back by British and French forces, who led other successful offensives in northern France. In the Eastern front, Russia was forced to retreat following pressure from the combined German and Austrian armies.

269   Leander George Macneill (1845–1913) was LMM's uncle and the eldest child of LMM's maternal grandparents. When living with her grandmother, LMM had criticized her uncle as "a very unpleasant guest" whose presence agitated her grandmother; see, for example, the journal entry for August 26, 1910.

struggles and cares. To-morrow our children will fill our places and our hands will be folded. Such a "scunner" of life has come over me since the outbreak of the war that such a consummation seems to me rather to be desired than dreaded. I am tired of this horrible rack of strained emotions. When every day brings a new horror or the dread of it the tortured consciousness grows very weary.

Corner of garden

We reached Montreal the next evening where we had to part from Frede. I looked back as we hastened to our train and saw her standing, a lonely figure in the crowded station. It made me feel very lonely, too. If Frede and I could only see each other oftener it seems to me that I would ask nothing else of life.

We reached the Island Wednesday evening and stayed all night in Charlottetown. Our journey down had a peculiar feature. When we left home Ontario was in full mid-spring—the maples on our lawn were in summer luxuriance, the grass lush, and the day of the daffodils over. But Ontario springs are a full three weeks earlier than Island springs at any time and this year, as Ontario had an early spring and P.E. Island an abnormally late one the difference was fully six weeks.

The maples on the lawn

As we got further and further east spring seemed to recede from us. The leaves grew sparser until they ceased. When we arrived on the Island last Wednesday the trees were as bare as in mid winter, there was not a hint of green anywhere and only one or two brave dandelions were peering out. I never recall so late a spring here. Always by the first of June at the latest the leaves were out. Was it this that gave me such a sense of being an alien? Or was it simply the effect of change and absence?

On Thursday we came to Aunt Christie's at Kinross. Friday the *Guardian* contained the bad news that the Germans and Austrians had retaken Prysmysl from the Russians.[270] It made me terribly nervous and depressed. Of course, in my present condition worries possess me abnormally and I cannot fight against them.

Saturday night we were at Annie's for tea. It was a cold gray night and as we walked back to Christie's in the darkness Ewan and I owned to each other that we were homesick for Leaskdale. *There* was our home—our interests now. Here, in this old Island, we had become as pilgrims and sojourners. It hurt me to acknowledge this—it seemed utterly disloyal to the land I have loved so well—that I still love so well. I think I might not have felt so if we had found the Island in the June loveliness it should have had by now. As it is, I have a sense of desolation and banishment.

Cavendish, P.E.I.
Wed. June 9, 1915

Chester and I are at Ernest Webb's. We left Kinross yesterday morning. I had dinner with Fannie Wise Mutch[271] in town and got to Hunter River in the evening. Ernest met us and we had a pleasant drive down, as the weather had suddenly turned warmer. But there was one heart-breaking feature about our drive. When we came over the crest of "Laird's Hill" I gazed about me in dismay. For years that hill road has been

Ernest Webb's

so beautiful, with the thick velvet growth of young firs standing up on either side like a green wall. Some vandal road m a s t e r — m a y jackals sit on his grandmother's g r a v e ! — h a s caused all those beautiful trees to

---

270   The Przemyśl fortress was located in what had been an Austro-Hungarian controlled section of Poland prior to the war. It was captured by the Russians in March 1915 but the Central Powers retook it in June of that year.

271   Fannie was an old friend from Cavendish.

be cut down leaving a most unsightly hillside of stumps and brush. Gods, how blind some people are! The sacrilege hurt me as if I had seen some beloved temple profaned. It *was* a temple of my soul—that once beautiful hill. There have been hours when I communed with the soul of the Universe there and rapt up into the seventh heaven, tasted joy unspeakable. I recall sunset musings and starlit rambles on that hill when almost, so it seemed to me, I heard an echo of that "random word" of the gods we all listen and yearn for. And now it was desecrated—made into a very abomination of desolation. The man who cuts down a tree, except when it is absolutely necessary that it should be cut down, should be hanged as high as Haman on a gallows made from the wood of it!

I did not hurry to Lover's Lane the first thing today. No, I stayed in the house and shivered over the stove. It was bitterly cold and a heavy north-east rain beat down all day. In the afternoon the Stirlings came over and it was good to see them again. Margaret looks a little thin and pale. Doris has grown to be a very pretty child.

Friday, June 11, 1915
Cavendish, P.E.I.

These two days have been fine but very cold. Yesterday I went thro' the dear old lane and again today. But alas, I did not really enjoy it. The lane is not beautiful yet—the trees are only budding out and the ground is so wet and muddy that walking over it was not pleasant. But the main reason I found so little pleasure in it is that it is becoming difficult and even painful for me to walk any distance. I get tired out in a few steps and from then am keenly conscious of little beyond physical discomfort

Lover's Lane

and a determination not to show it or complain about it.

And then I can't get any war news. There is absolutely nothing in the *Patriot*, and the *Guardian* is not much better. Things seem to be going badly with the Russians. I miss tremendously the daily *Globe* with all the fresh morning news and its splendid "War Summary."

Friday, June 18, 1915

On the whole this has not been an enjoyable week. It has been in-cessantly rainy and very cold the greater part of the time. I could not get out and time hung very heavy on my hands. I think longingly of my own home with its peace and quiet, its rus-tling maple trees, its books and flowers.

Trees and flowers

Last Sunday I was in church and saw several old friends but the congregation was small, the day dull and cold, and there seemed a certain deadness and dullness about it all that I do not associate with the past. Cavendish is not what it used to be in the matter of its people. As a class they are going backward. I fear I could not live here now and be content. Yet perhaps this feeling is largely the result of my own ever-present sense of discomfort and if I were perfectly well I might find all here that I used to find. The old fields and hills and blue shore are still unchanged—and while they are here I can never be wholly alien in Cavendish.

I have had several walks in Lover's Lane and the "Deep Hollow" and the gods of the wild wood welcomed back their own. But the persistent rain and mud spoil all such rambles.

On Thursday Mrs. William Simpson was buried and I went over to the graveyard when the funeral came there. She was one of the Caven-dish people until a few years ago and her sons and daughters were my schoolmates. Ella, a girl I always liked, had brought her mother home and I was glad to meet her again.

Mrs. Simpson died of internal cancer. I asked Ella how long she had been ill and Ella said that it was a certain week in March that she had just felt badly and had gone to a doctor about it. He had told Ella and Lottie that the trouble was cancer in a quite advanced stage and that there was no hope. It was the first time they had even suspected that their mother's symptoms betokened serious trouble.

I mention this because of a strange fact—too strange and marked to be a mere co-incidence. One night of that very week in March—I could not recall the exact night but I distinctly remembered the week, because it was sandwiched in between two visits to Toronto—I had a very vivid dream. I dreamed that I was in Eaton's store in Toronto, watching the throngs of people go by.[272] Suddenly, I saw Lottie and Ella Simpson passing, I hurried up and accosted them. They responded civilly but

Lover's Lane

walked on and seemed anxious to escape me, but I stuck to them, walking along by them and trying to engage them in conversation. They seemed troubled and disturbed and presently one of them said to the other, "We must tell her about mother or she will not leave us alone." At that I woke. The dream was so vivid that it haunted me and when I wrote Myrtle soon after I asked her if she had heard anything recently about the Wm. Simpson family. She wrote back and said that she had had a letter from Lottie a few weeks before and they were all well. I concluded my dream had meant nothing and did not think about it again. But when Ella told me that they had discovered the cause of their mother's illness that week in March I was struck by the co-inci-dence. I do not believe it was a co-incidence. I have had too many sig-nificant dreams to believe that. Somehow I received a telepathic mes-sage that night, sent out by the Simpson girls in their distress. Why *I* should receive it I don't know, since we were not anything in particular to each other. But come it did; and I feel sure that the night I dreamed it was the very night after their discovery.

After the funeral I went to the manse to tea, and Ewan was there, having just arrived from Park Corner. In the evening he drove me to Mr. Webb's and we said goodbye. He leaves for home tomorrow and the thought made me very blue and homesick. Somehow I wanted to go

---

272   The T. Eaton Company was Canada's dominant retailer in the early twentieth century. Its largest Toronto store was located on the west side of Yonge Street north of Queen Street.

back with him. I went to bed tired and lonely, when the rain was beating down outside. I couldn't keep the tears back. Dear little Chester was such a comfort. He got his chubby arms about my neck and kept saying, "Don't ky, poor nice 'ittle mother."

Today was a delightful change in that it was fine and warm. Suddenly the dear Island became beautiful again, with green fields and blue seas. Myrtle and I drove up to Walter Simpson's and had tea. When we came home in the evening Ernest took Belle Webb and me for a row down the pond. It was beautiful and dream-like. We landed on the sandhills and walked up to their tops. Below us lay the old sandshore and the wavelets were splashing on it, murmuring the old music I loved in childhood. That was one of the few moments the memory of which makes my summer sojourn seem worth while after all.

Sunday, June 27, 1915
The Manse, Cavendish, P.E.I.

I came here last Saturday night and leave tomorrow for Alec's.[273] I cannot say that it has been very enjoyable. A perverse fate seems to dog my travels this summer. It has rained torrents and been bitterly cold almost every day. I haven't felt well and Margaret and John have been so much occupied with certain sad occurrences in the congregation that they had hardly any time for social intercourse. It was too cold to stay in any part of the house but the kitchen. I spent most of the days lying on the kitchen lounge while my back and head ached continually, amid the noise of the children, longing for my own home and household gods.

The war news has been disheartening too. The Russians are being driven steadily back. I rage at the scanty details in the *Guardian* but if the news were good I suppose I would not be so hard on it. Now and then comes a *Globe*, the four-days-old news of which seems as out of date as ancient history; but its *War Summary* always heartens me up.

Wednesday I was to tea at George R's.[274] There is still no change there. It seems as if I stepped back into the past when I go there and the sensation is strange and sweet.

There was nothing strange or sweet about Thursday's visit though. I drove through the pouring rain to spend the day with Amanda but

---

273   See note 196. *Pat of Silver Bush* (Toronto: McClelland & Stewart, 1933) was dedicated to Alec and May Macneill.

274   "George R." is LMM's friend and cousin George Raglan Macneill, the son of Jane and Jimmie Macneill.

it was a doleful visit. And long ago an afternoon with Amanda meant an afternoon of fun. Oh, poor Mollie, if you had not changed so sadly!

But last night I had a very dear, very sad, very strange and unlooked-for experience.

When I was on the Island before I shrank from the very thought of going near my old home. This year I felt the same until last night. I was on the

The Manse, Cavendish

manse veranda. The dew was falling. In the south-east a large, hazy, full moon was rising. To my left lay the dark trees that screened the old house from sight. Suddenly an irresistible longing took posses-

George R's

sion of me to go to it once more—in that pale enchantment of moonlight when one might chance to slip back through some magic loop hole into the olden years. I could not withstand it. I slipped over to the church grounds and through the old gap in the fence through which I used to go to church. I walked along the meadow edge where the footpath used to be, past the grove of spruces, and on till the old house lay before me in a soft, silvery shadow. I turned aside for a moment to the old well and looked down it. The ferns that always lined its sides had grown completely across it.

I went on to the old kitchen door. Beside it, every summer a certain shoot of balsam poplar used to start up, to be trodden down under passing feet. Since the old house was closed it had been able to grow and so fast had it grown that the whole angle between the kitchen and the cook house was full of it. It was as high as the kitchen roof.

I went around to the end of the house and stood under my old window. The moon was floating over the valley below. I had looked on that very scene a thousand times on moonlit nights of long ago. My heart beat with mingled pain and pleasure

My old window

The Lane

The front door

until it almost choked me. Everything in that kind radiance seemed so much the same. For a space the years turned back their pages. The silent sleepers in the graveyard yonder wakened and filled their old places. Grandfather and grandmother read in the lighted kitchen. Old friends and comrades walked with me in the lane. Daffy frisked in the caraway. Above me my old white bed waited for me to press its pillow of dreams.

Most of the windows were boarded up but the south one in the parlor was not. Through it I could see the bare old room distinctly with the black colonial mantelpiece that was the admiration of my childhood. I went around and stood on the stone steps of the front door. The old "front orchard" and the grove beside it seemed more bowery and bosky than of yore but I think that was only because I have grown used to a thinner screen of trees on my Leaskdale lawn. How lovely and lonely it all was, and yet how unreal. I seemed to be in a dream— and yet it seemed the only waking. Oh, as long as that moonlit magic worked the past was mine once more—the *old* past, before the last sad years I had spent in the old home. Oh, beloved old place, that half hour I spent with you last night was worth the coming from a far land. You were glad, I think, to have me back—me, who loved you so. For there is not one living now but me who loves you—not one. As I stood there I seemed to feel a presence enfolding me as if it claimed me—as if something that had been forsaken and desolate were once more rejoicing in my affection. Have not old homesteads souls that cling to them until they crumble to dust?

I could hardly tear myself away from the spot. Perhaps the charm it had for me was not a wholesome one—not altogether one to which it was well to yield. Perhaps the dead past should bury its dead. It may not be well to linger too long among ghosts, lest they lay a cold grasp upon you and bind you too closely to their chill, sweet, unearthly companionship. Certainly all the pleasures and joys of my real life seemed to grow pale and fade into nothingness beside the strange enchantment of that shadowy tryst.

Tuesday, July 6, 1915
Cavendish, P.E.I.

This is the last night I shall spend in Cavendish for a long time—a long, long time. I do not expect to be here again for at least three years and much may happen ere then. And yet I am not sorry that I leave tomorrow for Park Corner. I only wish I were leaving for home. This past week has not been very pleasant. I had looked forward to it, but few of my anticipations were realized. Not that it is anybody's fault—I could not help feeling uncomfortable and languid; May, who was ill all the spring, could not help feeling far from well; neither of us could help the cold wet weather, or the bad war news. But all these things have worked together to spoil my visit here.

Last Monday Margaret and I had a pleasant drive around the shore road. It was a nice day; Margaret was free for a time from the household cares that seem to press upon her over heavily. I felt better than usual and so we had an enjoyable drive and

Alec's House

chat. In the evening I came down to Alec's. There is little to say of my sojourn here. As I have said, there has been but scanty pleasure in it owing to untoward circumstances. I spent one pleasant afternoon at Hammond's and got to the shore—the first and only time. It is not far from here to the shore but I never felt able to walk it and most of the days were wet and cold.

Park Corner, P.E.I.
Sunday, July 11, 1915

After all my vacation is not going to be a complete failure. This past week has been very pleasant, despite my physical discomfort. Frede is here—which ex-plains it. Were it not for her presence even Park Corner would be lonely for me now.

Park Corner

Alec brought me over last Wednesday. We chanced to have a lovely day and I enjoyed the drive over that beautiful old road very much. All here are much as usual. Poor old Uncle John is very feeble and childish. At first I think he hardly knew me but now and then during my visit he has seemed to waken up, as it were, for a while and talk something like his old self. But it saddens my heart to see him. Aunt Annie is well but has to work too hard. Her old age will not, I fear, be what she deserves after her life of hard work.

The old beech wood

Chester is having a glorious time. He seems to get on beautifully with the children here—I suppose because they are all of "the household of faith." He and Doris did not hit it off especially well and even among the Webb children he seemed rather alien. But with Amy and Jim he is among his own and they play happily in the old beech wood where Clara and Stella and I once played long ago—long ago.

The war news is mixed—one day fair, the next bad. But the Russians are being gradually forced back and now Warsaw, twice saved, is again in danger. My dread is that Germany will crush Russia and then hurl her victorious legions, flushed with success, against the western front.

Yesterday Frede and I spent a beautiful forenoon gathering flowers and ferns in the hayfield by the pond with the children. The most beautiful irises are blooming now all about the pond.

Park Corner,
Sunday, July 18, 1915

To-morrow I leave Park Corner. I regret it, even though my condition makes me long for home. I have had a pleasant visit here, with some very sweet things in it. It is over now, and I dread the trip home muchly. The care of Chester, the hot trains, all loom up darkly before me. If I were well I would not mind but as it is the grasshopper is a burden.

To-night Frede and I planned to have a walk together, over the bridge in the dusk—a last farewell walk, the last one we could have there for many years—perhaps forever. In the twilight we slipped away and had our hour. The western sky was full of the hues of a weird sunset. Before us the old pond lay in shadow and silver. The evening was very still, very calm, very clear. And through the stillness came the strangest, saddest, most unforgettable sound in nature—the soft, ceaseless wash on a distant shore of the breakers of a spent storm. It is a sound rarely heard and always to be remembered. It is more mournful than the rain wind of night—the heartbreak of all creation is in it.

Frede and I walked back and forth over the bridge many times, sometimes in silence, sometimes speaking lowly of the deepest thoughts in our hearts. We seemed a part of the night—of the dreaming water, of the dusk in the cloudy firs, of the far remote stars, of that haunting moan of the sea. And when the twilight suddenly was night and the shining new moon swung above the tree tops that bend over that old homestead, we walked away from the glamor in a silence that touched the lands of dream and tears.

The Manse, Leaskdale, Ont.
Saturday, July 24, 1915

Home again—the gods be praised therefor! Last Monday afternoon Aunt Annie drove me to Kensington. It was really delightful. The old Island basked in summer loveliness and bombarded me with beauty as

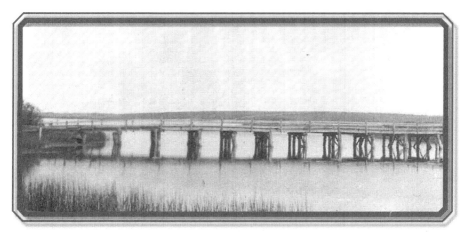

The Bridge

The dusk in the cloudy firs

if to say, "Be glad to leave me if you dare." No, dear old spot, I was not glad to leave you. I was only so tired that I could not find my olden joy in your beauty and only wished to flee away where I might be at rest.

I spent the night with Tillie Macneill—it is of no use to try to think of her as Tillie Bentley—in her Kensington home. I was glad to see Tillie again but she will be an old maid to the end of her life and her old-maidishness has lost the gentle charm it possessed in her old home and seems rather ridiculous in prosaic Kensington. She does not seem to "belong" there.

Tuesday morning I crossed in the boat. I had been dreading the journey home but, like so many other dreads in life, it turned out of no significance. My trip was rather pleasant. I felt much better than I had felt all summer, the weather was cool, Chester was very good, and the only part that was really unpleasant was the scramble and confusion in the change at Moncton.

But when I got into Montreal on Wednesday morning there was such bad war news that it rattled me. The Russians had been broken everywhere, driven across the Vistula, and Warsaw was about to fall. It all upset me so terribly that it's a wonder I ever got on the right train. I bought paper after paper feverishly in the irrational hope that some one of them might have better news—or, at least, present it in a little more favorable light. But each seemed worse than the last. Half way to Toronto a boy came through the train selling *Globes*. How delighted I was to see a Globe again! How comforting

Home again

was that blessed "War Summary" which admitted all the reverses, but gave so many excellent reasons why they could have no bearing on the final outcome of the war! What mattered it that I suspected the writer of the "Summary" to be a deliberate *Mark Tapley?* I was in that state where even a lie is a comfort, providing it is a cheerful lie! Nevertheless, when I reached Toronto, Wednesday night I was fearfully tired and gloomy. I spent a miserable night in the Walker house—couldn't sleep for worrying over war-news. A tiresome day of shopping followed and at five o'clock I got on that blessed old Uxbridge train. Most of the way we travelled through thunderstorms and I resigned myself in thorough pessimism to a terrible ride home. But we passed out of the storm belt before we reached Uxbridge and I arrived there in a pink-and-smoky dreamy summer evening.

On the night when Frede and I walked on the bridge at Park Corner I had said to her, "Is it not strange, when you come to think of it, how very *very* few things in life are *flawless*—how very few pleasures have no sting—how very few "good times" are wholly unmarred by some little, untoward circumstance—the secret pinching of the shoe?"

That is true; but now and again some things seem to slip past the grim fate whose mission it is to distil one drop of poison into every draught—an occasional hour *is* unmarred by the grim deity. My home-coming that night seemed one of them. It was perfect.

Ewan and Mr. and Mrs. Warner met us in their motor. We had a delightful drive home and arrived here just at sunset. The garden was beautiful, the lawn a green haven of peace. Lily came smiling to meet us and Chester announced that he was "awful glad to be home." It was all lovely and I looked about me with eyes that found everything good.

The Manse, Leaskdale, Ont.
Monday, July 26, 1915

The war news continues bad—still the Russians are retreating. What a horrible strain this long-drawn-out retreat of theirs has been ever since May!

I found "Anne of The Island" here when I got home—my seventh book. It is well-made, like all of Page's books. There is less of real life in it than in any of my other books. *Kingsport* is Halifax—more or less—but *Anne's* experiences there certainly are not a reflection of my own. I never liked Halifax—although I loved its park and "Old St. Paul's" cemetery. The afternoon spent there by *Anne* and *Priscilla* was sketched from an old ramble of my own in it and the chloroforming of "Rusty" was an echo of the time when Frede and I darkly did away with a homeless pussy cat which infested our back door. But all the rest of the story is "jest lies and nothing else."

With its publication my old contract with Page expires. It was a hard contract, even for a first book—and when my books attained such marked success it became an increasingly unjust one. Page has made a fortune out of my books—and

Cover design of "Anne of the Island"

spent it in gambling, I am told. I certainly have not received a fair recompense. Lately I have been hearing many things that have filled me with distrust of Page. I hate to believe them; for ties of association are strong with me and the Page Co. is bound up with my memories of my "arrival" at the goal towards which I had struggled for so many hard, disappointing years. *Green Gables* was refused five times before I sent it to Page and I cannot forget that it was his house that accepted it and so gave me my chance. But I cannot sacrifice my interests and, what is more, my children's interests, to mere sentiment, if Page is not "straight". Matters will have to be cleared up and settled before I give him another book. There will, I know, be a fight, and I dread it, because if Page is not honorable I am no match for him.

When I signed the contract for the "Chronicles of Avonlea" I would not sign it unless he left out the clause binding me to give him all my books for five years on the same old terms. Page was very loathe to yield and made a veiled threat that he would not continue to "push" my books if I would not sign. I persisted and eventually he yielded, with a very bad grace. If he had offered me better terms—the ordinary terms offered to any successful author—15% on the retail price—I would have signed. But he never hinted at such a thing—and I knew it was of little use to ask it. He wanted me to go on binding myself forever to his beggarly 10% on the wholesale price. This means only 7 to 9 cents per book, when I should have about 19. But the worst feature of it is that when the royalty is on the "wholesale price" there is absolutely no way in which an author can "keep tabs" on her publishers in the matter of a fair accounting.

The Manse, Leaskdale, Ont.
Friday, Aug. 6, 1915

News came today of the fall of Warsaw.[275] We have been expecting it for a week and knew it was bound to come but the announcement seemed as much of a blow as if it had been entirely unexpected. I have been so nervous and depressed since that I am "down and out." The weather, too, is horrible—almost constant rain and very close and hot.

Saturday, Aug. 7, 1915

I had a bad attack of nerves last night and slept wretchedly. I do not sleep well now at any time and very little suffices to give me a sleepless night. The war news worries me almost unbearably. So far the bulk of the Russian army has escaped but it is by no means out of danger yet.

---

275   Warsaw fell to the German Twelfth Army on August 4–5, 1915, as part of a "grand retreat" eastward by the Russian Army, which was faced with shortages of materiel and mounting casualties. The front stabilized in late September.

It would mean victory for Germany if she could surround Warsaw's retreating legions. Lacking that, all her successes will fall short of a decision. How wretched it is to wait from day to day for the papers, dreading to open them when they come. Oh God, the world has had a year of agony. It was a year on August 4th since England declared war. And not even yet is the end in sight—nay, worse, Germany has marched from victory to victory all summer.

The Manse, Leaskdale, Ont.
August 13, 1915

It is just a year to-day since little Hugh was born dead. Oh, that hideous day! Shall I ever be able to forget its agony? And will it be repeated in October? This thought is ever present with me. I have had some bad attacks of nervous depression lately—one last night that was almost unbearable. My condition—the war news—the weather—all combined to make me very miserable. Sometimes I feel so unutterably disheartened that if it were not for Chester it seems to me that I would rather not go on living.

August 31, 1915

Since my last entry I have been almost constantly ill with grippe and a persistent sore throat; and this last week Chester has been very miserable with attacks of fever and vomiting. I am really hardly able to wait on the poor child and yet he will have no one else when he is ill. I feel worried about him for he has had several of these sick spells this summer.

The war news is still bad—bad—bad! Oh, what will the end be? And now the Balkans are aflame and it seems as if Bulgaria would side with Turkey and Germany.

Friday, Sept. 10, 1915

I feel rather at the end of my endurance. I have been having a bad time with another ulcerating tooth. And I am so worried about Chester. He has been ill off and on ever since my last entry. He seems a little better now but the child has got so pale and thin that he frightens me. As for myself I am uncomfortable every moment. Will I ever feel well again? It seems to me quite impossible.

Wednesday, Sept. 22, 1915
Leaskdale, Ont.

Matters have mended a little lately. Chester seems to be pretty well again and is picking up. I, too, feel better in some ways. But the war news is bad—all bad. And today came two things that bowled me over. One was the *Globe* headline, "Bulgaria declares war on the side of Germany" and the other was a letter from Mrs. Aubin saying that, after all, she could not come to nurse me in October.[276] I had trusted in her promise and I thought the excuse she gave a trivial one. And now I must have a new nurse and I shrink from another stranger. Oh, if it were only all well over! As the time draws near my dread increases. If I should lose my baby again!

Friday, Sept. 24, 1915

Even yet in these woeful days we can sometimes have a laugh. Last night when Chester came to say his prayers he was in a very bad humor with Lily who had done something that displeased him. He always concludes his prayer with a petition to "bless father and mother and Lily and make me a good boy." But last night he omitted Lily's name. I supplied the omission—"and Lily." "No," said young Chester very decidedly, "make me a good boy *without Lily*, Amen." But my laugh did not bring me a good night. It was not exactly the war that kept me awake—rather my own discomfort. But since I could not sleep I *did* think continuously about the war. There is a gleam of brightness in the news that Greece is mobilizing on the side of the Allies. If she will only do so Serbia will yet be saved.[277] But in this war one is sure of nothing until it has happened. Constantine of Greece has a German wife![278]

To think that I should have to care what kind of a wife Constantine of Greece has!

---

276 Bulgaria had remained neutral at the outset of World War I, following recent exhaustion in the Balkan wars (1912–13), involving Greece, Serbia, Montenegro, and Bulgaria. Although it would be the smallest country in the Central Powers alliance, Bulgaria had a strong military and a strategic location, endangering Serbia and Romania.

277 A renewed offensive by the Germans, Austro-Hungarians and Bulgarians in October 1914 resulted in the rout of the Serbian army and most of Serbia falling into the hands of the Central Powers.

278 King Constantine I (1868–1923) ruled Greece from 1913 (following the assassination of his father, George I) to 1917 and again from 1920 to 1922. His wife, Princess Sophia of Prussia, was a younger sister of the German Emperor and a granddaughter of Britain's Queen Victoria. Allied propaganda painted Constantine as a German lackey but modern historians take a more nuanced view of his position.

Saturday, Sept. 25, 1915
Leaskdale, Ont.

The war-news is slightly better. The Russians seem able to make a stand at last, and their armies have escaped capture or a decisive defeat. And Greece continues to mobilize. That means much.

Monday, Sept. 27, 1915

Good war-news—great war-news! The British and French have scored a big victory on the western front.[279] Not a decisive one, to be sure. But they have made a great advance and captured a large number of prisoners. Coming after months of depression this might have gone to my head. In the earlier months of the war it certainly would—I would have danced and hurrahed. But now I feel only a sort of relief, as if a long painful pressure had been lifted. I could not exult. I could only feel thankful—and afraid. For somehow I cannot believe that this is anything but a rift in the clouds.

Sunday, Oct. 3rd, 1915

All this week the war news has been good. The British and French have gone on advancing: but now the advance seems at an end and nothing at all decisive has been achieved. The spot-light is again passing from the western front to the Balkans, where the situation is very muddled.

We have been housecleaning and I have found it very hard. I have done much more than I should have, I think. There are times when I get very discouraged. I have not been free from discomfort of some kind for an hour in eight months and sometimes it seems impossible that I ever will be. I expect the stork about the 17th of October. Miss Barnard, a friend of Mrs. Aubin's, is to be my nurse.

Wednesday, Oct. 6, 1915
The Manse, Leaskdale

We cleaned the parlor today and so I am very tired—so tired that, as I sit here at my desk, I dread the thought of climbing the stairs. Besides, I have been horribly worried over the war-news. Today came the an-

279 Probably the Battle of Loos, in which British troops used chlorine gas against German troops, enabling them to capture the strategic town of Loos in northern France.

nouncement that Constantine of Greece has dismissed Venizelos, the Greek premier who was responsible for the mobilization. This means that Greece will *not* enter the war on the side of the Entente—*may* mean that she will declare for Germany. Not for nothing has Constantine a German wife! Will there ever be an end to these wretched thunderbolts? We were all so sure that Greece would join the Entente. Will peace *ever* come? Yes, yes, it will—but peace will not mean a return to "that ancient world of 1914." We can never go back to that. Nothing will ever be the same again.

Saturday, Oct. 26, 1915
The Manse, Leaskdale

I am able to sit up all day today. All is over and well over—and I have another dear wee son. He came on the afternoon of October 7th, ten days before he was expected. Perhaps Constantine of Greece was responsible for that—and perhaps not. As all went well I was glad that I was spared ten more weary days, though I was taken by surprise with no nurse on hand. But Dr. Shier brought out an Uxbridge nurse for the day and Miss Barnard got here at night.

Stuart and Miss Barnard

Ewan Stuart Macdonald is another dear plump chubby little man of ten pounds.[280] I had a very easy time and oh how glad I was when I heard the baby's lusty cry. I had rather hoped he would be a girl but now I would not exchange him for a thousand girls. And I *am* glad that Chester will have a brother. Babykins does not look at all like Chester. He is thought to "favor" my side of the house. His eyes are certainly very like my father's. He is as good as a baby can be and so bright. When he was no more than half an hour old the nurse picked

---

280   LMM's son was named Ewan Stuart Macdonald, and died in 1980.

him up and he suddenly *lifted up his head* and looked all round the room for a moment with bright wide-open eyes. I shall never forget the look of the ridiculous mite, with his seemingly black eyes in his tiny white face, thus challenging the strange world in which he found himself.

Ewan named him Stuart—after some Stuart he had known at college. I did not really care for the name. I wanted to call him Sidney. But Ewan seemed to think that as I had my choice in naming Chester he ought to have his this time, so I gave way. I added Ewan to the name because I thought one of the boys should bear his father's name, though it is a name I never liked and Ewan does not like it himself.

Yes, I was thankful and happy. And yet my convalescence was a somewhat dreary time. The war-news was bad all through. Serbia was overrun and every day the papers were full of depressing despatches. I did not care very much for my nurse. I didn't actually dislike her but she was woefully dull and cow-like. I almost ached with loneliness. It all seemed very different from that gay time after Chester's birth. But then it was blessedly different from that horrible time last year after dear little Hugh's coming—and going.

For the first time the ache has gone out of my heart. And yet this baby does not, as someone said, "fill little Hugh's place." None can ever do that. He will always have his own place—that dear little shadowy baby who will always be a baby to me—a little phantom companion, unseen and unheard, of his brothers. Wee Stuart is doubly precious for his life was purchased by "little Hugh's" death. But he has his own place; he does not fill that where a little cold waxen form is shrined.

Monday, Nov. 29, 1915
The Manse, Leaskdale, Ont.

A day of "chilling winds and gloomy skies." But November has been like this most of the way through. And the war-news has been bad. The Serbian campaign has gone against the Allies and the attitude of Greece and Rumania is very dubious. It is becoming more and more evident daily that the Gallipoli campaign from which we all hoped so much at one time is a fiasco.[281] It is hard to keep up one's courage in the face of so many failures and reverses. Sometimes mine goes down

---

281   A peninsula running south-west, between the Dardanelles and Saros Bay (in modern-day Marmara, Turkey). The campaign was an ill-fated and costly failure, with many casualties on both sides, including heavy losses of Australian and New Zealand soldiers.

below zero. If it were not for the British fleet I would give up hope. But to that I still anchor my storm-tossed soul.

Baby is doing fairly well but does not gain as steadily as I would like, though he is very good. I daresay my constant mental disturbance is bad for him.

But I feel real well physically and it is really a delightful sensation. To be able to move easily, enjoy my food, sleep well, and wear pretty dresses again seems all rather too good to be true. I survey my slim shape in the mirror with an odd conviction that it doesn't belong to me.

We organized a Red Cross Branch here this month. I am President. I could not refuse for the need is urgent; but I felt and still feel that I had neither the time nor the strength for this, in addition to all my church societies. Nevertheless it is a demand that must be met and I must not shrink from a little sacrifice. What is it compared to that which some women have to make? But I do *not* shrink from it. Only, I must not neglect other duties for it and I do not honestly know whether I have sufficient strength to do all that seems expected of me. Household, literary and family interests—missionary societies, Guilds and Red Cross, endless visits—all seem to pile up before me and every night I feel so tired that I can hardly drag myself upstairs.

A few days ago I read in the *Guardian* of Toff Mckenzie's death. I can't picture Cavendish without Toff. He was a central figure in our social life as long as I can remember—jovial, friendly Toff. He never seemed to grow old. And yet he was seventy. His mother is ninety three. He was her first born; he had lived out man's allotted years; and still she survives him.

The other day I resumed work on a short story called "The Schoolmaster's Bride." I say "resumed" work. Nearly five years ago a month or two before grandmother's death I began work on it. I got it blocked out and I got no further. Never since then have I been able to take it up again. But this fall I am not at work on a book and I want to write a few short stories if I can. It is difficult to get the time for writing at all. But it must be managed. As matters are, I cannot afford to give it up, even for a time.

The Manse, Leaskdale, Ont.
Monday, Jan. 3, 1916

The New Year has opened amid bitter anxieties and worries. Chester was miserable all December with colds and sick stomach spells. About Christmas one of the glands in his neck swelled and we had the doctor last Friday. He looked grave and said it might possibly be a tubercular gland! I cannot believe it for the child has always been so strong and well until lately, but the worry is killing me. Neither Ewan nor I slept a moment Friday night.

But the thing to do is to *fight*— to build the child up so thoroughly and speedily that his vitality will kill the disease if it has got a hold upon him. Tuberculosis! The very thought of it makes my soul cringe with agony. Waking or sleeping, the thought is ever present with me. Dear, dear little Chester, the core of my heart since his birth—my first born.

Edith

On the first of December Lily, who had been with me for three years, left to be married to Rob Shier of Zephyr. I was sorry to lose Lily for she was a very good girl—neat, efficient, capable. But I was not quite as sorry as I would have been had she left a year ago. After her engagement to Shier she ceased to be as anxious to please as formerly and was not nearly so satisfactory in a great many ways. This reconciled me to her going. I have Edith Meyers, a Zephyr girl, in her place.[282] In a good many ways I really like her better than Lily. Her worst fault is that she is very untidy; but she is better tempered, more obliging, and really saves me much more time. And she does not take the morose melancholic spells with which the latter was afflicted. On the whole I certainly would not change back.

All the month the war-news has been bad, especially in regard to the British retreat from Bagdad, when they seemed on the point of

---

282   Edith was from Zephyr; her parents were John and Lillian Meyers.

capturing it, and the overrunning of Serbia by the Teutons.[283] It is hard to keep faith in the ultimate triumph of the Allies. It really seems that they are doomed to fail or bungle everywhere. And now a second New Year has come and the war seems no nearer an end than last year.

Frede came on December 23rd and left to-day—that has been the one bright spot so far this winter. Up to Friday night I took unmixed joy in her companionship and we had hours of old soul communion. Since Friday all has seemed a dream. I hardly felt regret when she went to-day. When one mighty emotion, be it joy or sorrow or anxiety, takes possession of the mind there is no room for any other.

Yesterday we had Will and Allan Mustard here to dinner. They leave in a short time for England to train in the artillery. They are such fine young fellows. Will they ever sit at my table again?

Tuesday, Jan. 4, 1916
The Manse, Leaskdale, Ont.

Ewan and I and the baby went to Mrs. Marquis's to spend the evening. Racked as I was with worry about Chester I had to sit the evening out, laughing and chatting and making small talk. I suppose I did it pretty well. I have had a good deal of it to do in my life; but it never gets any easier. I was thankful when we could get away and I could hurry home to find my dear boy sound asleep in his bed. I hate to be a moment away from him.

Monday, Jan. 31, 1916

I wonder if all the months of 1916 will be as hard as the first one has been. I hope not. It has been a wretched month. Chester had a couple of very sick spells. I was nervous and worried most of the month about him and had to be up so much at night with him that I am getting terribly run down. But thank God the swelling in his neck has completely disappeared so it could not have been tubercular. This past week he is beginning to look rosy and well again. I am so thankful for that that I feel I must not complain of anything else. Yet it *has* seemed a hard month. The war news has been scanty and rather bad—certainly nothing encouraging or hopeful. The weather has been depressing—

---

283   Baghdad was founded in the eighth century on the Tigris. An Indian colonial army confronted Ottoman forces in what is now Iraq. Serbia was under increasing threat following the entry of Bulgaria into the war (see note for September 22, 1915).

so much rain and fog and mud. I work doggedly through the day and when evening comes I am worn-out and nervous. Some of the nights are a terror to me for I cannot sleep.

Thursday, Feb. 3, 1916
Leaskdale, Ont.

Lately, for a few days, there has been no *real* war news. I fear it is the calm before the storm. Chester has had another sick stomach spell but seems pretty well today. Every time that he seems not quite well after this I shall be anxious, lest the gland trouble return.

Friday, Feb. 4, 1916

To-day Ewan came in saying, "Bad news! The worst yet." I turned cold with terror. Had the Germans smashed through on the western front? Or invaded England? I seized the *Globe* and opened it with shaking hands. The headlines announced that the Parliament Buildings in Ottawa had been burned—presumably by a German incendiary.[284] Bad enough news, indeed. But not what I had dreaded. New Parliament Buildings can be built; but if the British line were broken—well we might not need Parliament buildings in Canada! The Germans would see to that.

Monday, Feb. 7, 1916
The Manse, Leaskdale

Had an attack of grippe Saturday. But as I had promised to read a paper for the Hypatia Club today I drove to Uxbridge in the teeth of a furious gale and drift. I deserved to catch my death of cold, of course, and perhaps I did.

My royalty reports came from Page to-day and were rather disappointing. *Anne of The Island* did not sell as well as I had a right to expect—only 32,000 copies. There is certainly something wrong somewhere. The booksellers and retailers complain terribly of Page. They say he is so "hard" they cannot deal with him. Some have told me that they would not deal with Page at all if it were not necessary to get my books because the public demands them.

---

284   Fire levelled the Centre Block of the Parliament buildings in Ottawa on February 3, 1916. Subsequent investigation showed its cause was accidental.

Wednesday, Feb. 9, 1916

I should be in bed—but I feel as if I could not sleep. I am overtired, and worried and nervous into the bargain. Last night I got very little sleep. Ewan coughed incessantly. I fear he has bronchitis. He was so hoarse to-night that he could not go to the Guild, so I had to drag wearily over in his place and read his paper. It was cold and dreary and as I stumbled back home alone through the darkness and snow I almost let go of my "will to live" altogether. So I come to "growl it off" in my journal as of yore. Before the "congregation" I must wear a mask and assume a cheerfulness I am far from feeling.

Thursday, Feb. 10, 1916
The Manse, Leaskdale, Ont.

More growls! Last night Ewan became very bad—a most terrible racking cough possessed him without cessation. I was up all night trying to relieve him with hot applications etc., but nothing did any good and in the morning I 'phoned to Uxbridge for Dr. Shier who came and pronounced it bronchitis as I had feared. I'm afraid it will be some time before he will be able to be about.

The papers to-day were full of alarming rumors of 17-inch guns possessed by the German navy. The rumors may not be true. Many alarming rumors have proved false; on the other hand some have proved true; and no prophet can predict in which these belong.

Wednesday, Feb. 16, 1916

"Pray ye that your flight be not in the winter"[285]—ay, verily. Everything is harder to endure in the winter. Ewan is no better yet. His cough has improved slightly but his hoarseness has grown worse. He cannot speak above a whisper. Everybody in the congregation has a different remedy which is a certain cure and everybody is somewhat offended if his or her pet remedy isn't tried. We have experimented with most of them to no visible benefit. Flaxseed tea seems to be the staple. I make it by the quart and poor Ewan obediently swallows it.

Saturday I felt very miserable with an attack of what I think must be inflammation of the breast. Nevertheless I had to go and preside at the Mission Band and then help prepare for a Knox college student who was coming out to supply on Sunday. I kept up until I got him out

---

285   "But pray ye that your flight be not in the winter, neither on the sabbath day" (Matthew 24:20).

of the way in the spare room. Then I went to bed but not to sleep. I spent the night going from icy chills to burning heats, followed by drenching perspirations. In the morning I could not get up so had to spend the day in bed. By Monday the attack seemed to have spent itself and I got up.

That night Cuthbert McIntyre came and stayed till Tuesday night.[286] He has been in Edmonton the past two years and was paying a flying visit to Toronto. I was heart-glad to see him although in my wretched condition and with poor Ewan quite debarred from conversation I could not enjoy his visit as much as I would otherwise have done. How it brought old

Cuthbert and Chester

days back to see him! When he sat talking at the table I shut my eyes— and it seemed as if I must be back in the old dining room at Brighton and that when I opened my eyes I would see Bertie and dear little Aunt Mary opposite me. But Bertie is in Vancouver and Aunt Mary sleeps well in the cemetery at Charlottetown.

At present the ever shifting limelight of the war is concentrated on the Caucasus and Armenian fronts where the Russians are doing good work with the Turks. Elsewhere there is "nothing to report."

Cuthbert and Chester

286   Cuthbert, along with Jim, Laura, Harry, Lewis, and Beatrice ("Bertie") were the children of Mary Montgomery McIntyre (LMM's father's sister) and Duncan McIntyre. LMM became close to the family in 1893 while a student at Charlottetown's Prince of Wales College, and came to regard "Aunt Mary" (see below) as almost a second mother. (See also the note for July 17, 1913.)

Tuesday, Feb. 22, 1916
The Manse, Leaskdale, Ont.

Last night I had a very strange dream. I cannot shake off the impression it made on me. It was so vivid, so real, so strangely broken and resumed.

I was in my room at noon, standing by my dressing table. Outside the sun was shining on a summer world. Suddenly—nay, instantaneously—the sky became overcast with inky blackness, torrents of rain fell, thunder rolled and lightning flashed incessantly. Though alarmed, I stood my ground for some time. Then came a crash and flash that seemed to rive the universe. I was sure the house was struck. In a frenzy of terror I ran shrieking downstairs and through the hall, calling for Ewan. He, at the same time, came running in from the stable, and we met in the dining room, clasping each other in dismay. As we passed back through the hall I saw a man running up the walk. I opened the door and he dashed into the hall, out of the rain—a soldier in khaki.

At this moment the cry of the baby awakened me. At the instant of awakening the curious conviction flashed into my mind that my dream had to do with events of the war about to happen and I felt deep regret that I had wakened before I finished it and knew how it ended.

I arose, attended to the baby's needs, and returned to bed. I fell asleep and did what I never did before—I resumed the broken dream and dreamed it out. The storm was just over; the sun was shining and the drops of rain were glistening on the young grass like diamonds. The whole world seemed joyous and springlike. I was walking down the hill beyond the church—nay, not walking but dancing, as a child might dance, and I wore a wreath of white blossoms on my hair. I danced the whole way home and I felt inexpressibly light-hearted and jubilant. Then I awakened again.

Curious? Well, if the dream "comes true" and the storm breaks, we are to be happy after the storm has passed. I must remember that for any comforting.

Monday, Feb. 28, 1916

Did that strange dream of mine have any real significance? It has been most strangely fulfilled. Two days after I dreamed it came the news of the great German offensive at Verdun and since then the strain has been hideous.[287] Last Thursday the French line was broken. Every day since has brought tidings of a German advance in spite of the desperate resistance of the French. The situation is horribly critical. If the Germans capture Verdun the spirit of France may be broken, or the way to Paris opened.

Apart from the horrible strain of the war news this has been a dreadful week. Last Wednesday night I came home from a Guild social and went to bed feeling fairly well. In the night I wakened with another attack of inflammation of the breast—dreadful pain, chills and sweats. I had to spend the next day in bed and the pain and sweats weakened me so dreadfully that I could hardly stand on the following day. Get up I had to, though, for there was to be a "pie social" in aid of the Red Cross at Webster Fawn's that night and as I had charge of the programme it was necessary that I should be there. It was a cold, raw blustery night. I went up in Alec Leask's big sleigh. There were about twelve in the sleigh, the rest being young folks full of jollity and laughter—harmless and natural enough but not much in accordance with my then mood. I felt inexpressibly miserable—weak, chilly, tired, discouraged. Ewan's voice was no better—the Germans were advancing—the baby had been failing for three weeks—I was wretchedly ill. I gazed over the stormy fields in the bitter wind of night and wondered if it were any use to keep up the struggle. I have seldom been more sick at heart than I was that night.

But nobody knew it. Of course, I looked quite ghastly—hollow-eyed and haggard from lack of sleep, with a racking cough. But I smiled and laughed and jested and engineered the programme; I gave a comic reading that brought down the house; I ate a third of a pie with the purchaser thereof—an awkward schoolboy who could say nothing and to whom I could say nothing. We ate that pie in silence and I felt as if every mouthful must choke me.

I got home at one so overtired and ill that I couldn't sleep. Saturday seemed like a nightmare. It was stormy and bitterly cold. Ewan's voice was no better. The war news was bad and the baby was ill. Worst of all, my illness, lack of appetite and loss of sleep had their inevitable effect. I had not enough nourishment for him and what little I had didn't agree with him—has not agreed with him ever since my first attack. He has simply been fading out of life for three weeks. It is breaking my

---

287   Located in the northeastern part of France, the city of Verdun, whose very name comes from a Latin word meaning "strong fort," had been newly fortified following the end of the Franco-Prussian War in 1870. By early 1916 the Verdun salient protruded into the German lines and became the focus of unrelenting artillery attacks, followed by infantry assaults intended to bleed the defending French dry.

heart. He never cries—never complains—just lies in his little basket and gives a sweet, piteous little smile when someone bends over him. He weighs less than he did two months ago. Something must be done. I hate the thought of weaning him so soon, but I am going down terribly myself and if there is not a change for the better in him soon I will lose my baby. I have been so blue and nervous and depressed these last three days—so weak and ill, too, yet I must be on my feet constantly. I cannot sleep at night, between worry and physical pain. If Ewan were only better! I get so worried lest he lose his voice altogether. In fact, I seem to be the prey of a score of worries just now—worry over the war, over Ewan, over the baby, over myself. Verily, this is the storm of my dream with a vengeance. Oh, for Frede or Bertie—for any "kindred spirit" to help me out a bit with a little encouragement or laughter.

Thursday, Mar. 2, 1916
Leaskdale, Ont.

I am seriously alarmed about Ewan's voice. There is no improvement— nay, he is really worse. I have slept hardly any this week and when I do waken with a night sweat. It is probably the result of the trouble in my breasts but it is extremely weakening. I look like a ghost and feel like a lunatic. It seems to me that I *cannot* bear the suspense of that hideous struggle at Verdun, where men are being mowed down in indiscriminate butchery. "The snow around Verdun is no longer white" was the hideously suggestive sentence in a paper today.

I drag through the days like a doomed creature. There are times when I could scream aloud. It is dull and gray and cold. Chester goes about the house lustily singing that absurd old song, "Polly Wolly Doodle" which is his reigning favorite at present. The contrast between present conditions and that chorus is grim. Thanks be, *he* keeps well and rosy. Baby, too, has seemed better today. I began on Monday to give him some cow's milk. It is agreeing with him well and certain things have altered for the better with him.

Thursday, March 9, 1916
Leaskdale, Ont.

Verily, I think the Verdun struggle will drive me mad. I could scream when I think of the hideous carnage. And the Germans are creeping nearer and nearer. Almost every day this past week has brought bad news for strategic points taken. To-day, when Ewan went for the mail, my suspense was intolerable. I walked the floor until his return. The news was not as bad as it might have been. The French have re-captured the Crow Wood—an important point. But the situation is terribly critical. It seems to me that the whole civilized world is standing breathless with eyes fixed on Verdun. I believe that the fate of the war hangs on the issue of the Verdun struggle. If Germany wins there she will win the war. If she loses, the tide must set against her.

I think Ewan's voice begins to show a slight improvement—but it is very slight. I have been poorly. The night sweats continue and leave me weak and nerveless through the day. One bright spot is that baby is certainly improving. He has gained two pounds in a little over a week.

Friday, March 10, 1916
Leaskdale Manse, Ont.

I have had a rather strange experience tonight. To-day was hard. I had another sweat last night and could not sleep after it or prevent myself from picturing everything in the gloomiest colors. One of my breasts was sore again and I felt as if I could *not* bear another attack of inflammation. To-day a wild snowstorm raged and no mail came. It is a torture every day to get the mail—but it is a worse torture *not* to get it. Ewan's voice was worse again—baby was not so well—everything seemed as bad as it could be. I had no physical strength to fight off worry and at dark my nerves suddenly went to pieces as they have not gone since that terrible winter of my nervous breakdown long ago at home. I could do nothing but walk the floor in agony of mind and travail of spirit. This continued for two hours. I looked forward to a night of sleepless horror. All my misery seemed to centre around Verdun where "the snow was no longer white." I seemed in my own soul to embrace all the anguish and strain of France. Not for one moment would I tear my tortured thoughts from it.

Suddenly the agony ceased—a great calm seemed to descend upon me and envelop me. I was *at peace*. All unrest passed away from me. I seemed to have emerged from some awful crisis. The conviction seized upon me that Verdun was safe—that the Germans would not pass the grim barrier of desperate France. I was as a woman from whom some evil spirit had been driven—or can it be as a priestess of old who, out of depths of agony wins some strange foresight of the future? I feel as if I had wrestled with principalities and powers, with things present and things to come, and come off victor. Is it so?—or is it merely the reaction of tortured nerves, agonized to their limit?

Saturday, March 12, 1916
Leaskdale, Ont.

I slept well and feel much better today. And that strange calm continues—that strange conviction that the Verdun crisis is past, no matter how much longer the struggle may continue. It was not disturbed
when the mail came bringing bad news of the Germans again winning
the Crow's Wood. Yesterday that news would have agonized me. Today
it did not affect me at all.

Ewan's voice is certainly a little better and he means to try to preach
tomorrow. I don't envy his listeners but he has lost four Sundays and is
determined he will not lose another.

And so I finish this volume. It covers six years—a very full and happy
six years, in spite of some dark hours. How I love my old journal and
what a part of my life it has become. It satisfies some need in my nature. It seems like a personal confidant in whom I can repose absolute
trust. I shall begin a fourth volume with my next entry and I wonder
how many years it will embrace—what records of joy and sorrow, of
success and failure it will contain.

> "The Moving Finger writes; and having writ
> Moves on; nor all thy piety and wit
> Can lure it back to cancel half a line
> Nor all thy tears wash out a word of it."[288]

> [This marks the end of LMM's handwritten journal,
> labelled "Vol. III," containing entries from
> February 11, 1910 to March 12, 1916]

---

288   From Edward Fitzgerald's (1809–1883) translation of Persian poetry attributed to Omar
Khayyam (1048–1131), *The Rubaiyat of Omar Khayyam*, stanza 71.

Vol. IV
L.M. Montgomery Macdonald
March 1916–December 1919

[LMM]

Tuesday, March 21, 1916
Leaskdale Manse, Ont.

Last Monday I went to Toronto for a week. Ewan's voice, though not yet fully recovered, was considerably improved and I felt that I really needed a little change after the strain of the past four weeks. I had a good deal of shopping to do also, so I went, though not feeling very fit for it.

The war news of Monday was fair—the French lines still holding. Baby and I went to Toronto on the after-noon train and Norman Beal met us. I spent the week with the Beals. Mary is a dear jolly soul—"one of the race that knows Joseph"—and Norman is very nice. I should have had a good time that week but physical discomfort poisoned it all.

Tuesday the Press Club gave an afternoon tea for me and that evening Messrs. McClelland and Goodchild, of McClelland, Goodchild and Stewart, called to dis-

Mary

219

cuss the Canadian publication of my next book.[289] I have decided that I shall give them the Canadian rights. Hitherto I have not had a Canadian publisher, Page holding the world rights—a very unsatisfactory arrangement. I told Mr. McC. that I intended to give Page the U.S. rights. McC. and G. looked at each other. They *said* nothing against Page but all through the interview I had a feeling that they *could* say a good deal if I gave them a chance. I did *not* give them the chance. Whatever Page may be I shall not give rival publishers the chance to vilify him unless he gives me greater reason to distrust him as a publisher than he yet has.[290] As for the McClelland firm, they are well spoken of in quarters where I have confidence and I think I am safe in trusting them.

No definite arrangement was come to in regard to the new book but I have arranged with them to bring out my poems next fall. I have always wanted to do this—not that they are of any special merit but solely for my own satisfaction. Page practically refused to bring them out some years ago declaring that poetry would not pay. Considering the amount he has made out of my novels I thought he might have published the poems for me even if they did not "pay." So I felt that I did not need to consider him in this deal.

I had another attack of inflammation of the breast that week and of course it spoiled my visit—I had it all over again—the pain, the chills, the night sweats, the nervous restlessness. And I had to run around to afternoon teas and smile and talk. Of course, the sensible thing would have been to cut them out. But having promised beforehand to be present I felt that I could not disappoint hostesses whose guest of honor I was and who had invited their friends to meet me. Fame, as well as rank, imposes certain obligations!!

But I did feel disappointed that my little visit, to which I had been looking forward all winter, was completely spoiled.

Baby was in with me and was entirely good and adorable.

At one of the teas I received quite the most stupendous compliment that has ever been paid to me on account of my books. A lady came up to me, and said, "Oh, Mrs. Macdonald, I want to tell you how much my little girl loves *Anne*. I found her with *Green Gables* the other day and

289   Two former employees of the Methodist Book Room (later the Ryerson Press), John McClelland and Frederick Goodchild, established McClelland and Goodchild Ltd. in 1906. The firm became McClelland, Goodchild and Stewart after George Stewart came on board late in 1913. Goodchild left the company in 1918, at which point the company was renamed McClelland & Stewart—the name it still bears today as an imprint of Random House.

290   This is one of the early signs of what would become a very troubled relationship with her first publisher, L.C. Page.

I said, 'child, how often have you read that book?'[291] She said, 'Oh, mother, I don't know. I *just keep it and my bible together and read a chapter of both every day.'*

In my salad days I may have dreamed of rivalling Brontë and Eliot. I certainly never in my wildest flights dreamed of competing with the Bible!!!

Seriously, though, I thought that incense of a child's adoration the sweetest that has ever been offered me.

I came home yesterday and have spent the day putting things to rights. I am very tired tonight and, worse than tired, I am nervous and depressed as a result of my breast trouble. Ewan's voice is much better, though not normal yet. The German attack on Verdun still rages but so far they have made no further progress. The struggle at present centres around "Dead Man's Hill"—so named surely by some prophet—and "Hill 304."[292] The carnage is dreadful but the French watchword is "They shall not pass."[293]

I read a horrible statement in a paper the other day. It haunts me. When I cannot sleep at nights it tears my soul. "No child under eight years of age is left alive in

[Stuart] Grave

[Stuart] Gay

---

291   LMM often puts in a period where normal convention would require a question mark. We have silently corrected this punctuation for clarity.

292   Between February 21 and December 18, 1916, the Battle of Verdun took place on hills north of Verdun, in northeastern France. The German Fifth Army attacked strategic French positions overlooking the city. "Dead Man's Hill" (*Mort-Homme*) and "Hill 304" (*Côte 304*) were key targets of German assault.

293   *On ne passe pas* ("they shall not pass") was a phrase made famous by French General Robert Nivelle during the Battle of Verdun.

Poland. They have all perished from starvation or exposure."[294]

And this is the year 1916 of the Christian era!

Thursday, March 23, 1916
Leaskdale Manse, Ont.

I have been having some bad night sweats and the breast trouble seems to have become chronic. I have lost so much sleep that I am getting terribly run down. I weigh only 109 pounds. I never weighed so little in my life. I have lost sixteen pounds in the last six weeks.

Ewan is not any too well either. Baby, though, is thriving like a weed.

Saturday, April 1, 1916

The war news was bad today—the Germans have captured Malancourt.[295] This is serious and yet it does not worry me. I have never felt any real alarm about Verdun since that strange Friday night. Nevertheless, the slaughter is sickening. I have been much better this week, having weaned baby finally. My breast seems to have got quite well and my night sweats have ceased.

Tuesday, April 11, 1916

The fifty-first day of the Verdun struggle! "God of battles, was there ever a battle like this in the world before?"[296] The Germans seem determined to take it. I do not believe they ever will, despite the fact that they have recently won some important successes at enormous cost. Nowhere, on any other front, is there any especial activity. *When* will the British strike their blow? We have waited so long—so long.

Wednesday, April 12, 1916

Mr. Noonan, of the Britton Publishing Company was here today, trying to get my new book for them. Well, there was a day when publishers did not hustle over one another to get my books! Mr. Noonan was one of

---

294   While the report that LMM read was likely an exaggeration, the people of Poland suffered a great deal during the war, positioned as a battleground between the Central Powers and Russia. Given the threat of mass starvation, for example, between 1914 and 1922, it is estimated that the American Relief Administration (ARA), established by Herbert Hoover, fed 200 million people.

295   Part of the Battle of Verdun (February 21–December 18). When German forces failed to take Hill 304, they moved around it to the southwest, capturing the French fort of Malancourt on March 22, 1916.

296   From Tennyson's *A Ballad of the Fleet*, a long poem commemorating the Spanish-British Battle of Flores (1591).

Page's salesmen for seventeen years. I asked him candidly to tell me his opinion of Page and his methods. His revelations were rather ghastly. Perhaps too much credence should not be given them. Yet Noonan is highly spoken of by book sellers. He said he left Page because he could not tolerate his methods any longer. The offer the Britton Co. made seemed a good one. But I feel all at sea. I have not sufficient knowledge of the publishing business to protect my own interests. I don't know whom to trust. I am afraid of Page. There are times when I half regret my old free-lance days of magazine writing. I could steer my own bark then. Now it seems rather beyond me.

Monday, April 17, 1916
The Manse, Leaskdale, Ont.

Am in a condition of worry tonight caused by a telegram from Page. I foresee much trouble. He wires that he has had "a very unsatisfactory interview with McClelland" and asks me to do nothing further in the matter until I hear from him, adding that he will write fully on Monday—the wire was sent Saturday night. I have no doubt that the interview was unsatisfactory because Page could not get his own way in everything. He is, I understand, that kind of a man. Well, the battle is evidently on, this poem business being in the nature of a preliminary skirmish. God defend the right!

Tuesday, April 18, 1916

I wrote a letter to Page today in which I told him a few plain truths about the matter of my poems.

The war news is fair. The French still hold at Verdun; but Roumania's attitude is giving cause of alarm.[297] Every week some new worry

---

297   From April 1916, LMM writes a great deal about the role of Romania in the war. Romania had not entered the war in 1914 on the side of Austria-Hungary, as it might have done, given the existence of a 1883 treaty stipulating that it would go to war in the event that Austria-Hungary came under attack. Instead, Romania remained neutral in 1914, on the grounds that Austria-Hungary had not been attacked but been the belligerent. Romanian opinion was divided about how to orient itself in the war. Some members of the Romanian government hoped to use the war to achieve national unity and territorial gains, particularly in Transylvania. Others were concerned about Russian territorial goals in Moldova and Bassarabia. Romania negotiated with both sides. Romania possessed a large army, but by comparison with the Central Powers, the army was poorly equipped in terms of technology and armaments. This was one of a range of Allied concerns about Romania but nevertheless negotiations continued, and, on August 17, 1916, Romania signed the treaty of Bucharest with the Allied countries, in secret. In exchange for entering the war on the Allied side, the treaty stipulated conditions of territorial expansion after the war as well as military and logistical support during the war. On August 27, Romania declared war and Romanian forces

crops up re the war. Nine tenths of the rumors turn out to be void of truth but one cannot tell whether a fresh one belongs to the nine-tenths or the one-tenth.

To-night we had our social Guild and Chester recited. He did pretty well, too. Of course, it was only a verse. He is only three and a half. It seems but the other day that he was a tiny baby; and now he can stand up and recite in Guild.

Thursday, Apr. 20, 1916

Yesterday the war news announced the capture of Trebizond by the Russians.[298] This is good, though perhaps it will not affect the main campaigns. But we have not much to rejoice over these days so we ran up the flag for the fall of Trebizond.

Chester at three-and-a-half

I am dreadfully tired tonight and worried to boot. Mr. McClelland came out today and we spent the whole day thrashing out various matters. He and Page had a battle royal over the matter of the poems—which is their affair. It is very much *my* affair, however, that in the course of their stormy interview Page uttered the threat that "the courts would decide the matter" if I gave my new book to anyone but him. If Page were not merely "bluff-ing" to intimidate McClelland I do not know what he meant. We have had some correspondence about the literary contents of my next book but I feel sure that there was nothing in my letters to bind me. I wish I had kept copies of them. Anyhow, I have given McClelland the right of placing the book in the U.S. market. If Page has any unknown hold on me I must have good backing; and if he hasn't he must be taught not to make threats like that—and after making a fortune out of my books on his niggardly contract! McClelland confirmed what Noonan told me, as far as his own firm went. I have been making some inquiries about the Mac firm and find them very well spoken of. But Page has rather shaken my faith in everyone. I shall not sleep much tonight.

---

crossed the Carpathian Mountains into Transylvania (coordinated with, as agreed in the Treaty, a separate Russian offensive into Bulgaria). It would eventually be a costly invasion for Romania (suffering losses of some 220,000 soldiers over the course of the war). A large part of Romania was occupied by enemy forces until the fall of 1918. But profiting from the victory of the Western Allies, Romania gained extensive territories at the Versailles Peace Conference in 1919.

298   The Trebizon Campaign was a successful battle by Russian land and naval forces to capture Trabzon, a city located on the northeast coast of modern-day Turkey (then part of the Ottoman Empire). It was not then widely known that as part of the larger Armenian genocide, some 50,000 Armenians had been massacred by the Turks in Trabzon in 1915.

We begin housecleaning tomorrow. Now for a month of hard work, combined with worry over the war and over the Page affair. Nice cheerful prospect!

Wednesday, Apr. 26, 1916
The Manse, Leaskdale

Every week we can confidently count on some new and startling and unexpected war news. This week it is the Sinn Fein rebellion in Ireland. The authorities claim to have it in hand but the situation is nasty.[299] The Verdun struggle goes on without cessation while the world holds its breath.

Page has never written yet in spite of his promise to do so. I suspect the reason of his silence is that he hopes *I* will write and give away what McClelland said about their interview. Then Page would have the chance of denying everything he wanted to, whereas, if he writes first, he runs the chance of saying things that will incriminate him in my eyes. Well, I shall not write. If Page is playing a double game he will hang himself if he is given enough rope.

Mr. McClelland advises me to join the Author's League of America.[300] He says it is a capital organization and a great help to authors. So I have applied for membership. I understand that Page has a wholesome respect for the League, having run up against it several times in his dealings with authors.

May 1, 1916, Monday.

Kut-el-Amara has been compelled to surrender at last.[301] We have expected it for some time but that did not prevent us from feeling very

---

299   The Easter Rising of 1916 was first called the Sinn Fein Rebellion in newspapers, although the Sinn Fein party was not involved; however, Sinn Fein was opposed to Irish involvement in the war and its leaders were interned in the aftermath of the rising. The insurrection had in fact been organized by Irish republicans with the goal of establishing Irish independence at a time when the United Kingdom was otherwise focused on the war. British forces had captured a shipment of German arms bound for the Irish rebels on April 21, 1916. On Easter Monday, April 24, 1916, a rebel force of some 1,600 men took over parts of Dublin. Within 6 days the British army had quelled the uprising, with numerous civilian casualties caught in the crossfire. Many rebels were arrested (and later released), with 16 executions.

300   Now known as the Author's Guild, the Author's League of America was established in 1912 to advocate for authors on issues of copyright and freedom of expression.

301   Between December 1915 and April 1916, Ottoman forces laid siege to the British-Indian garrison in Kut (160 km/100 miles south of Baghdad). The garrison was forced to surrender on 29 April, with many Briton and Indian soldiers taken captive. The surrender was seen as a humiliating loss to the British Empire, with the two generals responsible being removed from command.

blue over it all. It is an encouragement to the Germans and a blow to Britain's prestige. I feel too depressed tonight to do anything.

Page has never written yet. His silence is getting on my nerves because I believe it means he is hatching some deviltry. I have got so that I cannot sleep at nights and really I think I'll end up in a hospital or sanatorium. I understand that Page worried another of his authors into an asylum not long ago—and she was his cousin, too. I wrote recently to Bertie McIntyre asking her to investigate Page's standing with the Vancouver booksellers. She has answered with some lurid disclosures. The booksellers, one and all, condemn Page's methods utterly; and one added the information that he was not "straight"—that he had repudiated his gambling debts etc. From another source I have recently learned that Mildred Page is his second wife, his first wife having divorced him, and that he is notorious for immorality. It is all very sickening. I suppose there is nothing to do but break completely with him. And if he is the man rumor paints him he will make all the trouble he can for me, there is no doubt of that.

Friday, May 19, 1916
The Manse, Leaskdale

This was quite a day in the annals of our little village. The 116th Battalion which has been training in Uxbridge all winter and to which many of "our boys" belong made a route march through the township and passed here

Chester under arch outside of our gate

at noon.[302] We had several arches erected for them and treated them all to fruit and read them an address. Poor fellows. I wonder how many

[116th Battalion]

of them will ever return.

The Verdun carnage still goes on. The Germans have crept nearer the fortress but their losses are enormous. So are those of France. "Dead Man's Hill" must be soaked to the core with blood. And *still* England does not strike! God, *when* will this strain end?

---

302   The 116th was an infantry battalion of the Canadian Expeditionary Force that had been authorized on December 22, 1915; it would depart for Britain on 23 July 1916. The 116th received a range of battle honours, including at Vimy, Passchendaele, and Canal du Nord.

Wednesday, May 24, 1916
The Manse, Leaskdale

On Monday the long-expected letter came from Mr. Page—a very lengthy epistle. He makes several statements in it that I happen to know are false and several more that I am almost sure are false. He asked me to give a personal interview to his salesman Mr. Mullen who was in Toronto. So I went in on Tuesday and conferred with Mac's first. They told me they were quite intimate with Mullen who was a very fine fellow and who intended to leave Page as soon as his contract was up, being unable to tolerate his methods. I met Mullen at the King Edward and had a long talk with him. The first question he asked me was, "Are you a member of the Author's League?" Evidently Page had told him to find this out. I said I was and declined to discuss the question of my new book, saying that I had appointed Mac. my agent and he must apply to him. We had a long talk on various subjects and it was plain to be seen he had no good to say of Page, though he did not positively say evil of him. When we parted he said, "Have you any other questions you would like to ask me, Mrs. Macdonald?" I said, "Yes, but it would not be fair to ask them of Mr. Page's salesman." He then said, "Sometime in the future you may ask me those questions and I will answer them"—a remark which I would not have understood had it not been for what Mac had told me of Mullen's intention to leave Page as soon as his contract was out. It seems Page cannot keep his salesmen at all unless he binds them by contract. Of course, Mr. Mullen meant that his answers would not be favorable to Page, otherwise there could be no reason for his not answering the questions at once. Well, the die is cast. The issue is on the knees of the gods.

Thursday, May 25, 1916
The Manse, Leaskdale

I have written to Mr. Page, telling him that I have appointed McClelland my literary agents and that he must negotiate with them for my new book. I told him he was to have the first chance for it. I had insisted on this, although Mac. was not any too well inclined that way. But I shall be fair if Page is not. He shall have his chance, even though I would prefer, in the light of recent revelations, to break with him altogether.

The war news is very bad. At Verdun the French have again lost Douamont and in Italy the Austrians have begun a drive that bids fair to have disastrous results for the Italian army.[303]

---

303   Douamont was the highest of several forts protecting the city of Verdun. It was lost and

We are having the wettest spring on record. It has rained almost every day since the first of April and is also very cold. We have had none of the lovely spring weather we usually have here. It all makes the worry and strain and suspense harder to bear. Well, "he that endureth to the end shall be saved."[304] But what about those who are not strong enough to endure to the end?

Thursday, June 1, 1916
The Manse, Leaskdale

The war news continues depressing and dubious. The Austrians are driving the Italians back and the Germans are slowly gaining ground at Verdun. There are rumors of strange doings at Saloniki also, and Greece's attitude is again causing anxiety.[305] I have been very busy, sleep poorly and feel tired and spiritless all the time. And rain! Will it *ever* stop raining? I don't think we have had three wholly fine days since the first of April. *Mark Tapley*, this would conquer even you!

Friday, June 2, 1916

I awakened this morning with an odd conviction that good war news was coming. But there was certainly nothing in today's papers to justify it—quite the reverse, in fact, because the news from the Italian front

---

recaptured several times before being taken by the French Second Army on October 24, 1916. Italy had been part of the Triple Alliance, with Germany and Austria-Hungary; however, it had not entered the war on the side of the Central Powers in 1914. Italy instead had entered into secret negotiations with the Allies, culminating in the 1915 Treaty of London, signed by the United Kingdom, Russian, France, and Italy. In May 1915, Italy entered the war on the side of the Allies. The Italian army engaged mostly with Austria in difficult terrain, and suffered heavy losses throughout 1915 and 1916. In May 1916 Austria launched what would be known as the Trentino Offensive.

304   "But he that shall endure unto the end, the same shall be saved" (Matthew 24:13).

305   Greece was a divided country in World War I. A treaty in place between Greece and Serbia stipulated that Greece would help Serbia in the event of a Bulgarian invasion. But Greece had remained neutral in 1914. King Constantine I—referred to often by LMM—was married to Kaiser Wilhelm's sister, Sophia of Prussia. Moreover, Constantine believed that Germany would win the war, and therefore Greece should stay out of the conflict. On the other side of the divide was Prime Minister Eleftherios Venizelos, who supported the Allies. When Bulgaria began mobilizing against Serbia in September 1915, Venizelos gave orders for a Greek counter-mobilization. King Constantine I resisted, favouring a policy of neutrality. Venizelos, however, allowed an Entente military base to be established in Thessaloniki ("Saloniki") and obtained a declaration of war from parliament. Constantine removed Venizelos from office, unconstitutionally, on October 5, 1915. The particular event that LMM is likely referring to took place in May 25, 1916, when the Athens government (loyal to Constantine) allowed Bulgarians to take over a military base—Fort Rupel—north of Thessaloniki. Venizelos's supporters saw this as an act of betrayal, calling for the overthrow of the Athens government. In the months that followed the schism deepened. In September 1916, Venizelos joined the pro-Entente provisional government of northern Greece, based in Thessaloniki, and began to raise troops in support of the Allies.

was very bad. There is also a report, however, that the long-looked-for British offensive is soon to begin. Perhaps this is true and my presentiment may have had reference to it. The French are still holding out at Verdun and there is a fresh crop of alarming rumors about Greece.

Saturday, June 10, 1916

It seems to me that *everything* has been crowded into the past eight days—as if every emotion possible has been experienced. It has been horrible beyond words. This war is slowly killing me. I am bleeding to death as France is being bled in the shambles of Verdun. On last Saturday came the first news of the battle of Jutland—and it was announced as a *German* Victory![306] I felt as if I had received a staggering blow in the face from a trusted friend. And the physical effects of that blow were not removed when on Monday the news came that the first reports were German lies and that instead it had been a British victory though a dear-bought one. Never shall I forget that intervening Sunday. If the British navy had failed in what were we to trust? On Monday morning I drove Ewan to the station on his way to the General Assembly in Winnipeg and the morning papers were a relief. On Tuesday Mrs. Oxtoby and I drove to Sunderland to attend a meeting of the W.F.M.S. Presbyterial. I went in good spirits, for the *Globe* had brought an encouraging report of a sudden blow and a big victory for Russia on the eastern front. But my elation was short lived. During the afternoon the word came of Lord Kitchener's death off the Orkneys![307]

I cannot describe the effect the news had on me. Since the Boer War Kitchener has seemed little less than a demi-god. He was the greatest man and the most dramatic figure in the British Empire. His death brought to me an agonizing sense of personal loss. I have felt as if I were in a bad dream ever since.

Well, perhaps Kitchener's death is the last sacrifice demanded by the god of battles and from now on the tide will turn.

On Thursday the war news was mixed. The Germans have captured Vaux[308] and so advanced a long stride towards Verdun; but on the Eastern front the Russians are sweeping onward in an amazing fashion and

---

306   On May 31 and June 1, 1916, the Royal Navy's Grand Fleet engaged Germany's High Seas Fleet in the North Sea near Jutland, Denmark. Fourteen British and eleven German ships were sunk, with great loss of life. Both sides claimed victory.

307   On June 5, 1916 Field Marshal Kitchener was one of 600 who drowned when the HMS *Hampshire* struck a German mine and sank west of the Orkney Islands, Scotland. He had been making his way to Russia to attend negotiations.

308   Fort Vaux, outside Verdun, fell to German forces on June 7, 1916.

have captured 75,000 Austrians.[309] This will certainly relieve the pressure on Italy and may even lighten that on Verdun. On Thursday came word that they had captured Lutzk.

I am ill at present with a bad cold and I am sleeping wretchedly. Sometimes I feel that life is *too* hard—that I cannot endure it any longer.

Monday, June 12, 1916
The Manse, Leaskdale

The Russian advance continues. Dubno has been taken and 108,000 prisoners.[310] The Austrian invasion of Italy has been checked and the whole situation eased up.[311] God grant that it continue.

Saturday, June 17, 1916

This has been a week of worry. I have neither eaten or slept much. I had a letter from Page on Tuesday threatening a lawsuit if I give the book to anyone but him. The letter reveals the scoundrel in the man and confirms all I have heard of him. I do not believe anything I have written can give him any hold on me, but I have not copies of my letters and it is of course possible that some incautious phrase, used innocently, may give him some ground for legal claim. On the other hand, he may be merely "bluffing." Anyhow, he shall not frighten me. I will fight him now to the last ditch. But my resolve cannot prevent his threats from worrying me and life has been nightmarish this week.

The war news has been good—the Russians continuing their advance and taking an immense number of prisoners.

The General Assembly has voted for church union.[312] I expected

---

309   The Brusilov Offensive of June to September 1916 involved a major Russian attack against the Austro-Hungarian army in what is now western Ukraine. The offensive was launched on June 4, 1916 with a huge artillery barrage and shock troops. Austrian forces began to retreat and on June 8 Russian forces took Lutsk, a town in northwestern Ukraine that had been seized by Austria-Hungary on August 29, 1915. Overall, the Russians took over 200,000 prisoners in what remains one of the most successful offensives in military history.

310   On June 9, 1916 Dubno in western Ukraine was another town successfully captured by Russian forces.

311   Throughout 1916 Italian and Austrian forces battled for territory in what is now northeast Italy. The situation became very serious in late May, when Austrian forces broke through Italian lines in the Trentino Offensive. However, on June 4 Russian forces advanced in Galicia (now western Ukraine) such that Austrian forces were withdrawn from the area for reinforcements elsewhere. In this way the situation was stabilized, although what was felt to be mismanagement of the Italian army would lead to volatility in Italian politics.

312   Union of three mainstream Protestant churches in Canada—the Methodist, Presbyterian, and Congregationalist—was considered from the start of the twentieth century. On June 10, 1925, the United Church of Canada was formed. About one-third of Presbyterian congregations, however, chose not to join the United Church as "continuing" or "non-concurring"

they would but I feel bitterly on the subject. I have never been in favor of union, although Ewan is. But when the whole world is rent and torn what matter another rending and tearing? Our old world is passed away forever—and I fear that those of us who have lived half our span therein will never feel wholly at home in the new.

I have a nasty, queer, crampy feeling in my hand nowadays when I write. I am really terribly run down. Since the New Year I have been constantly either worried or ill and often both, and there seems to be no prospect of a respite.

I began to write my new book on Friday—"Anne's House of Dreams."[313] I have been getting the material for it in shape all winter and spring. I am not likely to have much pleasure in the writing of it, with Page's threats hanging over my head. Oh, it all makes me heartsick.

Stuart is well and flourishing. He is known locally as "the baby who never cries."

Friday, June 30, 1916

"I should worry." [Stuart]

I have been miserable ever since my last entry with my old trouble cystitis. I know of no ailment that can poison life so utterly. This past ten days I have been abjectly wretched. And yet I must go about—attend to social and parish and Red Cross duties—see to my children and household—write—sew—plan. I love doing these things when I am well—but just now I don't know how I keep up from one day to another.

The war news is mixed. The Germans are still creeping up to Verdun and it really seems as if they might get it yet. But the Russian advance continues splendidly. *When will the British strike?*

Presbyterians. A Supreme Court decision in 1939 restored to the non-concurring Presbyterians the right to use the name "The Presbyterian Church in Canada," which still exists. Interestingly, the Leaskdale Church of which Ewan Macdonald was the minister chose in the end not to join the United Church.

313   The fifth in the Anne series, *Anne's House of Dreams* was published in 1917 by McClelland, Goodchild, and Stewart.

Monday, July 3, 1916
The Manse, Leaskdale, Ont.

Yesterday evening people came up from Whitby with the news that the British *have* struck at last. On Saturday they broke the German first line in the valley of the Somme.[314] To-day's mail confirmed the news. Has the "Big Push" begun? Are our long days of waiting over? One hardly dares to hope it.

Misery is still my portion physically. Woe is me!

Thursday, July 6, 1916

The British and French are still creeping onward. Verdun is still in danger, though. The weather is very hot and dry. Yesterday I enjoyed (?) an experience which has not been mine since I came to Ontario—picking wild strawberries in their native haunts. Had it not been for my persistent ailment I would not have needed to put the question mark after "enjoyed" in spite of the heat and mosquitoes. Edith and I drove ourselves and the children over to her home in Zephyr and picked in their clearing for the afternoon. But I never felt well and was worn out when I got home. Strawberry picking is not what it was in the good old days—or I am not!!

"It's hot—but

Sunday Afternoon
July 30, 1916

I am sitting on the veranda, trying vainly to get a breath of cool air. The children are asleep beside me—Stuart in his basket and Chester in the hammock—both suffering from the heat. July has been a terrible month—not a drop of rain and the most intense burning heat, especially for the past eighteen days. I never

—I feel pretty comfortable" [Stuart]

---

314   Between July 1 and November 18, 1916 British and French forces launched the Somme Offensive. It was one of the largest battles of World War I—and in human history—with more than 1,000,000 men wounded or killed.

recall anything like it in my life. I feel the heat all the more because of my ailment which has persisted now for six weeks. It makes life a burden to me and embitters everything. Yesterday was a nightmare of suffering from my trouble and the heat combined. To-day I feel fairly well, so suffer mainly from the heat. Ewan, too, has been miserable all the month with rheumatism or neuritis in arm and back. Fortunately, the children have kept well so far. Stuart is such a darling—just a big white dumpling with such large, lovely blue eyes. Chester is growing. His favorite post these days is perched on the gate post watching passing cars and teams. He sits there by the hour.

The Warden of the Gate [Chester]

It is well that with all this discomfort and suffering the war news is good. Were it like last July I don't see how we could live. The British and French are still creeping on in the Somme Valley—nothing spectacular yet—nothing to fly the flag for, but steady progress which all the German counter attacks cannot check. Russia is doing marvellously—her resurgence seems like a miracle. The Verdun crisis *seems* past—but it has seemed past many times before.

On July 12th I had a very nasty letter from Page re-iterating his threats of a law suit. I did not reply to it but of course it worries me. The next day I went into Toronto to meet Mr. Jewett of Appleton's who had come up to bid for my book. He made me an offer which made me gasp, comparing it to Page's niggardly contracts. The Mac. firm has been snowed under with offers. Humph! It was rather different when I was peddling *Anne* about from place to place!

In one of his letters Mr. Page referred to this and asked me to remember that *he* had accepted my book when other houses turned it down. Well, I *did* remember this—though he did not accept it out of pity or consideration for me but simply because he thought it would succeed. And his belief in its success was *not* due to his own superior insight in discovering its merit. I have recently found out just how *Anne* came to be accepted by the house of Page. Page himself was strongly opposed to accepting it—wanted to turn it down. But there were on his staff at that time two people. One was a Miss Arbuckle from Summerside, P.E. Island. *She* had been interested in the book because of its scene. She had read it with more care than most readers bestow on a manuscript from an unknown author and she had talked about it to the other readers and piqued their interest too. A young man—Hardress, or some such name, who was then on the staff, liked the book and insisted that it should be taken and Louis Page yielded to their opinions and accepted the book. Louis Page does not know that I know this and as I was told it in confidence by one of his salesmen I cannot retort upon him with it but must accept his reproach of ingratitude to him in silence.

I liked Mr. Jewett and Appleton's is a good firm. I think probably I shall accept his offer but the matter is not definitely settled yet. I went in last week to meet Mr. Dominick of Stokes who also made a good offer; but I think I prefer the Appleton firm.[315] I wish it were all settled. I do not want ever to have to change publishers again. I want to form "a partnership for life" as Mr. Jewett says.

Recently I had a letter from Annie Fellowes Johnston, the author of the "Little Colonel" series.[316] She published with Page for twenty years and has recently left him, as has also another popular author, Mrs. Porter of *Pollyanna* fame.[317] I wrote to Mrs. J. and asked her why she had left Page etc. She wrote fully in reply. He behaved as badly as possible to her—refused flatly to give her any better terms and then when she gave her last book to another firm bombarded her with insulting telegrams, letters and threats of law-suits etc. She says she seriously doubts the man's sanity—he does so many things flatly opposed to his own interests. The same thought had crossed my mind before her letter came. It is a consoling prospect truly to reflect that my seven books, which properly handled ought to bring me in good returns for many years yet are hopelessly in the power of so unscrupulous and vindictive a man.

The queer, persistent, indefinable distrust I felt regarding Mr. Page during that visit in Boston has been justified.

The only thing I regret in changing publishers is that my books will never be quite so nicely gotten up again. The Page firm are the best bookmakers in America. Everybody admits that.

Tuesday, Aug. 1, 1916
The Manse, Leaskdale, Ont.

Verily, no wonder we found Sunday hot. It was 98 in the shade. Yesterday a delicious cool wave reached us and today was delightful. But I am

---

315   The F.A. Stokes Company was not as well established as D. Appleton & Company. Appleton had been founded and 1831 and was known for publishing many important names. Stokes, however, was at this time rapidly gaining a good reputation in the publishing world.

316   Annie Fellows Johnston (1863–1931) was an American author of a popular children's book series beginning with *The Little Colonel* in 1895.

317   American novelist Eleanor Hodgman Porter (1868–1920) was a best-selling author of children's fiction and tales of adventure and romance. Pollyanna was the eighth best-selling novel in the U.S. in 1913, its year of publication.

still miserable and have a racking sick headache tonight also. Yesterday evening I felt fairly well and had a rare hour reading Rupert Brooke's poems.[318] They are very wonderful. His "Song of the Pilgrims" is one of the most exquisite things I have ever read. One feels that a great poet died in Lemnos, a victim to that fatal Gallipoli error. One drop of his blood was worth an ocean of Hun gore. If he could do such in youth what might he not have done in maturity? But he sleeps well and the Kaiser and his six sons are all well and thriving. So the world is not left wholly desolate!

Wednesday, Aug. 2, 1916

Woke early this morning and as usual could not sleep again. I have slept miserably ever since the New Year. My nerves have never recovered from the shock of Chester's illness, the strain of the winter and the agony of Verdun. Finding I could not sleep I sat up and read a bundle of Mr. MacMillan's letters I had wanted to look over.[319] They were all very delightful but seemed to belong to a world and a day gone by. I felt very miserable all day but had to "keep going" as raspberries and cherries had to be canned.

Tuesday, Aug. 8, 1916

If today had been like yesterday—but it was not!

The past week has been unrelentingly hard. Thursday was hot and close again. We were busy all day preparing for a Guild garden party. As I was on the committee of programme, was physically miserable, and had the two children to look after, I need not say that the evening was more or less of a nightmare to me. I breathed a weary, "Thank God" when it was over.

Friday, Saturday and Sunday continued hot. On Saturday E. went to Kirkfield to exchange with Mr. Lindsay who came Saturday night and stayed till this morning in order to lecture last night for the Red Cross. He was a rather nice fellow and quite an interesting conversationalist—or at least seemed to be by contrast with the residents of this community. I fairly starve at times for a little *real* conversation. But what matters it? If I could only feel well again and get rid of this horrible trouble I would not mind anything else. The inanities of current talk

---

318   Rupert Brooke (1887–1915) was a promising poet, particularly of war poetry. Brooke died from an infected mosquito bite while on active duty in Greece. LMM used a quotation from Brooke as an epigraph for *Anne's House of Dreams*.

319   G.B. Macmillan was a long-time correspondent (see note for July 19, 1911).

would not weary me then—they would slip unnoticed over my inner kingdom—a kingdom of which I am at present utterly dispossessed most of the time by the nagging discomfort of the flesh.

Yesterday was in some respects really the worst day I ever spent in my life. The heat, oppression and sultriness were terrible. The house seemed like a hot, wet oven. When night came I felt limp, flaccid, spineless. But I dressed up, took both the children, and went to the Red Cross lecture. I nursed the heavy sleeping baby, kept Chester in his chair—it's beyond the power of any mortal to keep him *still*—answered his ceaseless questions—for I believe children's questions *should* be answered if it is at all possible—and felt sick with my inseparable misery.

Today brought a truly blessed change—some nice showers and a cool fresh air. I could have danced with joy to see the good rain falling on the famished earth. I felt better to-day, too.

This evening I had a rather curious experience. I read the last chapter of a serial story, all the other chapters of which I read—thirty-three years ago!

When Well Nelson was in Cavendish his aunt sent him a magazine called "Wide Awake"—a capital juvenile. During the last year it came a serial by Harriet Prescott Spofford ran in it—"A Girl and a Jewel."[320] I revelled in it. But alas, it was not quite concluded before the magazine ceased to come. And it stopped just at the most exciting, dramatic point! I never found out what happened and who "Lucia" really was. And now, more than 30 years after, I read the last chapter and solve the mystery. Recently, I had a chance to purchase four bound volumes of the old *Wide Awake* and I got them for the children. It is impossible to tell how much I have enjoyed re-reading them and what delight they gave me—a strange, eerie pleasure as of a journey back into the past. It was not only that their contents had still a literary relish even for my maturer taste; but as I read I seemed to be back again in the surroundings of the days in which I read them first. I was back in the old home in Cavendish. Grandfather and grandmother, and Dave and Well were there. The blue gulf sparkled beyond. The spruces and maples crowded about the old house. The orchards were fairy-haunted. Our little playhouse waited for us in the fir wood. I went again to the white washed school on the crest of the hill; the stars were in their right places in the heavens; the cherries were ripe on summer evenings; a world utterly

---

320   Wellington Nelson and his brother David had lived for some years with with LMM's family following the death of the boys' parents. Harriet Elizabeth Prescott Spofford (1835–1921) was an American novelist and popular contributor of periodical fiction and poetry.

passed away was my universe once more. I felt curiously homesick and strange, every time I shut the book and came back to this one.

Sunday, Aug. 13, 1916
The Manse, Leaskdale

This has been a busy week—the Red Cross lecture Monday, a trip to Uxbridge and the Missionary society Wednesday, the Red Cross Thursday and the Mission Band yesterday—and two hours writing every morning at "Anne's House of Dreams." But I growl not; for it has been cool, with one beautiful rain and—mercy of mercies!—I have been well. My cystitis has disappeared with the suddenness that always marks its going; I have been sleeping splendidly, as I have not done for a year and a half—nay, more, as I have not done since Chester was born. Oh, if I can only get really well and keep well!

Thursday came the great news of the Italians' capturing Goritz— something they have been trying to do for a year and a half.[321] It is an important victory, as is also the Russian capture of Stanislaus.[322] We have victories tri-weekly now. How it is with others I know not but they bring to me no feelings of jubilation. All that passed forever in that dreadful summer last year and the still more dreadful last spring. Verdun has slain all exultation. I only feel a dazed relief, hardly vivid enough yet to be called thankfulness—as a man just loosened from the torment of the rack might feel.

I often recall that curious experience of mine that terrible March night last winter—when after hours of agony the sudden great peace came to me. I believe and always shall believe that on that night the Genius of Victory left the German lines and passed over to the Entente powers. Since then the Central Empires have won no lasting successes and they have sustained some serious defeats. But the end is not yet.

Saturday, Aug. 19, 1916
The Manse, Leaskdale, Ont.

This has again been a hot day but the past week has been rather cool and pleasant—and oh, so dry! Everything is scorched up. My flower

---

321 Following heavy fighting between Italian and Austrian armies, Gorizia ("Goritz") in northeastern Italy was recaptured by Italian troops, with heavy casualties on the Italian side.

322 LMM misspells Stanislau as "Stanislaus." This city in Galicia, western Ukraine (now most commonly called Ivano-Frankovsk) was taken by the Russians on August 7. Stanislau was near the maximum western advance of the Brusilov offensive (see note for June 10, 1916).

garden this summer is an utter failure. I was not able to water it as I have done in other droughts.

I was in Toronto Tuesday over this interminable business of contracts. A question of possible serial publication has come up and I have to prepare a synopsis of the book. I have been working feverishly at it every evening since and writing all the forenoon at the book itself. I do my writing in the parlor now, as said parlor possesses the only door in the house which young Chester cannot open. Besides, it is a pleasant, green, summer-like room and has an agreeable effect on me. Wednesday and Thursday I was miserable with an attack of bowel trouble. Naturally, visitors took that day for appearing.

The Russians have captured Tarnapol heights[323] and the British and French have renewed their offensive, which lately seemed to have been petering out. I am horribly tired. It is now 10.30 and I have been working at my synopsis for three hours.

Monday, Aug. 21, 1916

We have had two days of terrible heat—100 in the shade. Last night sleep was all but impossible from the heat.

I was intensely shocked on reading the *Guardian* today to find an account of the accidental drowning of Mrs. Bayfield Williams—Edith England—in Edmonton. In company with several friends she was out boating on a lake at a summer resort near Edmonton; a sudden squall came up; the boat went down and all on board were lost.

Edith and I lost touch with one another after she and Bayfield went west. But on seeing this notice of her tragic death the old girlhood affection revived in my heart. I was very fond of Edith once. She was a sweet, kind-hearted little girl. I remember our first meeting—that summer day twenty-two years ago when I alighted from the train at Ellerslie station and she and Bayfield met me. Edith and I were chums all that year. Many a night we spent together in her beautiful home and poured endless confidences into each other's ears, after the immemorial fashion of girlhood. And now one is taken and the other—as yet—is left. Poor little Edith! Her girlhood was very bright and happy, as the indulged and idolized only child of well-to-do parents. I used to envy her in some ways. But I do not think life was very rosy for her after her marriage. Bayfield was dissipated and more than once they were on the verge of financial ruin. I am sorry for her mother who is living alone in the old home at Bideford, husband and child both gone. "Why can't yesterday come back, mother?" Chester asked me the other day. Oh,

---

323   A city in western Ukraine (now Ternopil).

my little laddie, you asked one of the saddest and most unanswerable questions in life.

Tuesday, Aug. 29, 1916
The Manse, Leaskdale, Ont.

All this year, just as soon as I would get over one thing and begin to feel a little like living I would take some new misery. I have just had quite the worst attack of grippe I ever had in my life. On Friday afternoon Ewan and I drove down to Uxbridge to take tea with some friends. We drove around by the Brock road. It was a beautiful afternoon, cool and sunny, and I enjoyed the drive down very much, in spite of a touch of sore throat. It is so seldom in our busy life that we can get off for a little pleasant drive like that. Mostly when we go driving it has to be with the object of making a "pastoral call."

Coming home was quite another thing. It had turned bitterly cold and although I had a heavy coat I felt chilly all the way home. Just after I got home I took a most dreadful chill. I could *not* get warm. Bed, piles of clothes, and hot water bottle availed not. Finally after an hour's misery burning heat succeeded, shortly followed by floods of perspiration which lasted all night. Saturday I spent in bed, too weak to lift my head, and with a sore throat that grew steadily worse until Sunday morning. I could neither speak nor swallow. I was afraid of tonsilitis, so had the doctor; but he said it was only a bad sore throat and left medicine which helped me a little. Yesterday I dragged myself up. It was wash-day and Edith could hardly do all the work and attend to the children, too. I managed to keep going but the grasshopper was a burden. Unexpected company also arrived and stayed to tea. Today I feel somewhat better but very useless. I have no appetite and I never saw such a face on top of my body as a look in the glass shows me—thin, hollow, paper white. I am thinner now than I ever was in my life—I weigh only 107 1/2 lbs.

Roumania has declared war on Germany and Austria.[324] She has haggled and bargained for two years and as her motive for entry is strictly selfish I do not give her any great meed of admiration. But her help will be welcome and her entrance into the war is certainly the handwriting on the wall for the Central Powers. She would not have climbed down on the side of the Entente if she had not been sure that they were going to win.

---

324   See note for April 18, 1916. On August 28, 1916 the Romanian Army had invaded Transylvania, then part of the Austro-Hungarian Empire.

Saturday, Sept. 2, 1916
Leaskdale, Ont.

This has been for me a dragging profitless week. I don't seem to pick up. I have no appetite and have "gone stale" on everything. Ewan, too, has been suffering severely from neuritis in his arm with a resultant loss of sleep for him and myself.

Thursday Jas. Mustard's received a telegram stating that Allan had been shot in the back.[325] He had been at the front only for a few days. They do not know yet if the wound is serious or not. Poor Allan! He and Will were to dinner here when Frede was here Christmas week and I asked myself then what would be their fate.

I am tired and useless and don't care—at present—what happens to me.

Monday, Sept. 4, 1916
The Manse, Leaskdale.

The war news was good today—the Russians have won an important victory on the Dneister, the French have captured Clery and the British have taken Guillemont.[326] Good news? I wonder if the wives and mothers whose husbands and sons were killed for it will call it very good news.

Ewan and I spent the evening calling on an old couple in the village. The old lady is about as graceful as the proverbial feather bed with the string tied round the middle. She entertained me by showing me photographs and Christmas cards! Heaven save the mark! It was certainly an evening of boredom. And yet that same waddling, uninteresting old dame has two sons at the front. So I take off my hat to her. She may be prosy—but she has done her bit.

I could hardly drag myself home—not because I was worn out by old Dame Colwell's honest effort to entertain, but simply because I was utterly tired, listless, "stale." I feel tired all the time. I cannot feel keenly interested in anything. The rack and strain of this horrible year has played me out.

---

325 The Mustards were a prominent local family. Allan Alexander Mustard, James and Jennie Mustard's son, was a gunner in the 8th Canadian Field Artillery Brigade.

326 The Russian victory was probably the capture of Lemberg (the German name for L'viv in Galicia, western Ukraine) in early September 1916. British and French armies were involved in the long, costly Battle of the Somme in northern France, capturing the strategic villages of Cléry-sur-Somme and Guillemont. The account LMM was reading may well have reflected some overly positive reporting; attacks and counter-attacks would continue through September.

Saturday, Sept. 9, 1916
The Manse, Leaskdale, Ont.

Have had a very busy week and have been tired all the time. Yesterday the war news was bad—the Roumanians have met with a serious defeat at Tetarkai in the Dobrudja.[327] I never heard of the Dobrudja before. Now it looms up in my new war-geography with sinister importance. Hitherto the Roumanians have been doing well, overrunning Transylvania at their own will and pleasure apparently.

I was weighed today—107 pounds. I never went as low as that before.

I've been especially busy this week, preparing for a short visit to Warsaw Ind. where Ewan's brother, Dr. Angus Macdonald lives.[328] If I were not taking the children I would look forward to it with pleasure; but as it is I feel only dread of it and a wish that it were all over and I safe home again. I am tired already. What will I be after looking after two young children away from home for ten days? Chester hasn't been very well this week either—his stomach is unsettled and he has no appetite. He hasn't had a sick spell since last February, even in all the hot weather; but I always dread his taking one. When Angus wrote asking us, I would rather not have gone. But Ewan wished to go and would not go alone. So I agreed to go for his sake. Edith will take her vacation at the same time and we will lock up the house. Mrs. Warner will feed Daff and water my plants.

The Walker House, Toronto, Ont.
Tuesday, Sept. 12, 1916

We left home at one today. Mr. Warner—our next door neighbor—motored us to the station and we came in on the afternoon train and had dinner here. I like an occasional dinner at an hotel—I like the lights and guests and the change of viands. Stuart sat in his high chair, his great blue eyes like stars, his cheeks like roses, and attracted the atten-

---

327   See note for April 18, 1916. Romania had entered the war in late August 1916, declaring war on Austria-Hungary and invading Transylvania. The Romanian army initially won considerable territory, pushing back the Austro-Hungarian First Army to outside of Sibiu in Transylvania. But within weeks the Central Powers had despatched reinforcements. A multi-national force commanded by Field Marshal August von Mackensen (a name that LMM mentions many times below) soon assembled in the south on the Bulgarian border, and attacked on September 1; this was soon followed by the September 6 surrender of the Romanian garrison of Turtucaia in northeast Bulgaria (which LMM refers to as "Tetarkai in the Dobrudja"; Dobruja—Dobrogea in Romanian and Dobrudzha in Bulgarian—is a historical region shared by both countries).

328   Angus Cameron McDonald (1865–1944)—the tombstone in the Oakwood Cemetery and obituary confirm the variation in spelling of the last name—was a prominent physician in Warsaw, a town in central Indiana. He established the first hospital there.

tion of all in his vicinity. Everybody seems to love him at sight. Chester is at the hard age—it is difficult to get him to behave properly at the table. Not that he is bad—only heedless and mischievous, and very determined to have his own way! Now we are up in our room. Ewan is reading, Chester is asleep and Stuart is having a glorious romp all over the bed.

Warsaw, Indiana.
Thursday, Sept. 14, 1916

Yesterday morning we rose at 6 and took the Chicago train at 8. In the evening we reached South Bend at 7.30. There is nothing to be said about the trip. The children were good but we all got very dirty and tired. At South Bend we had to wait until nine for the Interurban car to

x Dr. Angus Macdonald's House xx His private hospital

Goshen. At Goshen we had to wait half an hour for the car to Warsaw where we arrived at twelve. Edith and Angus met us in their car and we got here and tumbled into bed.

Warsaw is a typical "middle west" city of about 5,000. Angus and Edith have a nice home but no family. This afternoon Edith took us in her car to Winona Lakes—a very pretty spot.

Friday, Sept. 15, 1916
Warsaw, Ind.

It seems so strange to be in a country that is not at war! I did not realize until I came here how deeply Canada *is* at war—how *normal* a condition war has come to be with us. It seems strange to go out—on the street or to some public place—and see no Khaki uniforms, no posters of appeal for recruits, no bulletin boards of war despatches. It all makes me feel that I ought to be back home in the thick of it. And we miss our Toronto papers so. The papers Angus takes are all Chicago papers. They give a few official reports—nothing else.

Chester hasn't been well today. He seems to have caught cold while out motoring with his father and uncle today. I did not know he was going and he did not have on his overcoat. They put him in the back seat alone and man-like, forgot all about him—went away out into the country where a very bitter wind was blowing. When they came back the child was crying with cold and his bare legs were simply blue, for they had not even wrapped a rug around them. I admit I was a little provoked with Ewan. He promised, when I consented to go to Warsaw, that he would look after Chester and take him entirely off my hands. And this was how he did it! Since then Chester is fretful and won't eat. He is so fussy at the table that I feel ashamed, for Angus and Edith know little about children and seemed to think the child is very finicky, whereas he is half-sick. He is hearty enough when he is well. Stuart has been fussy today, too, because of cutting teeth, so that, between the two, I have had a harder day than if I were home working.

Angus is a very nice man—a really remarkable man in many ways. I like him immensely; but I find nothing congenial in Edith. She has been very kind in one way—takes us out in her car every day and spreads most elaborate meals for us. But she is one of those "pizen neat" housekeepers who turn pale at a fleck of dust. I know it is absolute agony for her when Stuart is eating a biscuit on the floor. She watches him with a fascinated eye and before he has jammed the last bit in his mouth she flies for broom and dust pan. As a result I am in constant misery, trying to keep the children from making a litter. This afternoon I had to smile to myself. Chester had gone to the window to look out at a passing train. When he turned away Edith sprang up, crossed the room, picked up the corners of the curtains which he had—very slightly—pushed aside, and matched them with the most scrupulous care. Then she sat down again with a martyr-like expression. She has given me some rather nasty digs because the children don't always shut the screen door quickly enough to prevent an odd fly or two getting in. I suppose it is all such second nature with her that she is hardly conscious of it. She certainly has no idea how it makes me feel. I am never comfortable or easy one moment I am in the house. Stuart is creeping everywhere now and I follow him about and try to keep him out of mischief.

Sunday, Sept. 17, 1916
Warsaw, Ind. U.S.

I am rather done up. Imprimis,[329] I have not had a decent sleep since coming here. We are near a transcontinental railway and trains roar past every few minutes during the night. Not being used to them they

---

329   From a contraction of the Latin *in primis*, "imprimis" is here used to denote the first of a number of items on a list.

keep me awake. Then Chester continues unwell—fretful and listless by day, feverish and restless by night. I am so worried lest his neck get like it was at New Year's again. His illness is completely spoiling my visit which would otherwise be rather pleasant, despite some drawbacks. Last evening we dined with Dr. and Mrs. Dubois at a hotel and then spent the evening in their home. They are nice people and as I did not have the children I enjoyed myself, though with a secret grumbling ache of worry over Chester and the war—for things are going badly in the Dobrudja and the Germans have won a great victory over the Roumanians.

Monday, Sept. 18, 1916
Warsaw, Ind. U.S.

Chester was quite sick all night—high fever and vomiting. He can eat nothing. We cannot get his bowels to move normally and he is certainly very miserable. We all went out motoring this afternoon. It would be so enjoyable if matters were right. But as it is I enjoy nothing. I only wish our visit was ended and we were safe home again.

Wednesday, Sept. 20, 1916

Chester was a little better yesterday and today. The fever seems gone but he will not eat and is so pale and listless—so unlike his usual rosy, active self. He wants to be on my knee all the time, poor little fellow. Nobody but "muvver" does when one is ill. I feel horribly "dragged." Oh, for one good night's sleep! We had a very delightful motor drive to Yellowbanks Lake this afternoon but I was too tired to enjoy it.

Stuart has been very good and entirely adorable.

Thursday Afternoon, September 21st, 1916
Warsaw, Ind. U.S.

Last night I had the first decent sleep I've had since I came here and feel much the better for it. But I am thankful our visit is ending. I knew it would be rather strenuous but Chester's illness has robbed it of any pleasure there might have been in it for me. Ewan, however, has had a good time and a beneficial change so I am glad for his sake that we came.

The war news this morning was bad again—another defeat in the Dobrudja for the Roumanians.[330] Chester is not at all well. He has com-

---

330   See notes for April 18, 1916 and September 9, 1916.

plained all day about his feet—declares it hurts him to walk. He has complained of this off and on ever since last Friday. The others think it is his boots that hurt him but I do not think so. I shall be glad when I get him home where I can put him on the diet that brought him round last winter. There is no sign of any trouble in his neck but after last winter I cannot help feeling worried, though I say not a word to anybody.

We had a last motor drive this afternoon and it was pleasant. When we came back I packed up. We leave at 7.30 this evening and I shall be a thankful woman when I once more find myself under my own roof-tree.

My Own Roof-Tree,
Sunday Evening, Sept. 24, 1916

I *am* here—and besottedly thankful. There was a time when I almost gave up hope of ever getting here! Seldom have I undergone a more strenuous twenty-four hours than those which followed our departure from Warsaw. I can laugh over them now—but ye gods! It was no laughing matter at the time.

We left Warsaw at 7.30 last Thursday evening on the Interurban car for South Bend. We did not get to South Bend until ten. It was not a pleasant drive. Chester kept half-crying and complaining about his feet. Stuart got excited and past his sleep and for the last hour cried almost incessantly. When we got to South Bend I went into the waiting room with the two children, both of whom were now dreadfully tired and sleepy. Ewan went off to see about the trunk and after what seemed to me, alone with those two worn-out babies, an endless time, he returned with the cheerful news that our trunk had not come. It *might*, so the officials said, be along on the eleven o'clock car!

But just then I refused to worry about a trunk. My one thought was to get to a hotel and get those children into bed. We got a taxi and went to the Oliver. They were full. After much telephoning they got a room for us at the Sheridan. We got another taxi and started again. Poor Chester kept asking tearfully when he could get into bed. His feet were so sore he could not walk and in our peregrinations his father had to carry him and one suitcase while I carried 26-pound Stuart and the shawl-strap. Well, we got to the Sheridan—a shabby, dirty place. Had Ewan and I been alone we would have turned and left. I would rather have spent the night in the waiting room of the station than in such a place. But with those two children we were helpless. So we went to our room. It was certainly the dirtiest place I ever was in. But there were two beds in it with decent linen and I was not long in getting those children into them. When I came to take off Chester's boots and stockings

I was aghast. No wonder the poor child had declared he was unable to walk. His feet and legs were swelled as large as mine to the knees, and were covered with angry-looking red blotches. I was terrified. But I got him into bed and warmly covered up and in a few minutes both he and Baby were sound asleep. As it was now eleven Ewan said he would go out and see if our trunk had come and also try to get something to rub on Chester's legs. Left alone I undressed and prepared for bed. I felt like sitting down and crying. I was cold, tired, hungry—and, worst of all, sick with anxiety over Chester's condition. What *could* be the matter with the child? I had never heard or read of anything like this.

It was nearly twelve when Ewan walked in, his face like a tombstone. "Oh, the trunk hasn't come!" I exclaimed. "The trunk has come. *That* is not the trouble," he said gloomily.

My heart gave a horrible jump. The thought that whirled into my head was, "He has seen a doctor and found out that there is something dreadfully wrong with Chester."

"What is the matter?" I cried. "Tell me, quick." "That idiot of a station master at Warsaw told me that the Chicago train got here at nine in the morning. Instead it gets here at nine at night. We will either have to wait here until tomorrow night or catch the train that goes through at two o'clock tonight."

At first, in my relief that his gloom did not concern Chester I heard the news almost gaily. On second thoughts, I saw that we were confronted with two very disagreeable alternatives. We would have to waken up and dress those two tired children, one of them ill, and scuttle down to the station to catch that two o'clock train, with no likelihood of getting a berth at that late hour; or we would have to hang around that miserable hotel, till nine the next evening, we would not get home until Saturday night, there would be nothing to eat in the house and Fraser was coming to preach on Sunday; worst of all, suppose Chester was worse in the morning, there in that wretched hotel in a strange town. That last supposition decided me. I must at least get him to Toronto where we would be near friends and home.

I dressed and repacked. Then I dressed Stuart. The poor mite was so lost to the world that he lay like a log, never waking, while I pulled his clothes on. I dreaded waking Chester but the poor little soul was a brick. I told him when I waked him that we were going to get on the train to go home and he was so eager to get home that he made no fuss. We could not get his boots on, so I wrapped his legs in baby's shawl and Ewan carried him. We got our taxi and whisked to the station where we had to wait twenty minutes in a cold room as the train was late. E.

had to go out to see about our luggage and berths and Stuart, now too thoroughly wakened up, cried until I had to walk with him. Poor Chester kept saying, "Oh, will we soon get to our cosy home, muvver?" and from my heart I echoed the wish. I was desperately tired, hungry, cold and worried.

At last the train came. We could not get berths but a drawing room was vacant. We simply had to have it, though the expense was considerable and in the present tied-up state of my finances, with Page's threats hanging over my head, every dollar counts. But we had to wait twenty minutes in the smoking

Photo of Ewan, taken in Warsaw

room until it was made up and it seemed an hour. I don't remember any time in my life when I was more thankful than I was when I finally got into that section and got the children into those clean white beds. I was too tired to sleep myself but I *rested* and by morning the worst of our trip was over. When we went to the dining car for breakfast the first thing I saw was a *Mail and Empire* with a big headline, "Teutons defeated in Dobrudja,"—and then came a boy with Toronto *Globes*. I clutched one with the avidity of a starving man and ate my breakfast with an appetite sharpened by good news.

Chester's legs were much better. The red spots had gone and the swelling much reduced, although he could not put his boots on. He seemed much better and brighter also.

We reached Toronto just in bare time to catch the Uxbridge train. From Uxbridge we motored home and arrived here in a pouring thunderstorm to find, of course, the house dark and locked. But we soon got the key, got the house lighted and warmed, the kiddies in bed and a good old supper of fried steak on the table. Verily, I blessed the fates for my home.

Yesterday I was very busy, as Edith is still away. Chester seems much better and the swelling has quite gone from his legs, but he still limps a little and complains that it hurts him to walk. I cannot but feel anxious about him.

Wednesday, Sept. 27, 1916
Leaskdale, Ont.

Edith came last night, for which I am glad, life being rather strenuous with everything to do. Monday I washed in the morning and canned corn in the afternoon. Last night I had a night of sleepless worry about Chester. He still complains of his leg and I am haunted by the fear that it may be some form of tuberculosis of the bone. Shier's hints of last winter are ever lying in wait in my mind, to rush out and fasten on me in a downcast hour.

There has been good news from the Somme front lately—British and French have made important advances. But it is all so dreadfully slow—and at such a cost. Combles was captured yesterday.[331]

Wednesday, Oct. 4, 1916

Very busy all the time. Oh, for a rest! If I could just go to bed for a week and do *nothing* but just lie there! Instead, I must be a-going every waking minute. Monday there was bad news of the defeat of the Roumanians at Hermanstadt.[332] In the afternoon I went to Uxbridge and had a pleasant hour at the Hypatia club. Then we had tea at Mr. Willis' at night. Chester was with us. He looked well and behaved nicely. His legs have got perfectly well, so I suppose my anxiety was groundless. He is rosy and hearty again. Tuesday we had our Missionary Society Thank-offering meeting and tea in the afternoon—a most deadly bore. I gladly gave my Thank-offering but would have been more thankful still if I could have had the afternoon to rest. Rushed home from the tea, got everybody ready and went to a Guild Social at night, where Mrs. Lapp and I arranged for a Tag day in aid of our Red Cross at the Scott fair. Today I feel played out but wrote two hours at my book as usual and did a hundred other things.

Thursday, Oct. 5, 1916

Today I finished "Anne's House of Dreams." I never wrote a book in so

---

331 As part of the larger Somme Offensive, Combles, a small strategic village in north-east France, was captured on September 26, 1916, along with equipment, ammunition and engineering stores abandoned by the Germans.

332 Romanian forces had successfully captured considerable territory in Transylvania in central Romania in the early days following their entry into the war on the Allied side. However German reinforcements soon arrived and halted Romanian progress, retaking the Transylvanian city of Hermannstadt (now Sibiu).

short a time and amid so much strain of mind and body. Yet I rather enjoyed writing it and I think it isn't too bad a piece of work. I am glad it is done however. It has taken a lot out of me. Mrs. Lapp came this afternoon and we made the boxes for Tag Day.

Tuesday, Oct. 10, 1916

Had to go to the Scott fair today because of our Tag effort, and of course had to take the children as Edith was a Tag girl. It was bitterly cold, with a high wind and the whole thing was a nightmare to me. I got home very much disgruntled—but we made $50 for our Red Cross.

The war news has been bad of late. The Roumanian situation is very dubious.[333] Germany is putting forth every effort to crush Roumania and will, I fear, succeed. And yet—I had a strange dream before the German offensive against Roumania began—the very same kind I had before the Verdun offensive and once again before that when the drive against Russia began. And if it "comes true" as it did twice before Roumania will not be wholly crushed. Yet is not my faith strong enough to save me from worry.

Thursday, Oct. 12, 1916
The Manse, Leaskdale

There was good news today of a big Italian victory on the Carso.[334] That should help Roumania a little.

I had a letter from Aunt Annie today.[335] Poor Uncle John is very feeble and a great care. I hardly think he can live through the winter. The thought brings no *new* pain. I realized last summer that the Uncle John Campbell I had always loved was *already* gone—nothing but his outworn shell remained in the old home. And now, considering what his condition entails on Aunt Annie, I feel that it would be better if he were taken.

And yet—and yet—!

"So many friends I loved are gone,
Oh, death, be careful of the rest—
I cannot spare another one!"[336]

---

333   See entries for April 18, 1916, September 9, 1916, and October 4, 1916.

334   Italy took some limited ground in the Karst Plateau ("the Carso") in north-east Italy.

335   LMM's Aunt Annie (daughter of her maternal grandparents, Alexander and Lucy Woolner Macneill) and Uncle John Campbell.

336   From "How Many Friends I Loved Are Gone" by Richard Le Gallienne (1866–1947), in his

Tuesday, Oct. 17, 1916

Last Friday I had a bit of amazing news in a letter from McClelland—a clipping from a Boston paper stating that Mildred Page was suing for a divorce from her husband on the ground of cruelty and failure to support. I could hardly believe it. She seemed so happy when I was there six years ago in her beautiful home. I rather think Louis Page has gone down rapidly these past six years. But of course, he was always a bad lot and Mildred herself as I have recently discovered was not an angel. Annie Fellowes Johnston and Marshall Saunders between them have given me the history of the Pages.[337]

Louis Page has been married three times. His first wife died soon after they were married. His second wife was the daughter of a rich Boston banker, and a very beautiful charming and accomplished woman. She divorced him about ten years ago, the co-respondent in the case being Mildred who was then one of his office staff. She had a "past" of her own, having divorced her first husband—on what grounds I do not know. As soon as Louis P. was divorced he married Mildred and built the beautiful Brookline house for her. Now, it seems, that has come to an end, too. I rather fancy Louis was tired of Mildred and is compelling her to sue for divorce by ill-using her.

On Friday afternoon Mrs. Alec Leask and I drove to Whitby and spent the weekend with the Anderson's. I really enjoyed the outing. Saturday afternoon we were at a very nice afternoon tea at Judge McIntyre's. As a rule, I loathe afternoon teas but this was a nice one.

The war new is very bad. Roumania seems in a hard plight. Drat Roumania! We thought she would be a help to the Allies. Instead, owing to the blundering incompetency of her generals and plan of campaign she is an added weakness and danger point.

Saturday, Oct. 21, 1916
Leaskdale, Ont.

So far the Roumanians have checked the Teutons in most of the passes and driven them back in others. But Mackensen is beginning another drive in the Dobrudja. If anybody had mentioned the Dobrudja to me three months ago I would not have known whether it was a place, a

---

collection *New Poems* (1910).

337   Margaret Marshall Saunders (1861–1947), a Canadian author and early advocate for animal rights, was born in Nova Scotia but in later years lived in Toronto. Her novel *Beautiful Joe* (1893), written from a dog's point of view, has been likened by some to *Black Beauty*. More than seven million copies of the book were sold worldwide.

potentate or a germ. Now, it has for me the significance of Verdun and Ypres.

I had a sick spell Wednesday and Thursday that pulled me still further down. Today I began to write the story of "My Literary Career" for *Everywoman's World*. They want 30,000 words. I shall call it "The Alpine Path."[338] Years and years ago, when I was a child of about twelve I found in a magazine a bit of fugitive verse entitled "Lines to the Fringed Gentian" by some forgotten author.[339] The last verse haunted my memory and has been with me all these years as an aspiration.

"Then whisper blossom, in thy sleep
How I may upward climb
The Alpine path, so hard and steep,
That leads to heights sublime—

How I may reach that far-off goal
Of true and honored fame
And write upon its shining scroll
A woman's humble name."

It has given me the title of my article. The "Alpine Path" has been climbed after many hard years of toil and endeavor. It was not an easy ascent but in the struggle even at its hardest there was a delight and a zest known only to those who aspire to the mountain tops. The easy dwellers in plain and valley never know it.

Monday, October 23rd, 1916
Leaskdale, Ont.

We have had a beautiful October—a welcome thing after our awful summer. Yet, fair or foul, the weather seems to have little significance for me just now. I am always too busy to "take any stock" in the outside world.

To-day Chester went to the office *alone* for the first time and brought up our mail—my little man child. He is growing so fast—oh, where is the dear, tiny baby of 1912? He *was* such a "cute" little chap. Stuart

---

338 "The Alpine Path" was first be published as a series of autobiographical essays in the Toronto magazine *Everywoman's World*, between June and November 1917. (It was published in 1974 in book form by the University of Michigan Library.) See note for January 5, 1917.

339 This poem was identified by Carol Gaboury in 1989. LMM had cut it out of the March 1884 edition of *Godey's Lady's Book* and pasted it into her scrapbook. "The Fringed Gentian" was part of a continued story entitled *Tam, the Story of a Woman* by Ella Rodman Church and Augusta De Bubna.

is very sweet and beautiful and winsome but he hasn't Chester's clear-cut features and fine profile.

The war news was mixed today. The British have made an important advance but the news from the Dobrudja is bad.

Tuesday, Oct. 24, 1916

Very bad news that Mackensen has taken Costanza and is threatening Cernavoda.[340] This is a serious reverse for the Roumanians.

Four-square to all the winds that blow

I was very busy *all* day—but this is my normal state. I made pumpkin preserve and prepared tea for company. Mrs. Goforth, a missionary from China, came to speak. We all went and took both the children—which meant a rather tiring evening for me.

I wish I could go to bed and stay there for a month! I think that would set me up as good as new.

Wednesday, Oct. 25, 1916

I never thought that the name "Verdun" could ever have any pleasant significance in my consciousness. We have heard little of Verdun since the Allied offensive began in July. That put an end to the German hope of getting it. This morning I drove Mrs. Goforth down to the train and then went into an uptown store. A man was standing by the counter reading a *Mail and Empire*. I saw the headline "Great French Victory at Verdun."[341] It was a pleasant surprise for I had been expecting only more bad news from Roumania. And it *was* a great victory. In a few hours, by one splendid smashing attack the French regained almost all the ground that had been won by the Germans in their long and costly offensive. France is certainly very wonderful.

---

340   On October 19, 1916 a counter-offensive led by Field Marshal Anton Ludwig August von Mackensen (1849–1945) successfully captured the city of Constanţa ("Constanza") on the Black Sea coast in Romania. This was soon followed by the capture further inland of the city of Cernavodă. Mackensen's march into Romania would continue throught the winter. (For more on Romania, see the entry for October 4, 1916.)

341   On October 24, the strategic village of Douamont in north-eastern France was recaptured by French marines and colonial infantry. By the following day, some 6,000 German prisoners had been taken. As LMM notes of the French offensive, in a short period of time the French advanced some 2 km/1.2 miles into German-controlled territory in an important victory.

But the Roumanian news *is* bad. Mackensen is sweeping everything before him in the Dobrudja and Falkenhayn is pounding his way through the passes.[342] It is evident they hope to crush Roumania between them.

Friday, Oct. 27, 1916
The Manse, Leaskdale, Ont.

Have been busy housecleaning. The war news was scanty today but the Teuton rush seems halted somewhat. I read a most depressing article in the *Montreal Witness* today. It took a very pessimistic view of the whole situation. I could not see that all the pessimism was justified but still the article had a very bad effect on me—took away all my spirit and courage for the day. I just dragged through the hours thereafter. He prophesied two or three years of war yet. I fear *that* is all too probable. *How* can we endure to the end?

Saturday, Oct. 28, 1916

More depressing news—Russia, they say, is short of shells.[343] She has certainly not been doing anything of late. All she can do goes to help Roumania. The situation of the latter is still serious but not appreciably worse than two days ago.

Monday, Oct. 30, 1916

The war news was good today. The Roumanians have won victories in all the passes but one. That is well. But probably tomorrow the pendulum will swing back again. This see-saw of news is racking to the nerves.[344]

Thursday, Nov. 2, 1916

Lately the Roumanians have been doing pretty well—advancing in some passes—holding firm in others. One ventures to draw a long

---

342   General Erich Georg Anton von Falkenhayn (1861–1922) commanded the German counteroffensive in Romania. Meanwhile Mackensen was continuing a forward march into Dobruja, forcing the retreat of Romanian and Russian soldiers. By this time the Romanian army was demoralized and running low on supplies. (See notes for April 18, 1916 and September 9, 1916.)

343   Following the early success of the Brusilov Offensive (see note for June 10, 1916), Russian soldiers began to suffer from a lack of manpower and supplies.

344   Both the Romanian and Russian armies were struggling at this time. The Romanian army was being forced to retreat ever further from initial gains.

breath and hope fearfully that the crisis is past.

Our Red Cross met over on the Sixth today. I went, feeling dejected. I had a letter from Frede saying that she feared she could not come on Christmas—she felt she ought to go home and see her father. I dare not urge her—I recognize the condition of things. But I am inexpressibly disappointed. All that has helped me during this past hard year was the consoling hope of "talking it all out" with Freddy when she came at Christmas. Some virtue seemed to go out of me today when I read her letter. I went to the Red Cross and sewed and planned and talked like an automaton. My soul seemed to be somewhere else in a dark little torture chamber of its own.

Tuesday, Nov. 8, 1916
The Manse, Leaskdale

Another see-saw has begun in the Dobrudja. Mackensen having driven the Russo-Roumanians almost into the Danube has suddenly taken to retreating before them for the second time. There was no particular news from the passes. The Italians have won a big victory over the Austrians.[345] That *may* ease up the pressure on Roumania a bit.

I got weighed today—109 1/2 pounds. That is to say two more than I weighed in September. The gain is not great but I am thankful I haven't gone on losing. Perhaps I am on the up-grade again now.

Saturday, Nov. 11, 1916
The Manse, Leaskdale, Ont.

To-day my volume of poems "The Watchman" came from my Canadian publishers. It is very nicely gotten up. I expect no great things of it.

Mackensen is still retreating in the Dobrudja and the Roumanians are doing well.

Wednesday, Nov. 15, 1916

We have had two days of good news from the British front—they have won a big victory—captured Beaumont, Hamel and Boncourt and taken 6,000 prisoners.[346] But the situation in the Roumanian passes is

---

345   Between November 1 and 4, 1916, an Italian offensive against Austria-Hungary positions along the Isonzo River saw only modest gains, with heavy casualties on both sides.

346   Between November 13 and 18, 1916 the British Fifth army launched an attack on strategic German positions, located on both sides of the river Somme in northern France. The assault was costly but successful, capturing Beaumont Hamel, St. Pierre Divion, and Beaucourt, and destabilizing German positions elsewhere. Over 7,000 German troops were taken prisoner.

again very bad and ominous. Mackensen is still retreating in the Do-brudja but that is not a vital part.

Thursday, Nov. 16, 1916

We had good news today of a big Serbian victory on the Macedonian front. But the Roumanian situation is very very bad. I can't sleep at nights for thinking about it. This past month has been the Verdun agony of last spring over again—not quite so dreadful, of course, but very nearly. I wonder if I shall ever be able again to await the coming of the mail with feelings of composure—never to speak of pleasure. For over two years I have dreaded the arrival of the paper every day. I am always so thankful when Sunday comes—it is free from that nightmare. But I pay for its ease on Monday mornings when the agony of suspense seems doubly dreadful—so much may have happened in the long interval between Saturday and Monday.

I was reading over Bertie MacIntyre's old letters to-day. It is five and a half years since I saw Bertie. That is terrible. She is one of the few women in the whole world who really matter to me, and something is wrong when we have to live so far apart and meet so seldom. Surely in some former life I must have sinned terribly against friendship and I am punished for it in this by having always to live under circumstances wherein it is impossible for me to have any truly congenial friends near me save in random and fugitive glimpses—just enough to show me what I miss!

Monday, Nov. 20, 1916
The Manse, Leaskdale, Ont.

As per usual—tired. Ewan and I drove into Uxbridge this morning, to find very good and very bad war news. The French and Serbians have recaptured Monastir—but the Roumanians have met with a big defeat in the Jiul pass—a defeat which will, I fear, have serious consequences.[347] This afternoon

Red Cross Packers

347   The Allied victory in Serbia that LMM refers to here was part of a larger plan known as the Monastir Offensive, a strategy designed to relieve the pressure on Romania among other goals. The battle lasted three months with overall retreat by German and Bulgarian forces. On

I spent helping to pack our Red Cross collection of waste papers for shipment—a hard and dirty job. Then this evening I read and corrected the whole of one typewritten copy of *Anne's House of Dreams*. I fear I am too tired to sleep.

Tues. Nov. 21, 1916
The Manse, Leaskdale

The news from Roumania was so bad today that it completely upset me. I could not work and I foresee no sleep tonight. Falkenhayn is sweeping forward in Wallachia.[348]

Friday, Nov. 24, 1916

This was a rough, doleful day of high winds and squalls of snow. I have finished correcting the four copies of the *House of Dreams*, glory be. The war news is scanty but it is said that Russian reinforcements have arrived in Roumania, so one feels a little more optimistic—which seems to be an ominous feeling in this war for I have noticed that whenever we have dared to feel optimistic something dreadful happened soon afterwards.

We had to drive over to the Sixth tonight in the teeth of that wind and have supper with one of "our families." It was really a very dreary performance.

Saturday, Nov. 25, 1916

The "something dreadful" was not long in coming. To-day the war news was that Mackensen has crossed the Danube. This is the worst thing yet in the Roumanian campaign. I feel wretchedly worried and upset. And it always seems doubly hard when ill news comes on Saturday. We can hear nothing more until Monday and it seems as if the time would never pass.

November 19, French and Russian soldiers entered the town of Monastir. The front was moved 50 km/31 miles in favour of the Allies, but at a cost of thousands of casualties. In the meantime Romanian forces continued to lose ground in some regions.

348   General Erich von Falkenhayn (1861–1922) had been Chief of Germany's General Staff in the early years of the war, but after failures at the Somme and Verdun, was removed from the Western front. He took command of operations in Romania. While Mackensen was approaching from the north, von Falkenhayn attacked across the Carpathian mountains into central Romania. Wallachia is a historical region south of the Carpathian mountains.

Monday, Nov. 27, 1916
The Manse, Leaskdale, Ont.

Yesterday was Edith's Sunday to go out so I spent the day alone, so tormented by worry over Roumania that I could not even read. The hours dragged on as if they would never pass. This forenoon I spent in an intolerable condition. I was fairly sick when Ewan went for the mail. The news was bad—bad. We drove to Uxbridge after dinner and I was in a maze of mental misery all the way down and while there. I went about among the shops like a woman in a dream and started and stammered foolishly when anyone addressed me.

Thursday, Nov. 30, 1916

What a day was Tuesday! I had had a sleepless night and passed a wretched forenoon trying to work but unable to fix my thoughts on anything. The mail was late, which prolonged the agony; and when it did come the news was bad. The Germans are drawing near to Bucharest.[349] I shall never forget Tuesday afternoon and evening. I have suffered nothing like it in all the months of the war, not even in the dreadful Verdun struggle. I gave up all attempt to work. I did what *had* to be done and between times I shut myself in the parlor, walking the floor unrestingly, muttering incoherent prayers—prayers that will not be answered. I feel that Bucharest must fall.

At bedtime I took a sleeping powder and so obtained a few hours of loggy sleep and forgetfulness. At five I wakened to sleep no more, so lighted a lamp and tried to read. We left before the mail came Wednesday to attend a wedding. I talked and laughed and did all the proper didoes, with the under-ache of dread and worry gnawing at my soul. Drove home ten miles through the dark, sloppy, wet night, forced myself to look at the papers—and found the news bad. The Roumanian Government had left Bucharest. Then I dressed both children and took them to the Guild Social. Came home worn out in mind and body and slept the sleep of exhaustion.

To-day as E. was away I ploughed down through the mud for the mail. Still bad—still bad! The Russians have begun a counter offensive in the Kirlzbaba pass but I feel that it will peter out. They do not seem to have the munitions.

---

349   The Romanian Army continued to retreat throughout November. By December 6, the capital, Bucharest, had fallen to the Central Powers.

After I read the papers I drove over to the Sixth to a meeting for the Red Cross, sewed all the afternoon, and have come home tired and blue.

Sunday, December 3, 1916
The Manse, Leaskdale

The war news continues bad. Friday evening Edith and I drove over to Zephyr because I had to recite at a Red Cross concert there. I was very miserable all the evening with an attack of cystitis. It was pitchy dark coming home and it was one o'clock when we got here. Then up at seven in the morning and hard at work. But I am always thankful when I *can* work—when I can compose my mind sufficiently to think and plan and do. But I lost my usual Sunday rest today, wherefrom I usually obtain enough strength and grit to face another week. I was asked to go to a certain place to spend the afternoon and have tea. There were circumstances which made it advisable for me to go, so I reluctantly went, taking the children. I spent a miserable afternoon of worry and headache and boredom. Came home, exceedingly tired, to find that a certain worthy old dame from Zephyr had invited herself here to spend a week. At another time I would not have minded it muchly but just now when I am so nervous and worried it really seemed to me almost "the last straw."

Sunday, December 10, 1916
The Manse, Leaskdale

The calendar says it is a week—viz. seven days—since last Sunday. My soul cries out that it is seven years—for seven years would not have aged me in mind and soul as this past week has done.

Last Monday I got up, wondering how I could get through the morning and face the mail when it came. I held myself down to work until I saw Ewan leaving for the office. Then, as usual, I went to pieces, fled to the parlor, shut myself in, and walked the floor. There should surely be a path worn from corner to corner across that parlor carpet from my peregrinations there since the war began.

Ewan came back with the *Globe*. With icy hands, pallid lips, shaking fingers, and fluttering heart I seized the paper and looked at it. The news was unbelievably good. Mackensen's army had been driven back south of Bucharest and badly defeated. The papers were jubilant. Bucharest, like Paris, was to be saved at the eleventh hour etc.

Weak from reaction I fled to my room and flung myself on my knees to thank God. The rest of the day I passed in comparative calm, but when I got up Tuesday morning I felt even worse than before. It was a very dull, dreary day. The agony of waiting for the mail had again to be gone through—an agony even greater than if the previous day's news had been bad. After that short respite from torture it was unbearable to fear being stretched on the rack again. But "the Moving Finger writes"—and turns not back or falters for human agony. The paper came—the news was as bad as could be—the Germans were again closing in on Bucharest. Constantine of Greece had played the Allies false and in England a cabinet crisis had at last been precipitated by the war situation and the Asquith government had fallen.[350]

I passed a horrible afternoon and evening. And I could not even show my suffering. I had to repress every sign of it and go to a Missionary meeting, taking Mrs. Lockie[351] along with me. I sat there while the women talked local gossip before the meeting began, as if they had never heard of the war, and I made no sign. I occupied "the chair" while the officers for the next year were elected and I put the business through with composure and despatch; I read a lengthy screed from the Mission Study Book and knew not one word I was reading; and I walked home afterwards with some of the village women and talked gossip, too—harmless gossip, of course, such as is permitted to ministers' wives, as to who was ill, and whose hens were laying and whose hens were not—and smiled and bowed and went through the motions. And inside of me my soul writhed and gibbered on its rack!

I got tea over and then settled down to keep the lid on for the evening. I sat and crocheted a medallion and talked to Mrs. L. and listened to her. She is a fluent talker and never, even by accident, says a word worth saying or hearing. She talked about people I never knew—told

---

350   What became known as the "National Schism" in Greek politics involved forces loyal to the pro-German Monarchy of Constantine I vs. those supporting the liberal Prime Minister, Eleftherios Venizelos (see note for June 1, 1916). Following divisions and internal political turmoil, Venizelos had established a government in the north of Greece that was loyal to the Allies while Athens remained under the control of the Monarchists. Early December saw riots in Athens between both sides, with the involvement of Allied troops. The Allies were forced to withdraw and in the days that followed, supporters of Venizelos in Athens were attacked and imprisoned, and in some cases murdered. The government of Herbert Henry Asquith had fallen in May 1915, following what was seen as poor handling of the war effort. He formed a coalition government with Conservatives on May 25. The coalition government itself collapsed in December 1916. The creation of a cabinet under liberal David Lloyd George marked a change in British management of the war, with Lloyd George making decisions more quickly and involving the country moore deeply in the war effort.

351   The reference is to Elizabeth Imrie Lockie. Emigrating from Scotland to Upper Canada in the first part of the nineteenth century, the Lockie family was among the founders of the Presbyterian Church in Zephyr.

me who they married and where they were born and how many children they had. Ewan was away at a recruiting meeting and there was no one to take the edge off her. I smiled with the muscles of my face and compelled my tongue to utter sounds, while my mind spun round and round, impaled on one sharp point of torturing thought, unable to escape it. I thought over every possible chance of saving Bucharest, including a miracle, but I could see no hope. And Mrs. L. talked on!

The woman really amazed me. The war news seemed to have no more effect on her than if it were a conflict between the kingdoms of Mars. She asked what it was, agreed that it was very bad and very sad and then went placidly on with her fancy work and her biographies. If this had been the result of a fortunate strength of mind, such as I assuredly do not possess, which enabled her, after the first shock and pain, to go steadily on with the routine of life, suffering but calm, I should have admired and envied her. But it was nothing of the sort. It was simply the most inaudible insensibility and indifference. And if she had guessed what a turmoil of feeling I was concealing under my calm exterior she would have thought me crazy. Why, Bucharest was thousands of miles away! Why worry over what the Germans were doing there?

But bedtime came at last and I thankfully deposited Mrs. L. in the spareroom and fled to my own. Then the lid flew off. I had a nervous collapse, the result of my self-suppression all day. I had a wild fit of crying. When it was spent I felt calmer and finally fell asleep, but wakened up at two with a bad headache. I could not sleep again but lay there and listened to the high wind banging the shutters and rattling the windows.

Wednesday—bad news again, from Roumania, and *no* news from Greece. I worked doggedly all day and in the evening went to a Red Cross lecture in the church—an illustrated lantern affair. I looked at the pictures with blank eyes that stared straight through them and saw only the Huns closing in on the doomed Roumanian capital. Several soldiers were present and after the lecture they made recruiting speeches. Captain Cockburn, a boyish-looking fellow, whose brother was killed "somewhere in France" last spring, made a speech in which he drew a very gloomy picture of the war situation.[352] My reason told

---

352 Recruiting speeches were increasingly common as the war progressed and more manpower was required. In this case the speech was accompanied by pictures projected from a "magic lantern" consisting of a lens fitted to a box holding a light bulb. LMM's husband Ewan was president of the Scott Township League on Resources Committee, which had recently been authorized to raise 45 men as a township quota. Ross M. Cockburn—probably the person that Montgomey heard—was from Port Perry and formerly of the 34th Regiment (a regiment of Ontario County that predated the 116th Battalion).

me that, despite the Roumanian reverse, it was *too* gloomy—probably deliberately so, with an eye to stirring up reluctant recruits who might be disposed to think the war could be won without their aid. But reason has small power to help me in my present condition of nerves, and I felt as if Cockburn's speech was more than I could endure.

However, I slept well that night, being so worn-out that I ceased to suffer actively. And on Thursday came the news that Bucharest had fallen!

I was calm that afternoon with the calm of despair. Even the certainty of the worst is more endurable than the horror of suspense.

And Lloyd George is Premier of England—the ruler of the British Empire. It took the Roumanian crisis to bring that about. Nothing less could have put the foot of the Welsh lawyer on the neck of the aristocrats of England.[353] Perhaps that was why the Roumanian disaster was decreed in the Councils of Eternity—since the gods themselves, it seems, must work out their purposes by indirect means. I believe that Lloyd George is one of the greatest men Britain has ever produced and that he, if anyone, can yet snatch victory from the jaws of defeat. Well, it is something to live in such times as these in spite of the agony of them!

Thursday night I could not sleep for hours. Lay awake thrashing over the Balkan situation and wishing I could skin Constantine of Greece alive. I woke early, lighted a lamp, and read Wordsworth. The classic calm and repose and beauty of his lines seemed to belong to another planet and to have as little to do with this world-welter as an evening star.

There was little news of any kind on Friday. Had a letter from Ella Campbell, telling me of her new girl-baby which is named after me. I have six namesakes now.

Yesterday brought alarming rumors of Greece going in on the side of Germany. Still, I feel strangely calm now—as if the climax of the war were passed, for good or ill. Mrs. Lockie went home today. Poor old soul, she told me she had had a lovely time. I think she had. She got to see all her old friends and I tried to make her visit pleasant. It was not her fault that the week was such a dreadful one for me and I am glad I succeeded in hiding my unrest and worry from her. But I pray that if ever I have to live through such a week again I will not have to keep up appearances before a Mrs. L.

---

353   David Lloyd George, born to Welsh parents, had grown up speaking Welsh (he lived in both England and Wales, following changing family fortunes). Coming from a middle-class family that had seen its share of hard times, when he became prime minister he positioned himself as a champion of working people over the interests of the landed aristocracy—those he termed "the Dukes."

Monday, Dec. 11, 1916
The Manse, Leaskdale, Ont.

The war news was scanty to-day. The Roumanians have won a little local success near Ploesti but it is evident it is only a rear-guard action.[354] Still, I have that strange, composed conviction that the worst is over. Tonight, when I was in next door calling on the Warners, Mr. Warner was taking a gloomy view of the whole situation. I agreed with him because I could give no credible reason for the faith that was in me; but inside of me I felt like one who has had certain secret information the other does not share. I wonder if my feeling is truly prophetic. Or is it only the calm of my reaction from the dreadful agony of the past week?

Tuesday, Dec. 12, 1916

No war news except from Roumania—and that bad. The Teutons have crossed the Jablonitza River. Confound the Jablonitza River![355] An ultimatum is to be delivered to Greece to-day. It will take more than ultimatums to skin a snake like Constantine. But the little Welshman is behind this—so it behoves the kinglets to sit up on their hind legs and listen.[356]

Wednesday, Dec. 13, 1916
The Manse, Leaskdale, Ont.

The date should be written in capitals! Today came the news that Germany has offered peace.[357] This means that she realizes that she is nearing the end of her rope, despite her Roumanian campaign. In so far, it is good news. For the rest it means nothing. The Allies will not be fools enough to put their heads into the noose she dangles. I feel sure they cannot be so mad. Yet there is always a dark possibility where Russia is concerned, and so the news has upset me. It has also upset the world. Every stock-market on the planet quivered and rocked under the impact.

---

354   Germany had seized the oil fields near Ploieşti ("Ploesti"), 56 km/35 miles north of Bucharest. On December 5 a British Army operation destroyed production and sabotaged much of the infrastructure of the industry. Throughout December, there was heavy fighting around the area of Ploieşti; any ground gained by Romania in this period was modest at best.

355   Heavy fighting continued in the area north-east of Bucharest.

356   LMM had great faith in David Lloyd George ("the little Welshman"), a strong admirer of Prime Minister Venizelos and pushed for a resolution on the festering political divisions Greece.

357   In December, Germany offered to enter peace talks with the Entente powers. Allied countries rejected the offer, however, distrusting the Central Powers and counting on eventual victory.

As for Mackensen, he is still advancing in Roumania, though more slowly and gruesome rumors still come through from Greece. Constantine is said to be mobilizing. But I think the Allied Blockade will hammer some gumption into his head.

Thursday, Dec. 14, 1916

No good war news yet. The despatches were full of wild tales of fighting in Greece. The Globe seems to credit it but the other papers discredit it and I hardly see that it could be true. But the mere suggestion is disquieting.

Friday, Dec. 15, 1916
The Manse, Leaskdale, Ont.

Bitterly cold. How I dread the winter! Last winter was so dreadful. I do hope we will not have so much sickness this winter. But we will have the war and it is bound to grow more agonizing every day. The winter is hard on the children, too. They are so cooped up and cabined. I went to the Red Cross today but was very miserable with a cold. War news still bad.

Saturday, Dec. 16, 1916

To-day we had some splendid news to offset the usual bad—a pungent taste of victory to flavor the bitterness of our recent diet of disaster. The French have won another great victory at Verdun and captured 10,000 of the enemy. Douamont and Vaux are in their hands again.[358] Oh, Verdun, surely some new Homer will arise to sing you! What was Troy compared to you? The British, too, have made an advance in Mesopotamia, where there has only been dreary silence since the disaster of Kut-cl-Amara last spring![359] And Greece—'tis said—is consenting to all the Entente demands. But Mackensen has captured Buzen—a victory of evil omen to Roumania.[360]

Today I had a letter from McClelland. The Frederick Stokes Co. have got my book. This seemed best; but I feel slightly disappointed that the

---

358   Following a French offensive from December 15 to 17, 1916, these two strategic forts were recaptured, along with 11,387 prisoners.

359   British General Frederick Stanley Maude launched an offensive on December 13, 1916, advancing up the Tigris River, an important military success following the defeat in Kut-el-Amar.

360   On December 14, 1916 German forces captured Buzău, occupying the Romanian city until 1918.

Appleton dicker fell through. They split on the terms between them and Mac for the Canadian edition. I did not feel that I could insist on giving them the book, when Mac had been so generous in his contracts, so I told him he could give Stokes the book. Of course the standing of Stokes is equal to Appletons and they gave me the same terms—twenty percent on list price and five thousand down advance royalty. Such terms rather frighten me. Can I continue to write up to them? I am always haunted by the fear that I shall find myself "written out."

Mac writes enthusiastically of *The House of Dreams* and says it is so good he feels sure we shall have a record sale.

Monday, Dec. 18, 1916

Yesterday I felt all day that I *could not* bear it if the war news turned bad, or even *nil*, again. Nevertheless, it *was* bad and I bore it. Galatz and Braila are in danger—two very important Roumanian cities.[361] Perhaps I was helped to bear it by a letter from Frede saying that, after all, she is coming for Christmas. It sound inadequate to say I am thankful. It has seemed to me that I couldn't endure it if she didn't come—though I suppose, as in the case of the war news, I would have found that I *could* when I had to. But mercifully I am to be spared the test. She is coming; and I am not so sure as I was a few days ago that I have quite lost all my youth. Then tonight Ewan came home from Presbytery and brought an evening paper which said that the British were closing in on Kut again and that the Roumanian army was safe behind the Sereth.[362] The latter is *very* good news if confirmed.

Tuesday, Dec. 19, 1916
The Manse, Leaskdale, Ont.

I had a good sleep last night—which is not the matter-of-course thing with me that it was a few years ago. The war—the children—over-tired-ness—all combine to give me many a bad night. The Roumanian news was somewhat better today. The Russo-Roumanian army seems to be making a stand at last.

Mr. and Mrs. Petch, the Sandford Methodist minister and his wife,

361   Fighting continued throughout December on the Macedonian front, with two important Romanian cities (modern-day Brăila and Galaţi) on the Danube under threat.
362   Its source in northern Ukraine, the Siret or Sireth River flows 470 km/291 miles through Ukraine and Romania to empty into the Danube.

were here to tea and we went to a recruiting meeting tonight. Mrs. Petch and I recited. The meeting did not come out till eleven and I am very tired.

Wednesday, Dec. 20, 1916

Got up, very tired still, and Edith and I drove to Uxbridge. Lloyd George's first speech as Premier, for which the whole world has been breathlessly waiting, was in the papers today.[363] Never before, in the history of the race, I feel sure, was any speech so awaited by every nation in the world. The speech itself is a satisfying thing. The Kaiser will assuredly make some wry faces over it. There was no other war news of any importance.

Thursday, Dec. 21, 1916

All the papers were in a white fume of indignation today because that colossal old idiot, Woodrow Wilson, has been ass enough to send a peace note to the warring powers! They might save their splutter. He is a man of straw and not worth taking notice of. The Entente will put him delightfully in his place in due time.

I re-read Kipling's "Kim" tonight—that is, I finished re-reading it, having had it out several weeks—for alas, I get so little time for reading now, and what I do get I steal from sleep.[364] I read it many years ago when it first came out and cared little for it as contrasted with his short tales. But this time I found it charming. And yet how strangely *far away* everything written before the war seems now. I felt as if I were perusing some classic as ancient as the Iliad.

Sunday, Dec. 24, 1916
The Manse, Leaskdale, Ont.

There was no especial war-news Friday. We had our annual Xmas concert at night. As it was necessary to take the two children and look after them myself, since Edith was one of the performers, I anticipated a hard evening. But Stuart was exceedingly good as he always is and

---

363 Delivered on December 19, 1916, Prime Minister Lloyd George's speech began with the war situation: "I appear before the House of Commons to-day, with the most terrible responsibility that can fall upon the shoulders of any living man, as the chief adviser of the Crown, in the most gigantic War in which the country has ever been engaged—a war upon the event of which its destiny depends. It is the greatest War ever waged."

364 *Kim* by Rudyard Kipling was published in 1901. It recounted the experiences of an Irish orphan, Kimball "Kim" O'Hara, in British-ruled India.

Chester was good also. He is beginning to "have sense" when he is out and realize that he must keep quiet while a programme is going on. So I got on very well. Yesterday the war news was scanty but the Russians are still retreating in the Dobrudja.

The outstanding event of the week however, was Frede's arrival yesterday. We talked till two o'clock at night—a very orgy of confidences. Of course, I've felt rather rotten today as a consequence but who would regret it for so good a reason? I am going to have a real holiday while Frede's here—do nothing that I do not absolutely have to do but just have a good time. I am thankful that the Roumanian agony was over before she came. Were it going on now, it would spoil our visit.

Monday, Dec. 25, 1916
The Manse, Leaskdale

This has been an ideal Christmas day as far as weather is concerned. We had a nice, homey time. A Christmas tree in the morning gave great delight to Chester and we had a good dinner and lots of good talk.

Wednesday, Dec. 27, 1916

War news continues scanty and bad from Roumania. The British have won a rather important success in Syria.[365] The silence of the grave seems to have descended over Greece. Ewan and I drove over to Sandford this evening to have tea with the Petch's. The roads were good and the evening fine so I really enjoyed the drive. We had a pleasant tea also and I recited at a recruiting meeting in the evening.

Sunday, Dec. 31st, 1916

Thursday Frede and I drove over to Zephyr and spent the day with Lily Shier. Friday we had Mr. Fraser up to tea and Saturday we drove over to Wick and spent the day agreeably at the manse. Frede has certainly had Queen's weather for her visit.[366]

The war news from Roumania remains rather bad.

And so 1916 closes. Looking back over it I can say that I have never, in all my life, spent a year so physically hard—or indeed I may say more torturing mentally. From beginning to end it has been a hard year. It

---

365   Following important logistical improvements, British forces continued successful operations in the Middle East.

366   It was a matter of English folklore that pleasant weather always accompanied a visit from Queen Victoria.

dawned for me in the anguish of alarm over Chester's condition—an anguish that lasted through January. February brought Ewan's six weeks of bronchitis. March brought my dreadful attacks of mammitis, anxiety over Stuart, and the worst of the Verdun agony. Then followed my terrible worry over Page and over the Austrian offensive in the Trentino. The first reports of the battle of Jutland and Kitchener's death were followed by a summer of almost unrelieved misery with cystitis. Then in the autumn came the Roumanian disaster. Verily, 1916 has been a black year.

And what of 1917? This is the third year that has come in since hell broke loose upon earth. Surely—surely it will be the last New Year of war. I look forward to it with dread. Some things will certainly be dreadful. And the Page worry still haunts me. I had not received any communication from Page since his letter of June, threatening a lawsuit, until just before Christmas when one came. I turned very cold as I opened it. But to my amazement it was a most suave epistle, signed by George Page, but as I know from internal evidence, dictated by Louis, and saying that they were enclosing an advance royalty check thinking "it might come in handy about this time." Now, in the days of my most cordial relations with the Pages, they never sent me a royalty advance unless I asked for it. I am quite sure I know just what is behind the manoeuvre. Page imagines, because my book has not yet been announced by any firm, that his threats have deterred me from offering it or that I have failed to find a publisher. He therefore reasons that if he sends this nice "peace note" I may revert to him and give him the book after all. My curt and business-like acknowledgement of the receipt of the check will not give him much encouragement—or enlightenment.

But, as aforesaid, his attitude worries me. Still, matters are much better than at the dawn of 1916. Chester is a big rosy fat sturdy fellow, the picture of health. Stuart, who is walking now, and amusingly proud of it, is ditto. I am feeling much better physically than I did all summer and fall. So I hope 1917 will not be quite as nerve-racking as its predecessor.

Yet I dislike to be wished "a happy New Year." It seems like a tempting of the gods!

Monday, January 1, 1917
The Manse, Leaskdale, Ont.

The *Globe* today contained the anxiously awaited Entente reply to the German peace note—a document in which the Huns will not find much comfort.[367]
News still bad from Roumania and Greece still in a broil.

Thursday, Jan. 4, 1917

The Roumanian situation is still dubious. But certainly the German progress is much slower than before. Frede went away Tuesday. We had a delightful week and I think I can live comfortably on it through the winter. Wednesday night I entertained the Guild Executive and today I went to the Red Cross.

The Manse, Leaskdale, Ont.
Friday, Jan. 5th, 1917

I had an amusing letter from the editor of *Everywoman's World* to-day.[368] At least, it was amusing to me. I recently wrote the story of "My Literary Career" for them at their request—only I didn't call it *that*. I called it "The Alpine Path," taking as motto the little verse which I wrote in my port-folio over thirty years ago—one of the verses of a short poem "The Fringed Gentian" which was published in the old *Godey's Lady's Book*. I have forgotten if I ever knew the name of the author but I have never forgotten the poem. As literature it was *non est*; but as an expression to the restless dreams and desires in my own soul it seemed to me perfect; and I echoed the last verse to the core of my being.

> "Then whisper, blossom, in thy sleep
> How I may upward climb
> The Alpine path, so hard, so steep
> That leads to heights sublime.

---

367   The Allied response to the German "peace note"—an offer to enter peace talks—was despatched December 30, 1916, claiming that "no peace is possible so long as they have not secured reparation of violated rights and liberties, recognition of the principle of nationalities, and of the free existence of small states; so long as they have not brought about a settlement calculated to end, once and for all, forces which have contributed a perpetual menace to the nations, and to afford the only effective guarantees for the future security of the world."

368   *Everywoman's Magazine*, which arranged with LMM to publish several short memoirs, was the first Canadian magazine to post a circulation of more than 100,000. See also the note for October 21, 1916.

How I may reach that far-off goal
Of true and honored fame
And write upon its shining scroll
A woman's humble name."

When I grew discouraged and down-hearted in those old early years of struggle I used to repeat that verse over to myself and always there was something in it that inspired me afresh—and lured me on again to that "far-off goal."

Let me return to my sheep.

I sent "The Alpine Path" to the editor and he writes, professing himself as delighted with the story, but laments that there is nothing in it "concerning my love affairs." He is sure I must have had some! Will I not write an additional thousand words and tell my "adoring Canadian girls" of my pangs and passions!!!!!

Ye Gods! Suppose I were to do it!

I smile when I imagine what the "parties of the second part" would think if they picked up a copy of *Everywoman's World* and read a cold-blooded account of their "affairs" with me in it. But I do *not* smile when I imagine what their wives would think!

The dear public must get along without this particular tid-bit. I have snubbed that editor very unmistakably, telling him that I am not one of those who throw open the portals of sacred shrines to the gaze of the crowd.

But for my own amusement I *am* going to write a full and frank—at least as frank as possible—account of all my "love affairs." Possibly my grandchildren—or my great grandchildren—may read it and say, "Why, we remember grandma as a thin, wrinkled, little, gray-haired body, always sitting in a warm corner, with a hug-me-tight on, reading a book (If I ever am a grandmother I am going to do nothing but read books and do filet crochet!). Surely she couldn't really have lived these love stories."

Yes, dear unborn grandchildren, I did. For I was not always old and gray-haired and hug-me-tighted, you know. I was once young and brown-tressed, and wore lace and georgette crepe and silk stockings—and was called a flirt by my enemies; while my friends said "It is only Maud's way."

Well:—

I was twelve or thirteen years old, I am not quite sure which, when I first fell in love. There was a musical concert in Cavendish Hall one

Cavendish Hall

night, given by three graduates of the Blind School in Halifax.[369] One of these was a Mr. Chisholm—a tall, slender young man with little golden dabs of side-whiskers, a most angelic face, and a more than angelic voice. He sang several songs and I, small miss, gazing up at him from the audience, lost my heart completely.

It is the truth that I felt, for the first time a very strange sensation—a romantic yearning of hitherto unknown and of almost-terrifying sweetness. It mattered not at all that my hero was blind. He was perfection, that was all. When I went home it seemed to me quite intolerable that I should never see him again and the world was suddenly big and lonely. I thought about him for a week—and then forgot him.

Fifteen years afterwards in Halifax I met his widow. Her husband had recently died and she was heart-broken—for it seems that he had really been all my young fancy had painted.[370] I told her with a smile that her husband had been the first man I had ever been in love with and she laughed sadly and said that everyone who knew him loved

---

369   The Halifax School for the Blind was the first residential school for blind students in Canada. "Mr Chisholm" was likely Arthur M. Chisholm (1856–1902), a one-time student and later head of the music department of the School for the Blind.

370   Chisholm taught music at the School for the Blind in Halifax. Himself blind as the result of a childhood medical error, he was a much-loved teacher and headed the school's music department. The concert LMM refers to would have taken place in 1886 or 1887.

him. So I did not bestow my virgin passion unworthily.

It seems absurd to speak of that experience as *love*; but, save in intensity and duration, what I felt that evening, as I gazed at the young singer's pale, spiritual face—it really *was* spiritual in spite of the side-whiskers—and listened to his thrilling voice differed in nothing from the similar emotions of after years. There was no passion in it, save of the soul, but that night I crossed the threshold of life's temple, though I did not penetrate to the inner shrine.

When I was fifteen a boy of fifteen said to me "I love you." Nathan Lockhart and I had been good school friends for a year, finding in each other an intellectual congeniality which we could find nowhere else in Cavendish.[371] I liked Nate as a friend—and I liked to have him dangling after me, and "seeing me home" from the hall, and setting certain other girls wild with jealousy—not so much because they wanted him themselves; but they were Baptists and I was a Presbyterian and they were furious because their "minister's son" singled *me*, of a rival church, out. It really was glorious fun—I was a minx, I am afraid. But I did not care in the least for Nate, save as a friend. I wanted to because I thought it would be romantic; I tried to—I even wrote him some love-letters in response to various ardent epistles of his, which he used to while away the tedium of Sunday afternoons in the decorous parsonage by writing. But the fact remained that he meant nothing to me—had no power over me, either of the senses or of the heart. His memory, personally, means nothing to me. But he was the first male creature who said to me "I love you"—and no woman ever forgets the man who first says that. As a man he may mean nothing to her: as a symbol, he means more than any other ever can.

When I went out west in 1890 I was beginning to wonder how I could get free from the cobweb entanglement which linked me to Nate. He had talked boyishly and shyly about "after years"—when he "would be through college"—and I would be his wife. I had never said "yes" or "no." I knew in my heart I could never marry him but I hated to hurt his feelings by telling him so. He felt, so gossip informed me, very badly when I went away. But he went to college. We corresponded for a time but as years passed our letters grew cooler and less frequent—it happened that we did not meet again for a few years—we had both forgotten. At least, Nate never made any effort to resume the tenu-

---

371   As a girl, LMM was attracted to Nathan ("Nate") Lockhart, who was the Cavendish Baptist minister's stepson. They exchanged notes in school but also competed academically, as Lockhart was said to be the brightest boy at school. Details on the men LMM mentions in this entry may be found in Mary Henley Rubio, *Lucy Maud Montgomery: The Gift of Wings* (Toronto: Doubleday Canada, 2008), the definitive biography of LMM.

ous relationship that had somehow grown-up between us. Whether he would have done so had I been less cool and deliberately friendly I cannot tell nor does it matter. Somehow, I never like to think of my affair with Nate. Why I don't exactly know. It was a very innocent and harmless thing; perhaps the faint physical repulsion,—so faint as to seem as much spiritual as physical—which I always felt more or less conscious of when we were alone together colored subconsciously my memory of our friendship and affects it now. When a third party—Amanda, for instance—was with us I felt perfectly at home with Nate and enjoyed laughing and talking with him immensely. But the minute we were alone together, even if it were only walking primly down a country road, I felt ill at ease and conscious of a longing to escape. It was not shyness; I was never shy with Nate. It was simply the dissonance of two natures which required a third to harmonize them. If by any fluke Nate and I had ever married we would have been wretchedly unhappy.

Nate was not good-looking. He was tall and had curly hair, a pale face somewhat freckled, greenish-gray eyes which were apt to twinkle teasingly. Yet sometimes—especially when he wore a certain cap I remember well—he had decided distinction of appearance and used to make the other C. boys, even the handsome ones, look rather commonplace and "bumpkin-y." He was very clever and had a fine voice for singing. There was no charm of any kind about him—he was singularly lacking in it. Yet he was a very agreeable companion intellectually. I have most of his letters still—tied with ribbon in my old trunk. Once in a while I take them out and read them. They always bring those old days back very vividly. I have no photograph of Nate—there were no kodaks in those days; more's the pity.

Nate is a lawyer in some Western town—Estevan, Sask. I think. He does not seem to have risen as high as he should, considering his undoubted talents. He married a Miss Saunders of Halifax.[372] I never heard anything about her save her name. Sometimes I have thought Nate might have written me a line of congratulation on my literary success. I used to talk over my aspirations with him in those old days. But he has never done so (I always have felt that Nate felt a little resentful that I let him drift out of my life, even though he had ceased to care. His vanity suffered a little, I think.) I remember he once told me, a little condescendingly, that I had a "very fair intellect" and if I could have a college course I might attain to "some success" in the world of letters!

Well, I went out to Prince Albert. I was sixteen that winter—and still

---

372   In 1906 LMM wrote that Nate had married Mabel Saunders of Wolfville, Nova Scotia, and moved to Sydney, Nova Scotia, to practise law.

a minx. Poor John Mustard could testify to that.[373] I laughed at him, jeered at him, flouted him, made him the laughing stock of Prince Albert. And yet—when a man persisted in dangling after a girl who used him so didn't he deserve to be minxed? I hold he did.

I never could understand why John Mustard endured it. I was a pretty girl, but I was never such a distracting beauty that a man would be involved in such an infatuation because of my face; and in no other way did I try to attract him. Yet he kept up the crazy pursuit until he had to be flatly refused. There have never been any pleasant memories in connection with this one of my lovers. I have always felt queerly ashamed of the whole incident—I suppose because Mustard was such an awkward shambling shamefaced sort of lover.

Meanwhile, I was hand in glove with Willie Pritchard. I *liked* Willie I am quite sure better than any man I ever had as a friend. He was not in the least intellectual; but he was an exceedingly congenial companion. I always felt perfectly at home with him—enjoyed every minute I spent in his company. But I was not in the slightest degree in love with him, even sentimentally. He was as deeply in love with me as a boy of eighteen could be. We corresponded for six years—at first enthusiastically—then more coldly, till finally in the year before his death our letters were few and far between though very friendly. I think Willie had ceased to care for me save as a friend, though I never heard of him going with any other girl.

But while Will was my cavalier all through my P.A. year I had a certain *tendresse*—sentimental and concealed—for a young Englishman named Barwell who was in P.A. that year. I never met him but I used to hear him sing frequently at the many concerts and there was something about his *eyelids* that intrigued me. It was the eyelids with which I was in love, I am quite sure. My unrequited and unsuspected affection never bothered me in the least or prevented me in the slightest degree from having a splendid time with Will and tormenting John Mustard to the verge of insanity. Thus are we fashioned.

The next winter I was in Park Corner. Lem MacLeod and Edwin Simpson were both aspirants for the privilege of walking home with me from "Literary." I snubbed Edwin till he left me alone and went around with Lem. But all the time I had a romantic passion for Irving Howatt,

---

373 John Alexander Mustard (1867–1950) had been smitten with LMM when her high school teacher in Prince Albert in 1890–91; she viewed him as serious and well-meaning, though he had trouble controlling his classes. As discussed in earlier notes, he was called to the ministry, becoming a respected Presbyterian cleric in Toronto. He and Catherine Agnes McFarlane were married in 1896, and Ewan Macdonald and LMM visited the Mustards in July 1922 at their Muskoka cottage, a visit that provided a setting for LMM's *The Blue Castle* (1926).

who was not in the least interested in me. It went a little deeper than any of my previous ones. I did a great deal of day-dreaming that winter, with Irv as central figure; but I was not in the least unhappy because he was not in love with me. I had a jolly good time every way. I soon forgot all about Irv after I left Park Corner and as the years passed on began to find him a bit of a bore in our chance meetings. Then Fate played one of the jokes she loves. She gave me the "colored box" I had once so ardently wished for—and the spools were gone! Irv Howatt was at Dalhousie the winter I was on the *Echo* staff.[374] He began calling to see me and "seeing me home" from Fort Massey. He was very "soft"—yes, "soft" is exactly the word, horrible as it is. If I had wished I could have had him at my feet—have been engaged to him in short order. I did not wish it; he bored me to tears; I loathed his attentions; I could not imagine what in the world had ever attracted me to him ten years before. I snubbed him so pointedly that he took the hint and came near me no more. How relieved I was!

As for Lem I never cared for him in the least and liked him only moderately. He liked me about as well as he could like anyone and wanted to marry me but he was not capable of really *loving* anyone, I think.

As for Edwin Simpson—well, there is no need, nor any desire on my part to say much of him.

Alec Macneill drove me around for years during my Cavendish vacations. I haven't any idea whether he cared for me or not. I think he would have liked to marry me but had sense enough to know he never could and was too shrewd to make a fool of himself over a girl he couldn't get. Alec has always been an excellent friend of mine and is very fond of me in a harmless platonic fashion to this day.

During the winter I was at Prince of Wales I went around with Lem but it was John Sutherland I was in love with. John was my cousin, a tall homely fellow but with something very charming in his personality. I really cared a goodish bit for Jack, though still not enough to hurt at all. He liked me pretty well too—was a *little bit* in love with me I think but not enough to hurt either. But I *could* have cared for John quite deeply if I had "let myself go." But it wouldn't have lasted—I would have grown tired of him. He could not have held me.

In Bideford Lou Dystant cared terribly. He was a good sort who mattered nothing to me. In Belmont, Fulton and Alf Simpson made asses of themselves more or less. I loathed Fulton but I *had* a queer unaccountable attraction toward Alf. For a few months I let myself feel it,

---

374   LMM worked from 1901 to 1902 for the newspaper, the Halifax *Echo*.

though I never showed it. It was quite safe to feel it—I knew I had it easily in hand and could stifle it whenever it seemed good to me. Alf was homely and uncouth—but it was there, for all that. Finally, when I decided to marry Ed I said, "Now, this nonsense about Alf must end"— and end it did. That was all it amounted to.

Then I went to Bedeque and—for the first time—*loved*. Loved with heart and soul and sense—with everything but *mind*. For the first time I experienced the overwhelming power of the senses—of sheer physical passion. It had never touched me before. My infatuation for Herman Leard was undoubtedly, the *deepest strongest* feeling I have ever experienced. It lacked only mental subjugation to be all-conquering. But that it *did* lack—and so I escaped. But I left something behind in that fiery furnace of temptation—and I brought something out. Passion gives and takes away.

In the years after I gave up teaching to live with grandmother there were various men. Joe Stewart, a good-looking inanity, drove me around one summer and was quite madly in love and horribly cut up because he knew there was no chance for him. He never told me this but used to pour out his woes to Clara Campbell. Henry McLure was another. These two men meant nothing to me in any way—I did not feel even friendship—nothing but a tepid toleration. As for Will Houston—well, *that* was not one of *my* "love-affairs" certainly.

For Oliver Macneill I felt a certain mad infatuation of the senses— nothing else. I lived through a few hectic weeks on his account and then forgot him utterly.

I was never in love with Ewan—never have been in love with him. But I was—have been—and am, very fond of him. He came into my life at its darkest hour when I was utterly lonely and discouraged with no prospects of any kind, and no real friends near me. At first I thought I could never care at all for his type of man; but I did; and I married him—and I have not regretted that I did so. I have been contented in my marriage, and intensely happy in my motherhood. Life has not been—never can be—what I once hoped it would be in my girlhood dreams. But I think, taking one thing with another, that I am as happy as the majority of people in this odd world and happier than a great many of them.

But I write not of these things for the Editor of *Everywoman's*. My grandchildren may include what they like in my biography. But while I live these things are arcana.

There was a recruiting concert at Udora tonight.[375] Ewan and I drove

---

375 Udora, Ontario, a village originally known as Snoddon Corners, is about 10 km/6 miles

up in the teeth of a biting wind and stinging drift to speak and recite respectively. It was past one when we got home. I must cut this sort of thing out for I cannot stand it. I am willing to do my bit but I can serve neither my family nor country by wrecking my health.

The Manse, Leaskdale, Ont.
Saturday, Jan. 6, 1917

Bad war news—the Germans have captured Braila, one of the great Roumanian granaries.[376] This news depressed me all day. And the rumors regarding Greece continue very alarming. Possibly—nay, probably, they are the inventions of imaginative newspaper correspondents. But they keep one uneasy. One somehow expects that nothing good can come out of Greece.

I had a letter from Mr. Jewett today regretting that Appletons had not got my book. Well, I cannot help feeling sorry, too. But perhaps it will all turn out for the best. I am weary of the whole affair and in very truth am inclined to regret the old days when I was a struggling "free lance," making much less money but unhampered by these worries and perplexities.

Edith and I and the two children spent the afternoon paying a duty visit. I was bored all the time and feel dreadfully tired tonight.

Tuesday, Jan. 9, 1917
The Manse, Leaskdale

The war news has been mixed yesterday and today. The Germans have been winning at some points and losing at others. It looks as if their unchecked drive over Roumania was nearing its end. I pray God the Sereth lines hold.[377] The Greek situation is still alarming.

Today I had the women of the Missionary Society here for a Missionary Tea. This meant a lot of work and some worry but everything went off well and the function was successful of its kind. I did not dare read the war news until it was all over and everybody away, lest if it were bad I should be too disturbed to give the necessary undivided attention to my arrangements.

---

south of the Lake Simcoe shoreline and 6 km/3.75 miles north of Leaskdale.

376   Brăila, an important port city on the Danube in eastern Romania, was taken by German forces on January 4.

377   Cold weather was enabling Romanian forces to slow the German advance and eventually stabilize the front at the Siret ("Sereth") River.

Wednesday, Jan. 10, 1917

Got a check for $2,500 from Stokes to-day, being half of my royalty advance. Tonight I began work on a new book, that is, I began looking over my notebook for ideas, etc.[378]

Thursday, Jan. 11, 1917

The ills of 1917 have begun. Edith took ill today with German measles. I suppose we will all have them.

Today was mercilessly cold—15 below zero and a bitter wind blowing. A big Sunday School Convention met in the church. I attended the afternoon session—but felt miserably tired and draggy. The war news was somewhat better today. Greece is said to have yielded.[379]

Monday, Jan. 15, 1917

Have been exceedingly busy these days as Edith was not able to do anything. She is better today however. I put out the washing this morning and got along well with all my work but am very tired tonight. The weather has been very cold and the war news a mixture of fair and bad. The Germans have reached the Sereth. I cling to the hope that they cannot force it.

I am suffering miserably from an outbreak of eczema on my hands and arms. I am really very much run down. I must get a tonic. But the tonic I really need is a good rest, release from worry, and a thorough vacation from an endless round of missionary meetings, mission-band meetings and Guild meetings and papers.

Saturday, Jan. 20, 1917

Another week ended, thanks be—for it is one week nearer spring, for which I long ceaselessly.

I had a letter from Hattie Smith this week. Her youngest brother has been killed in France, and her son is in the U.S. army and has been on the Mexican border.[380] Is there a heart in the world that does not ache today?

---

378   This book would be *Rainbow Valley* (1919).

379   Newspapers in the British Empire were reporting that King Constantine of Greece had yielded to certain Allied demands. (See note for June 1, 1916.)

380   Harriet ("Hattie") Gordon Smith had been a favourite among LMM's Cavendish teachers, inspiring the character "Miss Stacy" in *Anne of Avonlea* (1909). Her brother, Milton MacLaren Gordon, born in 1880, enlisted in May 1916 and went to France as part of the Northern British Columbia Engineer Corps, 4th Canadian Division. Less than six months later, on October 21, 1916, he was killed in the Battle of the Ancre Heights, a series of British attacks that were part of the Battle of the Somme.

The war news has not been so bad. The Tigris has come into the despatches again and the British have won a victory there. The worst seems to have been over in Roumania. Wednesday was so stormy the mail could not get up and Thursday was the same. Then we could endure it no longer and Ewan drove down to Uxbridge despite the drifts and brought back the mail. It really seemed as if we had been a year without it. We had a regular debauch of reading Thursday evening—a feast after the famine.

Today I had a letter from Amanda, so compact of envy, malice and all uncharitableness that it made me sick at heart to read it.[381] She seems to be living in there at Mayfield, literally stewing in her own venom and exhaling it in everything she says or writes. What a tragedy to befall a nature that once promised fair. I never can get over the pity of it.

Sunday, Jan. 21, 1917
The Manse, Leaskdale

Really, this has been a dreadful day. All day a bitter and furious northeast wind blew. This is the only wind that affects us here and when it blows the house is really not fit to live in. All day the kitchen and dining room were literally as cold as a barn and the rest of the house little better. I was all alone from noon until Ewan came home from Zephyr church at ten. Storm outside and gloom and cold within. I put the children to bed after supper to ensure their being warm and then tried to read the evening away but was so blue and lonely I could not fasten my thoughts on my book. It is very seldom I feel as I felt tonight—like some imprisoned soul. I was very thankful when Ewan got home safe for I had been afraid the roads would be blocked. I seemed haunted all the evening by some dismal presentiment of impending evil.

The Manse, Leaskdale
Monday, Jan. 22, 1917

My presentiment came true. This morning word was 'phoned over that Goldwin Lapp had been killed at the front.[382] The news upset me for the

---

381   Amanda Macneill, LMM's third cousin, was the same age as LMM and her closest friend around age nine.

382   Goldwin Dimma Lapp (1893–1917), son of the Macdonalds' friends George Washington and Effie Loretta Lapp, had been was working in Toronto and studying to be a pharmacist. He had enlisted in January 1915, and was placed with one the first authorized units, the 20th of Central Ontario. By July 1915 he was training in Sandford, England, and later that year was on the Front, marching to St Quentin Cabaret in Belgium on September 28, 1915. On the morning of January 17, 1917 he set out with a special operations raiding party. The raid captured 100

day. I could not help crying all the time. The Lapps are especial friends of ours and Goldwin was the first Scott boy to go to the front. He has been in the trenches for a year and four months and went through the Somme offensive without a scratch. Poor boy! We drove over to Lapps' this afternoon. It was bitterly cold and the roads were dreadful. And it was a heart-breaking errand. But is not life a heart-break these days? It seems to me that the very soul of the universe must ache with anguish.

Sat. Jan. 27, 1917

This has been a very cold, stormy week and today we had another northeast storm, so the house was miserably cold. I do not mind for myself so much but it is so hard to keep the children warm and safeguard them from catching cold. I had Mabel Marquismost of the week sewing for me. There has been no important war news but Greece seems really to have given in at last.

[Chester and Edith]

Monday, Jan. 29, 1917

Ewan and I drove to Uxbridge this afternoon in the teeth of a cold, driving rain. I spent the afternoon in the dentist's chair and as a result felt very tired and useless ever since. I seem to have so little nervous energy now that when any extra strain comes on it I feel exhausted.

The war news today was good. The British have won a success on the west and also on the Tigris and the Russians have scored a win in Bukowina.[383]

The Manse, Leaskdale, Ont.
Tuesday, Jan. 30, 1917

To-day was fine though cold. Ewan and I had to go over to a family on the 5th to tea. The lady of the house shouted at me as if I were deaf

---

prisoners, 40 dug-outs, exploded three ammunition dumps, and took two machine-guns. During this operation, 40 Canadians were killed and 135 injured. LMM dedicated *Rainbow Valley* to him and two other men.

383   British forces continued to push ahead in Ancre, France, north of the Somme River—both McLaren Gordon and Goldwin Lapp had been killed in this region. Bukovina ("Bukowina") is located between modern-day Romania and Ukraine; the Russians had pierced the Austrian line.

and the "old man" remarked feelingly, "You bet your boots," whenever I said anything he agreed with. So it may be inferred that our sojourn there was not exactly a feast of reason. But we had a most excellent supper—for which I pardoned all, as my long cold drive had given me a ravenous appetite. But oh, these "pastoral visitations"!

Saturday, Feb. 3, 1917

Ewan went to Toronto Wednesday morning for a three days visit to take in the Social Congress.[384] We have had it frightfully cold ever since—everything way, way below zero. On Thursday came the terrible news that Germany had declared her intention to indulge in unrestricted submarine warfare.[385] It *sounds* very alarming but can she really do much worse than she has been doing? I doubt it.

I got Kenneth Cruit's photo today.[386] He is an English boy with whom I have corresponded for four years at occasional intervals. He first wrote me when he was fourteen to tell me that he was delighted with my books. Last summer he wrote to tell me he had enlisted and would like to send me his photo in uniform "if I would not think it presumptuous." Needless to say I wrote and told him that I would be delighted to have it. So it came today—two of "it." I shall have one framed and hung on my "khaki row." He has such a pure winsome boyish face. I never saw a more attractive countenance. And it is this boy and thousands like him who must be sent away for cannon fodder because a crowned madman has set the world on fire. Oh, it is iniquitous! Kenneth's photo made me cry.

[Kenneth Cruit]

384 Supported by Canada's major Protestant denominations and an outgrowth of the "social gospel" movement, the Social Service Council of Canada held congresses beginning in 1914 that focused on issues such as temperance, child welfare, and social reform.

385 Germany hoped its policy of unrestricted submarine warfare beginning in February 1917 would force Britain from the war. Though losses were heavy, the British ultimately devised effective anti-submarine measures, notably the convoy system, and the German policy provoked the United States into entering the war on the side of the Allies.

386 Kenneth Cruit from England had enlisted in July 1916. He served with the 8th Yorkshire Regiment and as a First Lieutenant with the Kings African Rifles. Rilla's love-interest in *Rilla of Ingleside*, LMM's 1921 novel about the home-front during the war, is also named Kenneth.

Yesterday the house was uncomfortable all day because of the cold. The gloom of the weather was increased for me by the receipt of a letter from Stokes saying that Page had written them claiming to have a contract for my next book etc. Of course I had expected Page would do this as soon as he had found out that I had given the book to Stokes. But it upset me miserably. Mr. Dominick asked for a copy of all the correspondence between Page and me, so I spent the afternoon copying it out—in so far as I have it, for unfortunately I have only memoranda of the contents of my own letters.[387] I was very tired when it was finished and between over-exhaustion and worry I passed a sleepless night.

To-day was very stormy. Ewan got home in the afternoon. Shortly after his arrival a telephone message came up from Uxbridge saying that the U.S. have severed diplomatic relations with Germany because of the submarine outrage. Edith and I made some candy to celebrate the event![388]

Sunday, Feb. 4, 1917
The Manse, Leaskdale, Ont.

Today was cold and the roads so blocked that only a few village people got out to church. Ewan suffered all day from an ulcerating tooth. I feel somewhat calmer in regard to the Page matter but there is always an undercurrent of worry poisoning everything.

Tuesday, Feb. 6, 1917
The Manse, Leaskdale

Still very cold. Ewan's tooth aches constantly and keeps us all in misery. Besides, today he has developed German measles!

The war news was scanty but the reports from the Tigris are good.[389] But oh, that wretched Page affair! What will be the outcome? I find life bitter because of it.

387　Maynard Dominick was an executive with the Frederick A. Stokes Company, founded in 1890. A *New York Times* story from 1912 describes him as the company treasurer. Stokes became LMM's American publisher from 1917 onward, with the exception of one book, *Further Chronicles of Avonlea*, that was published by L.C. Page under contentious legal circumstances. Even though *Anne's House of Dreams* was under contract with Stokes, Page claimed it held the rights to the book, and went so far as to arrange a reprint edition with Grosset & Dunlap.

388　President Woodrow Wilson announced on February 3, 1917 that the United States had broken off diplomatic relations with Germany, following the German announcement of a policy of unrestricted submarine warfare.

389　British and Indian forces were advancing along the Tigris in modern-day Iraq, retaking the strategic town of Kut on February 23 (Kut had been lost to the Ottomans in April 1916).

Wednesday, Feb. 7, 1917

When I went to the office today and found two letters, one from Stokes and one from McClelland, I was much upset—for I dreaded what the contents might be. But I had to assume a calmness I did not feel and chat to Mrs. Cook and Zella Mustard. I walked home with the latter, trying to talk; but my legs were trembling beneath me. I did not dare open the letters till after dinner. Even so I could not eat. Then I put Stuart to bed and shut myself up in the parlor to face it alone. But there was no further bad news so I felt great relief for the time being. Mac does not think that Page will really carry the matter to the courts. But Page is not a reasonable man so there is really no knowing what he will do.

Thursday, Feb. 8, 1917

Fine and mild—a most welcome change. War news bad as regards the subs but the British have captured Grandcourt.[390] I went to the Red Cross at Jas. Cook's and sewed and smiled and talked, and worried over the war and Page all the time.

Friday, Feb. 9, 1917
The Manse, Leaskdale, Ont.

I do not know when I have ever endured a more utterly *lifeless* day. I feel like a squeezed orange—I have neither animation nor hope nor energy nor interest in anything. Life was gray—gray—gray. I suppose this is nervous exhaustion due to worry and intensified by certain physical conditions. The war news was fair, the British having captured an important fort.

Saturday, Feb. 10, 1917

Bitter cold again. With mail came a letter from Page. I took it in my hand as if it were a snake. Did not dare open it until after I had been to Mission Band for I did not want to be unfitted for my duties. When I came home I opened it. It was not about the new book which was a relief. But it is a most barefaced attempt to cheat me out of a thousand dollars due me on my 1916 royalties on the ground of an alleged discovery of a "mistake" in the royalty reports of three years ago.[391] I have

---

390   Part of the larger strategy of British operations in the Ancre region of northern France, Grandcourt—a village on the Ancre river north of Courcelette—was evacuated by the Germans.

391   Page's deduction of $1,000 from LMM's 1916 royalties was one of two claims made by her in her first suit against the firm, the other being Page's sale of the reprint rights for *Anne's House*

written to Mac about it, asking if he advises taking legal action in the matter. Page is certainly a most thoroughgoing scoundrel. I shall likely lose this money and I cannot afford to do that, especially at present.

I was reading the proof of *Anne's House of Dreams* tonight. It should have been a pleasant task but there was no pleasure in it as matters are.

Sunday, Feb. 18, 1917
The Manse, Leaskdale, Ont.

A hard, hard week. Last Sunday was exceedingly cold. I felt very draggy and listless the whole day but went to the church in the afternoon and superintended the decorations for the memorial service for Goldwin Lapp at night. In spite of the fearsome cold the church was crowded. The service was sad and impressive. Oh, God grant that we do not have to have another.

Monday was the coldest day this winter—22 below zero.[392] I thought my feet would freeze while I was working in the kitchen.

I had a letter from Stokes. Dreaded to open it; but there was nothing in it to cause fresh alarm—on the contrary, it was encouraging, for they are in possession of all the facts and are evidently of the opinion that Page cannot do much except "bluff." Nevertheless the possibility hangs over me like a sword of Damocles. All week I lived in dread of the next letter from them, telling what happened when Page received their reply. Every day I dreaded the mail. Yesterday the letter did come, enclosing one from Page, uttering all sorts of threats and stating that he had put the matter into the hands of his lawyers. Whether this necessarily means that he is really going to take the affair into court I do not know and cannot find out for a few days. The suspense will nearly drive me wild I think. I can neither sleep nor eat. My face frightens me when I look in the glass—it is so pale and haggard and hollow-eyed. Page worried another of his authors into an asylum and I verily believe he will drive me there, too. At present I have nothing to distract my thoughts. I am cooped up here by cold and snow and even if I could get out Leaskdale society offers no attractions to me. Ordinarily this does not matter. My work and my books furnish me with plenty of interest and amusement. But in this state of mind I cannot read or do anything but necessary routine work and I find it very hard to get through the days. It is the *uncertainty* that is so terrible. If I knew that I *had* to fight

---

of Dreams.

392 Canada used the Fahrenheit temperature until March 31, 1975, when, as part of an overall "metrication" program, the Celsius scale came into use. A temperature of –22°F. is the equivalent of –30°C.

and *what* I had to fight I think I could summon up enough "grit" to face the issue squarely. But I *know* nothing and I torture myself with a hundred conjectures and suppositions.

The war news yesterday was not good either. The Germans have scored a local win in Champagne.[393] In itself it is not very alarming but it may be the opening of another terrible offensive. *That* is the dreadful thought. It was just about this time last year that they opened their Verdun offensive.

Life has been so full of terror and worry these past two years. I begin to feel a certain weariness I never felt before. And how I dread the coming week. What news will it bring? This afternoon I am alone with the children. They have to be amused, poor little souls, and I find it hard, for my heart is not "at leisure from itself"—it is eaten up with worry and dread.

Sunday, Feb. 25, 1917
The Manse, Leaskdale, Ont.

Have been nearly "visited" to death this week. The war news was good on Monday from both the Ancre and the Tigris.[394] Went to Uxbridge and had another dental seance. Drove home over the wildest roads in a snowstorm. Tuesday I had a young bride and groom to tea and was busy all day preparing for them. Then sat and talked to them until eleven, while my soul yawned and my back ached and my mind whirled around on the Page matter.

Wednesday was a fine and pleasant day—a great rarity this winter. A reassuring letter from MacClelland buoyed me up and relieved my mind to such an extent that I enjoyed our evening drive when we went out to tea. The enjoyment ended with the drive, however.

Thursday I went to the Red Cross at Jas. Mustard's and when Ewan came for me we stayed the evening.[395] The Mustards are nice people and ordinarily I do not look on a visit there as an unpleasant duty. But I was too tired Thursday night to enjoy myself and only wished I was home in bed. Friday we again had to go out to tea and then to a Guild

---

393   German forces had launched several attacks in the Champagne region of northern France, penetrating French positions and taking several lines of trenches as well as many prisoners.

394   The Ancre River is a short (38-km/24-mile) stream in France's Picardy region that flows in a south-west direction into the Somme at the small town of Corbie. In the region that is modern-day Iraq, British and Indian forces were advancing along the Tigris, and on February 23 successfully re-captured the fortified position of Kut (the British-Indian garrison at Kut had been lost to the Ottomans in April 1916; see note for May 1, 1916).

395   See the entry and note for October 3, 1911.

social in the evening with both children. Stuart, being made too much of, could not sleep and grew very cross and fretful. Edith was away so by the time I got them both home and to bed I was too tired to sleep. Yesterday we again had company to tea and were late in getting to bed. Today was Sunday and I have had a blessed rest. Fred Leask came down and took Chester up for the afternoon and Stuart was good. So I had a good "read"—to my great content, as dear Pepys says. I am at present reading *Pepys' Diary*.[396] I never read it before though I have heard of it all my life. It is the most unique book I have ever read. No one but an Englishman could have written it. It is a book without a spark of wit, without a gleam of conscious humor, without passion, imagination or insight. It is a book which deals almost wholly with commonplace people and incidents. And yet it is packed with interest from cover to cover and is irradiated on every page with unconscious humor. Its great charm is its sense of reality. It is impossible to believe that it is over two hundred years since Pepys lived. He must have been alive yesterday. The people he mentions—his neighbors and servants and sweethearts—are alive. We know them. Pepys himself is a most naive and engaging old sinner in his love of fine clothes, of "good eating" and of "gadding abroad looking for beauties." The book is delightful. I always come back to my own world after reading it with a jolt as if I really had been back in the 1660s.

Sunday, March 4, 1917
The Manse, Leaskdale, Ont.

The war news has been uncannily good all the week. The British have been advancing steadily on the Somme front and on the Tigris also. In the latter theatre they have recaptured Kut and wiped out the disgrace of last spring.[397]

The children have both had a very severe cold all the week. Stuart took it Monday night with an attack of croup which gave me a bad scare. But he has had no return of it although his cold has been very bad.

Looking over this journal I find that I have written little of Stuart compared with what I wrote about Chester. This may be partly because he is not such a novelty but more, I think, because I about "wrote my-

---

396   Samuel Pepys (1633–1703) was an English politician who kept a diary from 1660 to 1669.

397   In a systematic campaign that moved up Tigris River, British Forces recaptured the British-Indian garrison in the town of Kut (see note for May 1, 1916).

self out" in that line and could only repeat myself if I went into raptures over Stuart. It is certainly not because I love him less, or find his development any less enthralling and delicious.

He is entirely different from Chester in every way—in personality as well as appearance. He seems to have less aggressiveness—he is a much quieter baby. He is what might be called "a sweet child." He looks like a big wax doll and has dear, appealing ways and delicious little gurgles of laughter and fun. He has remarkably beautiful eyes—large, soft, sky-blue, clear, full of vivacity and yet dreamy, crimson cheeks, and silky

Grace before meal [Stuart]

thick hair that curls in dear ringlets all over his head.

The Ontario government has given the suffrage to women.[398] So I may vote yet ere I die! I wonder! Certainly I shall never vote along merely party lines. But I am glad it has come. Soon, I think, all the provinces will fall into line and then we will have Dominion suffrage. But I truly doubt whether it will make as much change in things as its advocates hope or its opponents fear.

Wednesday, Mar. 7, 1917
The Manse, Leaskdale, Ont.

Have been miserable with grippe and cold. The war news continues fair but not very important. Tonight I finished *Pepys* to my great regret. Would that he had been able to write thirty years more of his diary.

Saturday, March 10, 1917

My cold continues to worry me. This has been a rough blustery week. Have been reading "A Diary of the Great War" by "Pepys Junior."[399] It

---

398   The Wartime Election Act of 1917 extended the vote to women who had husbands, sons, or fathers serving overseas; the meansure was intended to increase support for the pro-conscription vote. In Britain a bill to partially enfranchise women had been introduced on March 28, 1917.

399   Robert Massie Freeman (1866–1949), an English journalist living in Surrey, writing as "Sam Pepys, Junior," published three parodies of Pepys' diaries during the First World War: A

is very amusing but it is not *Pepys*. It is a good imitation but you never forget that it is only all imitation. The modern Pepys *tries* to be funny on every page—which is the vital difference between him and the original Pepys who never dreamed of trying to be funny but was always in deadly earnest. Perhaps if I had not just read the real Pepys I might have had a higher opinion of his "descendant."

Monday, March 12, 1917

We should have hoisted the flag to-day—the British have captured Bagdad.[400] But somehow I have lost heart for flag-raising. I do not think I can again feel any keen emotion in regard to the war news. If I were to hear tomorrow that the British fleet had been defeated I would experience a dreary realization that the empire was lost and we must resign ourselves to the fact; and if a series of unbroken and brilliant victories was to come I would feel a dull thankfulness that the empire was saved; but I would not want to run out and hoist the flag.

At least I think I would not. But who knows what stimulant wormwood or wine might prove?

Tuesday, March 13, 1917

Stokes had planned to issue the *House of Dreams* in August. But Mac writes me that they are going to bring out a small trial edition in June to test the reality of Page's threats. It will shorten the period of suspense. But how I shall dread June. The whole spring will be embittered for me by my anxiety and worry.

Friday, Mar. 16, 1917
The Manse, Leaskdale, Ont.

I did not think any development of the war could surprise me. But one has come. Today word came of a Revolution in Russia and the abdication of the Czar.[401] The whole thing is so stupendous that I feel

---

Diary of the Great Warr [sic] (1916) as well as a *Second Diary* (1917) and a *Last Diary* (1919). LMM discusses Pepys in her journal entry of February 25, 1917.

400   Following successful operations on the Tigris, Baghdad was captured by British Forces without a fight on March 11, 1917.

401   Russia had been approaching military and economic collapse throughout 1916 and 1917. Much was blamed on Nicholas II, who had ruled since November 1, 1894. The Russian high command had handled the war poorly, leading to considerable suffering. In early March 1917, strikes and riots brought the city of Petrograd (now St. Petersburg, Petrograd was then capital of Imperial Russia) to a halt. Nicholas II was unable to control the riots and government forces retreated.

dazed. Internal conditions in Russia have been disquieting for some time but no hint of this was ever foreboded. What the outcome will be God knows. Most of the despatches take the view that it is a good thing for the Allies since the Russian court was infested with pro-Germans. It *will* be a good thing if it holds. But no one can tell what will come of such an overturn. It is not likely the reactionaries will give up without a struggle and if Russia is distracted by internal broils her power of assisting her allies will be lessened. But why worry? It is all part of the Great Plan. After the strange series of dreams I have had since the war began I have become a fatalist. I believe that all is planned out in the councils of Eternity—yea, in the words of the old theology, foreordained. Some day, when I have time, I shall write out those dreams in this journal. To say the least they have been curious.

Sunday, Mar. 18, 1917

To-day I read "A Hilltop on the Marne"—a quite delightful little thing, though lacking the charm of "My Home on the Field of Honor."[402]

No sign of spring yet. To-day was bitter and wintery. These winter Sundays are dreary enough but not so dreary as they used to be at home in those few winters before I left it. How terrible they were! I have been glancing over some pages of my journal written then. Life is a very different thing now. I am often—very often—tired and worried. But I never have any of the terrible days or hours of nervous agony I suffered then. They seem like strange terrible dreams to me now. But— for nothing is perfect—there were some very sweet-things in my life then that are lacking now and which I often long for—walks of wood and shore, accompanied by invisible companions of dream and fancy— friends and lovers. I hanker often times for their wild, elusive flavor.

But my two little sons—they fill life and heart and soul. When Chester puts his arms about my neck and says *"Dear little mother"* or when Stuart cuddles his curly little head against my breast I miss nothing, lack nothing of bliss. Life is full and perfect and complete at such moments.

But—I *would* like an old-time walk in Lover's Lane at sunset—or along the old haunted sandshore in the twilight!

On March 15, 1917 Nicholas II removed himself at the advice of Army Chiefs and a provisional government was established. (This would be the first of two revolutions in Russia, with the second recorded by LMM below in November 1917.)

402   *A Hilltop on the Marne: Being Letters Written June 3–September 8, 1914* (1915) by Mildred Aldrich; *My Home on the Field of Honour* (1916), a memoir from Frances Wilson Huard.

Sunday, Mar. 25, 1917
The Manse, Leaskdale, Ont.

Last Monday Ewan came home with the mail and to me, waiting in the usual tense suspense, said, "Great news today." Well, it *was* great news, and it has so continued all the week. But whether it is *good* news is not yet established and until it is I shall permit myself no rejoicing. But the Germans have begun to retreat on the Western front and are still retreating.[403] The Allies have captured all the objectives for which they fought last year, in the campaign of the Somme. But *why* are the Germans retreating? It does not seem on the face of things that they are compelled to just now. Has Hindenburg some deep-laid scheme on hand? Does he mean to turn on the advancing allies when he has allured them from the shelter of their trenches? I fear it. On the other hand, he may be only doing, while weather conditions favor him, what he knows he would be obliged to do in a short time under less favorable conditions.

All this week we have been "visiting" frantically in an effort to overtake our work in that line before the roads break up. We have been home only one evening and I am deadly tired. It has been, for me, a wasted week.

Yesterday I read a "ten year letter"—one Frede Campbell wrote me ten years ago. I suppose she also read mine. It is a rather gruesome business—too much like opening a grave. At thirty-two I still had the courage to write such letters. Now, at forty-two, I could never dare to write another. What changes there have been since those letters were written! Frede was in Stanley then, teaching school, and I was in the old home, an unknown, obscure scribbler, past my youth. Now I am a wife and happy mother and have written "the famous book" Frede predicts and which I only dreamed of then. The ten years have made a vast change in almost everything that concerned us. And those letters were written before the war! That in itself would be change enough.

The changes for me have been for the better and I think for Frede also. But all change, even if it be for the better, has an element of bitterness in it and bitterness is something which makes itself felt above and before all other flavors.

---

403   Between February 9 and March 15, 1917 German forces in France began a strategic retreat back to the Hindenburg line, a more easily defended position from two territorial projections on the front lines that projected into Allied-held territory, and therefore required defense on three sides (these German-held regions were located between Arras and Saint-Quentin and from Saint-Quentin to Noyon, east of the River Somme). In their retreat, the German army destroyed roads and villages, and took some 125,000 able-bodied civilians to other regions in occupied France. Paul von Hindenburg was Chief of the General Staff of the German Army.

Sunday, Apr. 1, 1917
Leaskdale, Ont.

The "break-up" came the first of the week and now we have spring, albeit a drab and muddy one as yet. The news from the western front is still fair but there are alarming rumors of a German thrust at Riga.[404] We have been still visiting wildly, despite the condition of the roads.

This week I read Butler's "Way of All Flesh."[405] It is a clever book but not by any means the great novel some have pronounced it. It is full of truths and half truths and yet it is on the whole a very false book. It impresses me as having been written by a man who was himself congenitally incapable of feeling any lofty or inspiring passion or even any decent, pleasing ordinary emotion. He therefore refused to believe that any other person could feel such, and proceeded to docket anyone who claimed to as a hypocrite or a fool. Real pleasure I found not in reading the book, but a certain titivating intellectual delight I did find.

Last night, being alone, I read over all Nate Lockhart's old letters—for the first time since my marriage.[406] Their charm for me now lies in the power they possess to transport me back into the past—into a world unrent by the tragedies of the present. For a time, I was again a girl of fifteen, exulting in my newly discovered power to win the love of men. Nate was a clever lad, just wakening to the lure of life and therefore bound to make a goddess of the handiest girl. I was that girl, as it happened. And I was flattered by his devotion and entranced by the love of love. After all, nothing can ever quite equal the wonderful moment when a woman first suspects she is loved. Nate and I had a charming friendship. All that summer and fall before my fifteenth birthday and the winter after it was a delightful period for me. Then came the climax, when Nate and I—both knowing perfectly well what it meant to tell and discover—agreed to tell each other whom we "liked" best. Last night I read again, with a little mockery *and* a little envy that note of Nate's in which he told me the name of the girl he not only liked but *loved*. To be sure, after he had written the "love," an access of shyness or terror must have overcome him for he had marked it out. But the red ink of the original word was quite distinguishable behind the black of the blot and the context would have betrayed him in any case. Well, I received my *cachet* of womanhood that day.

---

404   Riga (now the capital of Latvia), a major Baltic port, would be captured by the Germans on September 3, 1917.

405   *The Way of All Flesh* (1903) by English author Samuel Butler (1835–1902), a best-selling novel with a strong autobiographical component that criticizes aspects of Victorian-era culture.

406   See note/entry for January 5, 1917.

It was, as I have said, the climax. And it spoiled our friendship! That was the price I paid for my rapture. After the fumes of emotional intoxication cleared away I found that I had lost a friend I wanted and gained a lover I did *not* want. But to be adored as Nate adored me was quite pleasant and served for a time to take the place of our vanished comradeship. Then, alas, it palled; and my romance, having no root, withered away.

I have not got all Nate's letters—in fact, I have very few of those he wrote after our mutual confession. They were for the most part too sentimental and I never read them with anything but distaste. So I burned them long ago and kept only the few earlier ones in which Nate confined himself to tentative skirmishings around the great theme.

It is a long time since I heard anything of Nate save the fact that he was living in Estevan, Sask., was a lawyer, and had two boys. It has always been a little wonder to me that Nate should have chosen the law as his profession. I remember one spring evening twenty-seven years ago—yes, it *is* twenty-seven when Nate and I were loitering

The spot on the road

home in the twilight from somewhere and holding high converse on destinies and ideals such as youth revels in. Nate, in speaking of what he would like to be, said emphatically—I recall the exact spot of the road where he said it and the stars that were glittering over the dark firs in the school woods, just beyond—"I would *never* be a lawyer! Making a living out of other people's quarrels seems to me a dirty trade."

Hum! Ha! Well, alas and alack, Nate is not the only one of that philandering couple who has been compelled or allured to forsake or compromise with the ideals we cherished then. I have surrendered many of mine.

Oddly enough, for the last eight years I have carried on a very delightful correspondence with an uncle of Nate's—the Rev. A.J. Lockhart of Winterport, Me. He is a writer of essays and verse and is known in the literary world as "Pastor Felix."[407] Years ago Nate's possession of this uncle cast a glamor over him in my eyes. It was to me quite wonderful that I actually knew a boy whose uncle had written and published books. Nate had one of his books—a volume of poetry entitled

---

407   Methodist clergyman Arthur John Lockhart (1850–1926), Nathan Lockhart's uncle, was best known for *The Papers of Pastor Felix* (1903), but also published several books of verse, including *The Masque of Minstrels, and Other Pieces* (with Burton Wellesley Lockhart; 1887) and *The Isle of Song: A Dream of Arcadia and Other Poems, 1870–1918* (1918).

"The Masque of Minstrels."

When "Anne" was published "Pastor Felix" wrote to me about it. Of course, he knew—and knows—nothing regarding my old love affair with his nephew. He is now an old man. His verse is rather weak but he writes delightful prose and his letters are among the most enjoyable I receive. Well, Nate's letters are re-tied and relocked away. It is not likely I will think of them again for many more years. But neither can I ever quite forget them.

This week, too, I saw a paragraph in the Charlottetown *Guardian*, under the elegant caption, "An Island Booze Fighter," stating that the Rev. Edwin Simpson had resigned his pastorate to become the leader of the Anti-Saloon Association of Rhode Island.[408] I wonder if Ed has got tired of preaching doctrines he doesn't believe in. The last time I talked with him he told me that he could no longer believe in the divinity of Jesus; and when I asked him why he preached it then, he replied that he thought "*e*luding the people was not *de*luding them." Possibly "eluding" people grows wearisome in time.

Sunday, Apr. 15, 1917
Leaskdale, Ont.

A cold, bleak spring so far, no "lure of April days" yet. There has been a fortnight of "good" war news—with huge casualty lists. The British and French are slowly advancing on the western front, purchasing a little village or so a day with the lives for which mothers have agonized. The U.S. has formally declared war at last.[409] I wonder if future historians will acclaim Wilson as a great statesman or a man of straw. It seems impossible to decide just now. I incline to the straw theory. He is too fine a phrase-maker to be anything else.

I went to Toronto on the third and spent a very enjoyable week. I kept the fact of my being in out of the papers so was not bored with "teas" etc. but got around quietly and saw a lot of people I wanted to see. Also did much shopping with great detriment to my purse—for the prices of things are alarming.

I spent most of my time with Mary Beal who is a chummy congenial creature.[410] My last evening I went up to South Drive and spent it

408   LMM accepted Edwin Simpson's proposal of marriage in 1897, but broke off the engagement the next year. The Eighteenth Amendment to the American Constitution, which prohibited the production, transport, and sale of alcoholic beverages, was ratified in January 1919 and came into effect in 1920. Of the 48 states in the union, only Rhode Island and Connecticut never ratified the amendment, which was repealed on December 5, 1933.

409   President Woodrow Wilson declared war on the German empire in April 1917, having tried to keep the United States neutral.

410   Mary Gould Beal was one of the founding members of Uxbridge's literary society, the

with the MacMurchy's.[411] They are as baffling and inhuman as ever. I always feel when I am with them that I am among the inhabitants of another planet. Their mannerisms intensify with passing years and are now so strongly marked as to be much less amusing and much more disagreeable.

I dropped into Mac's and saw the cover design of *Anne's House of Dreams*—a pretty, *sellable* thing. Of course it does not in the least resemble the house or setting I had in mind but "the trade" all seem to be charmed with it and that is the main thing when it comes to "big sellers." Page has been trying his best to make trouble but the Stokes Co. seem to know just how to manipulate him. He has backed down sufficiently to ask us to "arbitrate the affair" but we have all declined with thanks. I begin to believe that all his threats have been only a gigantic "bluff" but I shall be uneasy until the book is published. He *did* try to get his Toronto lawyers to take up the Canadian end of the case but I found out that they refused, telling him he had no chance. His American lawyers may be less scrupulous.

Thursday, Apr. 19, 1917
The Manse, Leaskdale, Ont.

Another of the little heart breaks of motherhood! Chester last night moved into a room of his own—poor little man. He has always slept in his little crib in the corner of our room. Night after night I have looked on his chubby, rosy face just before I turned out the light. Always in the darkness I felt and loved his nearness. Always in the morning his roguish smiles gleamed across to me. But last night he slept alone—like a little hero, too, making no fuss about it. The change, painful as it is to me, is necessary. Stuart has

Stuart and Edith

been sleeping all winter with Edith; but I do not like this and he must henceforth have the crib. He is a rosy, adorable occupant—but oh, my little first-born man! Another step away from me.

We are in an orgy of housecleaning. Amen.

Hypatia Club. She continued to attend even after moving to Toronto.

411   Marjory MacMurchy, author of *The Woman—Bless Her* (1916), an address to women to support the war effort, and other books. Helen MacMurchy, Marjorie's sister, was the first woman doctor to intern at Toronto General Hospital; she made important public health contributions to Canada and in 1949 was named one of the leading women physicians in the western world (MacMurchy also held outdated views on eugenics).

Sunday, Apr. 29, 1917

A strenuous week! We cleaned the library—a task involving the carrying out, dusting and carrying back of about 1200 books!—the parlor, and papered the kitchen. Friday night I was as tired as a beaten dog. But instead of going to bed as my bones yearned to do I had to dress and drive myself and Mrs. Oxtoby to Udora, four miles away, to recite at a "Maple Syrup Social" given in aid of the Methodist church there—more fool I! It was one o'clock when I got to bed.

Sunday, May 6, 1917
The Manse, Leaskdale, Ont.

Praise be, we have finished housecleaning. The weather keeps very cold and the war news only fairly good. The situation in Russia is alarming. I fear we can expect little from her this season and there is even a growing dread that she may be deluded into a separate peace.

I am exceedingly tired. Chester had grippe all the early part of the week. I had to trot out night after night to practice for a Red Cross social we have been getting up. It came off in the township hall Friday night and was a success of its kind but oh, how weary I was yesterday. It is shameful that our Red Cross should have to resort to such methods of raising money. The Council should give us a grant large enough to do away with such a necessity.

Monday, May 7, 1917

Today I wrote to the Attorney of the Author's League and put my case re Page and the royalties into his hands. I am dubious about the outcome but I will not tamely sit down and let Page cheat me at pleasure.

The Russian situation continues precarious but the crisis seems past for the time being.

Wednesday, May 9, 1917

The news was rather depressing today. The Germans have retaken Fresnoy, captured with the loss of so much Canadian blood.[412] It is, I suppose, only an incident—but such incidents are disheartening enough.

We were out to tea tonight and I'm afraid I caught cold. I was over

---

412   Canadian operations had been successful on the French Front in spring 1917, particularly in capturing Vimy Ridge. Following this, Canadians and British continued to push eastwards in France, reaching Fresnoy in the north. Canadians captured the village on May 5, but it was retaken through German counterattacks two days later, May 7.

tired and there was a bitter wind. It keeps so cold. There has been no spring like this since I came to Ontario. The crop outlook is not good and this is serious. The spectre of famine is threatening the whole world and the submarine menace is growing. What will be the outcome? Prices now are terrible. Potatoes are four dollars a bag and may soon not be obtainable at any price. We allow ourselves a ration of *five* a day. Did I ever dream I should come to that with *potatoes*. I can remember when they sold for ten cents a bushel at home and even just before I was married twenty cents a bushel was a big price.

Sunday, May 13, 1917

Still cold. Stuart has been sick all the week and I have been sick since Thursday with stomach and intestinal trouble. The war news has been scanty and every day the prices go up. We finished our garden this week. Not an inch of space has been left unutilized this year.

[Stuart]

On Monday Ewan leaves for a short trip to the Island. I have not been thinking of it for I cannot go down this year. But now that he is going I grow very homesick and wish I were going, too. When he comes back I plan to go up to Macdonald College and spend a week with Frede—and then settle down to work for the summer.

Monday, May 14, 1917
The Manse, Leaskdale, Ont.

I drove Ewan to the station this morning and saw him off for the homeland. Then I came home to find a letter from Bertie McIntyre.[413] I have been slightly intoxicated ever since, I think, her news was so unthought-of and delightful—or rather predictive of delight. There is a strong likelihood of her coming to Toronto to live! Laura and her husband are going to move there and Bertie thinks she will come, too, if

---

413 LMM's cousin Beatrice ("Bertie") McIntyre now lived in Vancouver. Laura and Cuthbert were Bertie's siblings.

she can get a position on the Toronto teaching staff. With Frede at Macdonald and Bertie in Toronto, I should really have little more to wish for. But it will not happen—it would be too beautiful. I will not think of it or build on it lest I taste the bitterness of disappointment.

Thursday, May 24, 1917

A nice, warm, pleasant "24th" surely! It has blown a hurricane and been bitterly cold, with showers of *snow*. All this week has been cold.

On Tuesday I got the shock of my life. A letter from Frede Campbell informed me that she had been married the preceding Wednesday in Montreal to Lieut. Cameron Mc-Farlane two days before his expected sailing on his return to the front![414]

I said, when the Czar of Russia abdicated that I should refuse ever to be surprised again. So I was *not* surprised by this—I was only dumfounded, flabbergasted, knocked out and rendered speechless!

I suppose it is because I feel the thing so deeply that I write this frivolously about it. Something about it seems to hurt me terribly—the element of change and doubt that enters into it all I suppose. I knew that Lieut. McFarlane had been courting her ever since his return home on leave but she had written me more than once that nothing could come of it; and though I did not feel sure of *that* I did not dream that she would be

Lieut. Cameron MacFarlane
of the Princess Pats

married before the war was over—nor, it seems, did she, until about six hours before the ceremony.

---

414   Frede had met Nathaniel Cameron McFarlane (LMM spelled his last name "MacFarlane") after they were both hired in 1913 by Macdonald College, part of McGill University. McFarlane, a chemistry instructor, enlisted in 1915 in the Princess Patricia's Canadian Light Infantry and also served with the so-called "New Brunswick Kilties," the 236th Battalion of the Canadian Expeditionary Force. While with the Kilties McFarlane returned for a year to Fredericton, his home town, to assist in recruiting efforts. It was at this time he courted Frede. Home on a six-day leave, the now Lieutenant McFarlane proposed on May 16; he and Frede were married the very same day. McFarlane and his regiment soon returned to France to participate in some of the bloodiest battles of the war.

It hurts me to think that I did not see Frede married. We had always planned that, if she should marry, her wedding would be in this old manse where we have had such good times, and Ewan was to marry her. But plans! The war has upset a few!

Oh, I hope poor Frede will be happy! She has never had much happiness. I have always had a nasty feeling that Frede was not *meant* for happiness—that her nature was and her life must be, essentially tragic—and this in spite of all her laughter and jollity and race-of-Joseph-ness. A war marriage to a bridegroom who is on his last leave is a dubious thing.

Well, perhaps, Bertie *will* come to Toronto, now. I felt that I dare not hope that she and Frede could *both* be so near me. But if the events of the near future will remove Frede to God knows where, I may be permitted to have Bertie, that my soul be not utterly starved of friendship. But not even Bertie can fill Frede's place.

There has been rather good news from the Italian front this week and Russia is struggling terribly to pull herself together. In spite of the hurricane of rumors about a separate peace I do not think there is any real danger of that.[415] The very real and dangerous certainty is that her army is wholly disorganized and, come the best that can, will not be anything to reckon on or with this summer.

Yesterday I took Chester to Zephyr and left him with Lily. He will stay with her until my return. Ewan returned today.

I leave tomorrow for Macdonald where poor Frede is pluckily going on with her work by way of a honeymoon.

Saturday, May 26, 1917
Teacher's Residence, Macdonald College, Quebec

Yesterday morning Ewan drove me to Uxbridge. 'Twas a delightful day for a wonder. A fine day is such a novelty this spring. I reached Toronto at noon and stayed there until eleven. Rung in with Mary Beal and had a jolly time. Saw Balfour in the street procession.[416] Wound up with a "movie" at the Strand at night and motored to the train afterwards. Spent a poor night as usual on the train and reached St. Anne's about nine the next morning. Frede met me and we proceeded to talk!!!

---

415   Following the overthrow of Nicholas II there were growing concerns that Russia would default on its commitment to Allied powers and organize a separate peace with Germany.

416   Arthur James Balfour (1848–1930), who had succeeded Edward Grey as British foreign secretary in 1916, travelled to the United States to confer with American leaders in April and May of 1917. He also came to Canada to address Parliament on May 28, 1917, and to speak to the Montreal chapter of the Canadian Club two days later.

I have a nice room in the teacher's residence. Frede gave a little tea to the house girls this afternoon which I enjoyed very much.

We spent the evening in my room thrashing things over. I found out that Frede had sent a telegram to me the day she was married which I never received. This cured a little ache which I admit I had felt ever since I got her letter. I had thought that she had let three days elapse after her marriage before letting me know and that *did* hurt. I might have known Frede

[Teacher's Residence, Macdonald College, Ste-Anne de Bellevue]

[Macdonald College, Women's Residence]

[Frede's Wedding Announcement]

wouldn't do such a thing.

But I hardly know what to think of her marriage. She is eight years older than Cameron MacFarlane. It is all very well to say that he is old for his years. No doubt he is—two years in the hell of the battle front might reasonably age a man! And Frede is young for hers. Nevertheless, while 34 and 26 is not so bad 50 and 42 sounds dubious and Nature's logic is very relentless.

Again, I do *not* think Frede loves him in any real sense of the word. They have been friends for years—she likes him—but—but—but! However, it all may turn out better than I expect and little worse than I hope.

Cameron has not left Canada yet after all. He is with his regiment in New Brunswick, as all their orders were recalled after conscription was mooted.[417] The vexing side of this is that had they known it was to be so they could just as well have come down to Leaskdale and been married as not. Poor Frede is in a rather trying position here, on a gossipy campus, amid acquaintances who are not all friends or all friendly. I think my presence is a help and comfort to her—a bit of family backing and countenance, as it were. The gods grant us all pluck and patience and good digestion! We need it.

Saturday Night. June 2, 1917
Macdonald College, Quebec

This week has seemed as long as several weeks—judging by what we have crammed into it. I have been having a delightful time— the pleasantest "vacation" I have had since my marriage.

Macdonald College is a beautiful place, especially now in the opening bloom of spring. The buildings and equipment are wonderful. I have been feeling a queer, half-resentful feeling of regret that I could not have spent some of my formative girlhood years in such a place. There is no sense in feeling resentful about it. Nobody was to blame— except the fates. Yet I feel as if I had

[The Campus]

[St. George's Church]

417   Until 1917, enlisting in the Canadian Expeditionary Force had taken place on a volunteer basis. Following Vimy Ridge, Prime Minister Robert Borden began to move toward compulsory military service by way of replacements for the thousands of dead and injured. Quebec as a whole did not favour conscription.

been cheated out of something I would have enjoyed enormously and which would have been of great benefit to me. I envied the girls who sat under the trees of the campus. And *they* envied *me*, and stood in my presence with timid awe and admiration such as schoolgirls feel when they meet the writer of books they love. And so the world wags—truly "a mad, world, my masters."

[The Practice Dining Room]

I have met a great many delightful people—and some not at all delightful, but all interesting to me because I have heard Frede talk of them so much.

Sunday evening Frede and I went to St. George's church.[418] We sat nearly at the top and as we came out we became aware that the organist—a rejected suitor of Frede's by the way—was playing Mendelssohn's *Wedding March*. There were significant smiles on several faces. If "Chippy" were trying to get a bit of revenge I must say he took a peculiar method. I think it was an abominable trick.

[The Teacher's Residence]

[A corner of the dining room]

Frede and I spent Monday in Montreal shopping—and talking so continuously that we were "dead beat" on returning home. Tuesday afternoon a friend of Frede's gave one of those abominable teas at which I was the guest of honor, terribly bored. In the evening

---

418   St. George's Anglican Church is located in Saint-Anne-de-Bellevue, Quebec, about 35 km/22 miles south-west of Montreal and roughly a quarter-hour's walk from Macdonald College, where Frede taught.

Mrs. Fisher gave a dinner for Frede and me in the Practice Dining Room at which the Ladies of the faculty were guests. I rather enjoyed it. The dinner itself, cooked and served by the Household Service Girls, was exquisite. But these undiluted "hen parties" are rather cloying affairs—especially when they are formal. Oh, for one agreeable, sociable rooster!

[The Ottawa, from the College]

Afterwards Frede and I sat up until an unearthly hour and thrashed over her problems. We laughed so much during the process that we did not make any great headway in solving them.

Wednesday we went into Montreal and heard Balfour speak in the Royal Victoria College—and incidentally saw heaps of raw crude human nature in the crush.[419] I was somewhat disappointed in Balfour's speech. It was commonplace—even hesitating; and he seemed to have as much difficulty in disposing of his hands as the rawest recruit at some rural "debating society." But the might of Britain was behind him and there was something about him that said "English Gen-

[The Ottawa]

[The Ottawa]

tleman" very unmistakably. As we sat on the steps of the Residence that evening, Frede said, "The Germans can do what they like to increase their population after the war but they'll never be able to get anything that looks like him." That's about it.

---

419   Established in 1899, Royal Victoria was McGill University's women's college. The residence did not become co-ed until 2010.

We have our meals in the College dining room—and Institutional meals seem alike the world over. Wholesome—oh, very wholesome!

We were out to tea twice this week and enjoyed it. Friday was spoiled for me by a letter from Ila saying that Carl had had his leg blown off above the knee at Vimy Ridge and was now in a hospital in England.[420] Poor little fellow! It seems dreadful that he should be maimed for life like that. But Ila says he is very cheerful and plucky over it. I suppose he is almost thankful to escape from that inferno even at such a price.

Last night Frede and I had the most beautiful walk along the river road in the moonlight and talked of a thousand things in past and present and future. The moonlight danced on the silver river and the banks dreamed in shadow; and somehow Frede and I drew very near to each other in spirit and knew what was in each other's hearts without need of words.

The war news has been scanty this week and the Russian situation seems to be going from bad to worse. The Montreal papers give fearfully pessimistic views possibly with the idea of inducing Quebec to accept conscription. But I long for a good, optimistic "Globe" *Summary*, just to brace me up. There was an editorial in the Montreal *Star* Friday night that almost squelched me.

Wednesday, June 6, 1917
The Manse, Leaskdale, Ont.

I left St. Anne's at 11.30 last Sunday night. It was a cold, windy, lonely night and I felt horribly blue over leaving Frede but glad, in spite of my good times, to be going home to my darling boys. How I had longed for them! Every night after I went to bed I could feel Stuart's dear little chubby arms around my neck.

I reached Toronto the next morning, spent a satisfactory day from a business standpoint, and got on the Uxbridge train exceedingly tired, but promising myself a good rest on the way out, varied by a refreshing dip or two into a new book Mr. McClelland had given me. But I am not one to whom is allotted rest. The train was crowded and an elderly commercial traveller shared my seat. That man deliberately set out to talk me to death! He poured out on my weary ears a ceaseless stream of facts concerning politics, the war, conscription, woman suffrage, and the way he and his wife brought up their family and apportioned their income. Had I gone on to Blackwater I should have been a dead

420   Ila May Montgomery was one of three children by Hugh Montgomery's second marriage to Mary Ann McRae, and hence she and Carl were half-siblings to LMM.

woman. As it was, I staggered off at Uxbridge with a faint spark of life still in me which a pleasant drive home with Ewan in the spring twilight fanned into a respectable flame once more.

Friday, June 8, 1917
Leaskdale, Ont.

After a weary time of inaction the war news was good today. The British have captured Messines Ridge—a notable success.[421] The Russian situation seems to be clearing up a little.

Mrs. Hugh Mustard

Hugh Mustard died to-day. Ewan and I feel his death keenly. He was not only our right-hand man in the church but our warm personal friend. He and his wife met us in Uxbridge when we came here after our wedding trip and I have always remembered his hearty handshake. I feel his death as I have not felt any other death in the congregation.

Thursday, June 14, 1917
Leaskdale, Ont.

Yesterday I almost felt like running up the flag—although the flag raising spirit has pretty nearly left me. The news came that Constantine of Greece has "abdicated"—that is the Allies have finally packed him and his German queen out of Greece, bag and baggage—a year and a half too late.[422] Venizelos will come to his own now and have a chance to retrieve what he can out of the wreck of his hopes.

Last night Edith and I drove ourselves to Zephyr where I had promised to recite at a Red Cross Social. A terrific thunderstorm came up and we had to stay there all night and had a bad time all round. Came home early this morning, rushed through my work and went to Red Cross over on the 6th in the afternoon. Oh, for my bed!

---

421   Capturing the village of Messines, Belgium, was part of a British campaign to relieve pressure on French positions as well as to deprive the Germans of a region of high ground along the front, near Ypres. German losses in this successful campaign were heavy.

422   See note for June 1, 1916. King Constantine I was pro-German, while Prime Minister Eleftherios Venizelos supported the Allies. After much internal political turmoil, with increasing pressure from the Allies, Constantine left Greece on June 11, 1917.

Sunday, July 1, 1917

There has been *no* war news of any importance since the capture of the Messines Ridge. It seems so hard to *wait*. The Russian muddle is certainly clearing up a little and the danger of a separate peace *seems* past. I have been busy— so busy—too busy. And I never seem able to get a good night's sleep now. It is seldom we can get to bed before eleven and Stuart wakens so early and then—good-bye, slumber. I know I am over-working—but what can I do? Certain things *must* be done—and there are so many of them. I feel tired, body and soul, tonight.

Stuart picking roses

Saturday, July 7, 1917
Leaskdale, Ont.

Chester's birthday—he is five years old! It seems hard to believe that it *can* be five years since I saw that wee baby-lad of mine. He is a big, sturdy fellow, rosy and tanned, the picture of health. In some ways he has been a rather difficult child to manage—he is so determined and so full of ebullient energy. But this period seems almost over. He is now beginning to develop an understanding and self-control that should

Three Good Pals [Ewan, Stuart and Chester]

"Chums" [Doug Madill, Cameron Leask, Chester]

gradually make my task much easier. He is a very loyal, straightforward little soul, with a very tender heart. He seems free from deceit or low cunning—from "mean" faults in general.

We arranged to celebrate his birthday by a picnic in the woods up the old mill-race, to which we invited his bosom chums, Cameron Leask and Douglas Madill. But we had no sooner reached our picnic ground than a thunderstorm came up and we had to flee home and have our picnic on the veranda.

The war news this past week has been good. Russia has had a wonderful sort of resurrection and Brusiloff has opened an offensive that seems to be sweeping everything before it.[423] But will it last? Somehow, I haven't much faith in the stability of Russia's efforts. Every offensive she has begun has petered out. It is to be hoped that this will be an exception. Yet I have little confidence in her revolutionary army.

Saturday, July 21, 1917
Leaskdale, Ont.

Cover Design

Verily I say unto you put not your trust in Russians. After a week of wonderful successes they are being driven back so rapidly that their retreat is alarmingly like a rout.[424] Traitorous regiments are deserting their posts—probably bribed thereto by German gold. The situation could hardly be much worse than it is at present.

Today I got my author's copies of "Anne's House of Dreams," although it will not be "published" until August 24th. Stokes gave up his idea of bringing out a trial issue in June. I have not been worrying over the matter lately. I know Page can do nothing and I feel tolerably sure he will not be such a fool as to try.

The House of Dreams is nicely "made," with a pretty cover design. The latter is very illogical of course. Twenty-five year old Anne looks

---

423   The final Russian offensive of World War 1 was the Kerensky Offensive, organized by Russian Minister of War Alexander Kerensky, taking place in July. Russian forces attacked Austro-Hungarian and German positions in Galicia (now western Ukraine).

424   The Russian Army had been suffering from poor morale and discipline. The Kerensky, or "July," Offensive in Galicia, Ukraine—the last offensive to be launched by the Russians and widely felt to be ill timed—had collapsed.

like a girl of seventeen. But it is all very dainty and will "catch the trade." I do hope the book will be a success. It would be humiliating to me if it failed to make good, for I would feel that Stokes would think they had been led into giving "big terms" to an author who could not "deliver the goods." Then, too, its failure will make glad the heart of Page. Myself, I think the book is the best I have ever written not even excepting *Green Gables* or my own favorite "The Story Girl." But will the dear public think so? The Canadian advance orders are 12,000 copies—a huge advance on the numbers sold by Page, who never sold more than 3,000 and very seldom more than one or two.

The scene of the story is laid mainly at "Four Winds Harbor"—New London harbor was in my mind, though I altered the geography to suit my requirements. "Captain Jim" is a pet creation of mine. He had his first incarnation several years ago in a short story of mine published under the title "The Life Book of Captain Jesse." Some of the stories he tells were ones I used to hear Grandfather tell many years ago—especially the one about Father Chiniquy.[425]

Sunday, July 29, 1917
The Manse, Leaskdale, Ont.

An exceedingly hot day has ended in as hot a night. However, this has been a cool summer so far—more like an Island summer. The Russian war news has been bad all the week. Kerensky is virtually dictator now.[426] But the question is, can he dictate? I fear me, no.

I have been very busy all the week canning fruit and vegetables, in obedience to the behests of the newspapers. I think it will take more than a thrift campaign to put Russia on her feet again.

Sunday, Aug. 5, 1917

Somehow I feel horribly depressed. This has been a hard week. The first part was swelteringly hot. Monday, Tuesday and Wednesday nights were so hot that it was impossible to sleep in the house. So we slept outside, Ewan and the boys behind the bamboo screen on the veran-

---

425 "The Life Book of Captain Jesse" appeared in the August 1909 issue of the American magazine *The Housekeeper*. Charles Chiniquy (1809–90) was ordained in Quebec as a Roman-Catholic priest, but following disputes with the Catholic Church became a Presbyterian minister in the USA. He also became an anti-Catholic activist, authoring books such as *The Priest, the Woman, and the Confessional* (1880).

426 Alexander Kerensky—the Russian Minister of War in 1917—succeeded Prince Lvov (the first Prime Minister following the removal of the Romanovs) as Russia's Prime Minister.

da, myself in the hammock under the big apple tree that never
bears any apples.

All my life I have nursed a secret wish to "sleep out." I have
always wanted to go camping.
Now my wish was attained. It
was a beautiful clear night with
a full moon in the south-west.
The breeze whispered softly, the
perfume of flowers floated on
the dewy air—all was according

The Veranda

to Hoyle.[427] But alas! There were mosquitoes—scores of them. Mosquitoes don't know the horn-book of romance. I stood it until two o'clock
and then retreated to the library floor.

The war news has been bad. The Russians are retreating—and retreating—*and* retreating.[428] The whole army seems demoralized. Brusiloff has resigned or been dismissed—a bad thing, for he was a great
general. Where will it end?

Wednesday, Aug. 8, 1917
Leaskdale, Ont.

Monday afternoon I went in to Toronto and met Bertie McIntyre that night
in the Union Station.

It is six years since I saw her last. I
expected we would feel a little strange
at first—that those six years would
hang between us like a misty little veil.
But there was nothing of the sort. We
were at one from the moment of our
meeting. For all the difference, our
parting at Kensington Station might
have been yesterday. Bert is the same
dear girl, as full of fun and philosophy

Bertie

427   "According to Hoyle" is a phrase meaning "in keeping with the rules" or "in accordance
with how things should be done." It stems from the work of Edmond Hoyle (1672–1769), a writer
who codified the rules for a variety of card games, beginning with whist and moving on to back-
gammon, piquet and other games.

428   The Kerensky Offensive (see entry for July 7, 1917) was widely considered to be a poorly
judged military campaign in the wake of widespread political change in Russia; by July 23, Russian forces had retreated some 240 km/150 miles.

as ever. We came home yesterday and last night sat in the parlor until the wee sma's, settling up a number of theological and ethical problems that had lain over since our last sederunt.[429]

Saturday, Aug. 11, 1917

The Russian situation is still obscure but seems to be clearing a little. Bertie and I have been having a dear week. This afternoon we suffered the fearful boredom of a Mission Band picnic for which we afterwards gave the reward of merit by going for a drive in the twilight by ourselves—through the shadowy, beautiful side road, down the Sixth, across to the Seventh, and so home. Nothing exciting—and yet it was one of those pleasures that shine forever in memory with a soft starry radiance.

[Horse and trap]

Wednesday, Aug. 15, 1917

To-day Mr. Warner motored us to Lake Simcoe where we had a picnic, a delightful row, and a glimpse of an aeroplane.[430] As I watched it calmly soaring over us I quoted to Bertie a random verse that came into my mind.

"With the majesty of pinion
Which the Theban eagles bear,
Sailing with supreme dominion,
Through the azure fields of air."[431]

---

429   "Sederunt" is a Scottish term for the sitting of a court or like body; it came to be applied to any prolonged discussion. The root is the Latin sederunt, meaning "they sat."

430   Isaac Warner and his wife Fannie (née Colwell) lived near the Macdonalds; Warner was the village blacksmith and his son William also took up the trade. Lake Simcoe, about 18 km/11 miles north-north-east of Leaskdale, has a surface area of 722 square kilometres/279 square miles, about 4 percent that of Lake Ontario, the smallest of the Great Lakes, and empties into Georgian Bay through Lake Couchiching and the Severn River.

431   LMM misquotes lines from a poem by Thomas Gray (1716–1771), "The Progress of Poesy: A Pindaric Ode" (1757) (and in *Rilla of Ingleside* (1921) Anne Blythe similarly misquotes Gray). The relevant lines are: . . . Though he inherit / Nor the pride, nor ample pinion, / That the Theban eagle bear / Sailing with supreme dominion / Through the azure deep of air . . ." (lines 113–17, from the online Thomas Gray Archive).

It is all very wonderful. But will humanity be any the *happier* because of aeroplanes? It seems to me that the *sum* of human happiness remains much the same from age to age, however it may vary in distribution, and that all the "many inventions" neither lessen nor increase it. After all, "the kingdom of heaven is within you."

Friday, Aug. 17, 1917
The Manse, Leaskdale, Ont.

Ewan and I drove Bertie to the station this morning and I saw her depart with a sick heart—for she is not going to stay east after all. I knew *that* was too good to be true. We have had a lovely time during her visit; but life seems lonely now that it is over.

[Montgomery and Bertie McIntyre]

Bertie and I had a most memorable and glorious walk at sunset last evening up the north hill and sought pictures in the clouds until we must certainly have been adjudged utter lunatics if anyone were watching us from the houses along the road—as probably someone was. We would walk along our faces fixed on the sky, then suddenly stop, grasp each other excitedly by the arm and point cloudward. No doubt when one

[Ewan, boys, Bertie, and Montgomery]

of the Jones' cows was killed in their pasture by lightning this afternoon Mrs. Jones would attribute it to our weird incantations of last evening. But—Bertie has gone. The house is so empty tonight.

Friday, Aug. 31, 1917

After all, that was not my last taste of Bertie. Fate has been kind and has given me an unexpected box of bon-bons. When Bertie reached Toronto she found a telegram from Vancouver giving her an extra week's holiday. So Monday last I went into Toronto and stayed at Laura's till Wednesday morning. Laura, Bertie, and I took in the Exhibition and the Grand Stand show at night and we had a lovely time, which seemed to us like one of our gay old revels of long ago, when I would go into Charlottetown and the three of us would gad off to the opera for an evening's fun.[432] It *is* so jolly to be able to shake off for a few days the everlasting incubus of Missionary meetings and mission bands and guilds, and have a little carefree enjoyment.

Earl Grey has lately died after a somewhat long illness. I felt sorry to hear it. Well, I shall not have any more heart to heart talks with him on the steps of unmentionable resorts and thereby drive his countess into agonies of jealousy.[433]

The war news from the Western front has been fairly good this week but that from the Russian theatre has been very dispiriting. We have entered upon our fourth year of the war. I wonder how much more humanity can bear. And there were some who said, when the war broke out "It will be over by Christmas." Ewan was one of them and I can yet see his look of tolerant amusement when I said, "It will last at least three years."

Saturday, Sept. 8, 1917
The Manse, Leaskdale

The war news from Russia has been very bad this week. The Germans have crossed the Dvina and are marching on Riga with every likelihood of taking it.[434] Of course treachery is again at the bottom of this. The Italians have been doing well and winning some important successes which may eventually mean the elimination of Austria.

Tuesday evening when I got home from a boresome "missionary tea" at Zephyr I found that my half-sister Kate had been here, having motored over from Beaverton with some of her cousins whom she is visit-

---

432   The Toronto Industrial Exhibition was founded in 1879 (it was preceded by provincially sponsored fairs that were held in different cities, including Toronto). From 1912 its name was changed to the Canadian National Exhibition. The "Grand Stand" was built in 1907 and could accommodate a crowd of up to 16,000. In 1947 it was destroyed by fire. The 1917 edition of the CNE featured an automobile show, a "women's building" showcasing 18,000 square feet of exhibits, and displays inspired by the war effort, including "bombing on the lake front" and "bayonet demonstrations." The fiftieth anniversary of Confederation was also marked by a lavish pageant.

433   Albert Henry George Grey, 4th Earl Grey (1851–1917) had served as the ninth Governor General of Canada from 1904 to 1911. Grey had been a fan of LMM's books, and at his request had met her in 1910. (See her entry for September 16, 1910.) He should not be confused with Edward Grey, the British Foreign Secretary, 1905–1915.

434   During the first three weeks of September, the German 8th Army advanced on the retreating Russian forces, pushing them back across the Western Dvina River (now known as the Daugava; it rises in the Valdai Hills to flow 1,020 km/630 miles into the Baltic Sea) and toward the city of Riga, now the capital of Latvia. With her use of the term "treachery" in the next sentence, LMM is no doubt contemplating the prospect of a separate peace between German and Russia.

ing there.[435] I was sorry to have missed her, so next morning Ewan and I drove over to Beaverton. He left me at the MacKenzies and I stayed there about three hours—quite the longest three hours I have endured for many moons.

I was much disappointed in Kate—though why I should have been disappointed I don't know, for I remembered quite well what she was like when she called at the Oxtoby house six years ago. I never met so listless, dull, and uninteresting a girl. I tried my best to talk to her but no subject, personal or impersonal, seemed to hold the slightest interest for her. There was *nothing* of father about her, save a physical resemblance in eyes and nose. Neither was she much like her mother, who was a person of considerable force of character, however disagreeable it might be. I was deeply thankful when Ewan finally appeared. After chatting for half an hour we left. "And so *that* is your sister," he said as we walked away. "What an inane person." "Inane" was the very adjective.

Kate is studying nursing in Winnipeg hospital and will graduate next spring. She evidently does not care much for her work, having taken it up, I fancy, because she hated teaching and found herself "getting on" and no available man emerging from the horizon mists. Kate is about thirty. In one thing she is certainly her mother's daughter—her restless craving for "a good time" and extraneous excitement and her dislike of work. Mrs. Montgomery was one of the laziest women I ever met.

In short, my heart did not warm to Kate in the slightest degree. We are not "next of kin" in anything save the accident of birth.

Sunday, Sept. 16, 1917
Leaskdale, Ont.

A rather hard week. More bad Russian news—this time of Korniloff's revolt.[436] At latest reports Kerensky was crushing the revolt. Perhaps that is best but I must confess that I wish Korniloff had succeeded. I believe that Kerensky is a weakling, unable to control the elements of the Russian situation. Korniloff would have been a strong leader and would have tolerated no nonsense along military lines. But he has thrown and lost and it remains to be seen what Kerensky will be able to do. The Italians have won a great victory on San Gabriele which may open the way to Trieste.[437]

---

435   Kate Montgomery, daughter of LMM's father Hugh John from his second marriage.

436   The Commander-in-Chief of the Russian Army, General Lavr Kornilov, led a coup against the Russian Provisional Government, headed by Alexander Kerensky. While the coup failed, it reflected widespread unrest in Russia.

437   Another of many battles along the Isonzo River (now known as the Soča River, running through Western Slovenia). The Italians made what would turn out to be some short-lived

Ewan has been a martyr to a severe attack of neuralgia in arm and shoulder all the week. He has suffered greatly night and day. As a result I, as well as he, get little sleep and feel rather seedy. I had a pleasant little outing yesterday when I motored to Whitby with the members of the Hypatia Club. Mrs. Dr. Bascom entertained us all and we had a very nice time. I paid my usual fee for pleasure, though, for when we got back to Uxbridge I had to drive myself home alone, through a very dark night, meeting an endless stream of buggies and cars bound for the Saturday night's attractions there. I was so tired when I got home that I hardly thought it worth while to have gone at all.

Sunday, Sept. 23, 1917
The Manse, Leaskdale, Ont.

This has been a very busy, hard week and I feel almost worn out. Ewan is no better. He has really had a dreadful week of it. What with losing sleep and rushing madly through the days to overtake a thousand duties I feel almost discouraged. This has been such a busy summer—and I foresee a yet busier fall. And over us all the time—*all* the time—the ever-deepening shadow of war.

Tuesday, Sept. 25, 1917
Leaskdale, Ont.

Busy all day pickling and preserving and then wound up by spending the evening at George Leasks where Mrs. Geo. and I, between us, wrote out 144 appeals for money for our local Red Cross.

Geo. Leask's [same as "View from front door," March 22, 1912; the Leask family lived across the street.]

A letter today from Frede made me feel down-hearted. She writes that she cannot come here Christmas— that she must go home to cheer up her mother. I had rather been expecting this, for I knew poor Aunt Annie was having a very hard time with broken-down Uncle John, who has wholly lost his memory and suffers

territorial gains between August 18 and September 12, 1917; armies on both sides were exhausted.

from miserable delusions and has to be tended like a child. So I think Frede is right, but the disappointment is none the less keen.

There was also the usual crop of alarming rumors from Russia—but that is a matter of course. One may as well make up one's mind to the fact that Russia is, to all intents and purposes, a non-combatant from this out, unless a miracle happens.

Thursday, Sept. 27, 1917

Ewan's neuritis is no better—worse, indeed. It seems strange that nothing does him any good. Even the doses of phenacetin etc which give temporary relief in most people have no more effect on him than so many doses of water.[438] The only thing that alleviates it even temporarily is applications of hot water.

There was some encouraging news today of a British advance—only those "advances" never seem to get very far on. And I had a dreadful letter from Amanda, bewailing her unhappiness and abusing her husband in unmeasured terms.[439] It was disgusting. She knew what George Robertson was when, without either love or respect, she married him merely to escape "old maidenhood." If she would but control her own diabolical temper he would be good enough to her. If she does *not* control that same temper she will end up as her wretched old father did, in insanity and suicide. Shall I ever forget that night after his death and the way Amanda behaved! It was enough to make one believe the old legends of devil possession. To my dying day I will see the picture of Amanda, her face convulsed with rage, shaking her fist in my face when I tried to coax her to leave the kitchen and go upstairs before the men brought in the stark dripping body they had found in Clark's pond. Grief she never felt—nothing but the most fiendish rage and fury with her father for "bringing this disgrace" upon them. Her own temper had done much to drive the poor old man to his terrible end. And I much fear me it will yet drive her to a similar one. Poor unhappy woman—who was once so nice a girl. What a tragedy her life has been and all because of the twin demons of temper and jealousy! Even yet, when I recall those old days—our walks and talks and nights and outings together—it seems to me that the Amanda I loved so much then *must* be somewhere yet and that this changeling is none of her.

438　Phenactine (or phenacetin) was one of the first widely used analgesic (or pain relieving) drugs, first brought to market in 1887. It was withdrawn from sale in Canada in 1973 and the U.S. in 1983 because of side effects.

439　Amanda Macneill, LMM's third cousin, had been her closest friend around age nine.

Friday, Sept. 28, 1917
The Manse, Leaskdale, Ont.

Still Ewan is no better. We had all our arrangements made to leave on Monday for Boston to spend a week with Flora; but we have decided that we must put it off for a week.[440]

I canned pears today and then went to the church in the evening and presided over the social guild—something I do not like doing when Ewan is not present, owing to the fact that prayer has to be offered.

Wednesday, Oct. 24, 1917

October so far has been a busy month. On the first Edith went away for her vacation and I had the busiest week of my life I think—doing all the household work, getting the house ready to be left, getting ourselves ready to go and doing up a lot of canning and preserving. Ewan's neuralgia improved slowly but our sleep was broken and when we started on our trip on Monday I was so tired, so utterly tired that I would much have preferred to go to bed. We left Toronto at eleven that night and got into Boston Wednesday morning. A little later we were at East Braintree where Flora—now Mrs. Eagles—and her husband have a very cosy and convenient little bungalow.

It was very different from my last visit to Boston. For one thing there was no calling at the office on Beacon St. I sighed a little over this. That Boston trip was very delightful and Mr. Page very kind. If only he hadn't been a scamp!

By the way, Mildred divorced him last spring! I have made some ghastly discoveries of late about them, of which I had no inkling when I was their guest. Mildred it seems was Louis' *third* wife. His first wife died it seems

The Eagles' Bungalow

very soon after their marriage. He then married a Boston girl, very beautiful, accomplished and charming. Eventually she suspected him

---

440   Flora Macdonald Eagles (1862–1924) was the only child and namesake of Ewan's father Alexander and his first wife Flora (1833–1860). She married New Brunswicker Amos Braintree (1853–1941); they lived in Braintree, Massachusetts, a town of about 10,000 16 km/10 miles from Boston.

of unfaithfulness. One of his office staff was a girl who had divorced her husband—why, I do not know. Mrs. Page had her husband shadowed, found that her suspicions were correct and divorced him. He then married his new love—Mildred. They had been married about six years when I was there. Of course I knew nothing of all this then but it explains several things that puzzled me a bit when I was there. Last spring Mildred sued him for divorce—on the ground of *cruelty* and failure to provide—and got it. So that's that! He has to pay about $10,000 a year alimony to each of his two ex-wives, so no wonder he has to cheat his authors.

We had a very nice time in our week's visit, though I did not go about much because of the children. Both were very good and attracted attention wherever we went—especially Stuart, who won everybody with his delightful smiles. I spent one afternoon in Boston with Alma Macneill and we had a pleasant time. On our way back we got to Montreal at 10 P.M., were met by Frede and her husband, and had an hour with them. Cam was leaving for the front in a few days. And yet we spent the whole hour, jesting, laughing, and talking nonsense. Somehow we could not strike another note. Cam has since left. I hope he may come back; but it seems like asking too much to expect any man to come back scatheless from that hell twice. I am glad I saw him once at least. He seems real to me now. Heretofore, he has seemed like a myth and that did not seem right in the matter of Frede's husband.

Brothers

Three of a kind [Chester, Ewan, Stuart]

Every time I go away for a visit those miserable Russians do something to spoil it. I felt sure that trouble was coming in that quarter for I had had another of my curious "snow" dreams just before I left. Sure enough, the capture of the Riga Island by Germany followed, with its threat of an advance on Petrograd.[441] This has not

---

441 Riga, Latvia was captured by German forces on September 3, 1917. On September 11 they captured the Island of Saaremaa in the Gulf of Riga. Saaremaa could have allowed sea access to Petrograd (now St Pet-ersburg).

followed, however, and the incident seems almost closed. I wish I could think my dream *did* refer to it, for then I could believe that the danger was over. But, bad as it was, it somehow does not seem anything like bad enough to "justify" my dream, and I have an uneasy feeling that something worse is coming yet—the worst thing that has so far happened to Russia.

Both British and French have won some dashing local victories lately.

Tuesday, Oct. 30, 1917
St. Paul's Manse, Leaskdale

Every fall there is some catastrophe in regard to the war to embitter the waning days. Two years ago it was Serbia, last year it was Roumania, this year it threatens to be Italy.[442] Oh, the agony of the past few days!

It has come like a bolt from the blue. All summer the Italians were gaining important victories, working their way foot by foot towards Trieste, which seemed almost within their grasp. On Oct. 25th came the first alarming rumors of a huge German offensive against the Italians. On Friday, the despatches were bad but nothing very disastrous seemed in sight. On Saturday the bolt fell. It was a beautiful day and we were enjoying ourselves out cleaning up the lawn and garden. Then the mail came with the news that the Germans had broken through the Italian line to the north, capturing 30,000 and, what was far worse, endangering the whole Italian army and all the gains of the past three years. All Saturday afternoon I worried. At night Edith telephoned down to Uxbridge to ask what the night despatches were. I did not prevent her though personally I had not the courage to do it. I

Corner of lawn

have never dared, when a crisis was on, to 'phone on Saturday night and thereby risk greater anxiety for Sunday. But I let her do it, wildly hoping that the news might be better. It was infinitely worse. Sixty thousand were captured and many guns.

---

442   Austro-Hungarian forces along the Italian front had been weakened by successive fighting. Germany agreed to reinforce the Austrian army in the region, with the goal of pushing the Italians back across the Isonzo river (now known as the Soča, running through Western Slovenia), further if possible. Six German divisions and nine Austrian divisions broke through Italian positions near Caporetto (now Kobarid, Slovenia). The Italians suffered heavy losses between October and November: 10,000 killed, 30,000 wounded, and 265,000 taken prisoner.

I passed a dreadful night. I took a veronal powder in my desperation but even it could not overcome my unrest and I got only an hour or two of troubled slumber.[443] In that brief sleep, however, came another strange dream and, if it came from the gate of horn, Italy will not be utterly defeated. Sunday was a most miserable day. I went to church and sat with my mind pivoting on the Italian situation and spinning around it as on a wheel of torture. In the afternoon I couldn't read. I walked the floor and wrestled with principalities and powers. Sunday night I slept from sheer exhaustion. Yesterday morning I worked feverishly until Ewan left for the office. Then I could work no more but locked myself in the parlor and paced the floor in an anguish of suspense. The news was terrible—Goritz taken, 100,000 Italians taken and the whole Italian army in full retreat.[444]

I went all to pieces. The only thing I could do was plain sewing that required no attention. So I sewed madly until five and then again retreated to the parlor and paced the floor for a twilight hour of agony. Evening brought a reaction of calmness and I was able to read but got little good of it, while torrents of rain poured down outside. I have had many bad days since the beginning of the war but all added together could scarcely equal yesterday. It was by far the worst of them all. Last night I slept poorly and all through this cold, autumnal forenoon I worked hard at routine tasks requiring little thought. When the mail came the news was slightly better. For the first time there seemed a gleam of hope that the Italian armies might yet escape supreme disaster.

Wednesday, October 31, 1917
The Manse, Leaskdale

The Italian retreat still continues but it is not the panic rout of the first few days, and, there seems some ground for hoping that they will be able to make a stand at the Tagliamento.

We cleaned the trunk room today. I am thankful to be able to work again.

Thursday, Nov. 1, 1917

Housecleaned in forenoon, went to Red Cross in afternoon and Guild at night—all in a dull maze of worry and foreboding. Cadorna seems to

---

443 Veronal is the trade name for the barbiturate barbital or barbitone. It was brought to market by the Bayer company and remained a widely used sleeping aid until the 1950s.

444 "Goritz" (now Gorizia in northeastern Italy) had been under Italian control since August 1916; it was lost to Central Powers in October 1916.

have rallied his men but the situation is still very critical.[445] I foresee weeks of racking suspense. In the early days of the war we had the strength to endure it. But in this, the fourth year, when we had hoped for victory, it is very hard to bear it. The Russian collapse is mainly the cause of the Italian reverse, of course—Austria has been able to take her men from the eastern front and hurl them against Italy.

Saturday, Nov. 3, 1917

Cadorna has got his army safe behind the Tagliamento, though with the loss of 70,000 more men. Pray God he may be able to hold it but I fear he cannot. The news from the Western front is fair as the Germans have had to retreat a little. But what is that compared to their victorious march in Italy?

Tuesday, Nov. 6, 1917
The Manse, Leaskdale

Alarming news that the Teutons have forced the Upper Tagliamento.[446] Worried all day over this. Oh, what will become of Italy—and then of France?

Wednesday, Nov. 7, 1917

The Italians are retreating in good order to the Piave River. A strange calm fell on me when I heard this—as if I had received also some psychic message that the worst was over as far as Italy was concerned— and this though military critics think that the Piave line cannot be held and predict a further retreat to the Adige. But the Piave line *must* hold or Venice will fall to the Hun—an unthinkable catastrophe. *They must not get it.* They must *not!*

I put faith in my message and went out to tea and enjoyed myself for the first time since that hideous Saturday night. The Canadians have taken Passchendaele—a victory that would have been blazoned

---

445   Luigi Cardorna (1850–1928) was Chief of Staff of the Italian Army in the early part of World War 1. Cadorna's poor handling of the Italian army's response to Austro-German offensive at Caporetto is partly blamed for the heavy Italian losses that LMM recounts. Following the retreat he was removed from immediate command.

446   The Italian army retreated across the Tagliamento River, establishing defensive positions. Newspapers reported that on November 2 a German division established a bridgehead across the river further north; given the exhaustion of soliders on both since in the region, however, this maneuver did not advance further.

in headlines a fortnight ago, but which now, in the gloom of the Italian disaster is hardly noticed.[447]

Thursday, Nov. 8, 1917

The Italians are retreating in good order to the Piave—alas for the fact that they are *retreating* successfully should be good news—and the British have taken Gaza.[448] This unlooked-for-resumption of the Palestine campaign comes as a surprise.

We drove over to Zephyr this afternoon, had supper in a house where we almost perished with cold and where the people were dreadfully dull, went to Guild and had a cold dismal drive home through an exceedingly dark night. How tired I was—and with what a gasp of thankfulness did I creep into my comfortable bed!

Friday, Nov. 9, 1917
Leaskdale, Ont.

My "Russian" dream was a true one. To-day came the worst news from Russia yet—that Kerensky's government is overthrown and that the Bolsheviki is in power led by two notorious pro-Germans.[449] This means that worse things are to follow.

Monday, Nov. 12, 1917

Dreaded the mail unspeakably. The news in the *Globe* was fairly cheering but the *Mail* and the *World* seem to think that a retreat to the Adige is inevitable and that means that Venice—but no, I will not think it—I

---

447   The Battle of Passchendaele was a costly and controversial series of operations on the Western Front involving Allied attacks launched between July and November 1917 to gain control of a strategic ridge near Ypres, Belgium. Several British offensives, carried out under appalling conditions, had failed to capture the ridge and resulted in heavy casualties. In late October 1917, four Divisions of the Canadian Corps under Canadian General Arthur Currie led three separate attacks, successfully gaining control of the ridge, but at the high cost of 15,600 casualties.

448   At the end of October 1917, the Egyptian Expeditionary Force (a multi-national army led by British General Edmund Allenby) broke the Ottoman lines at the town of Be'er Sheva, entered Southern Palestine and fought their way north and later to the east. About six weeks later they were in Jerusalem

449   A provisional government had been in power in Petrograd (now St Petersburg) since the removal of the Russian Tzar in March 1917, following the first of two revolutions in Russian in that year (see entry/note for March 16, 1917). On November 6 and 7, 1917, the "Red" army, organized by Bolshevik party leaders Vladimir Lenin and Leon Trostky, overthrew the provisional government, with a goal of establishing soviets—or worker's councils—across the country to improve conditions for the working people. The war had caused massive suffering in Russia; the Bolksheviks also had promised to remove Russia from the war.

will not believe it.[450] Venice *shall* be saved. There are wild mixed rumors from Russia. Kerensky is said to be marching on Petrograd. But I lost faith in Kerensky long ago. He is too weak and indecisive.[451] Russia is on the knees of the gods. I shall give up worrying about her.

Tomorrow I go to Toronto to see my brother Carl. He is home from the front and will spend the winter in Toronto having his leg treated. Frankly, I dread going to see him, having in mind my meeting with Kate.

Wednesday, Nov. 14, 1917
The Manse, Leaskdale, Ont.

Yesterday was a very beautiful day. Ewan drove me to Uxbridge and I got on the train. Far down the car a man was reading a *Globe*. I caught a partial glimpse of the headline—*Great Battle in Italy*. There I sat in miserable terror and suspense. If there had been a great battle it could not have resulted in victory of the Italians or there would have been a different headline. They had lost it—Venice was lost. For God's sake, why didn't some trainman come along with papers!! If I hadn't wanted one they would have passed by the dozen. None came— none came—none came— and half the way to Toronto I

Carl [and Stuart]

sat there wretchedly trying to figure out what the whole head line was

---

450   A retreat to the Adige River in northern Italy would have meant the loss of the famous Italian city of Venice. However, the speed of the Austro-German advance had caused logistical supply problems, and the advance was halted at the Piave River, 30 km/19 miles north of Venice.

451   Alexander Kerensky had served in the Provisional Government following the overthrow of Tzar Nicholas. He lost support and was overthrown by the Bolsheviks. Although he did rally some loyal troops, he eventually fled the country.

and looking, I doubt not, so dazed that the conductor glanced at me sharply evidently wondering if I ought to be out alone. Finally a news-boy *did* come, I feverishly bought a *Globe* and found, that the headline which had caused me such misery was only "Allies Prepare for Great Battle in Italy"!

The situation is very critical. On the outcome of that battle depend great issues beyond even the loss of Venice. The rumors from Russia are wild. There has been fighting and both sides claim to be successful.

I hied me up town to Rosehill Ave. where Carl was staying with his mother's cousin. He came hopping on his one leg to the door to meet me. I just caught hold of him and kissed him. No need to dread that meeting. He is father's son and my *full* brother—the dear, plucky, jolly little chap. He is *so* like father in his ways and personality, and very like him in looks, too. In short, he is just a darling. It was a great relief to me. It would have hurt me horribly if I couldn't have loved Carl—worse, much worse, than it did in Kate's case. We had a jolly afternoon together. He has father's own knack of telling laughter-provoking sto-ries. He was so like father that I had the most ridiculous sensation that he *was* father and that I was his daughter, instead of being, as I am, quite old enough to be his mother.

I came home last night. Today there was the same old dread of the mail. I will drop dead some day when Ewan comes in at the door with it!

The news from Italy is dubious. The Austro-Germans are making tremendous attacks on the northern front and if they smash through there the Piave line is turned. There is no satisfaction in the news from Russia. Ow!

Thursday, Nov. 15, 1917
The Manse, Leaskdale, Ont.

A hard day for those in anxiety—dull and drizzly and cold. Lived once again through the coming of the mail. The news was good as far as it went. The Italians are putting up a gallant fight and so far are holding but the situation remains critical. The sub. losses are small and the British have won a victory in Palestine.[452] After this I took heart and went to a Red Cross meeting and from there over to tea in Zephyr. A very good tea, too, the creature comfort there of being needed to brace

---

452   Following the successful capture of Gaza (see entry/note for November 8, 1917), British operations in the region continued to push north. LMM may have been referring to the capture of the strategically important ridge of Wadi el Hesi, east of Gaza, on November 9.

me up for the ensuing dismal walk through a wet muddy night over a muddy, unknown road to one of those ghastly performances known as "cottage prayer-meetings." And so home and to bed—*a la* Pepys—for which I was good and ready.

Sunday, Nov. 18, 1917

One of those dull, gray, autumnal Sundays I always dread, when the babies and I are alone here from noon and get tired of everything lawful. This past week has been a very hard one in its increasing suspense. But still the Italians hold back the Huns from the Venetian plains.[453] There is nothing definite from Russia but the British are making good progress in Palestine. It begins to look as if they might capture Jerusalem. But there have been too many "almosts" in this war. It is useless to think about Jerusalem until it is actually taken.

Tuesday, Nov. 20, 1917
Leaskdale, Ont.

The Italians still hold but the situation seems to be at a crisis. I feel ceaseless anxiety over it. I worked two hours at my new book today and then went to eat supper and spend the evening. We were with a nice family and I enjoyed myself after a fashion but there was always the undercurrent of worry which made itself felt continually. I laughed and talked with one part of my mind and with the other haunted the Piave front. I feel at present as if I *could not* face the war news for the rest of the week—for this week will probably decide the fate of Venice. But perhaps by morning I shall have gained from wells of slumber a little fresh strength to go on with.

Wednesday, Nov. 21, 1917

Dull, gloomy, drizzling. Walked the parlor floor while waiting for the mail. Once more it was not so bad. The British are near Jerusalem and the Italians still hold Mt. Tomba. But the despatches are full of hints that they must retreat to the Adige and Russia seems in a worse state than ever. I felt very dull and depressed the rest of the day but compelled myself to work doggedly.

---

453   The Italians, reinforced by six French and five British divisions, held their positions at the Piave River (see entry/note for November 12, 1917).

Friday, Nov. 23, 1917

This has been positively a wonderful day. Yesterday we had such a storm that we had no mail so today my dread was doubled. But the news was splendid—the British have won the biggest victory of the war on the western front.[454] Such tidings were almost intoxicating after the unbroken brew of wormwood we have been drinking this past month. And the Italians hold still. This afternoon I felt like a released prisoner. I cheerfully got ready and drove five miles through heavy snow and bitter cold to Zephyr to take supper with a family that is one of my pet detestations. I don't think I *could* have stood them had the news *not* been good. As it was I gulped them without a grimace and even looked pleasant afterwards.

Saturday, Nov. 24, 1917
The Manse, Leaskdale, Ont.

Italians still holding. But Russia—or rather the scoundrels who have got her in their power—are offering Germany an armistice.

Monday, Nov. 26, 1917

We drove down to Uxbridge this afternoon to hear Sir Robert Borden and Mr. Rowell speak.[455] I am especially interested in the coming election not only because it will be the most momentous ever held in Canada, not only because it will or will not show Quebec that her long day of domination is over, but because I have a vote, by the grace of my brother Carl.[456] All Canadian women will have the vote soon. Sir Robert is certainly no orator, yet he has a forceful, direct way of speaking and what he says sticks in your memory. Powell is more flowery and eloquent—more interesting to listen to, but rather too emotional for

---

454   On November 20, 1917 a massive British force—nine infantry divisions, five cavalry divisions, and three tank brigades—launched a surprise attack on German positions near Cambrai. The attack was successful but the follow-up was not, and ten days later the Germans counterattacked, regaining most of the lost ground.

455   Newton Wesley Rowell (1867–1941) was leader of the Ontario Liberal Party in 1917. A supporter of conscription, in 1917 Rowell left the Ontario legislature to join Borden's government. He won a seat as a Unionist MP for Durham in the December 1917 federal election.

456   Canada needed to raise more troops to meet its commitments to its allies, but public opinion in the country was divided. Many Canadians, including a large number of French Canadians, did not fully support the war effort, and were even less supportive of compulsory military service. Prime Minister Robert Borden had introduced the Military Voters Act in August 1917, which extended the right to vote to women (partly in the awareness that women who had sons and husbands in active service would be more likely to support conscription).

strength. If I had not already believed every word he said I don't think he would have convinced me.

Thursday, Nov. 29, 1917
Leaskdale, Ont.

General Maurice says that he considers the Italian crisis past—as far as this offensive is concerned at least.[457] I believe that there will be another one—I have been "warned in a dream" of it—but I believe that it, too, will fail. Meanwhile I frizzle in torture just the same.

There are a thousand rumors from Russia but one thing stands out in bitter certainty. The Bolshiviki are arranging an armistice.[458]

Saturday, December 1, 1917

We are having a breathing spell before the next turn of the rack. There was no especial news yesterday or today. To-night I had a treat—a quiet, undisturbed evening for reading. I am reading Lecky's "History of Rationalism."[459] Gods, through what seas of blood and over what red-hot plough shares of torment has humanity reeled in its onward progress. Was it necessary? Could not Omnipotence have made the ascent a *little* less hard—difficult, perhaps, but not agonizing. Were the rack and stake and thumbscrews the *only* way? These questions are idle. But the mind persists in asking them.

Monday, Dec. 3, 1917
2 Nina Ave., Toronto

Came in this morning to spend a week with Mary Beal. I need the change and enjoy it, and yet it wrenches at my heart

Miss Bollert

457　Major-General Sir Frederick Barton Maurice (1871–1951), British Army officer, correspondent, and writer.

458　The new Bolshevik government had vowed to stop Russian participation in the war. An armistice was under negotiation that would come into effect on December 15, 1917.

459　William Edward Hartpole Lecky's (1838–1903) *History of the Rise and Influence of the Spirit of Rationalism in Europe* (1865) surveys aspects of the intellectual history of eighteenth-century Europe.

[Sherbourne House Club Dining Room]

strings to leave my home and my darling boys. The war news is none too encouraging. The Germans are trying with all their might to undo the effects of the British win at Cambrai and I fear they will partially succeed.

This afternoon I gave a little talk on "The Responsibility of Women in the Future" to a chapter of the Daughters of the Empire. I dislike trying to speak in public but I did it today and tried to say as simply as possible some things that are very near my heart—especially in regard to the fate of the children of the future. I suppose I did fairly well for one of my listeners, Miss Bollert, asked me to repeat the speech tonight to the girls of the Sherbourne House Club. Mary and I dined at the club and I spoke to the girls afterwards. As a result I am "all in" tonight and have no yearnings whatever to become a platform speaker.

Tuesday, Dec. 4, 1917
2 Nina Ave., Toronto

I went to Mac's this morning and among other things discovered this curious fact. L.C. Page, after declaring repeatedly in his letters to me and his letters to his lawyers that he would "under no circumstances" have any dealings with McClellands regarding my new book, wrote to his lawyers about three weeks before the book was to be published and asked them to find out on the sly—I don't say those were his exact words but that was his meaning—if there was any chance of re-opening negotiations with them. Mr. Page's return to sanity came too late. But as he knew that the contract with Stokes was signed and the book advertised by them it is difficult to understand what chance he thought there could be for him, even supposing the unsupposable that I would have considered such a suggestion for a moment after the way he had behaved.

I lunched with Mac at the National and this evening dined at Mr. Stewart's where Carl also was. He is such a dear little chap—I like him better every time I see him.

Wednesday, Dec. 5, 1917
2 Nina Ave., Toronto

War news from Italy bad again—they have sustained a serious reverse which may result in the smashing of their northern line. I do not believe it will—though no military critic would agree with me. Things are not going overly well at Cambrai either—the Germans have retaken considerable of their lost ground.

I shopped furiously all day and am exceedingly tired.

Friday, Dec. 6, 1917
2 Nina Ave., Toronto

Yesterday at four o'clock I came out of Eaton's brilliant noisy store into the dull gray light of the late winter afternoon. I felt a little tired and dull. A newsboy went past waving a paper across which I saw a big black headline "Halifax City Wrecked." I looked at it indifferently and thought, with a feeling of disgust, "Another of those fake papers."

A few weeks ago, in the stress of the Victory Loan Campaign some enterprising canvassers brought out a fake newspaper, purporting to be published in 1921. It assumed that the present war ended in a draw. Germany recuperated and in four years time struck again—this time at a solitary Britain. The British fleet had been demolished and the paper dealt with the subsequent descent of the Germans upon Canada. Its headlines had been "Germans Land in Canada—Halifax and St. Johns in Ruins" etc. and the despatches gave the details. It was all quite clever and amusing and nearly frightened some of the good people in Toronto into fits. They thought it was genuine.

But I thought a repetition of it was rather silly and wished that the gov't had hit upon a more effective dodge for opening the eyes of Canadians to their peril. With a shrug of impatient contempt I walked down to my car corner. Here a second newsboy went past and I saw that the paper was no fake but a genuine "Star." Still, I was not alarmed. I concluded that some steamer named "Halifax City" was wrecked and although this would have been a sensation in the *Lusitania's* day it is a mere commonplace now. However, I bought a paper out of mild curiosity and opened it.

Twenty minutes later I came to my senses upon an uptown car without any recollection of how I got there. Luckily it proved to be the right one which I had boarded automatically while my brain was trying to take in the magnitude of the disaster when a steamer loaded with munitions blew up in Halifax Harbor and laid fully half the city in ruins.[460] The loss of life is said to be appalling and the whole thing is sickening. It is hard to think that the Germans had no hand in it. It comes so pat to the moment, just before the conscription election. But in so far as appears on the surface the explosion was the result of an accidental collision between two ships.

Laura [McIntyre Aylesworth]

I got here just in time to receive a bevy of Jarvis St. Collegiate girls who had asked for "the honor of an interview."[461] I went through the hour talking like a machine, while my whole consciousness centred around the Halifax horror. Those poor girls sat in an adoring circle and gazed at me with the awed, reverent eyes of idealizing girlhood. I wish I did not feel so ridiculous in these interviews. But the contrast between my real self and what those worshippers of *Anne* believe me to be is too ludicrous. And yet there is something very sweet in the admiration of those innocent young souls. They are so uncritical and ungrudging.

Today I finished shopping. The Halifax story grows worse in each despatch. I hope Edith Russell and her family escaped.[462] There were many killed in Dartmouth where her home is.

This evening I went and had dinner with the Aylsworths. A jolly evening. Laura has such a tang of the old stock.

Monday, Dec. 9, 1917
The Manse, Leaskdale

I had planned to come home Saturday but a terrific blizzard prevented and I could not come before tonight. It is so good to be home again. But I had a nice time in Toronto.

This afternoon when I got on a downtown car I saw a big black headline on a "*Star*" at the other end of the car. "Jerusalem surrenders

---

460   On December 6, 1917 a French cargo ship carrying high explosives and a Norwegian ship collided in Halifax Harbour, causing an explosion that killed 2,000 people and injured 9,000.

461   Jarvis St. Collegiate, in Toronto, is the second oldest school in Ontario, originally founded as a private school in 1797. Dr Archibald MacMurchy—the father of LMM's friend Marjory Mac-Murchy and doctor Helen MacMurchy (see note for April 15, 1917)—had been principal from 1873–1899.

462   Edith Russell, a cousin, was the child of Emily Macneill Montgomery and John Malcolm Montgomery, LMM's aunt and uncle.

to the British."[463] I wanted to give a wild hurrah but I had to do my hurrahing internally. It is wonderful to think that the Cross once more flies over Jerusalem, after so many centuries of the Crescent's rule. Surely it will never again be displaced. After all, it is worth while to live in the days which sees the object of the old Crusades attained. Surely the ghosts of all the old Crusaders should crowd the walls of Jerusalem tonight, with Coeur-de-Lion at their head to welcome the English conquerors.[464]

The Italians, too, are holding bravely, but the Russian muddle goes from bad to worse apparently.

Tuesday, December 11, 1917
Leaskdale, Ont.

A letter from Frede today gave the coup-de-grace to a faint hope that has hitherto refused to die utterly out of my heart. She cannot come for Christmas. Poor old Uncle John is so ill she feels she must go home. She is right. But how lonely Christmas will be. And this year of all years.

Courage! "He that endureth to the end shall be saved."[465] Verily, yes. But what about those who fall by the way? We are not all born with equal powers of endurance.

The storm-cloud is gathering on the western front. All the prophets are busy predicting a supreme effort there by Germany with the men and guns taken from the Russian front.[466] We all feel like a creature cringing away from a threatened blow. God defend the right!

---

463   Jerusalem had been under Ottoman control since 1517. In World War I, capturing Jerusalem became part of the larger Allied strategy within the Middle East. Throughout 1916 and 1917 Allied forces in the form of the Egyptian Expeditionary Force (a multi-national army led by British General Edmund Allenby) had been fighting Ottoman positions combined with German reinforcements in the Sinai Penninsula. From late October into November 1917, a series of successful military campaigns had broken enemy lines south of the city; the British then continued pursuit to Jerusalem. Ottoman forces evacuated the city on December 8–9 and allied soldiers entered on December 9 (Jerusalem was not technically "surrendered"; an Ottoman official involved in the evacuation had left a letter with the Arab Mayor stating that the departure was as effort to avoid harm to the ancient city). The allied taking of Jerusalem was a huge boost to morale across the British Empire, with General Allenby being portrayed as a modern-day Richard Lionheart ("Coeur-de-Lion"). Army officials avoided the Crusades connection, however, given that there were many Muslims in the EEF, not to mention fear of a negative reaction from the local Muslim population.

464   LMM's reference to the Crusades—a series of European military campaigns between 1047 and 1487 to improve Christian access to the Holy Land—reflects her historical imagination and patriotic reporting within the British Empire (the Crusades had long been seen by historians, including those LMM herself read, in a more critical light).

465   Matthew 24:13.

466   Post-revolutionary Soviet Russia was negotiating a peace with the Central Powers. This was concluded on December 15, 1917.

There is also such a constant strain of worry over the election and it intensifies now with every passing day.[467] If the Union Government does not win Canada will be dishonored before the world. And it is so desperately uncertain whether it will win or not—the issues are so tremendous. There is no predicting the outcome from the results of past elections. No election like this was ever fought in Canada before. Estimates of the final result differ hopelessly. Let me add my predictions to the others. Shure and haven't I as good a right to prophesy as anybody? Ontario will balance Quebec, B.C. and the Maritimes will break even and the Prairie Provinces will turn the balance in favour of Union Government.[468]

On the knees of the gods be it!

Wednesday, Dec. 19, 1917
The Manse, Leaskdale, Ont.

On Monday, Dec. 17, I polled my first vote![469]

I have never, I admit, felt any particular interest in politics. Perhaps this was because a woman could take only a theoretical interest anyhow. But I never felt any especial desire to vote. I thought, as a merely academic question, that women certainly should vote. It seemed ridiculous, for example that an educated, intelligent woman should not vote when any illiterate, half or wholly disloyal foreigner could. But it did not worry me in the least. And now that women have, or are soon to have, the vote I do not at all expect a new heaven or a new earth as the result. I hope and believe that certain reforms will be brought appreciably nearer by the women's vote. But I suspect that matters will jog on in pretty much the same old way for a good while yet—or if they do not, it will be owing to the war and conditions arising from it and

---

467   Liberal leader Sir Henri Charles Wilfrid Laurier had served as prime minister of Canada from 1896 to 1911. He was a highly respected bilingual statesman and the dominant political figure of his era. Laurier favoured Canadian involvement in the war and even spearheaded recruiting meetings, but feared conscription would alienate Quebec and divide the country. In this he was right (see the note for December 11, 1917, above). Montgomery's views of Laurier are also reflected in her novel *Rilla of Ingleside* (1921), in which an overfed, poorly behaved dog is named after Laurier.

468   Borden's Union government went on to win 56.9% of the popular vote. Ontario voted 62.3% in favour of Borden (Quebec, by contrast, was 24.7%); BC voted 68%, with the maritime provinces voting less enthusiastically (New Brunswick 59.4%, Nova Scotia 48.4%, and PEI 49.8%). The Prairie provinces also voted in favour of Borden.

469   LMM was one of some 500,000 Canadian women who cast a first ballot in a Federal election on December 17, 1917, the result of Borden's Wartime Elections Act that gave the vote to wives, mothers, and sisters of Canadian soldiers. The same law removed the right to vote from Canadian citizens who had been born in "enemy countries" after March 1902 unless a close family member was on active duty.

not to the franchise.

It is rather too bad that I, who have called myself a Liberal all my life, should have to cast my first vote against Wilfrid Laurier—whom at one time I thought little lower than the angels.[470] This was simply because I was brought up that way. In P.E. Island in the old days—and even yet for that matter—one was born Grit or Tory and so remained. My earliest political recollections are of anathemas hurled at old "Sir John A." whom Grandfather Macneill seemed to regard as a demon in human form.[471] Wilfrid Laurier was Grandfather's political idol and I, who was nothing if not loyal to my clan, worshipped him also. Our feeling was rather ludicrously like that of the old Quebec habitant in a story that used to be told at Liberal "rallies."

A visiting Yankee once remarked to the said habitant, "You Quebec people seem to be crazy over Laurier. I believe you think him as good a man as the king." "Oh, yes, yes, he good as de king—yes, yes." "Well, I suppose you don't think he's as good as the Pope?" "Oh—y-e-e-s,"—more doubtfully but still with assurance, "Oh—ye-e-s, he good as de Pope." "Well, surely you don't think he's as good as God?" The old habitant scratched his head uneasily. "No—no," he admitted reluctantly, "no, 'course he not so good as God—but"—brightening up—"but den, *he's young yet.*"

[The vacant store where Montgomery polled her first vote]

Well, Wilfrid Laurier is an old man now and he has outlived his glory and betrayed his country. Why? Senility—superstition—base political cunning? It is vain to ask. Perhaps even Laurier himself does not know. But on Monday I voted, with a queer little qualm of regret and a queer feeling of disloyalty to my old traditions, for the Government which is Union but which is headed by Laurier's long rival, the Conservative

---

470   Liberal leader Sir Wilfrid Laurier had been Prime Minister between 1896 and 1911, a highly respected bilingual statesman and dominant political figure of his era. Laurier agreed with Canada's involvement in the war but as a French Canadian himself understood that compulsory military service would alienate the majority in Quebec. See also entry/note for December 11, 1917. Canada was bitterly divided over this issue. In *Rilla of Ingleside* (1921), "Wilfrid Laurier" is the name given an overfed, poorly behaved dog.

471   Sir John Alexander Macdonald (1815–1891) was Canada's first Prime Minister, from 1867 to 1873, and again from 1878 to 1891.

chief, Borden.

The poll was held in a most disreputable old vacant store next to the manse. I append a photo of it by way of a souvenir of my first polling booth. The candidate I voted for was Major Sam Sharpe who has always been a rank "Tory." If Hogg, his opponent, had not been an equally rank anti-conscriptionist I would have found it much harder.

Having voted, there was nothing to do but wait. After supper Ewan went to Uxbridge to hear the returns and I hied me to the church where a practice of kiddies for our Sunday School concert was being held. In this occupation I contrived to pass the time with outward calmness until ten when I came home to find that Edith had been listening in on the phone and had this "news."

Sam Sharpe was in with a big majority and Ontario was almost solid for the Gov't.—*but they had done nothing in the west.*[472]

I went to bits. If the West had gone against us, all hope had vanished. Edith went to bed. I could not work or read or sit still. So I began to walk the floor. I walked it until half past eleven when my legs gave out and I sat down perforce. I do think "politics" is too strenuous for women.

At twelve Ewan came home. I met him in the kitchen and looked at him but I did not speak. I was quite past speaking and I was as cold as ice from head to foot. When he told me that it was Laurier who had "done nothing in the West" and that the Gov't was in with a majority that was already fair and would probably be a large one, I could have sat down and cried with relief.

For the first night for a week I had a sleep untroubled by three o'clock visions of a rejoicing Kaiser and a Quebec-bossed Canada. Yesterday the full returns came in and gave the Union Gov't a majority of from 45 to 50. My prediction was about as correct as predictions usually are so I think I may count myself in Class C. of the prophets. British Columbia instead of breaking even went almost solid for Union, whereas the Maritimes gave a small majority for Laurier. The rest was by the book,—Ontario matched Quebec and the West turned the scale lavishly.

It is over—and well over. I hope such an election need never be fought in Canada again.

This afternoon I got a telegram from Frede saying that her father

---

472　Samuel Sharpe, originaly a lawyer in Uxbridge, had been elected MP in 1908. In November 1915, Sharpe raised a new battalion, the 116th from Ontario County; Sharpe recruited many of its soldiers personally. Shortly after he served with distinction in Vimy Ridge in 1917, he was relected to his seat in Parliament.

had died this morning.

I knew Uncle John could not live long, nor was it desirable that he should, for he has been so miserable this past year. His mind was quite gone. He suffered from such terrible delusions and was as helpless as a child. Poor Aunt Annie was almost worn out and a few more months of it would have killed her.

But the news brought a sudden pang of realization of the change that had come over that old, beloved place. Uncle John Campbell was a man I always loved deeply. For no other uncle, of marriage or blood, did I have such an affection. He was the kindest, most hospitable of men. I never heard a harsh word from him.

Uncle John, Aunt Annie, and Frede

He was 84. I cannot "sense" it. To me he always seemed to be about forty or fifty, as he was when I first knew him. He was not an intellectual man and so had poor judgment and "no head for business." But he had all the qualities that make for lovableness.

Well, he has gone. How very few of those "who danced my infancy upon their knee" are left now. I shiver, as with a sensation of physical cold when I think of Uncle John's place being vacant—when I think that never again when I go to Park Corner, will I be met by his hearty handshake and his blithe jest. When I was there last he was sadly failed. But he could still sit down in the parlor and bear his part in the conversation as he always delighted to do. "I'd rather die in the trenches than live under German rule," he repeated several times as he talked about the war.

In the old picture I have placed here Uncle John is shown as he loved to be—surrounded by a crowd of gay young people. He was never so happy as when there was a houseful of guests—especially if he was

The Campbell's House

The house at Park Corner

at the head of the table carving a fat goose and contriving to give everyone a special tidbit.

He has left no son who can take his place. Poor George resembles his father in nothing save his lack of business ability. Possibly a grandson may yet rise up to restore the old place and traditions. I have hopes of some of George's children, if they are not ruined in their upbringing. But oh, for the dear old days when the girls were all home and George was only a chubby little boy and Uncle John and Aunt Annie were in their prime. I am so horribly lonesome to-night—for Ewan is away and I am all alone in the dining room—that my heart aches unbearably, and I have a miserable irrational feeling that my place is "out there" with my kindred.

"Whether 'tis ampler day divinelier lit
Or starless night without."[473]

I look up at the picture of the home at Park Corner hanging on the wall before me—a spacious old house, built in the days when lumber was cheap and large families

Park Corner pantry

---

473   From English poet William Watson's (1868–1935), "The Great Misgiving."

were to be housed. I have always liked its arrangement better than that of any other house I have ever known. I only wish I could have a house of my own like it and I would be satisfied. Roomy old hall, fine pantry, open fireplaces, large airy rooms. And I suppose that now, while I am writing here, that old house so far away is hushed and darkened and in the old parlor Uncle John is lying at rest. At last he sleeps well. God send him good slumber—and a happy awakening.

Tuesday, Dec. 25, 1917
Leaskdale, Ont.

I am glad Christmas is over. I was lonely for Frede—and very busy. As Edith went home I had all the work to do alone and a big dinner to cook, so it took all my time to get everything done. There was nothing really Christmassy about it for me. But the boys had a good time, and that is the main thing. They hung up their stockings last night and found them full of all delectables this morning. Chester still believes fervently in Santa Claus and this year Stuart has realized him—"Santy Tosh" as he calls him. I have only a very hazy recollection of ever believing in Santa Claus. I was beginning to feel very dubious as far back as I can remember.

Friday, Dec. 28, 1917
Leaskdale

This has been a hard day in many ways—hard on muscles and nerves. It was bitterly cold. The war news is none too good as the Huns are making another fierce effort against Italy and have won several important points.

Then this morning Edith told me that she could not stay longer than the first of March, as she intended to be married. I was surprised, as I had not expected it to happen so soon. I think I can get her sister Lily—but I hate changes. And I am rather sorry to lose poor Edith, too, for she isn't a bad little soul. Her two drawbacks were her untidiness and an annoying habit of making inane or out-of-place remarks

Edith [and Stuart]

when company was here and then bursting into a guffaw of laughter. In spite of this, however, she was really a more agreeable co-worker than Lily Reid was.

I went to a business meeting of our Red Cross in the afternoon. After supper we had a Guild Committee meeting here and then went to Guild in the church. I was very tired by this time and a certain well-meant but tactless remark made by a member of the Guild suddenly got under my skin. I came home and cried good and hard. Tomorrow I'll be all right. It's mainly nerves and fatigue.

Acknowledgements

The list of people to thank for this volume is a long one. It begins with an acknowledgement of the ground-breaking work of the first generation of L.M. Montgomery scholars: Mary Henley Rubio, Elizabeth Hillman Waterston, Elizabeth Rollins Epperly, Father Francis W. Bolger, Gabriella Ahmansson, and the late Rea Wilmshurst. (To give an idea of span in my own lifetime: Mary Rubio is my mother and began working on Montgomery when I was a teenager; my own daughter, who has had some involvement in all this, is now 13.) The wonderful research by Mary Beth Cavert for *The Shining Scroll* (among other sources) has been beyond indispensable. There is not space to mention help from many others, including Lisa Bode, Lesley Clement, Ben Lefebvre, Jenny Litster, Allan McGillivray, Bernadeta Milewski, and Emily Woods. And where would Montgomery scholarship be without the archivists at the University of Guelph's Montgomery Collection?

I am grateful for the help of an "army" of historians, military and otherwise, who helped me with the notes. This starts with J.L. Granatstein and Jonathan F. Vance. Thank you also to so many others who took the time to share their expertise, including Richard Butterwick-Pawlikowski, Professor of Polish-Lithuanian History at UCL's School of Slavonic and East European Studies; Jan Lencznarowicz, Associate Professor of History in the Department of History of International Migration, Jagiellonian University, Kraków; John J. Kulczycki, professor in the Department of History at the University of Illinois at Chicago; Maria Bucur-Deckard, John W. Hill Professor of East European History at Indiana University; Keith Hitchins, Professor of History at the University of Illinois at Urbana-Champagne; Ina Baghdiantz McCabe, Professor of History and Darakjian Jafarian Chair of Armenian History at Tufts University; Peter B. Brown, Professor of Russian, Eastern European, Baltic, and Eurasian-Global Studies at Rhode Island College; André Gerolymatos, Director, Stavros Niarchos Foundation Centre for Hellenic Studies, Simon Fraser University; Greta Jones, Emeritus Professor of History, University of Ulster; Ian McBride, Professor of Irish and British History, King's College London; Peter Gray, Professor of Modern Irish History, Queen's University Belfast; Thomas W. Gallant, Professor of Modern Greek History and Archaeology University of California San Diego, and Eran Tearosh, Chairman, Society for the Heritage of World War I in Israel.

Jen Rubio, Hamilton

Index

Index of Photography

Arch of St. John's Chapel, Chester   1

Clock Tower and fountain at Exhibition   3

Mr. Geo. B. MacMillan   3

Oban   4

Climbing over the Staffa rocks to Fingal's Cave   4

Entrance to Fingal's Cave [Staffa]   5

[St Columba's Trail and St. Oran's Chapel] Iona   5

Tomb of Kings   6

[Auld and New Brigs o' Doon]   7

Loch Lomond [Loch Lomond from Luss (Mist Effect)]   8

Coaching [Loch Katrine]   9

Stronachlacher Hotel   9

Lower end of Katrine   9

"Silver Strand" [path by the Loch, Loch Katrine]   9

Stronachlacher Hotel   9

[Path by the Loch Katrine]   10

[Katrine Path, Trossachs]   10

Loch Achray   10

Hotel   10

Ben Venue   11

346

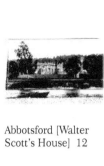

Abbotsford [Walter Scott's House] 12

Scott's Burial Place 13

[Melrose Abbey from SE] 13

Ruin of Dryburgh Abbey 13

The Den 14

The Den 14

The Den 14

Hut on Culloden Moor where Cumberland spent the night before the battle 15

Cumberland Stone, Culloden Moor 15

Tomnahurich 15

Scene on the crest of Tomnahurich 16

Berwick on Tweed 17

[Roslin Chapel] 17

Arthur's Seat 17

Ewan, Miss Allan, M. McMillan 18

On the path to Gartmoor Dam 18

The Lake at Gartmoor Dam 18

Dollar Glen 19

River Forth, Wallace Monument] 20

Wallace Monument 20

Stirling Castle 20 Berwick Pier 21 Spittal Cliffs 21 [Lindisfarne Priory, Holy Island] 22

View on Holy Island 22 Marmion Gateway 22 The Tweed 23 House where we had tea 24

[Keswick and Derwentwater] 26 [Grasmere and Helm Crag] 26 [Buttermere and Honister Crag, Keswick] 26 Druid's circle 28

[Ewan McDonald] 28 The biggest Stone in the Circle 28 Past and Present 28 York Minster 29

Gog and Magog 29 [Russell Hotel, London] 30 "So Green and cool" [Lover's Lane] 32 [The Ford, Kenilworth] 33

[The Ford, Kenilworth]
33

[Entrance to
Banqueting Hall, Ke-
nilworth Castle] 33

[Kenilworth Castle:
The Banqueting Hall
and Mervyn's Tower]
34

[Warwick Castle from
the Mound] 34

[Salisbury Cathedral]
36

[A Bird's Eye View of
Dunwich] 39

Lover's Lane 39

Old Woolner House
40

Granary of old Wool-
ner Place 40

[Woolner house] 41

Old Church Tower,
Dunwich 41

Uxbridge Station 43

Ewan's boarding
house, Leaskdale 44

Leaskdale Church
44

Outside and In 44

[Leaskdale Manse]
45

View to left of lawn
45

View to right of lawn
45

Front Walk 46

The Side Road 49

Inside the Manse 51   [Corner of Parlor] 52   Parlor view showing dogs and jug 52   Library view—my secretary in corner 53

Library view showing entrance door 53   [Interior of manse] 53   Dining Room showing sideboard 54   Dining Room showing china cabinet 54

My Dressing Table 54   Corner of our room 54   The Landing 55   Spare Room 55

Daffy 58   Marjorie MacMurchy 59   Frede 60   Hugh Mustard's House 60

Cuthbert McIntyre 60   Mr Fraser 61   Mr McKay 61   Mrs McKay 62

Winter view from front door 63

A weird picture of Stella and myself at Niagara 67

A corner of our lawn 68

Frede, Miss Fergusson and Daffy 70

Frede at time of her graduation 71

First pictures of Chester, three weeks old 71

Leaskdale Manse where Chester was born 72

Chester and Miss Fergusson 72

Chester in his christening robe 75

Stella 77

A flashlight photo of our supper table 80

"The Dweller On The Threshold" and "One-Eyed Oxtoby" 82

Queen 83

Punch [Chester] 83

Punch [Chester] 83

Abbreviated Punch 84

Aunt Mary Lawson 87

Winter on the Lawn 88

Mr Fraser 89

Punch "au naturel" [Chester] 90

Punch and Mrs Reid 97

[Chester in a high chair] 98

Chester in creepers 99

[LMM, Chester, Mrs Stirling, and Doris] 101

Punch trotting on all fours 102

The veranda 103

[Looking seaward, Tea Hill, PEI] 105

Chester at one year old 106

The curve under the maples 108

The spruces by the gate 109

The Pond Bridge 111

"Silent and shadowy and still" 112

Aunt Mary's 113

Stell 113

Ernest Webb's House from Back 114

Lover's Lane 114

Chester, the Webb children, and Polly 114

The row of wild cherry trees 115

Lover's Lane 116

The other gate 116

A very pretty vista 117

The bridge over the brook 117

The gate in the hill field 119

"Home as it was long years ago" 119

The old lane 121

Tillie 121

The front door step 122

Chester and "Polly" 124

The Manse [Cavendish] 125

Basking in sunshine 125

Amanda's Home 127

"The church beside" 131

"The rock-bound land" 131

Uncle Leander 136

Uncle Leander 136

Aunt Janie 137

[Mrs. George Dickson, of Toronto] 140

Grave and ... 146

... Gay [Chester] 146

Chester and Lily 150

The west window 156

[Chester] 157

[Chester] 157

[Picnic] 158

The side road 160

[Chester] 160

Chester 164

[Newspaper announcement: stillbirth, Hugh Macdonald] 164

["Zion" Cemetery] 167

The old home 171

Carl 177

[Chester] 180

"See my daffodil" 181

[Chester] 180

[Chester] 180

Corner of garden 188

The maples on the lawn 188

Ernest Webb's 189

Lovers Lane 190

Trees and flowers 191

Lover's Lane 192   The Manse, Cavendish 194   George R's 194   My old window 195

The Lane 195   The front door 195   Alec's House 196   Park Corner 197

The old beech wood 197   The Bridge 199   The dusk in the cloudy firs 199   Home again 200

Cover design of "Anne of the Island" 201   Stuart and Miss Barnard 206   Edith 209   Cuthbert and Chester 213

Cuthbert and Chester 213   Red Cross Packers 255   Mary 219   [Stuart] Grave 220

[Stuart] Gay 220

Chester at three-and-a-half 223

Chester under arch outside of our gate 226

[116th Battalion] 226

"I should worry." [Stuart] 231

"It's hot—but 232

—I feel pretty comfortable" [Stuart] 232

The Warden of the Gate [Chester] 232

x Dr. Angus Macdonald's House xx His private hospital 241

Photo of Ewan, taken in Warsaw 246

Four-square to all the winds that blow 251

Cavendish Hall 270

[Chester and Edith] 279

[Kenneth Cruit] 280

Grace before meal [Stuart] 286

The spot on the road 291

Stuart and Edith 293

[Stuart] 295

Lieut. Cameron MacFarlane of the Princess Pats 296

[Teacher's Residence, Macdonald College, Ste-Anne de Bellevue] 298

[Macdonald College, Women's Residence] 298

[Frede's Wedding Announcement] 298

[The Campus] 299

[St. George's Church] 299

[The Practice Dining Room] 300

[The Teacher's Residence] 300

[A corner of the dining room] 300

[The Ottawa] 301

[The Ottawa] 301

[The Ottawa, from the College] 301

Mrs. Hugh Mustard 303

Stuart picking roses 304

"Chums" [Doug Madill, Cameron Leask, Chester] 304

Three Good Pals [Ewan, Stuart and Chester] 304

Cover Design 305

The Veranda 307

Bertie 307

[Horse and trap] 308

[Montgomery and Bertie McIntyre] 309

[Ewan, boys, Bertie, and Montgomery] 309

Brothers 315   Corner of lawn 316   Carl [and Stuart] 320   Miss Bollert 324

[Sherbourne House Club Dining Room] 325   Laura [McIntyre Aylesworth] 327   [The vacant store where LMM polled her first vote] 330   Uncle John, Aunt Annie, and Frede 331

The Campbell's House 331   The house at Park Corner 332   Park Corner pantry 332   Edith 334

Printed in Great Britain
by Amazon